David West is a freelance writer who has been covering combat sports since 2003. He was the British correspondent for the US magazine *Full Contact Fighter* for six years and his work has appeared in *MMA Unltd, Fighters Only, Fight Sport, Fighting Spirit* and many more. His feature writing includes an article exploring the legacy of the London Prize Ring for *Fighters Only* and a look at Britain's forgotten wrestling heritage in *MMA Unltd*. David is the author of the book *Chasing Dragons – An Introduction to the Martial Arts Film* (IB Tauris, 2006).

D1081148

Recent Mammoth titles

The Mammoth Book of The Beatles
The Mammoth Book of Best New SF 23
The Mammoth Book of Best New Horror 21
The Mammoth Book of Great British Humour
The Mammoth Book of Drug Barons
The Mammoth Book of Fun Brain Training
The Mammoth Book of Dracula
The Mammoth Book of Best British Crime 8
The Mammoth Book of Tattoo Art
The Mammoth Book of Bob Dylan
The Mammoth Book of Mixed Martial Arts
The Mammoth Book of Codeword Puzzles
The Mammoth Book of Best New Sci-Fi 24
The Mammoth Book of Really Silly Jokes
The Mammoth Book of Best New Horror 22
The Mammoth Book of Undercover Cops
The Mammoth Book of Weird News
The Mammoth Book of Lost Symbols
The Mammoth Book of Conspiracies
The Mammoth Book of Antarctic Journeys

The Mammoth Book of

MUHAMMAD ALI

Edited by David West

ROBINSON

RUNNING PRESS
PHILADELPHIA · LONDON

Constable & Robinson Ltd
55–56 Russell Square
London WC1B 4HP
www.constablerobinson.com

First published in the UK by Robinson,
an imprint of Constable & Robinson Ltd, 2012

A copy of the British Library Cataloguing in Publication
Data is available from the British Library

UK ISBN 978-1-84901-734-3 (paperback)
UK ISBN 978-1- 84901-735-0 (ebook)
3 5 7 9 10 8 6 4 2

First published in the United States in 2012 by Running Press Book Publishers,
A Member of the Perseus Books Group

Books published by Running Press are available at special discounts for bulk purchases
in the United States by corporations, institutions, and other organizations. For
more information, please contact the Special Markets Department at the Perseus
Books Group, 2300 Chestnut Street, Suite 200, Philadelphia, PA 19103, or call
(800) 810-4145, ext. 5000, or e-mail special.markets@perseusbooks.com.

US ISBN: 978-0-76244-293-5
US Library of Congress Control Number: 2010941557

9   8   7   6   5   4   3   2   1
Digit on the right indicates the number of this printing

Running Press Book Publishers
2300 Chestnut Street
Philadelphia, PA 19103-4371

Visit us on the web!
www.runningpress.com

Printed and bound in the UK

Contents

Introduction   vii

PART 1 – THE LOUISVILLE LIP

A Look at Cassius Clay: Biggest Mouth in Boxing
Alex Poinsett   3
God Save the King, God Save Boxing   *Bob Mee*   11
Clay vs Cooper – The Louisville Lip Tastes Henry's Hammer
John Cottrell   17

PART 2 – SONNY

Legacies   *Reg Gutteridge*   27
He's Just a Little Boy in the Dark and He's Scared
Bob Mee   34
What the Hell is This? What Did They Do?   *Bob Mee*   46
The Devil and Sonny Liston   *Nick Tosches*   66

PART 3 – ALI VS THE USA

The Young Radical   *Jack Olsen*   91
The People's Champion Takes On Canada   *John Cottrell*   117
Intimate Look at the Champ   *Isaac Sutton*   132
Kicking the Cat   *John Cottrell*   140
Negroes and the War   *The Times Editorial*   150
Beyond the Confines of America   *Mike Marqusee*   152
The Unconquerable Muhammad Ali   *Hans J. Massaquoi*   169
The Great Fixed Fight   *Neil Allen*   180

PART 4 – ONCE MORE UNTO THE BREACH

Mr Anonymous is Angry, But Not With Cassius Clay
Neil Allen   185
Sting Like a Bee   *José Torres*   189

PART 5 – SMOKIN' JOE

Soul Music in Frazier's Workshop   *Rex Bellamy*   215
For God, for Country, and for Perenchio   *Budd Schulberg*   219
If At First . . .   *Felix Dennis and Don Atyeo*   241

PART 6 – ON THE ROAD AGAIN

The Big Fight Part 1 – In Living Colour   *Dave Hannigan*   271
The Big Fight Part 2 – Ali vs Al Lewis   *Dave Hannigan*   289
Bugner Loses a Gamble in Which Few Finish Ahead
   on the Tables   *Neil Allen*   303
Is Muhammad Ali All Washed Up?   *A. S. (Doc) Young*   307

PART 7 – THE RUMBLE IN THE JUNGLE

Bundini Brown, the Witch Doctor at the Court of King Ali
   Neil Allen   317
The Rumble in the Jungle   *George Foreman*   320
Walking With Kings   *Reg Gutteridge*   338

PART 8 – THE LONG FALL FROM GRACE

The Thrilla in Manila   *Ferdie Pacheco*   345
Can "Old Man" Ali Accomplish the Impossible?
   Gregg Simms   365
McIlvanney on Boxing   *Hugh McIlvanney*   371
Pal Ali   *Reg Gutteridge*   402
The Lost Legacy of Muhammad Ali   *Thomas Hauser*   409

Muhammad Ali's Professional Boxing Record   429
Acknowledgements and Sources   435

Introduction

Muhammad Ali has been called many things in his life: The Louisville Lip, Gaseous Cassius and The Greatest, the last being self-chosen. It was a long time before the general public accepted that one. When Ali, then Cassius Marcellus Clay, first came up the professional ranks, he was sometimes dismissed as a kid with a big mouth whose ambitions exceeded his ability. Opinion in the boxing world was split. There were those who were just happy to find a fighter that had the charisma to get people talking about boxing again when the sport was on the decline. In the other corner were those, and there were plenty of them, who thought Clay's apparently tireless mouth needed to be shut, preferably by way of a fist to the jaw. But love him or hate him for his pre-fight predictions, his often appalling poetry and his constant boasting, he knew how to bring a crowd to a fight. He was a character and good for the sport.

That all changed when his membership of the Nation of Islam became public. The Nation's anti-integration politics, their condemnation of white people as devils and Ali's very vocal embracing of the Nation's views saw his popular support plummet. His refusal to serve in the US military produced a public backlash of an intensity not seen against any boxer since Jack Johnson horrified white America half a century earlier. Ali was no longer merely a braggart, he was an unpatriotic draft dodger, a bad example to the youth of America and a disgrace to his title, far worse than his unloved predecessor Charles "Sonny" Liston.

However, Ali's stand against military service and his three-year struggle to get his boxing licence back came to be seen against the wider context of the growing anti-war sentiment and the civil rights movement. Whether or not Ali's personal issues with the government were ever intended to be construed in a larger context is open to debate, but it began the process of transforming Ali from public enemy to national treasure. His claim to be "The Greatest" was surely given the ultimate seal of authenticity in 1978 in DC Comics' *Superman vs. Muhammad Ali*, in which Ali even defeated the Man Of Steel. When he lit the Olympic Flame in Atlanta in 1996, his transformation from pariah to hero was complete. A man who earned his living by beating other men with his fists and who was once vilified by his government was now a symbol of tolerance, of racial integration and of America itself. It could only happen in boxing.

PART 1
THE LOUISVILLE LIP

Cassius Clay began his professional fight career on 29 October 1960 with a six-round decision victory over Tunney Hunsaker. The fight took place in Clay's hometown of Louisville, Kentucky. After the win, Clay moved to Miami and joined the stable of fighters at Angelo Dundee's 5th Street Gym. With Dundee's guidance he learned his trade and built his record and reputation over the next two years against a series of carefully chosen opponents.

On 15 November 1962, Clay got his first "name" opponent – the former light-heavyweight champion Archie Moore. The Old Mongoose was arguably the greatest knockout artist in the history of the square ring. His professional record, as listed in Bert Sugar's The Great Fights, *consisted of 229 fights and an extraordinary 141 knockouts. The two men had crossed paths before. At the outset of his pro career, Clay had been sent to Moore's training camp to see if the veteran could take him under his wing as he set out on the path to pugilistic glory. It was not to be. Moore expected his fighters to pull their weight and perform the chores that kept the camp shipshape. Clay, who was used to being spoiled by his doting mother at home, refused to wash dishes or mop floors and was sent home.*

Two years later, Clay was on the rise while Moore was well past his prime when they met in the ring. In a one-sided affair, Moore was dispatched in the fourth round. The Old Mongoose fought just twice more before hanging up his gloves for good. As for his youthful vanquisher, now undefeated in sixteen outings, he was just getting started.

A Look at Cassius Clay:
Biggest Mouth in Boxing

Alex Poinsett

Ebony Magazine, March 1963

"POET-PROPHET" SAYS HE COULD STOP SONNY LISTON IN EIGHT

This is the story about a man
With iron fists and a beautiful tan
He talks a lot and boasts indeed
Of a powerful punch and blinding speed

The boxing game was slowly dying
And fight promoters were bitterly crying
For someone, somewhere to come along
With a better and a different tone

Patterson was dull, quiet and sad
And Sonny Liston was just as bad
Along came a kid named Cassius Clay
Who said "I will take Liston's title away"

His athletic prowess cannot be denied
In a very short time it has spread far and wide
There's an impression you get watching him fight
He plays cat and mouse then turns out the light

This colorful fighter is something to see
And heavyweight champ I know he will be
*   —Cassius Clay*

Poet, prophet, propagandist, Cassius Marcellus Clay – less pretentiously nicknamed "Gee Gee" ever since his diaper-wearing days – is, by his own modest admission, "the greatest" happening in boxing today. At the very least, he is certainly "the most talkingest fighter," a compulsive phrase-maker fascinated by his own verbage. In a rhyming mood, the brash, twenty-one-year-oldster insists heavyweight champion Sonny Liston "is great, but he must fall in eight." Then he solemnly warns he will let Liston tarry only six rounds if the champion keeps "popping off" about the challenger's inability to hit hard enough to crack an egg. While his "poetry" only tickles the imagination, his uncanny and sometimes lucky knack of predicting the exact knockout round for ten of the sixteen professional opponents he has faced smacks of a voodoo witch doctor sticking psychological shafts in his victims.

In the fight which boosted him from seventh to fourth among world heavyweight title contenders, Cassius knocked out Archie Moore in the fourth round just as he said he would. Many of the 16,200 Los Angeles fans (a California indoor record), mildly angered because of Clay's boasting, had come to see him lose. But as always, the boxer, who preens himself with "I'm too pretty to be hit," prayed about twenty minutes before the scheduled twelve-round bout: "Lord, millions of people are waiting for me to fail. As long as you're with me, I can't fail."

Then in the second round Cassius caught the hardest punch he has ever felt in his life, a right smash flush on the jaw. "My legs got rubbery," he admits, his baritone voice going soprano in the excitement of the telling. "I was dizzy. But I couldn't let Archie know I was hurt. Man, I couldn't lose! And after all that talking, too?" So he hung on, had Moore in trouble in the third round but "played cat and mouse" with him until the fourth to make his prediction "come out right." Indeed, the only time Cassius has ever ignored his forecast came last March when he disposed of Dan Warren in the fourth round instead of the fifth as predicted. "He wouldn't shake hands with me when the bell rang," he apologizes now, "so I subtracted one round for poor sportsmanship."

Cassius was more gentle with a sweet, little old lady who later told him: "I read a story in the newspaper that said you're a nice boy. I always knew that you really were a nice boy!" He wanted to inform her the complimentary story had, in fact, wrecked months of national image building. "Like man, if you make your living as a professional villain, how would you dig it if somebody clipped your horns?" Cassius laments. "I don't want to be no nice boy in the press. That don't get it. More people come to a fight just to see a big-mouthed, bad guy fall."

Sparring with logic that is not nearly as sharp as his punching, Cassius figures any publicity – good, indifferent and, especially, the bad – helps him revive public interest in a sport grown humdrum from a lack of excellent fighters and captivating personalities. If, for instance, the heavyweight champion is popular, colorful and talkative, if he draws crowds on the streets, if he is idolized by youngsters, then boxing, as a whole, benefits. What boxing needs, therefore says Cassius, "is more Cassius Clays."

As if proving himself really as obnoxious as he appears, Cassius plays to a grandstand stretching from New York to Los Angeles. Tossing back his head, he stares wide-eyed through bifocals perched invisibly on the tip of his nose, passionately telling a television interviewer: "I am the greatest!"

"Yes, Cassius, we know," the interviewer replies wearily.

"I don't want you to forget it," huffs the boxer.

Cassius, of course, never, never will. Striding down the street in his Louisville, Ky. hometown, he is stopped by a boy who promises: "I'm going to be like you."

"What am I?" Cassius wants to know.

"A boxer."

"What kind of boxer?"

"A champion boxer."

"That's right," Cassius agrees. "The greatest!"

An idle boast? A front for fear? Arrogance? Immaturity? Perhaps all of these convenient catchalls. Perhaps none of them. For when Cassius declares "I am the greatest," he is not just thinking about boxing. "I'm talking about a whole lot of things," he explains. Lingering behind his words is the bitter sarcasm of Dick Gregory, the shrill defiance of Miles Davis, the utter contempt of Malcolm X. He smiles easily, but, behind it all, behind the publicity gimmicks and boyish buffoonery, behind the brashness, Cassius Marcellus Clay – and this fact has evaded the sportswriting fraternity – is a blast furnace of race pride. His is a pride that would never mask itself with skin lighteners and processed hair, a pride scorched with memories of a million little burns like the paper cup he drank root beer from at a New Orleans stand while his white companion sipped from a glass. He does not talk publicly about racial discrimination, preferring instead to leave protests to race leaders. But a hint of feelings, searing the very depths of him, surface even in his most jocular moments. Thus while eating breakfast, he asks his brother, Rudy, to pass the cream. "I want to integrate my coffee," Cassius quips. "I don't want to drink it black. Think I'll have my coffee weak this morning."

Later he bounces down the street, tall and proud, rhapsodizing: "I feel free since I learned the truth about myself and my people."

During other flights of the imagination Cassius talks of some-day building a $500,000 housing project for Negroes, a roller skating rink staffed with pretty, brown girls and a cab company to furnish jobs for his unemployed friends. But the race pride at times becomes almost a caricature of a cause, a confusion in Cassius's mind between love of his people and himself. And he calls the four-room clapboard, Louisville house he was born in "the eighth wonder of the world," claiming: "It should be turned into a national shrine where sightseers from all over the country can come and say, 'Gee, this is the birthplace of Cassius Clay.'" For this glory, he seriously considers repurchasing the family's former homestead.

The main stuff of Cassius's varied financial dreams is a healthy respect for the dollar – almost to a fault. It pops out when he drives up to a filling station in his long Cadillac and orders $2 worth of gasoline. It shows in a sparse wardrobe sporting a $40 suit. It turns farcical as he eats chili with his father, brother and two reporters in a Louisville restaurant. Two of his companions buy milkshakes to wash down the meal. Cassius thirsts for a thirty-five-cent milkshake, but does not buy. Instead, he "borrows" a glass full from each of the other two. "Most reporters pay my tab," Cassius announces at the end of the meal to the two newsmen. And when he leaves he does not pay.

It is as if the dollar he guards jealously will soothe him in blankets of green security. For beside the housing project Cassius wants to build for Negroes, he wants to wrap himself in a $200,000 home with all the trimmings. It irks him that most of his earnings in these, his most productive years, are gobbled up by income taxes. Cassius complained to Sen. Ted Kennedy, youngest brother of the President, while in Boston in December to receive a B'nai B'rith sport award. "I've been doing OK in the ring," he told Kennedy, "but I've been stopped by Uncle Sam. He's taking 85 per cent (actually about 65 per cent) of my earnings." Cassius asked for help from Washington.

"I'll not only ask my brother, the President, but I've got another brother down there," Kennedy answered. "He's in the Justice Dept. and you may need him!"

On another occasion, Cassius said: "There're a lot of things I want to be in this fight game, but I sure don't want to be a Joe Louis. That is, I don't want to have the income tax trouble he had. Man, you can't fight or do nothing without peace of mind. I don't want anything to take my mind off going straight up–up–up."

Cassius, after all, has promised the world he will reign as its next heavyweight king and with characteristic bravado added: "If I say an eagle dips snuff, look under his wing and get the can." His title prediction is shared by veteran referee Ruby Goldstein who officiated bouts of all the champions since Joe Louis. "This kid reminds me of Patterson when he first started," Goldstein said at the time. "He's like a combination of a young Ray Robinson and Floyd Patterson with the fast moves and quick hands. He's kind of a picture fighter. He's the kind you got to say to yourself, he can't miss."

Other fight experts, however, are dubious about the title chances of a boxer with hands once so brittle they had to be X-rayed after every fight by an orthopedic specialist. "He knows nothing about in-fighting," claims Bud Bruner, a Louisville fight manager, "but you have to catch him to make him fight inside."

Some critics claim Cassius lacks punching power. While it is true he is a boxer-type heavyweight who wears down his opponents with a tic-tac-toe pattern of lightning blows, his trainer, Angelo Dundee, warns against notions that he cannot put an opponent away with a couple of punches – or one. "He stopped Alejandro Lavorante with one punch," Dundee recalls, "and his punching is developing. I can see it. He sets and spots now. And he has something very few fighters have – a good left uppercut."

For fight experts who question his punching power, Cassius has answers of his own. While visiting his mother, Mrs Odessa Clay, in a Catholic hospital where she was recuperating from an operation, he argues rather loudly: "Who says I can't punch? Ask Alex Miteff, ask Willie Besmanoff, ask Archie Moore. They say I don't know nothing about in-fighting." *He is on his feet, now, shadow-boxing to prove his skill.* "The way I fight I don't need to. I'm sticking fast," he says, flicking out his left jab like a cobra. *His ailing mother smiles approvingly.* "I'm hitting him with a right cross. Ying!" *He snorts, blowing hard through his nose at the end of each punch, the way fighters do to conserve their wind. His mother giggles.* "Then a big left hook." *He is John Henry driving a human spike in the ground.* "I'm doing the twist, light on my feet, looking pretty. I'm clean, Jim!" *His mother holds her chest to soothe the pain of laughter.* "With me, you're wrong if you do and wrong if you don't attack. I don't see nobody whipping me. I'm too fast!" *Liston, he claims, is too slow for him.* "Sure he can punch, but a big punch don't mean nothing if you can't hit nothing. I'd smother Liston!" And a tiny, nurse-nun eases into the hospital room wanting to know: "Who's making all this noise?"

A doer as well as a talker, Cassius heeds a little of the fatherly advice from Joe Louis who warned him recently: "Boy! You better not believe half the things you say about yourself. You better train hard." The fighter puts in long days at the Fifth Street Gym in Miami Beach, Fla., to perfect moves and toils many hours outdoors running, chopping wood and performing other tedious tasks to develop his physique. The six-foot-two, 200-pounder neither smokes, drinks, dances nor becomes seriously involved with girls. Single-mindedly, he has been aiming for boxing glory since he was twelve when he learned how to box so he could punch the nose of the thief who stole his bicycle. Weighing 89 pounds, Cassius made his amateur debut winning a split-decision in the featured bout of a Louisville television program hopefully called "Champions of Tomorrow." Between the ages of twelve and eighteen, while struggling through high school with a D-minus average, he lost only eight of 108 amateur bouts. The momentum of his ambition carried Cassius to national Golden Gloves and Amateur Athletic Union light-heavyweight titles in 1959 and to the Golden Gloves' heavyweight, A.A.U. light-heavyweight, and Olympic light-heavyweight championships in 1960.

His Olympic success was like nectar attracting bees. Cassius accepted more than $400 worth of watches for all the members of the Clay family from Reynolds Metals Company Vice President Billy Reynolds, then rejected Reynolds's offer of a $20,000 bonus to sign because the contract included no plans for his future. Cassius and his attorney, Alberta Jones, also rejected managerial offers from Floyd Patterson's manager, Cus D'Amato, boxers Pete Rademacher and Archie Moore. Finally, three days before his first professional fight in October 1960, Cassius came to terms with a group of 11 white multi-million-aires – nine from Louisville, the other two from New York and Plains, Va.

Cassius's unusual contract, brilliantly negotiated by Miss Jones, netted him a $10,000 bonus and the entire $2,000 proceeds of his first pro fight. Signed for six years, he receives 50 per cent of all his earnings the first four years and 60 per cent thereafter with the sponsors paying his expenses out of their share. During his first two development years, which ended in January, he was guaranteed a minimum annual salary of $4,000. Thereafter the fighter started drawing against his purses. For his own protection, 15 per cent of his salary was invested in US bonds and 15 per cent of all his earnings throughout the tenure of his contract goes in a trust fund (now more than $10,000) which he cannot touch until he is thirty-five or until he retires. His sponsors' attorney, Gordon Davidson, reveals they are technically in the red, having spent about $40,000 so far for Cassius's salary and expenses.

When Cassius signed the 1960 contract he set for himself the goal of becoming boxing's youngest heavyweight champion. For months he has complained to trainer Dundee: "Don't give me those 'ducks.' There's nothing to beating a bum." Dundee admits he has been trying to sit on the youngster's ambition, explaining: "Cassius has lots of time ahead of him. If it were up to me, I'd book him against nothing but ordinary fighters for the next year and a half. Twenty-two, twenty-three, that's a good age to be challenging for the heavyweight title. But what can I do? He hollers, 'no ducks, no ducks,' and his Louisville sponsors agree."

William Faversham Jr., chairman of the sponsoring group which up to now has not tried to rush Cassius into a title bout, says because of the fighter's ambition: "I owe it to him to get him a fight with Liston next September." For if Cassius is to win the heavyweight championship by the time he is twenty-one, he must move swiftly. Patterson became champ at twenty-one; thirty-five days before his twenty-second birthday. Cassius has until Dec. 12, 1963, thirty-six days prior to his twenty-second birthday – to break Floyd's record. "This is the jet age. People are going to the moon," says boxing's verbal astronaut. "If you don't break a record, you're nothing. I want to be the youngest champ!"

God Save the King, God Save Boxing

Bob Mee

When Cassius Clay won his Olympic gold medal in 1960 in Rome, Floyd Patterson was world heavyweight champ. However, the uncrowned king of the heavyweight division was Charles "Sonny" Liston, a scowling ex-con with brutal power in both hands. After his second spell in prison in 1957, Liston had moved up the ranks in impressive style. With wins over contenders including Zora Folley, Cleveland Williams and Eddie Machen, Liston's claim to a title shot was hard to dispute, but Patterson's manager Cus D'Amato wanted no part of the hard-hitting challenger. Weary of accusations that he was ducking Liston, Patterson accepted the bout and the pair clashed in Chicago on 25 September, 1962. Most of the press and public were rooting for clean-cut, polite Patterson. They were to be disappointed. Bob Mee picks up the tale.

Nearly 8,000 in the ultra-modern, carpeted, circular Las Vegas Convention Centre stood and cheered Patterson into the ring, then booed and yelled abuse at the heavyweight champion of the world. Rocky Marciano, Joe Louis and Billy Conn were announced to the crowd, then Cassius Clay shook hands with Patterson, went to cross the ring to Liston, then stopped and dashed out in mock fear – to applause and laughter.

After both had pawed out jabs, Liston landed a short right hand to the body about ten seconds into the fight. Patterson seemed to feel it, moving away as soon as he could. Liston connected with a left jab. Patterson held. It was as if he were waiting for something bad to happen. He didn't have to wait long.

A seven-punch burst, including a right uppercut that jerked Patterson's head back and almost seemed to take him off the floor, and at the fifty-second mark of round one, the challenger was down.

After the mandatory eight count from referee Harry Krause, Patterson retreated, then held and spoiled, clinging to Liston's right glove. Sonny belted him in the ribs with his free hand until Krause called break.

As soon as Liston found the room, he marched forward, this time unleashing an unanswered burst of eleven blows, a final chopping right hand sending Patterson sprawling on the canvas. He hit the floor as the clock reached ninety-nine seconds. This time he was dazed, hurt and plainly demoralised, but he got up.

Some vestige of pride made Patterson fire a right hand, but it missed, and Liston finished him off with two rights to the side of the head and a left hook to the jaw. There was no point in another count, but referee Krause went through the formality, completing it at an official time of two minutes ten seconds. Patterson had not landed a single punch. Then again, he had only thrown five – three jabs and two right hands.

The condemnation of Patterson's pitiful challenge was pretty much universal. Lester Bromberg called him "a mouse of a man". A bookmaker at The Dunes in Las Vegas, Sid Wyman, may or may not have had his own agenda, but was angry when he told writers: "If he couldn't make a better fight, he shouldn't have gone through. It was an insult to the people."

Patterson, wrote John Gold for the *London Evening News*, went down "beneath a raging tide of human violence. It was a fight that should have been held in an abattoir not a sports arena packed with celebrities." At the end, Gold wrote:

> From some hole in the ring, up bobbed the irrepressible Clay, shouting and gesticulating and wrestling with the ring attendants as he tried to reach Liston. Clay gets his chance next. He will be fortunate if it isn't his comeuppance.

No deal would be signed for Liston to defend against Clay until 5 November 1963, but even in July, when Liston destroyed Patterson again, everybody knew there was no other fight that mattered, that it had to happen.

To roars of "We Want Clay" from the back of the hall, Cassius climbed into the ring and gave an interview. "It was a disgrace to the boxing game," he said. "It wasn't a heavyweight championship fight. It was just an eliminator to see who's going to fight me." After declaring himself tired of talking, he said Liston didn't have enough experience to deal with him. "If the bum whips me, I'll leave the country."

Clay said he was going to New York to cut an album for Columbia Records. "Maybe after Liston, I'll go into the movies," he said, opening his eyes even wider. "After all, I'm the greatest actor there is."

He anticipated boxing Liston in front of the biggest live crowd for a boxing match anywhere, bigger even than Dempsey and Tunney, then let his imagination loose:

> I'm gonna make my entrance surrounded by beautiful queens wearing gowns that drag on the ground . . . I'll be wearing a crown on my head and a beautiful robe, like in Pharaoh's days. One queen will take the crown from my head and place it gently on a silken pillow. Another queen will help me out of my robe. The others will be rubbing me down with cocoa butter and manicuring my nails. That's what we need in boxing. Beautiful girls!

Donald Saunders, in the *Daily Telegraph*, said: "Liston's biggest worry will not be losing the title but trying to find opponents who will be good enough to attract customers into arenas and television theatres." Liston made a good point when he said there were no real contenders because he had beaten them all on the way up. Saunders felt American fans were missing out by refusing to accept him. "He may not be the most likeable of world heavyweight champions but there have been, and still are, many people in boxing less deserving of sympathy and support."

Joe Louis said: "Nobody going to beat Liston except old age."

Robert H. Boyle, in *Sports Illustrated*, wrote: "Sonny Liston is still the heavyweight king. God save the king. God save boxing."

At the post-fight press conference, Liston seemed initially reluctant, seemed to hesitate as if he wanted to leave. Willie Reddish called out: "Ask the questions and get it over with."

The first was a dumb one – "Was this a better fight than the one in Chicago?"

Liston said: "Didn't you see it?"

Liston said he would have finished Patterson even quicker but for the mandatory eight count, said it "had me handcuffed".

A New York columnist asked Liston, who had on a straw trilby, sports shirt and casual slacks: "How does it feel to have made it after all these years of having nothing?"

There was a pause. "Well," said the champion . . . and no more.

The writer tried again: "You know what I mean, ten years ago you were in the can and had nothing. Now you're on top of the world. Anything you want is yours. How does it feel?"

The past, the past, always the past.

Liston stared back, let loose a slow smile and said: "It feels pretty good . . . but sometimes there are too many people bothering me."

When writers asked him whether he thought Patterson should retire, he turned the question around. "Would you tell a bird he can't fly?" he said.

Was Patterson afraid of him? Liston grinned. "Yes, I think he is. He gave me that hurt look."

On the other side of a partition in the Convention Centre's gold room, Patterson seemed like a man in a psychological trauma, like a man who was already so haunted by what had happened he wouldn't sleep for a year. He said he had no plans to retire. "In Chicago and here, Liston showed he's a much better fighter than I am . . ."

Someone asked what he had planned to do in the fight.

"Try to make him miss and counter."

Was Liston such a great fighter or had he developed a "sensitivity to a punch"?

"It could be a combination of both," said this painfully honest man. "I wasn't afraid. Perhaps I should have been. I wasn't tense, although maybe I was a bit nervous. Liston was a better fighter than I thought he was."

Someone asked what he planned to do now, perhaps a less direct slant on the retirement question.

"I'm not in the picture any more. I prefer to fight my way up. I eliminated myself."

After a couple of questions about details of what punch had

nailed him, Patterson was asked if he planned to put on a beard again on the way out of the building.

"I do feel disgraced terrible . . . but there will be no beard, no moustache, no nonsense this time . . . and I came here so you wouldn't say I ducked out."

There was some applause – and it was all over.

Back in his half of the room Liston was asked about Cassius Clay.

"Who is Clay? It would take me one and a half rounds to catch him, the other to knock him out."

Later that evening, Liston was enjoying his victory party when Clay walked in "just to make him mad". He made his way through the crowd to Liston's table and yelled at him: "You're just a sucker. My brother could have beaten Floyd Patterson."

Liston indulged him. "Come on over here and sit on my knee and finish your orange juice!" They made as if to go for each other, were kept apart.

People speculated that during his stay in Vegas Liston lost between $900 and $20,000 shooting dice.

Financially, the breakdown of this briefest, most damning of mismatches was as follows:

Attendance: 7,816
Gross live gate: $286,180
Estimated net gate: $260,000
Estimated Liston share: (30%) $78,000
Estimated Patterson share: (30%) $78,000

Each fighter was also on 30 per cent of the theatre TV gate, which was estimated at $700,000, which meant $210,000 each.

Given the nature of the charade, it was probably more than anybody could have expected.

The lords of the Las Vegas casinos didn't care. A short fight meant punters were back on the tables sooner rather than later. Sin City's love affair with the heavyweight championship of the world had begun.

Barry Gottehrer, who was not a boxing writer but a New York political and social analyst, did his best to unravel what Liston was about:

Servile before mobsters, he remains distrustful of most other people and feels – with good reason – that most writers are trying to crucify him. He feels secure only with his wife and, though childless, delights in the company and admiration of children.

He would like to be liked, but, realistically, he is prepared to live with the boos and catcalls that greeted him when he entered and left the ring in Las Vegas.

Liston had said: "The public is not with me, I know, but they'll just have to swing along until somebody comes to beat me."

Jim Murray, columnist for the *Los Angeles Times*, said: ". . . the world of sport now realises it has gotten Charles (Sonny) Liston to keep. It's like finding a live bat on a string under your Christmas tree."

In its December 1963 issue, *Esquire* magazine had a front cover photo of Sonny in a Santa Claus hat. A story circulated that for that shoot, which was in Las Vegas, Liston posed for just one photo in a room at a casino, then got up and walked away. The *Esquire* art director George Lois tried to stop him leaving and put his hand on Liston's arm. Liston stood and stared at him; Lois removed his hand. In a panic, Lois asked Joe Louis for help. Joe found Liston shooting craps and brought him back.

Two days after beating Patterson for the second time, Charles and Geraldine flew back to Denver, where they lived at 3395 Monaco Parkway, a four-bedroom house in an integrated neighbourhood. This time at the airport there were 1,500 people and the mayor and his wife. Liston was genuinely moved. "I was thrilled," he said later. "It's one of the nicest things that ever happened to me."

Geraldine was pleased with their new life. "It's really nice, you can hear the birds sing," she said.

Sonny said he enjoyed Denver's clean air. "No smoke, no smog," he said.

His home phone number was ex-directory, but the phone in his car was in the Denver telephone book. He took to cutting his grass and riding a bicycle. He felt as if he could live like that for the rest of his life.

Clay vs Cooper – The Louisville Lip Tastes Henry's Hammer

John Cottrell

One day in April, 1963, Warden E. V. Nash received an unexpected visitor behind the spiked walls of the Missouri State Penitentiary, Jefferson City. In a big white Cadillac, prisoner Old Boy No. 63723, better known as Sonny Liston, rolled up for a sentimental visit to the boxing school he had joined in 1950 when he was given a five-year sentence for armed robbery. Liston, who was paroled in 1952 and crowned world champion ten years later, declined an invitation to dine with prison officials. Instead, he joined the inmates lunching on chipped beef, potatoes, beans and milk. He found several of his old "colleagues" there, and they welcomed him like a famous old soldier at a regimental reunion.

Sonny, seeming more at home there than in the plush hotels of Miami and New York, passed by his old cell and quipped: "They should put a plaque in there." He popped in the prison barber shop for a short back-and-sides. "I always got a good trimming here," he joked. Then he handed the convict barbers the biggest tip they had ever seen and drove away.

It was all part of the Liston campaign to build up a new public image of a clean-living, good-humoured, reformed world champion. After capturing the heavyweight crown in September, 1962, he had promised to be "a fighting champion", defending the world title twice, maybe three times a year. But for many months he saw the inside of more hospitals and orphanages than boxing rings and was photographed with such respectable citizens as then Vice-President Lyndon Johnson more often than with sparring partners. Fighting did not seem all that important;

after all, many experts rated him the greatest heavyweight of the century. "He'll be champion for five to seven years," said manager Jack Nilon. "No one will touch him. I don't see anyone in sight."

For the moment at least, Liston, the former social outcast, was doing a pretty good public relations job in presenting himself as a "nice guy" if not as an active champion. But not so Clay, now the second ranked contender for the heavyweight crown. By this time, the immature Clay had firmly established himself as America's No. 1 Big Head. He had been hailed as the greatest attraction in boxing. He had made himself the most talked-of fighter in years and he had infused new life into the heavyweight division. But his disappointing showing against third-ranked Doug Jones had greatly diminished his reputation. Critics who had praised him in the past began to think again. Some concluded he lacked strength and stamina; almost unanimously they were agreed that he could not live in the same ring as Liston. Cassius's plans to become the youngest-ever heavyweight champion had suffered their biggest set-back.

Boxing generally suffered a severe body blow around the time of the Clay–Jones fight. It was in March, 1963, that world featherweight champion Davey Moore, after taking terrible punishment in defence of his title, fell into a deep coma and died three days later, thus sparking off a new outcry for boxing to be banned. That same month, the heavyweight championship was thrown into confusion by the curious news that Sonny Liston had damaged a knee – probably straining a ligament – while swinging a golf club for a freelance photographer. He would not, after all, be able to meet Floyd Patterson in the return bout scheduled for April 4th in Miami Beach Convention Hall. The fight was postponed until April 11th to allow the champion sufficient time to rest his knee; then it was put off for an indefinite period because, unexpectedly, he was still troubled by the injury.

Under the terms of the much-criticised return match contract, Patterson had authority to name the date and site for the title bout, but Liston's manager and business adviser, Jack Nilon, wanted the fight to be staged in Baltimore where he held concessions for the new sixteen million-dollar civic centre. Now, as weeks passed by, and wealthy Miami visitors began their winter migration, it became necessary to seek an alternative site. Miami had never been an attractive choice in end-of-the-season April, and possibly Patterson only insisted on that venue out of superstition, recalling that it was there, on March 13th, 1961, that he had defeated Johansson in the sixth round of their third meeting. Madison Square Garden, where Clay versus Jones had been a sell-out, was the obvious venue, but Liston was not eager to crawl to the New York Commission and beg for the licence which was refused him before he went to Comiskey Park, Chicago, on September 25th, 1962, and clobbered the world champion in two minutes, six seconds. Baltimore was discussed again as a possibility. Finally, after lengthy negotiations, it was agreed that the big fight should be staged in Las Vegas in July, even though this desert gambling city had an arena with fewer than 8,000 seats.

All these procrastinations seriously frustrated and finally killed Clay's cherished ambition to become the youngest world heavyweight champion of all time. At the end of February, when he was training at Miami's Fifth Street Gym, he regularly visited Liston's camp in an effort to lure the "big bear" into a fight. Liston laughed at Clay's first prediction that he could beat the champion in six rounds. "By the time of the sixth round, I'll be halfway through the victory celebrations." But at this time there did seem a remote chance that the moody champion might rise to the bait and accept a challenge after disposing of Patterson again.

When the return fight was scheduled for July – and there was no guarantee that it would take place then – Clay's chances of surpassing the record of Patterson, who had won the world title in November, 1956, at the age of twenty-one years ten months, faded considerably. Clay's deadline was November, 1963, and his aim was to meet Liston in September, but he still had to prove himself a worthy contender for the title. Most fight experts at this time reckoned that Clay needed two more years' experience to become ready to fight Liston, who would then be that much older and slower.

While he remained undefeated, Clay's prestige had fallen sharply as a result of his performance against Jones. He had failed to fulfil his prediction. He had failed to score a knock-out. He had failed to win over his sterner critics. On the other hand, as Clay saw his world title timetable delayed, he could secretly reflect how much grimmer the situation could have been if the points decision had gone against him in the Jones fight, as it might so easily have done but for his determined rally in the last two rounds. Defeat by Jones could have eclipsed Clay's image as the most dazzling title prospect in the world and set back his championship campaign several years. In his own words, he would have had to get down on his knees, crawl across the ring, kiss the feet of Jones, call him "the greatest" and then catch the first plane out of the country. Instead, victory, however unconvincing, had put him in direct line of succession to the heavyweight crown, as the man seen as the natural challenger to the winner of the Liston–Patterson return.

With Liston unfit and Patterson all geared up to fight, a Clay – Patterson match was an obvious possibility. Moves to stage this meeting reached an advanced stage and it was agreed that Clay would have a 175,000-dollar guarantee and Patterson 200,000 dollars. But negotiations broke down when the Madison Square Garden Corporation refused to enter into a joint promotion with Patterson's backers. Then the second Liston–Patterson fight was fixed for July and plans for a Patterson–Clay bout had to be shelved indefinitely.

Tired of waiting for Patterson, Clay signed for his first professional fight overseas – against Henry Cooper, five years British and Empire heavyweight champion, winner of twenty-seven out of thirty-six bouts. For Cooper it provided a long-awaited opportunity to prove himself a deserving world title challenger. Several times before he had come within an ace of fighting for the championship only to miss the heavyweight gold-rush. In January, 1959, a Patterson–Cooper fight was mooted but negotiations broke down and the privilege went to Brian London, whom Cooper had only recently defeated on points in defence of his two titles. Luckless Cooper then had a long wait while Patterson and Johansson settled their title dispute, and in December, 1961, just when the prospects of meeting Patterson were bright again, Cooper blotted his copybook by taking a second round knock-out defeat by Zora Folley at Wembley

Pool. Now, with time running out for the twenty-nine-year-old British champion, the attraction of a Clay match was considerable. The match was also another example of the shrewd planning of Clay's progress. Everyone wanted a return fight with Jones, a bout regarded as a sure sell-out, but another long struggle with the lower-ranked New Yorker would scarcely have speeded Clay's climb to the top.

In meeting Cooper, fifth in the World Boxing Association's rankings after Liston, Patterson, Clay and Jones, the Louisville Lip was as confident as ever – almost too confident. He broke off training in Miami a full month before the bout, drove his Cadillac to Louisville where he stayed up late at night, worked on his poems and played *Monopoly* with local kids. "I'm tired of training to fight stiffs," he grumbled, "all I want is a crack at Liston." Then he drove to New York, sometimes staying up to six o'clock in the morning, and arranged to cut a disc of his verses. Following reports that Cooper had no wish to meet Liston at present, he asked: "How can I be worried about a guy who's afraid to fight the Big Ugly Bear?"

In June, 1963, the Cassius Clay cyclone hit the shores of a Britain braced in readiness for the impact and prepared for anything after recently being rocked by the Profumo scandal. The British fans knew all about the Loudmouth. No one was surprised when he advertised himself as "the uncrowned heavyweight champion of the world", offered his autograph for a £5 note, posed outside Buckingham Palace ("a swell pad"), went on training runs in stately Regent Street and Pall Mall, and then called at the outfitters to H.R.H. the Duke of Edinburgh and came away with a new bowler and red brocade cocktail jacket with a dragon motif. The fans were ready for the bombast, too. He declared: "After five rounds Henry Cooper will think his name is Gordon Cooper; he'll be in orbit. It ain't no jive. Henry Cooper will go in five." But when Cassius tried working on his usual hate campaign, some sensitive Britons took extreme exception. They did not like to hear "Our 'Enery", the quiet, likeable ex-plasterer, being called "a tramp, a bum, and a cripple not worth training for".

Cooper himself took it all good humouredly, knowing that Clay was only building up the gate for both of them. But BBC

television interviewer David Coleman took Gaseous Cassius
much too seriously. "You talk too much," he told Clay during a
live programme, and he proceeded to lecture him on the British
view of good sporting behaviour. That was too much for the
master of monologues. Offended, he groused, "I don't have to be
on your programme. I'm leaving." And, true enough, he stormed
out of the studio in the middle of the interview. Later he threatened to go home for a week to cool down and complained, "The
English people don't understand me".

During his two weeks in England, Cassius worked as hard as
ever on building up the fight. He Rolls-Royced to a boxing
promotion in Nottingham, climbed into the ring with a great
placard: "Round Five". He held press conferences (to which one
newspaper sent its drama critic). He attracted a record 2,000
crowd to the televised weigh-in at the London Palladium. Clay
borrowed the dressing room of singer Susan Maughan and came
on stage signalling "Five". Cooper joined in the show by pluck-
ing a hair from the Kentuckian's chest.

It was an unforgettable big fight occasion at Wembley Stadium,
with the noisy entrance of Liz Taylor and Richard Burton and
the 55,000 crowd singing in the rain to the music of the
Coldstream Guards. Then, heralded by six trumpeters, came the
two gladiators. From one side emerged the British champion,
wearing a blue and white gown, simply marked "Henry Cooper,
England". From the other came the Kentucky rooster in a £25,
London tailored red and white satin gown emblazoned with the
words, "Cassius Clay the Greatest". Perched at a jaunty angle on
his head was a magnificent crown.

How gallant Henry raised British hopes that cold, rainy night,
the 148th anniversary of the Battle of Waterloo. Cooper, eight
years older and 22 lb. lighter than his rival, surprised Clay by
opening fast and furious. The American, fighting at his heaviest
ever weight of 207 lb., was forced to hold on and earned an
admonishment from a finger-wagging referee. Henry was really
aggressive. He forced Clay back against the ropes, and more
than once Mighty Mouth looked appealingly at the referee when
he was hit at the end of a break. Now he was bleeding slightly
from the nose for the first time in his career.

They were evenly matched in the second round, with Clay

carrying the fight to Cooper and jabbing much more effectively. Then poor Henry was hit by his old hoodoo – a cut had opened beside his left eye. With vision blurred, he bravely attacked in the third while Clay began toying with him contemptuously, dropping his hands and dancing teasingly around him. Between rounds Bill Faversham shouted to trainer Dundee to instruct Clay to cut out this exhibition of bad taste and fight properly. But in the fourth round, though carrying his hands higher, Cassius was again showing off unnecessarily, taunting his crimson-faced opponent, using only his feet to elude him, even taking the grave risk of leading with his right. Finally he swayed once too often – smack into the arc of Cooper's big left hook.

To the screaming delight of the fans, proud, arrogant, bombastic Clay was dumped unceremoniously on the seat of his pants. It was only the second time in his professional career that he had been put down, Sonny Banks having achieved the distinction in 1962, also with a left hook. All Wembley now roared for Humble Henry to thrash Gaseous Cassius, but it was too late in the round for him to follow up his unexpected advantage. Clay's pride was hurt more than his jaw; shaken, he rose at four, just before the bell brought respite. After round one, Dundee had observed a tiny slit between the thumb and fingers of his boxer's right glove. Now, by choosing this moment to complain about it, he shrewdly gained Clay an extra thirty seconds rest while officials searched in vain for a spare pair of gloves. Those extra seconds could have been vital for his man to regain his full senses. As it happened, Clay did not need more than a minute to recover from that left hook. It was now time for the prophet to keep his word – "Cooper in five". He threw off his casual approach, came out mean and determined, and revealed his superb combination punching as he rocked the Englishman with his first blow and then relentlessly hammered his grotesquely blood-stained opponent with both fists. Henry fought on bravely, hopelessly. One eye closed and slow-footed, he was taking so much punishment that the fans, including Liz Taylor, were yelling "Stop it". London referee Tommy Little duly obliged after one minute fifteen seconds of the round. "The fight's over, chum," he told the dogged Englishman. Cooper shrugged and, as he climbed out of the torture pit, he cracked: "We didn't do so bad for a bum and a cripple, did we?"

Cassius was more polite in victory. He had called the round correctly once again, but he refused to redoff his splendid crown. "Cooper's no longer a bum," he said. "He hit me harder than anybody else I have met. I underestimated him." But he explained that he had turned his eyes towards Cleopatra (Elizabeth Taylor) at the time he was caught by Henry's haymaker, having been distracted by her cries of "Stop it". Cooper, the placid realist, had no excuses. "Our 'Enery" simply stated the cold facts: "'E said 'e would, and 'e did it, and that's 'ow it goes. It can't be 'elped."

The fight did not raise Clay's standing as a boxer. His old defensive faults were more glaring than ever. But he had conducted such a brilliantly daring publicity campaign and had been so shrewdly managed that his claims for a world title fight could no longer be ignored. After the Cooper battle, the Louisville Lip had a surprise visitor to his dressing room – Liston's manager, Jack Nilon. "We want you bad in September, Cassius," said Nilon, taking another victory over Patterson in July for granted. "I've come 3,500 miles to get your okay." The site would probably be Philadelphia's 100,000-seat Municipal Stadium on September 30th.

Though his own management preferred him to wait a year, Clay assured Nilon that he would fight "if the price is right". After two and a half years of professional boxing, after only nineteen paid bouts, the strutting twenty-one-year-old pretender to Liston's throne was just one step away from the world crown. And there was still time for him to beat Patterson's record as the youngest heavyweight champion.

PART 2
SONNY

Legacies

Reg Gutteridge

The press almost uniformly portrayed Liston as an ogre, but British sports commentator Reg Gutteridge saw beyond Liston's fearsome, scowling front. The following is from Gutteridge's autobiography and provides an insight into Liston's character away from the ring.

> *"Teach us delight in simple things,*
> *And mirth that has no bitter springs."*
> *—RUDYARD KIPLING*

Sadly, like Dad and Uncle Jack, Mum also died before her time, at the age of sixty-one. She lived long enough to experience the joy of having grandchildren – my daughters Sue and Sally were six and three when Mum passed away.

Having to live with nothing but boxing, wrestling, dog racing and football chatter all her married life, she was delighted to be able to indulge herself in some girl talk, at last, with Connie and the babies.

As for me, and more importantly for my artificial leg, it meant that there was no need for me to make excuses that I was unable to get down on my knees and nag them to keep their chins tucked in behind the left lead or teach them to hook off the jab, as I imagined I would have had to if they had been boys.

I decided that the best way for them to get used to the fact that their old man had a wooden leg was to laugh about it, especially as I invariably took it off indoors and they were always having to shift it around like a piece of furniture when they were helping their mother with the housework.

In fact, they both became quite attached to it. Never more so than when we were on holiday and the leg became a status symbol to go with the bucket and spade.

The girls' favourite beach game, when they were toddlers, was to bury the artificial limb in the sand with the false foot sticking up and then to submerge me far enough away for them to tell any passer-by who was interested that I was a "daddy longlegs".

There was one incident, when they were still children that did shock them a bit and embarrassed them even more. That was when the bloody thing fell off in the street and Connie had to shove it in her shopping bag.

It was not just any old street, either, it was on a main drag in Gibraltar. I had splashed out to take us all on a cruise aboard the *Canberra*. We were all indulging in some sightseeing ashore when I heard this tearing noise coming from inside my trousers. The flesh coloured gauze surrounding the wood, or more accurately the hard cork, had ripped as the lower leg came away from its moorings and the foot fell off into the roadway.

It was the one and only time this type of accident ever happened to me, so we were all a bit flustered. I had to hop to the nearest wall and perch on it while we tried to cover up our collective embarrassment. Connie popped the offending leg in the bag she had been hoping to fill with souvenirs.

Some people who had been on the ship with us were close behind when this mishap occurred. One of them, a woman, who had previously had no idea that I was handicapped, asked me whether she should send for a doctor. I replied: "Not really, thank you, my dear, but I could do with a carpenter, just as long as it's not Harry." By this time the girls were bent double with laughter and this kind woman was able to take them off our hands while Connie and I retreated back to the ship in a cab. As I hopped up the gangway, the Master at Arms gave us an old-fashioned bemused look, as he hadn't noticed a one-legged passenger until now.

As for the girls they experienced the satisfying thrill of learning to swim in the pool on that ship so the last thing on their minds at that exciting time for them was old daddy longlegs.

Outside of the family, I decided the best way to cope with one leg was to tell as few people as possible about it, so that it did not become a source of boring conversation.

I've resolved to indulge myself just a little on these pages in the knowledge that after fifty-eight years of living with it I've paid my dues and am entitled to cash in at last.

As I'm told by my most ferocious critic – her indoors – this is the only story that still makes her grin. I'll begin these few shaggy leg stories with the one about Sonny Liston.

I'll have more to say about Charles "Sonny" Liston as a boxer and a man later, but suffice it to say, that anyone who can remember him will surely agree with me that, as monsters go, he made even made Mike Tyson look like a choirboy.

Against all the odds and certainly against my better nature, Sonny and I became genuine buddy boys. He was, if you can be persuaded to believe this, a bully with a soft centre. He possessed that precious gift of sometimes being able to laugh at himself, although you had to be very careful when choosing your moment.

I usually pick my friends on the "what-you-see-is-what-you-get" basis, as is most definitely the case with a gentleman like Henry Cooper. But, if you had the time, opportunity and patience to look for it, there was a rough charm beneath that well-rehearsed Liston scowl. So much so that I felt the need to go and pay my respects at Sonny's Las Vegas grave when he met his untimely and mysterious end.

His was the introduction from hell. He was attired in, of all things, a kilt. He was in Scotland on a tour of Britain at the time. Sonny told anyone who would listen that his Scottish hosts had only put the sporran on him to cover up his lunch box and so prevent the local ladies getting killed in the rush to take a closer look at him.

Instead of shaking hands with me at that, our first social meeting, he flicked his enormous fingers at my unmentionables and as I bent double with pain, he drawled: "Take a bow". Then he gave out a great belly laugh. When I had recovered my composure enough to tell him that I did not think it was funny and that I would have to go to the mens' room to inspect the swelling that was already growing, he just grinned again and said: "Mention my name and they'll give you the best seat."

Our jobs meant that we were destined to see a lot of each other. My chance for revenge came one night in a hotel bar when we were resting between engagements and were both, to coin a well-worn cockney phrase, slightly Brahms and Liszt.

Milking his bogeyman image for all it was worth, Sonny suddenly said to me: "Why is it that you white guys think black guys look like gorillas?"

"Come on," I protested, "I've never said anything like that in my life." I did not realise he was setting me up for another of his favourite party tricks. And for winning a bet which, as a notorious gambling man, he was very partial to, of course.

"Bullshit, man," rasped Sonny, "you're just like all the other white guys, you think us blacks are just big hairy apes. Well, I'm issuing you a challenge here and now – I'll bet you any money you like that you've got more hairs on your goddam leg than I have. So, come on, put your money on the table and roll up your trousers."

For the sake of my health, I went easy on him and only bet a tenner. Then I slowly rolled up my left trouser leg and exposed the hairless imitation in all its temporary glory.

Sonny called me, among other things, "a cork-legged limey son-of-a-bitch" but laughed heartily and paid up.

Between that meeting and our next he had other more pressing matters on his mind, such as a possible upcoming fight with Cassius Clay, for instance. By the time we came into contact again, he had forgotten that earlier betting skirmish.

On this occasion and in this particular hotel bar we happened to be drinking together again and I was addressing him as "Charles" in a phony upper-crust English accent, as I always did, when Sonny suddenly said: "You Brits are a bunch of faggots. All you got is horizontal heavyweights."

Game for another life, I got lippy and said: "Your tough guy act is so much bullshit. As old as I am I could show you what a real tough guy looks like. I've got $50 that says I'm tougher than you."

Astonished, intrigued and decidedly forgetful Sonny pulled out his $50 and covered mine, saying: "What you gonna do little guy – arm wrestle me?"

His mouth dropped open when I rolled up my trouser, took an ice pick out of the drinks bucket and began plunging it into what he thought was my bare leg.

It was only after ten "stabs" that he suddenly remembered who I was. He was so taken with me this time that every time I saw him subsequently he would beg me for an encore so that he could win some easy money from "some other sucker". Poor old Sonny never lived long enough to enjoy many more party tricks, his own or anyone else's.

These fun and games backfired on me, too. I had to go back to Roehampton Limb Fitting Centre to have the leg repaired. It looked as though a woodpecker had been at it.

The leg legacy that affords me most pride, however, came when I applied for life insurance in middle age and was sent by the insurance company to be examined by Dr Adrian Whiteson in Upper Wimpole Street. By coincidence, Adrian is chief medical officer for the British Boxing Board of Control, which means he and I have been friends for years.

He was astonished to discover that I was one leg short of a full set and, like so many other people who knew me well professionally, he had no inkling of my handicap.

I still thank my lucky stars that I was not wounded at Waterloo under Wellington. From my layman's knowledge of history it is more than probable that I would have had to go around begging for alms for the rest of my life.

This luxurious jet-set lifestyle of mine still has its niggling disadvantages for the disabled. Nothing was more irritating than when I asked a British airline if I could have one of those seats with leg room near the exit. They refused on the grounds that disabled people could not be allowed to sit there in case they obstructed other passengers in the event of an emergency exit. Pardon me for living!

That little grouse apart, I have managed to turn the handicap into a reason to have a giggle or two. By the time I went to commentate on a fight in France quite recently my missing leg had been revealed by Muhammad Ali's doctor, Ferdie Pacheco in his autobiography, *Fight Doctor.*

Armed with this information, a French journalist working for the local paper had worked out that my leg had gone missing very near the venue for this particular fight. This resourceful young Frenchman suddenly tapped me on the shoulder at ringside and inquired: "Monsieur Gutteridge, I believe you lost your leg near here."

I could not resist this smart ass reply: "Why, have you found it, my son?" I'm slightly ashamed of that lack of courtesy, but sometimes I can't resist the clown that is in me.

On another occasion, I was changing planes at Singapore airport, where I was bound for Alan Rudkins's world bantamweight title fight in Tokyo. There was a five-hour stop-over involved and I found myself sleeping on a bench opposite legless war hero Douglas Bader.

When it came to going through the security gate, I happened to be the next one behind Bader in the queue. As the inevitable bleep sounded the security man recognised Douglas and promptly saluted him. When I went through immediately afterwards and when he could find no metal in my pockets, he scratched his head and started examining the machine for a possible fault. It was only when I rolled up my trouser leg that the guard permitted himself a bewildered smile, which turned to a grin when I told him: "English is vellee funny people!"

The lack of a leg provided a laugh or two in my younger days when on trips to sunny climes where other newspaper lads would goad me into hopping out of whatever ocean we just happened to be lucky enough to be in at the time and clearing the beach by shouting "sharks!"

I still grin, too, at the young car salesman who was attempting to sell me my first car. He pointed out that as the vehicle in question was an automatic: "You won't have a clue what to do with your left leg." I told him to take a refresher course in his selling techniques.

One of the funniest automobile stories I have heard concerned my old pal, Henry Cooper, in the days before the phrase "road rage" was invented.

Henry, his twin George and their old manager, Jim Wicks, were involved in a contretemps over rights of way in a dark country lane one night. The driver of the other car came over to them shaking his fist and shaping up to fight whoever was inside what he considered was the offending vehicle.

Imagine his astonishment when the twins and old Jim all got out of the car to confront him. The other guy recognised them but they so appreciated his cheek and his courage when, in backing down, he said: "It's only because there's three of you," that they couldn't stop laughing.

He's Just a Little Boy in the Dark and He's Scared

Bob Mee

William B. MacDonald Jr owned a stud farm near Delray Beach, a baseball team in Tampa, a yacht, 45 per cent of a racetrack . . . and wanted to promote the heavyweight championship of the world.

He liked to make people happy. "You can't sell to everybody," he said once, "but you can be everybody's friend."

In order to do this, he handed out cufflinks with his face engraved on them. He entertained guests on a two-hole pitch-and-putt course in the grounds of his Florida home and on a fifty-foot cruiser named *Snoozie* after his wife – "She's still harder to wake up than a bear" – moored yards from his front door. His car of preference was a Rolls-Royce. Whoever you were, it was likely he would address you as "coach".

His eight-year-old daughter's treehouse contained a fridge, stove and jukebox. His son's sixth birthday present was a railway engine with 800 feet of track meandering through the gardens.

Bill MacDonald had met the President, he had met Jayne Mansfield, and he had the photographs on his wall to prove it. He was negotiating to buy Channel 10, the Miami-area television channel affiliated to the American Broadcasting Corporation. "I've spent $165,000 in legal fees, but if I get it, it's bingo – seven or eight million right away."

He estimated he had lost $200,000 staging golf tournaments "but made a million friends". And now he wanted to promote the heavyweight championship of the world.

He had bankrolled the promoters of the 1961 world championship "decider" between Floyd Patterson and Ingemar Johansson in Miami to the tune of $400,000 but had not promoted it himself. He had enjoyed the publicity and had lost nothing. He also revealed that at one point he had been approached to act as manager for Liston. He was vague about the details but said in an interview with *Sports Illustrated*: "Someone once approached me to manage Liston. He was looking for a front man. But it's an ugly business to begin with, and I make too much money other ways to be bothered wet-nursing those kids."

In 1961, the city of Miami Beach had awarded him a plaque in recognition and appreciation of his "work and accomplishments". He was a member of the board of trustees at St Francis Hospital, a founder-member of Mount Sinai Hospital, a member of the board of Miami Heart Institute and Cedars of Lebanon Hospital, chairman of the eighth annual brotherhood dinner of the National Conference of Christians and Jews, and a member and trustee of the Eaton Foundation at the University of Miami. A publicity handout distributed with the fight media pack described him as "a great philanthropist contributing to the betterment of his fellow man". One stop short of a saint, it seemed.

Chris Dundee, who had promoted fights in Miami for a generation and more, suggested MacDonald spread his philanthropy to Liston – Clay. Dundee's view, or the one he offered MacDonald, was that they could make a million dollars as easily as breaking sticks. And on the back of that tip, MacDonald bought the rights to promote the fight from Inter-Continental Promotions Inc., the company Jack Nilon had set up supposedly to guarantee Liston's future. MacDonald paid Inter-Continental $625,000 for the live promotion but did not buy the theatre TV rights. That was a monumental blunder. By fight time, there were more than one million seats available for the closed-circuit screening across the United States.

MacDonald said he just went straight in with his maximum offer, didn't mess with negotiating and wasting time. "I figure if this man Jack Nilon don't take it, he can't count. And him being in the concession business, coming up from a bag of peanuts and a hot dog, he ought to know how to count."

MacDonald said, with other expenses, he needed to raise $800,000 from the live gate to break even. The best he could do, with a full price sell-out of all 16,448 seats, was $100,000 profit.

As, perhaps, it dawned on him that there was no chance of this happening, he accepted the probability of losses but satisfied himself that he was doing something positive for the Miami Beach area. He was in it, he said, for the kick of making it happen and making it a success. He wanted people to want to come out of their homes and queue, even sleep, in the street to be able to watch it. He said he enjoyed the "motion" of being involved. He said moving the ringside seats at $250 would not be an issue. It was persuading the ordinary man to part with his hard-earned money to be there in the cheaper seats that was the difficult part of the job. "This promotion is going to be as clean as possible," he said to *Sports Illustrated's* Gilbert Rogin. "It's going to be a breath of fresh air."

Surprisingly, MacDonald had a shrewd analytical take on the fight itself:

> I figure Clay wins it. He'll take the title if he stays away, jabs and runs. But the little jerk is so egotistical he thinks he can punch Liston's nose sideways. It's liable to be a stinky fight to watch, but if Clay gets by seven or eight he's liable to win it.

Technically, prizefighting for reward was still illegal in Florida. MacDonald and Dundee circumvented that in the usual way by declaring that the occasion was sponsored by the Veterans of Foreign Wars charity (VFW). For the privilege, MacDonald and Dundee were to pay the organisation $500. They also had about 20 VFW members at ringside. This done, the Miami Commission licensed the fight.

In a subsequent financial wrangle between Inter-Continental and MacDonald, Harold Conrad told the court hearing:

> Well, I think there was some kind of a handout that these guys [VFW] had been having for years in this town. You can't put on a fight unless they are at the door. I don't know what the details are."

VFW representative Max Lenchner testified that he had received the $500 cheque and recalled the conversation he had with Chris Dundee, who told him: "We are having a fight next week, Max. Be here with the men." And Lenchner said: "That's the way it is."

Chris Dundee had begun in boxing in 1926 when another of his brothers, Joe, was fighting. Chris would go with him whenever he could. The family name, incidentally, was Mirenda. They were Italian immigrants, but somewhere along the way Joe took the name Dundee. Chris, who worked his corner, did too. He moved from Philadelphia to New York, where he was based at the Capitol Hotel, and looked after top-class fighters like Ken Overlin, who was world middleweight champion, Midget Wolgast, the flyweight champion, and contender Georgie Abrams. (Joe Dundee, incidentally, was not the fighter who used that name and held the world welterweight title.)

Chris's younger brother Angelo, meanwhile, learned cornerwork from leading trainers Whitey Bimstein, Chickie Ferrara, Ray Arcel and Charley Goldman. He talked to them all, watched them all, held the bucket in corners they ran. He watched how they wrapped hands. "I learned how to keep my mouth shut and my ears open," Angelo said.

This is the way you learn. I got to be known as a dependable kid. Chris gave me some four-round fighters to handle, and I was in Stillman's Gym day and night, working with them and hustling fights for them.

Chris moved on to Miami when the small clubs in New York began to die out and the television money was controlled by the IBC. In Miami, Angelo set up his own gym on Fifth Street. "The Cuban era came along when a lot of good fighters came to Miami to get away from the Castro regime," he told Graham Houston in a *Boxing News* interview in 1974. "We had Luis Rodriguez and Sugar Ramos, Doug Vaillant and Florentino Fernandez, who got robbed against Gene Fullmer for the middleweight title."

Chris Dundee had promoted almost 400 shows by the time of his involvement with the Liston–Clay fight, including twelve at the Convention Hall. He knew the business backwards, sidewards and any other wards you could think of. The publicity pack for the promotion declared him "a solid citizen of the ever-growing

Miami Beach area", with wife Gerri, daughter Susan and son Michael.

Liston arrived in Miami four weeks before the fight. He was taken from the plane in an electric cart across the tarmac to the VIP room. Clay, who was training as usual at Angelo Dundee's Fifth Street Gym, made sure he was there to greet Liston by running after the cart across the tarmac. The girl driving the cart stalled it. Liston got out, telling MacDonald he would break Clay's arms. MacDonald pleaded and cajoled him back into the cart, and they drove away with Cassius still yelling. MacDonald's stressed-out publicist Al Taylor saw the episode as an embarrassment that did not help people believe the fight was an occasion they needed to be at.

Liston was ushered through the airport terminal, his face its usual mask, a trilby on his head, a raincoat over his arm. The only man looking grimmer than him was MacDonald, who had his arm through Liston's, guiding him. Taylor was much more animated on the other side of the champion.

Liston had hired an expensive house at 6351 Pine Tree Drive, Miami Beach, for himself and his closest associates. Among those who visited him there was Ash Resnick.

Harold Conrad was still with the Liston public relations team. He says Liston simply could not believe he could lose to Clay. Instead of training, he took life at his leisure – and pleasure. "He thought he was invincible," said Conrad, in an interview with Dan Hirschberg for *Boxing Today*:

> He scared the shit out of Patterson just by looking at him, and here comes this big-mouth kid. He didn't train at all for that fight. He worked out a little, went to the gym. He would hang out at a beauty parlour banging on some of the chicks.
>
> I'd tell him, "This kid is big and strong, he's fast, he can hit."
>
> Sonny would just answer, "Ah, you're kidding. I'll scare the shit out of that nigger-faggot. I'll scare the shit out of him at the weigh-in. I'll put the eye on him . . ."

Jack McKinney also felt Liston's superiority over Clay in the two incidents in the Thunderbird the year before were the worst thing that could have happened to Liston. "Sonny thought all he had to do was take off his robe and Clay would faint," said McKinney. "He made that colossal misjudgement. He didn't train at all."

Harry Carpenter remembered the only time Liston ever gave him a long quote. It was when he asked if Clay's psychological tactics were getting under his skin. Liston said:

You ever hear that saying "whistlin' in the dark"? You know what a small boy does walking through a graveyard at night when he's scared. He whistles. Well, that's Clay. He's just a little boy in the dark, and he's scared.

Joe Louis also said Liston's preparations were not what they should have been. His sparring partners were not good enough. One of the best of them was his old friend from St Louis, Jesse Bowdry, who was a light-heavyweight. Bowdry would box on the undercard in Miami – the last bout of his long career. It would be his tenth defeat in his last twelve fights. He didn't have it any more.

Leotis Martin, a top-class amateur who would eventually turn into a worldclass heavyweight – and would be the last man to beat Sonny – was another. He bobbed and weaved, moved as quickly as he could, but as imitations of Clay went, it wasn't very useful. Liston didn't look good. Louis said: "He can't hit some of them, they're too small . . . One guy should have had his licence taken away, he was so bad." Even so, Louis said he thought Clay stood very little chance.

In Miami, after an impromptu doorstepping job at Liston's rented house, British writer Reg Gutteridge was leaving with nothing more than a stare and rebuke from the champion, when he chanced on Louis, who was sitting on a bench outside with his wife Martha. Louis called him over and told him:

This is an angry man and he can't afford to be angry fighting Clay. I keep him cool. Cassius is a master of psychological warfare. He irritates and disturbs, and whatever Sonny may think, maybe, Clay bothers him.

I am a practical guy, and I face realities. I tell Sonny, "Nobody saw me losing to Max Schmeling, but I did." It

curbs his over-confidence. His title is a passport to respecta-
bility. He has got to hang on to it.

Liston agreed to press workouts at the Surfside Civic Centre,
afterwards answering questions. At one he was asked if he had
met anyone bigger than him before. It was the kind of dumb ill-
researched enquiry that on another day might have provoked
him into a bitter "yeah" and a slow, steady stare. He was relaxed,
though, and offered: "Nino Valdes, Cleveland Williams, Julio
Mederos . . ."

Someone else suggested Clay might be too fast for him.

"Is he fast? Can he catch bullets or something?"

It was the same line he had used before the first Patterson
fight.

"The faster he is, the faster it will be over."

Liston felt Clay would be no faster than Patterson. I shouldn't
have to be training all this time to go just one round."

A large sign in front of the workout area invited fans to "Have
Your Picture Taken With Sonny Liston". At a price, naturally.

Peter Wilson for the *Daily Mirror* enjoyed an incident outside
the civic centre when Clay, with nine equally noisy friends, came
to bait Liston and was threatened with being arrested for breach
of the peace and blocking the sidewalk. The local police chief
who almost threw Cassius into the slammer was named Wiley B.
Barefoot. "So help me, I'm not making him up," chortled
Wilson. "I'm not that clever!"

Meanwhile, as the good Officer Barefoot was doing his duty,
Clay's "official photographer", Howard Bingham, managed to
slip inside to see Liston's workout, only to be ejected by a security man, whom Wilson discovered was named Gene Buffalo.
(Mr Buffalo, incidentally, had been a fighter. He was knocked
out in one round by Sugar Ray Robinson in 1949.)

Liston did throw writers a few morsels every so often. "I don't
hate Cassius Clay," he said with a week or so to go:

I love him so much I'm giving him 22½ per cent of the gate.
Clay means a lot to me . . . He's my baby, my million-dollar
baby. I hope he keeps well and I sure hope he turns up.

When pressed a little further, he said three rounds would be enough. "The poor guy can't fight," he said. "That's why he talks so much."

When someone brought up the question of ring-rust being a possibility, Liston seemed exasperated:

> Jeez, how good do I have to be? If I knock 'em out any quicker, the other guy won't even show up. The less I fight, the better I get. You say I've won three fights in three rounds in three years. So OK, so after next week it will be four fights in four rounds in four years.

According to George Whiting, after the question-and-answer session Liston was so irritated that he went out and took it out on sparring partner Leotis Martin. "But for the 16 oz gloves, I feel that brother Martin might no longer be with us," wrote Whiting, who said nobody could accuse Liston of not taking the job seriously and suggested that Clay should stick to show business.

He did have his moments of good temper. When he was late for one press conference four weeks before the fight, he actually apologised to the media and told them: "The only way Cassius can hurt me is not to show up for the fight."

Father Edward Murphy arrived and said he had never seen Liston so relaxed:

> Security has made a different man of him. He wants people to like him . . . Sonny has suffered frustrations all his life . . . He has no religion, but he believes in God. He comes to my church once in a while.

Willie Reddish, as trainers will, said Liston had been good to work with all the way through the camp and was in the best shape he'd been in during their four years together.

Confidence in Clay's chances did not even extend to members of the syndicate that backed him. Bill Faversham admitted he would have preferred to have given him more time, to have him fight Doug Jones again and do a better job, perhaps fight Machen and Patterson before risking everything against Liston:

But what the hell. The guy's of age . . . All he wanted was
Liston. So now he's got Liston. But we figure he can win, if
the young fool doesn't get too ambitious or too impetuous in
the early rounds. He's got speed, a good left hand, good
enough to peck Liston to pieces after seven or eight rounds.

George Whiting quoted Faversham, and added his own incredulous rider: "Peck Liston to pieces?"

Whiting said he and Faversham went to the Fifth Street Gym
to watch Clay's workout. "But I fear we each saw something
different, he wrote:

The chairman of Cassius Clay Inc. enthused over the smooth
dexterity with which the company's gangling asset slipped
kidney punches, moved away from clinches and countered
Liston's right hooks. But from where I was standing, these
same manoeuvres looked remarkably amateurish.

Whiting said Clay's father was watching the workout in a pair of
pea-green pants – and did not seem enamoured when his offspring
was hit on the nose three times in succession by a sparring partner's
left jab. When it was over, the young man declared himself satisfied.
"I believe in myself so much it's embarrassing," he said. "My fight
will be to hit and not get hit. I can't be beat. No one can beat me."

Jack Nilon talked up a bizarre idea he had of taking Liston to
the Soviet Union after he had beaten Clay. The peanut and
popcorn mogul felt a fight between his champion and a leading
amateur would be huge and also helpful in terms of developing
international business interests.

Liston said he would rather fight Cleveland Williams. Since
the second of his defeats by Sonny in 1960, Williams had won
twelve, drawn one and lost one – a split decision to a rising
contender from Chicago, Ernie Terrell – in fourteen fights. He
had just knocked out Roger Rischer in three. Only Liston and
Terrell had beaten him in the past ten years. But Nilon wasn't
interested in Williams. Liston asked:

So why doesn't some guy fight himself into a position where I
cannot ignore him? That's what I did . . . Joe Louis did all

right for himself fighting the bum of the month. But times have changed. I don't think I could make a score doing that.

Betting was holding steady. It had been somewhere between 5–1 and 6–1 against Clay for weeks. Clay went on enjoying himself. "After I finish with Liston," he said, "he'd rather run through hell in a gasoline sports coat than fight me again." He also told reporters: "If Liston beats me, I'll crawl across the ring, kiss his feet and take a jet out of the country."

Someone called his bluff, very quietly asking: "What would you really do?"

Clay paused for a moment, smiled and said: "I'll go to my dressing-room, collect my money and go home . . ."

Willie Pastrano, the world light-heavyweight champion, also trained in the Fifth Street Gym under the guidance of Angelo Dundee. He had seen Cassius develop and admired his talent, as well as his ability to drum up publicity. "It's his show," said Pastrano. "Cassius has trouble getting off stage."

After sparring extensively with him over the past couple of years, Pastrano also gave him a real chance of victory. "Cassius might be scared and tense at the start, but when he finds Liston slow and easy to hit he will box like a dream."

Pastrano also said that behind the scenes Clay was not bragging, that he admitted he was nervous, "half-scared", but Willie worried for him that when he danced around with his hands too low and leaned away from punches, which every young amateur was taught not to do, he was wide open for a left hook. Henry Cooper had already dropped him heavily, Sonny Banks put him down too. Pastrano worried what might happen if he made those kinds of errors against Liston.

In one verbal exchange at a press conference with the television cameras rolling, Clay used the same line on the champion face to face that he had already given to the press: "If you whup me, I'll crawl across the ring and kiss your feet."

Liston said: "I ain't gonna wait around all night until you're able to crawl."

Angelo Dundee said if Clay listened, followed instructions, he had the ability to take out Liston late in the fight. "We have many assets," said Dundee to Tex Maule of *Sports Illustrated*:

Clay has a style Liston has never seen before. He is much faster than Liston. He has the faculty of getting under Liston's skin, and he will not be browbeaten by him.

Cassius respects the champion, but really, deep down inside himself, Clay thinks he is unbeatable. And he can hit Sonny with every punch he has. Sonny isn't hard to hit . . .

We can hit him with uppercuts. Left and right. Cassius is the only heavyweight in the world with a good left uppercut . . . If you built a prototype of what kind of fighter can whip Liston, you couldn't improve on Clay. He hits hard, he moves, he has every punch in the book.

We can knock Liston out in the eleventh or twelfth round by wearing him down with the quantity of punches. If Cassius will do what he's told.

Solomon McTier, who helped Dundee after his own career had been ended by a detached retina in 1961, was a quiet member of the team but saw in Clay a touch of greatness that many still overlooked:

You see this kid, the way he can go, the things he can do. He can be a great man if he only does what he is told. All he needs to be afraid of is Clay.

If he keeps his cool and outboxes and outfoxes Liston – which he can do with ease – he can win without any trouble. He's the most wonderful boxer there is. Liston could be just another sparring partner for him. But he gets carried away. He's young and restless and foolish sometime . . .

Another time Clay said:

Maybe I can be beat. I doubt it. But the man is going to have to knock me down and then I'll get up and he'll have to knock me down again and I'll get up and he'll have to knock me down and I'll still get up. I've worked too hard and too long to get this chance. I'm gonna have to be killed before I lose, and I ain't going to die easy.

And he said: "I'll uppercut him stupid. I'll upset the world. I talk too much to lose."

Once while on his back having his Cuban conditioner, Luis Sarria, work on him, he talked quietly as the press gathered round in chairs; sometimes it seemed he was talking to them, sometimes perhaps to his handler, or even to himself:

I'm a pretty fighter. I don't get hit. I'm pretty and smooth. I don't get cut. I'm not marked. I'm something new. The game is alive. Before I came it was dead. The reporters have got something to write about now.

The peanut man is going to make money, the popcorn man is going to make money, the beer man's going to make money. The town is alive.

This is the biggest sport. I am participating in the biggest sport that ever took place in the whole wide world. Nothing is as great as me. The biggest thing in the world is the heavyweight champion. And I'm not going to be just an ordinary heavyweight champion. I'm going to be the greatest of all time.

What the Hell is This? What Did They Do?

Bob Mee

Before the fight, the dignitaries in the twenty-foot-square ring included Jake LaMotta, the middleweight champion who had admitted to the Kefauver Committee that he had taken a dive on Mob orders against Billy Fox in 1947. A long-time Miami resident, the legendary Bronx Bull was now largely ostracised by the boxing community. He took his bow anyway.

Sugar Ray Robinson stepped into the ring as immaculate as ever. He had lost his unbeaten record to LaMotta in Detroit in 1943 but had won four out of four meetings with him after that. Their last fight, in Chicago on 14 February 1951, was remembered as the St Valentine's Day Massacre. "We fought so often I got diabetes," said LaMotta.

Angelo Dundee's world champions Willie Pastrano and Luis Rodriguez were called in, too, as was Eddie Machen, who had taken Liston 12 rounds in 1960.

As challenger, Clay was first into the arena and, according to New York Yankees legend Yogi Berra, had to wait seven or eight minutes in the ring for Liston to appear. If it was deliberate, it was an old trick. If Clay had been feeling the tension, the wait could have all but destroyed his mind.

Ring announcer Frank Freeman introduced Liston as from Denver, Colorado, as if Sonny wanted to embrace publicly his new home town. Willie Reddish, though, wore a T-shirt advertising the Thunderbird Hotel, Las Vegas. Athletic director of the Thunderbird, Ash Resnick, was in the corner team, for no reason anybody could guess. Years on, when the fix theories were discussed, Resnick's presence was used in the argument that Sonny quit to order.

When the referee, Barney Felix, drew them together in the centre of the ring, Cassius met Liston's stare with one of his own. As they waited in their corners for the first bell, Clay danced around, ready to go. Liston shifted his weight ponderously, foot to foot.

The first round saw Clay moving and Liston trying to press, but too quickly, missing with one huge left swing. Clay was first to land with his left jab. He concentrated on movement, then towards the end of the session a sharp right hand connected solidly and he let go a barrage of shots that had the crowd roaring. Reddish was calling to Liston to shorten his punches, to narrow his stance.

The second was quieter. Liston landed a good left hook, but Clay rode it and kept dancing.

The third saw Liston rock from a right hand. He was having trouble with Clay's speed and long, raking blows. The jab was bothering him. Suddenly, Liston was leaking blood from a gash beneath his left eye. Over the second half, though, Liston came back with body punches, his own jab and some clubbing rights. Clay concentrated on damage limitation.

By the fourth, however, the challenger was blinking. Mostly he kept on the move, reluctant to get involved at all. Liston plodded after him, unable to cut the ring down but landing most of what punches there were.

In the corner at the end of the round, an agitated Clay told Angelo Dundee: "Cut the gloves off." He wanted the world to know that somebody had pulled a stunt, that something was fixed – his right eye, especially, was stinging from some kind of solution. Dundee was always convinced it was simply some solution Joe Polino was using on Liston's cut that had somehow got into Cassius's eyes. The young challenger was close to panic, insisted he couldn't see, but Dundee got him up for the next round, told him to run. One story emanating from, among others, the Cubans in the Fifth Street Gym, was that Dundee actually hesitated and it was the Cuban, Luis Sarria, who decisively told him to push Cassius back out because it was "for the big one". Barney Felix said, as they stood in the corner, still trying to put Clay's mouthpiece in, he was a second or two away from stopping the fight.

Liston ploughed forward, chasing, missing mostly, but landing sometimes, and Clay kept wheeling around the ring, buying himself recovery time. He did it.

By the sixth, his eyes had cleared, his jab was working again, and Liston looked terribly tired. Not to mention old. The champion was painfully slow on his feet and slow to react. A barrage of seven unanswered punches peppered Liston, but he continued to stand off. He took jab after biting jab as Clay picked him off in his own time. At the bell, Clay had the jaunty swagger back; Liston trudged to his corner, a ridge of flesh under his right eye, the cut on his left still visible.

In the corner, he said something to Willie Reddish. Jack Nilon was leaning through the ropes, and it became clear something serious was happening. Reddish touched Liston's shoulder. Sonny seemed uninterested, but his facial expressions were never a reliable guide to what was going on in his head. Then referee Felix was called over to the huddled group and after some discussion he turned and spread his arms to signal the end.

By then, Clay was already on his feet, early for the seventh that would never come, and spotted what was happening before anyone else in his corner – and probably before most in the hall. He raised his arms and shuffled and danced, then as his people dived between the ropes to congratulate him, he opened his mouth and eyes wide, almost in disbelief, and raced to the ropes to celebrate. "I told you, I told you," he yelled at ringside reporters. "I shocked the world, I shocked the world."

Liston just sat forlornly in his corner, the first world heavyweight champion since Jess Willard in 1919 to lose his title while sitting on his stool. Willard had a little more excuse: he had been floored seven times by Jack Dempsey, had his cheekbone and orbital eye socket fractured and swollen, and had lost some teeth. Liston had what amounted to a sore arm.

The *Miami News* reported that when Barney Felix raised Clay's hand in victory it began to dawn on the audience that Liston had quit. Muttering could be heard around the hall but no cheers or wild screams. It was five minutes before it was announced that the cause of Liston's retirement was a shoulder injury.

Dan Parker, in the *New York Journal–American*, described what it was like in the minute or so immediately after Liston's surrender became apparent:

> Clay's supporters stormed the press section, climbed over the broadcaster's bench and broke the plant supporting their

instruments, scattering them in all directions . . . A doctor appeared from somewhere, equipped with heavy bandaging tape with which he plastered the fallen champion's shoulder – the one on the same side as his heart.

The crowd booed its lungs out as Sonny Boy, the tame bogeyman, arose and, with shoulder bared to show the bandage, lumbered down the aisle . . .

In a ringside seat, Rocky Marciano slapped his head in astonishment. "What the hell is this?" he said. "What did they do?"

On his way from the ring, Clay paused long enough to call out to writers: "I came, I saw, I conquered." He pulled an angry scowl, then winked at them. "I borrowed the line from Caesar," he said, pointing out helpfully that in his day Caesar was the greatest, too. He was kissed by his mother and hugged by his brother. He shook hands with his father. Sugar Ray Robinson and the pro footballer Jim Brown walked alongside him.

Yogi Berra, who like Liston had grown up in St Louis, sat with Yankees manager Ralph Houk and the long-retired Joe DiMaggio, who had once been married to Marilyn Monroe. Berra was impressed by Clay. "He's a big guy, and he surprised me how good he could move."

As Liston was led away from the arena with two strips of tape patching up his cut eye, it was claimed he said in a voice scarcely above a whisper: "I tried to throw a left hook. It missed. I felt something snap. I just couldn't throw a punch. Not the jab anyway. My arm was killing me."

Maybe he said it, maybe he didn't.

There was an unsubstantiated suggestion that Clay's agony in round four was the result of skulduggery ordered by Liston himself. The word was that, in case of emergency – that is, the fight lasting more than three rounds – cutman Joe Polino was to smear a caustic solution, which Clay later described as carbolated Vaseline, onto Liston's gloves and shoulders. Like so many other possibilities, it's just a rumour, but Polino allegedly confessed to it many years later in a conversation with Jack McKinney. Maybe he was telling the truth, maybe he had other reasons for saying what he said. Nobody will ever know.

Liston was ferried to St Francis Hospital, from which he

would eventually emerge with his left arm in a sling attached at the shoulder and hip. Eight doctors had consulted and come to the conclusion that the injury was genuine and debilitating. The shoulder muscle was torn. Dr Alexander Robbins, the chief physician of the Miami Beach Boxing Commission, who had been in charge of the pre-fight medicals, read out a statement to say that Liston had been with doctors for three and a half hours:

> We came to the conclusion that Sonny Liston suffered an injury to the long head to the biceps tendon of the left shoulder with the result there is separation and tear of muscle fibres with some haemorrhage into the muscle belly. This condition would be sufficient to incapacitate him and prevent him from defending himself.

Robbins also said: "There is no doubt in my mind that the fight should have been stopped."

Jack Nilon, standing to the side of Robbins, asked writers: "Please make this positively accurate." He also said six stitches were inserted in the cut below Sonny's left eye, which would need plastic surgery. Nilon also said: "Put a Bible before me and I'll swear this was on the level."

When the scorecards were revealed, they showed the fight was even at the time it ended, the officials split three ways. Referee Barney Felix scored 57–57, judge William Lovett 58–56 Liston, judge Gus Jacobsen 58–56 Clay. The scoring system was not as it is today. The points gap between the fighters in a round was more liberally applied, while today 10–8 rounds are given only if one fighter is knocked down or a round is particularly one-sided and gruelling.

The scorecards in terms of rounds were as follows (C for Clay, L for Liston, E for Even):

	1	2	3	4	5	6	Total
Barney Felix	C	L	C	L	L	C	3–3
William Lovett	C	L	E	L	L	C	3–2–1
Gus Jacobsen	C	E	C	C	L	C	1–4–1

For what it's worth, under today's rules, the scores would have been: Felix 57–57, Lovett 58–57 Liston, Jacobsen 59–56 Clay.

After six rounds, Peter Wilson said he had Liston ahead by one point.

Bill MacDonald joked that boxing writers were as bad as political commentators in their lack of ability to predict outcomes. "We had over four hundred sportswriters from many parts of the world and only three or four gave Clay a chance," he said.

In Britain, the *Daily Mirror* would run a front-page piece headlined "The Men With Red Faces", followed by nine photos of British boxing writers with their wrong predictions. In that hall of shame were the *Mirror's* own Peter Wilson, Sam Leitch, Peter Lorenzo, J. L. Manning, Desmond Hackett, Donald Saunders, Reg Gutteridge and George Whiting, along with Rocky Marciano, who had done a ghostwritten prediction in the *Daily Sketch*. The scandal of the ineptitude of the British boxing press relegated the latest in the Jack Ruby trial to page two and news that nine Russian Jews were to be shot for running a knitted goods racket to the back page.

Harold Conrad said Liston's woeful preparation was to blame, nothing else:

> He was there for just three rounds. His tongue was hanging out. He aged twenty years in four rounds. Even though he was chasing the guy, he was way behind on points, and I could see he looked like an old man by the way he sat there on his stool.
>
> He was cut for the first time in his life, and it was a bad one. He was bleeding, and he had never bled before, not in all of his tough fights. When it came to the seventh round, he just couldn't get off his damned stool. He just couldn't catch him, and he just . . . well, don't forget he was no kid any more.

Clay had to be persuaded by Angelo Dundee to give the traditional post-fight interview to writers. "Hypocrites," he said. "I shouldn't be talking to you." Then he eased into full flow, taunting writers that they had criticised him for holding his hands too low, pulled away from punches, couldn't take a punch:

Well, I'm still pretty, and he's in the hospital. I'll fight anybody the public wants me to fight now. Boy, I whipped him bad. I tried to tell the world it was going to happen, but you didn't listen. Hypocrites, hypocrites, hypocrites . . .

I don't know what happened to Liston. All I know was he was floundering around, and I was flying like a bird. They tell me he had to stop because of shoulder trouble. All I know is he kept throwing lefts and was still throwing them in the fifth when my eyes were troubling me.

Wasn't the old man the one who said last week he could fight with one leg and one arm and still beat me? Hail the champion! Look at me! Not a mark on me. The old man was cut up around the left eye from the third round on. They made Liston the 7–1 favourite. That was a foolish thing to do. I never could be an underdog. I am too great.

Bundini Brown laughed and sang out: "Hail the champion!"

"Say it again," said the champion, and together they yelled: "Hail the champion!" He said he would fight Liston again, or Eddie Machen or Doug Jones. "Anybody," he said.

Angelo Dundee defused any suggestion that they were accusing Liston and his team of deliberately attempting to blind Clay. "It was just an unfortunate accident," said the victorious trainer. "They are too nice and too fair to resort to such tactics." Dundee also said:

I've been telling everybody that this kid is a great fighter. The talk's only an act. The kid's different, that's all . . . He did exactly what he had to do . . . So what if he fights with his hands down. So what if he pulls back to evade punches. He does everything different.

Liston would never again intimidate a world-class fighter and therefore would never again be the fighter he used to be. He understood that as well as by his power and ability he had beaten opponents by dominating them psychologically. He would not be able to do that to world-class opponents from then on.

It happened a couple of generations later with Mike Tyson.

When he was taken apart by Buster Douglas, the aura of invincibility that had surrounded him for more than three years simply evaporated. After that, even fighters of ordinary talent, for that's all Douglas was for most of his career, knew they could beat Tyson.

Harold Conrad and his wife went to see Liston. He was propped up on the pillows in his bed, hazy from medication. "What are they saying out there? What are they saying?" he said.

Conrad told him the people felt he "dumped" the fight.

Liston threw a glass against the wall and yelled out: "Don't they know what that title meant to me?"

Conrad believed Liston was being honest. "He said, 'You see me, you know what it means to me to hear a kid say, "Hello, champ"?'"

Johnny Tocco, the Las Vegas gym owner who knew Liston and the ways of the Mob well, didn't subscribe to a fix theory. "Sonny was tired, so he quit," said Tocco.

Jimmy Cannon said the fight was "peculiar even by the standards of this mean racket".

Dan Parker was scathing:

Real champions don't quit, even for dislocated or broken limbs, as many of them, much less fearsome looking than this straw bogeyman, have proved down the years . . .

Sonny the Bullyboy, realising that the phony image created by his press agents that represented him as a creature so awesome no human being could stand up against him was about to be revealed as a colossal fraud, lost heart and decided to chuck it . . .

The climax to this strange promotion, which, from the start, seemed like something out of Alice in Wonderland, came without warning at a time when the judges' cards showed they had it scored evenly.

An angry Parker suggested Liston "should be sent back into the oblivion from which he was rescued by that great American patriot, Blinky Palermo" and suggested that while Liston's purse was held temporarily by the Miami Commission "you can bet that the boys who split it up behind the scenes will get theirs". As to Clay, Parker said the victory had effectively made Elijah Muhammad, leader of the Nation of Islam, the new ruler of boxing. The *New York Journal-American* also reported that complaints had flooded in to the office of Governor Bryant. An aide to Bryant tried to calm things down: "I think it was an honest fight and I am sure the Governor feels the same."

George Whiting's ringside report, sent back to London for the *Evening Standard* front page, said: "Cassius Marcellus Clay, the lissome Kentucky kid the world derided as a shrill and raucous false alarm, is now heavyweight champion of that same world. The horizon is his, and all its rainbows."

Clay moved on from the Convention Centre to Hampton House, a Miami hotel, for what he termed "a private party with some friends". Among them, to nobody's surprise, was Malcolm X. Even the most blinkered of Clay apologists realised the truth: the new heavyweight champion of the world belonged to a religious group that preached its own form of segregation.

The day after Cassius Clay beat Sonny Liston, it was announced by Elijah Muhammad before a gathering of 5,000 followers in Chicago that the new heavyweight champion of the world was a member of the Nation of Islam. On 6 March, Elijah renamed him Muhammad Ali.

The public acknowledgement of his change of faith hurt his bank balance. Bill Faversham told Joe Williams: "We had a choice of two national product endorsements, each guaranteeing him $500,000 spread over three years, and both were withdrawn the day after the story broke."

Cassius was unrepentant:

I go to a Muslim meeting and what do I see? I see there is no smoking and no drinking, and the women wear their dresses down to the floor. I come out and you tell me I shouldn't go in there. Well, there must be something in there . . . I know the truth and I don't have to be what you want me to be.

The Temple of Islam in Detroit was opened by Wallace Fard Muhammad around the end of 1929 or the beginning of 1930. He preached there until his disappearance in 1934, a mystery that has not been solved. According to the FBI, he was born Wallace Dodd Fard on 25 February 1891. The Nation of Islam said the FBI had the wrong man, that their founder was born in the 1870s and arrived alone in Detroit from Mecca in 1930. There is a First World War draft registration card for a Wallie Dodd Fard from 1917. At that time he was in Los Angeles working as a restaurant owner, claiming to be born in Shinka, Afghanistan. By the 1920 census, he was still in Los Angeles with a wife named Hazel, still running a restaurant, but by now claiming to have been born in New Zealand. The date of his immigration was left blank, as was the space for the birth country or US state of his parents. After this, the historical record becomes darker: in 1926, Wallie Dodd was sentenced to jail on drug offences, and he spent the next three years in San Quentin prison. In 1932, two years after the opening of the Detroit temple, a Wallace Fard was arrested. His fingerprints matched those of Wallie Dodd. However, the Nation of Islam claim a smear campaign, that this was not their man. There are two known photographs, one provided by the FBI, one by the Nation of Islam. Aside from the hairstyle, the men look similar.

Upon his disappearance, Fard, by then Fard Muhammad, was replaced by Elijah Muhammad, who presided over the faith for the next 40 years. Elijah was born Elijah Poole, one of thirteen children in a family of sharecroppers in Georgia. By 1917, he was married and by 1923 had settled into life as a car worker in Detroit. When he took over the temple, he took on Fard's theories and developed them. His view was that black people needed to be politicised under the moral code supplied by Islam. He denounced drinking, gambling, the physical abuse of women, and believed black men should enable themselves to stand up physically against the violent element in white America. Beyond that, he felt that if equality for the black race could not be established within America, it made sense to work towards a separate territory and nation. Like many religious zealots, he decided they were living in the last age before a righteous tumult devastated and rearranged the world. Astonishing as it sounds, he allowed the leader of the American Nazi Party, George Rockwell, to address the Nation of Islam, on the grounds that both were separatist organisations. In 1943, Elijah was arrested in Washington, DC for preaching a message of non-cooperation with the draft. He was cleared of sedition but jailed for four years for instructing his followers not to serve in the US Armed Forces during a time of war.

By 1952, the organisation was still tiny, with about 500 members, but a decade later it had 30,000. A major factor in its increased popularity was the arrival of the charismatic, enigmatic Malcolm X, who had taken on the Harlem temple in 1954. He was born Malcolm Little in Nebraska in 1925. His father, a Baptist named Earl Little, supported Marcus Garvey's Universal Negro Improvement Association. Earl was run over by a street-car in 1931, when Malcolm was six. The official verdict was suicide. The same year the family home was burned down. Malcolm's mother, Louise, went insane and by 1938 was housed in a state psychiatric unit. Eight years later, in Massachusetts, Malcolm was sentenced to eight to ten years for grand larceny and breaking and entering. It was around 1948 that he heard of the Nation of Islam, and when he was paroled in 1952 he changed his name to Malcolm X. The FBI had a file on him that eventually concluded he showed the symptoms of a pre-psychotic paranoid schizophrenic. His influence was huge, and he became an increasingly high-profile figure. However, he upset Elijah Muhammad first with a tactless attack on the Civil Rights march on Washington and then on the death of President John F. Kennedy when he said he could not be sad about chickens coming home to roost. Elijah banned him from public speaking.

Mary Turner Clay, Cassius's aunt, insisted her nephew's first contact with the Nation of Islam came when he boxed in the Golden Gloves in Chicago when he was 16 but said he was really drawn into full involvement with them when he was in Miami and in contact with both Malcolm X and a Muslim called Sam Saxon, who changed his name to Abdurrahman. Abdurrahman said:

> I started to teach Cassius the tricks of the white man and how we, as blacks, became slaves and were skilfully deceived by the white man in this country. I started to talk to him about the

African empires and how great these empires were in their heyday when the whites were still living in caves.

In September 1963, Cassius had attended a rally in Philadelphia when in a three-hour sermon before 5,000 followers Elijah Muhammad called white Americans the most evil people on earth. During the weeks leading to the fight, Clay's house filled with Muslim brothers to the point where his father, who had been staying with him and attending his training sessions, found somewhere else to live. Cassius Sr was exasperated. He told Pat Putnam for the *Miami Herald* when everything became public:

> They've ruined my two boys. They should run these Black Muslims out of the country before they ruin other fine young people. The Muslims tell my boys to hate white people, to hate women, to hate their mother . . . I told Malcolm X that my grandparents were Christians, that my parents were Christians, that my wife is a Christian and that I was a Christian. And that we would all die Christians . . . They wanted me to change our last name to X. I laughed at them. I told them I had a good Christian name and it would stay that way. I told them that after a person learns to read and write he don't have to use any X.

Cassius was to reiterate the theory that the black man was damaged by the presence of white blood inflicted on him through slavery: "My white blood came from the slave-masters, from raping. When we were darker, we were stronger, we were pure."

He explained he felt more comfortable in the company of black people. He trusted them, could be himself:

> If I see a girl I want to wink at, I don't have to worry about getting strung up to a tree . . . I just want to be with my own. I'm no longer a Negro. I'm no longer a slave. I am with myself and my own kind.

The day after the fight, press conferences were held in a room in the Convention Hall. Clay said he felt sorry for Liston because he had been built up into something he wasn't. "He's an old man. He's beat up, and he's overrated. They called Liston the equal of Joe Louis and Rocky Marciano. This must mean that I'm the greatest!" This time he didn't shout, just quietly, thoughtfully made his point. He was planning to return to Louisville for a victory party.

Clay explained his problems at the beginning of the fifth round:

> It happened in the middle of the fourth round. I felt something burn my eyes and my face. It came off Liston's glove or head, I don't know which. I couldn't see. My eyes were on fire. My face was burning . . . There was something hot in my eyes, and I couldn't even see where I was. Angelo pushed me out. And then it made sense to go on.

Dundee said: "I told him this was the big apple, that this fight was for everything. He only had his mouthpiece halfway in his mouth when he went out for the start of the round."

Clay said he had been warned before the fight "by a wise, wise person" that somebody might try something. He said he was watching out for it, even from Dundee himself. Dundee took the apparent insult calmly. He knew that fighters are complex, sometimes paranoid souls, especially in a situation as tense as a world championship fight – and Cassius Clay was more complex: than most.

Liston appeared in sunglasses, with his left arm in a sling, half an hour late at 1.30 p.m. He felt his defeat was an accident, plain and simple. "After a hook in the first round, I knew it went out." He said he did not have the injury going in and didn't ask for the fight to be stopped. That decision, he said, was taken by Reddish and Nilon. He said Reddish told him in the corner after round six that he had to double up the left hook. He told Reddish he couldn't do that because he could not lift his arm. "He told the referee, the referee stopped it," he said. Liston said the arm injury had prevented him carrying out his plan of working Clay's body, and his left hooks didn't have their normal power.

When asked how good Clay was, Liston's response was odd, as if the tactics of boxing on the move and using his speed disqualified Clay from any right to the usual respect one fighter has for another. Because he fought on the "run", he somehow wasn't real.

"He's not as good as Machen or Folley or Williams," said Liston. "They came to fight. He's not as good as Patterson either. He came to fight, too. I was never tired. And he didn't hurt me either. I thought I could make it. Even fifteen rounds. Even with one hand."

The questions were soft, as if everyone knew they had in front of them a broken, demoralised man who couldn't be expected to give proportionate answers because he could not come to terms with the catastrophe that had struck.

"Sure, I want to fight him again," said Liston.

Asked how he felt at losing his title, he said: "Like I did when the President got shot. I never wanted to quit . . ."

Liston's physician, Dr Robert C. Bennett, intervened to show an enlargement of the X-ray of Liston's arm. He said there had been a "direct trauma", a torn muscle. Contrary to what Liston had said, Bennett said there had been a problem in training:

Sonny felt a little pain in his left arm during training, but we let it go. The first time he threw a left hook last night, he got a pain in his left shoulder, which got progressively worse. By the time the seventh round began, his hand was completely numb.

After Liston's death, his widow Geraldine was to say to *Esquire* magazine that Sonny had hurt the shoulder before the fight but was afraid to pull out because of the bad press it would cause him. Nilon was more specific: Sonny had not sparred between 3rd and 5th February, nor again on the 14th, because of soreness in the shoulder. "We thought we could get away with it," he said.

Nilon, who once declared that the amount he knew about boxing could be written on a postage stamp, said he had stopped the fight, Liston had not retired. "I was the one who made the decision," he said:

Sonny wasn't tired. He simply lost all sensation in his left hand after being hit in the left shoulder at the tail end of the first round. He got hurt when he tried to throw a punch and block one at the same time. He kept complaining about it, but we didn't pay much attention to it.

Willie Reddish said Liston had told him he had no feeling in his left arm, that it was like a paralysing sensation.

Liston said he wanted to go home to Denver and would then see a preferred specialist in Philadelphia. "I don't want any surgery," he said, evidence perhaps of his reluctance to undergo any kind of needle-induced anaesthetic. "Last year I had trouble with my right knee. I wouldn't let anybody cut me. I figured nature would cure me. So it did."

Morris Klein, for the Miami Commission, said he was happy that the fight had been "clean, well run and well ordered" and that the public had been given a "good run for their money". He said he was satisfied that Liston had not gone into the fight carrying the injury. Ed Lassman, president of the World Boxing Association, said the medical report was satisfactory. However, Florida State attorney Richard Gerstein was more inquisitive. He asked the commission for records and medical papers dealing with Liston's situation and helpfully reminded those involved that, under Florida law, "altering the outcome of an athletic event" carried a maximum sentence of ten years in jail. He did say he had received no public complaint, and no apparent evidence had been presented before him, but he wanted to see the reports because the conclusion to the fight had, in his words, "left me wondering whether what I had seen happen actually did happen".

Gerstein said he wanted further opinions on the medical report and X-rays, both from the Dale County medical examiner, Dr Joe Davis, and from the medical-legal adviser to the Attorney's office, Dr Franklin J. Evans. Klein also ordered reports from two orthopaedic surgeons to examine Liston the day after the fight and temporarily withheld his purse, or at least the "live gate" part of it – $367,000.

It was also disclosed by the Inter-Continental attorney, Garland "Bill" Cherry, in an article by Hugh Bradley, in the *New York Journal-American*, that $50,000 had been paid by the promoter to Clay's lawyers in the twenty-four hours before the fight as part of the contract relating to their rights over Clay's

next fight should he win. "We have the right to name the opponent, the site and the date. I would guess it would be Liston as
his opponent." As Liston was president of Inter-Continental, he
might therefore be said to have had a financial interest in the
outcome. While technically true, this does not mean he threw
the fight. Fighters having a piece of a promotion is more preva-
lent fifty years on. It has also become common practice for the
promoter of a world champion to secure options on the services
of a challenger (except in the case of a mandatory defence, where
the rules of most organisations prevent it).

There was also at least one heavyweight championship prec-
edent. When James J. Braddock defended against Joe Louis, his
manager Joe Gould negotiated a deal whereby, in the event of his
losing, he would be entitled to a percentage of Louis's promotional profits for the next ten years. Braddock, it should be said,
was managed by Joe Gould, who had, according to legend, sold
part of the contract to Pete "The Goat" Stone, who worked for
Bill Duffy, and Owney "The Killer" Madden, who ran Hell's
Kitchen.

Compared to the deal Gould was accredited with striking with
Louis's promoter Mike Jacobs, this one involving Liston and
Clay was clean as fresh snow. In 1964, however, given the general
atmosphere of mistrust and suspicion, and given Liston's connections – and for that matter Clay's – the questions seemed to carry
great pertinence.

Bill Faversham, the Louisville businessman whose syndicate
had hit the jackpot, said there was a moral obligation to give
Liston a rematch, but "I don't think he'll want it."

"We'll grab a return bout if they are good enough to give us one,"
said Jack Nilon. He knew about the return clause, so was playing
the part of humble loser for public consumption. "We're out of
business. Sonny will keep fighting, of course – if he wants to."

The financial breakdown shows just how badly MacDonald
was burned:

Bill MacDonald: staked $625,000 plus another $140,000 in
   expenses. Receipts at gate $402,000; loss $363,000
Sonny Liston: received $1,360,500 (gross, including 22.5%
   share in Inter-Continental Promotions receipt)

Inter-Continental Promotions: received $813,000, broken down between Jim and Bob Nilon (72.5%, $589,425), Liston as above (22.5%), Garland Cherry, Inter-Continental lawyer (5%, $40,650)

Cassius Clay: received $315,000

Louisville Syndicate: received $315,000

Theatre Network Television Inc: received $362,000

Closed-circuit exhibitors: received $1,750,000

By the day after the fight, Rocky Marciano had gathered his thoughts. "I thought Clay fought a real good fight," he said. Cus D'Amato went further. "He fought the perfect fight. He did everything right."

Jimmy Cannon wrote:

Clay was not intimidated by the thug who learned his mean business breaking heads for the mobs of St Louis. He came to Clay in the first round in heavily clumsy hops, like an aged chophouse waiter with bad feet carrying a heavy tray. The laughter of the multitude rose to mock Liston, as the kid moved nimbly out of range. Liston heaved punches as if they were cobblestones.

Clay impressed Cannon: "He ran, but he paused long enough to bust up Liston. It was the tough guy who folded up."

Reg Gutteridge, in the *London Evening News*, called it the biggest upset since Sitting Bull slaughtered General Custer. "Sonny Liston," he wrote, "was exposed as a fumbling automaton."

Sam Leitch, for the *Sunday Mirror*, wrote:

A smell has gone round the world since Sonny Liston sat on his backside and spat away, along with his gumshield, the title for which any man would give his left arm – the world heavyweight boxing championship . . .

Clay, the challenger, wanted to quit; his corner said No.

Liston, the champion, didn't want to quit; his corner said Yes.

I was one of the last of the red-faced writers to leave the bizarre atmosphere of Miami Beach. But the longer I stayed, the less sense it made . . .

Jimmy Cannon pointed out that the only man in the ring whose courage wasn't questioned was the referee.

Joe Louis didn't buy the shoulder story. "I don't think the shoulder made him quit," said the old champion.

"What did?" asked Cannon.

"I'm not sure. I don't want to say what I think unless I'm sure . . ."

Louis tried to explain more precisely: "He definitely hurt his shoulder. I don't want to say no different. He told me he hurt his shoulder. But a guy as tough as Liston, I don't figure it hurt him that much."

Louis, who went into the Liston corner straight after the fight was stopped, was insistent that manager Jack Nilon was telling the truth when he said he stopped the fight. In the *New York Journal–American* on 4 November 1964, during the lead-up to the ill-fated rematch, Jimmy Cannon revealed a conversation he had with Louis. Surprisingly, given that Cannon was a wise man with a strong news sense, this information was way down in paragraph eighteen of a twenty-eight-paragraph column.

I was the first one in Liston's corner Nilon say he stopped the fight. I looked at Liston. He don't say nothing, just smooth and calm sitting in the corner. Liston wasn't mad. He didn't say nothing. Nilon was doing all the talking.

Louis accompanied Liston to the rented house where he had been living at 6351 Pine Tree Drive, Miami Beach. Again, contrary to what Harold Conrad said, the deposed champion seemed to be a little too short on despondency for Joe's liking. "At home he wasn't too upset," said Louis. "He told me his arm was hurt . . . I didn't see no sign that he was mad at what Nilon did."

Doug Jones, who had taken Clay ten hard rounds eleven

months earlier, said: "I was shocked because I saw things that Liston could have done, but he didn't do them. I don't know why . . . I should be next in line."

Whenever a big upset happens in boxing, there will be those who will claim the loser took a dive, or deliberately did not perform at his best, or a fix was in. It's in the nature of things: people like to have an opinion on what will happen in big sporting events, like the satisfaction of knowing their opinions are proved right, that "here, look, there is evidence that I know what I'm talking about". Picking the right horse, picking the right fighter, bolsters the ego. Getting it wrong – getting it as wrong as so many people got Liston v. Clay wrong – makes people look as if they don't know what they're talking about, makes them feel angry. Therefore, they look for reasons.

And when the fighter who should have won but somehow didn't is known to have been involved with the Mob, then the "fix" is an easy answer. How could they have picked right when, unknown to anybody, "the fix was in"? By whispering "fix", "scandal", "corruption", all those people who got it wrong get themselves off the hook. They're not stupid after all; they can still talk about boxing as if they know something about it. And then again . . . there were those who said the word was out before the fight that something was wrong. Some felt that it was not the Mob but the Nation of Islam that had applied pressure to Liston himself. Nobody will ever know.

Former champion Ingemar Johansson said that rather than Clay winning the title it was a case of Liston losing it. He said he didn't think Clay would be champion for long: "I don't regard Cassius Clay as a worthy champion."

Nilon said they would have Liston's injury treated in Philadelphia and then look at working for the rematch. "We'll win it back," said Nilon. "I know it. This guy has pride – you can't imagine such pride. This thing is killing him. For the next one, I'll take him up to the woods, and when he comes down he'll be hungry." Nilon talked well but was on his way out and knew it.

A month after the fight, on 24 March 1964, in the investigation into the outcome, District Attorney Richard Gerstein recommended that boxers "should be compelled to disclose prior injuries – and that medical examinations should be clinical, rather than cursory, made routinely for the benefit of photographers."

On 29 May, in Denver, Liston was fined a total of $600 for speeding and possessing a firearm soon after returning home upon losing his title. It seemed a surprisingly lenient sentence given that according to police he was driving at seventy miles per hour in a zone restricted to thirty, he was drunk when arrested and was, according to police, aggressive in the police car as he was driven to the station. Colorado laws ruled it an offence for an ex-con to be carrying a gun. An unknown woman who was in the car with him was let go. It seems when Liston got home, he went off the rails again.

The Devil and Sonny Liston

Nick Tosches

If Liston quitting on his stool in the first fight provoked outcry, that was nothing compared to what happened in the rematch. Both fights remain mired in controversy, although the image from the second encounter of Ali standing over Liston has become part of The Greatest's legend, a defining moment in his rise to boxing immortality. Did Liston take a dive? Was the anchor punch for real? Let us take a small step back to before the first fight and take another perspective, this time from Nick Tosches's The Devil and Sonny Liston.

It was the end of the road. Here history took the pen from the player's hand, where, for a moment, a heartbeat, no matter how tentatively, it had seemed to rest. What remained was epilogue and epitaph, chords like wind of death-song, of threnody.

America did not want Sonny as her champion. "It is hard to discern any merit in Liston," wrote Dan Parker in his column of February 13, 1964. And America saw Liston much as Parker saw him: "a sinister creature, full of hatred for the world." Liston had likened boxing to a cowboy movie. "There's got to be good guys, and there's got to be bad guys." The "bad guys are supposed to lose. I change that," he had said. "I win." But in his winning, he seemed invincible. There seemed no good, or other bad, that could conquer or stay him; and, in the cowboy movie of his championship, the good guys never had a chance. There was no showdown in the ring, no battle, no melodrama – only fast and predictable victory for the villain America despised. The cowboy movie of his championship was a box-office failure, and in a racket built on suckers' money, Sonny as a champion was bad, bad news.

Moose Grayson had said that there had been a "settlement."

Yes, said Foneda Cox. "They made a settlement with Moose." By "they," he meant the Mob. "They paid Moose off. I don't know how much, but a lot. I think they even bought him a house. The Mafia picked up all of Sonny's tabs when Sonny got into trouble. I think maybe they got sick of it."

As the Clay fight approached, Liston was not only a bad draw and an unwanted champion. He was a man who could be exposed as a rapist at any time. This exposure would not only certainly cost him his title and end his career: with his record and reputation, he very likely could be returned to prison as well. Whoever had power over this exposure had power over Liston.

It was at this time that Ben Bentley quit, claiming that he was owed money and that the Nilons had reneged on an agreement to let him have the rights to the Chicago closed-circuit action for the Clay fight. "I don't blame Liston at all," said Ben.

Before the fight, the sportswriter Jimmy Cannon spoke with the former light heavyweight champion Billy Conn, whose career had spanned the years 1935–1948 and who was now forty-six years old.

"The first punch Liston hits him, out he goes," said Conn. "He can't fight now," he said of Clay, "and he'll never be able to fight. He hasn't the experience. The only experience he'll get with Liston is how to get killed in a hurry." Conn said – as Cannon noted bitterly – that Clay "took all the dignity away from the heavy-weight title by acting like a big phony wrestler."

Look magazine ran a story entitled "Sonny Liston: 'King of the Beasts,'" in the February 25, 1964, issue. "In essence, Sonny epitomizes the Negro untouchable, the angry dark-skinned man condemned by the white man to spend his life in the economic and social sewers of his country." A photograph pictured him at home in Denver, sitting on a couch between two matching and ornate fringed lamps: "*The Listons pose for their first family portrait: from left to right, daughter Eleanor, 13, wife Geraldine, Sonny, his mother Helen and daughter Arletha, 17.*"

Of the Negro untouchable: "His pleasures are simple: he drives a two-toned 1964 Fleetwood Cadillac and likes *The Beverly Hillbillies* on television ('Whatever mah wife's watchin', Ah'm watchin')."

The night of the fight was February 25, 1964. It had been barely three months since the Kennedy assassination, and this was the first blood revelry that a post-hysteric America had allowed herself. The crowd that gathered at Miami's Convention Hall, and all the other crowds that gathered in the closed-circuit showrooms and theaters throughout America were there not so much to see a contest, for no contest was foreseen. This sense of the inevitable was evinced by the lackluster gate at Convention Hall, where only about half of sixteen thousand tickets, priced from twenty to two hundred and fifty dollars, were sold. What crowd there was seemed to be a part of a masque in the season of psychic plague, a ritual, a spectacle that pitted the embodiment of callow spirit and whistle-in-the-dark braggadocio against that of the Adversary of the American Dream. The air of festive anticipation was unsettling. The scent of dear perfume and fancy cologne mixed with that of cheap aftershave, smoke, and sweat. The oversized head of tough guy manqué Norman Mailer was no longer alone in blocking the view at ringside. Beside him sat fellow tough guy Truman Capote and Gloria Guinness of *Harper's Bazaar*.

Clay's pulse had raced to 120 during the weigh-in, and the adrenaline of fear seemed still within him as he entered the ring. That fight-or-flee rush drove him forward and into Liston with a frenzy, and he took the first round. Sonny began to grind him down in the second, but his blows were delivered with none of the awesome power that in the past had felled man after man. In the third, Clay opened a cut under Sonny's eye, drawing forth what Sonny had given no other man since the days of those whippings. In the fourth, Sonny connected repeatedly, but again, his blows seemed oddly restrained, and Clay came in again to bruise Sonny's fearsome face.

At the end of round four, Clay came to his corner screaming surrender. "I can't see," he wailed to his trainer, Angelo Dundee. "Cut off my gloves. Call off the fight." At the sound of the bell, Dundee pushed Clay to his feet.

In the fifth, Clay, who claimed difficulty seeing, had no difficulty in dodging Sonny's punches, which seemed at times designed not so much to hit Clay as to punctuate the air of his blind bob and weave. Clay reached out his left arm, rested his gloved fist against Sonny's nose, as if to keep the beast at bay; and, though Sonny's reach was greater, he never struck or swatted that arm away.

At the end of the round, Clay's vision returned, and Barney Felix, the referee, who had been about to stop the fight and award a technical-knockout victory to Liston, allowed the match to continue. After six rounds, the fight was even on points. When the bell sounded to signal the start of the seventh round, Liston just sat there, refusing to rise and telling of a numbness that ran from his left shoulder down to his forearm.

In the halls and cellblocks of the Jefferson City penitentiary – the one true stronghold of Sonny's popularity as a champion – the blare of radios was suddenly overtaken by howls of anger and disgust. The son of a bitch had thrown the fucking heavyweight championship of the motherfucking world. Shit, some reckoned: a thief for a penny, a thief for a pound.

A few days after the fight, there came to light a contract that caused no small amount of speculation. Long before the fight – the contract was dated October 29, 1963 – Inter-Continental Promotions, of which Sonny was a partner, had contracted with the eleven-man Louisville Group to purchase for fifty thousand dollars the rights to promote Clay's next fight after the Liston match. This was a staggering amount to pay for the future rights to a single bout by a fighter who was seen as facing almost certain defeat in his upcoming match with Liston. Jack Nilon, trying to explain the suspect pre-fight contract, said that "Clay represented a tremendous show-business property."

Liston later said that he had injured his shoulder in the first round of the fight. Jack Nilon said the injury came long before the fight, during training.

But the training and training camps of both fighters had been the object of much coverage by the press, and there had been no hint of any injury. During training just a year earlier; the news of a less debilitating injury, to Liston's knee, was pursued and covered as a major story, and that knee injury had been sustained off the training grounds and away from the eyes of the press.

When the Senate Subcommittee on Antitrust and Monopoly announced, on March 1, that it intended to investigate the contract between Clay and Inter-Continental, Nilon said, "We never dreamed Sonny would lose the title." The contract, he said, was just "a lucky fluke."

That was two days after the Internal Revenue Service filed liens totaling $2.7 million against Sonny: $876,800 against him and Geraldine; $1,050,500 against Inter-Continental Promotions, Inc.; and $793,000 against Delaware Advertising and Management Agency, Inc., a Nilon-run sister corporation of Inter-Continental.

Sonny was taken after the fight to be examined at St. Joseph's Hospital. Three hours later, it was announced by Dr Alexander Robbins of the Miami Beach Athletic Commission that Liston did indeed show evidence of an injury to his left shoulder that was "sufficient to incapacitate him and to prevent him from defending himself."

Officials at the fight had withheld the fight purse on suspicions that things were not right. The announcement by Dr Robbins served to counter those suspicions and expedite the release of the purse.

Later, a Detroit physician, Dr Robert C. Bennet, would state that he had been treating Liston for bursitis in both arms and shoulders for the past two years. He said that Sonny had been taking cortisone shots for this bursitis almost continuously in the months preceding the fight. In his medical opinion, the bursitis was not connected to the injury that had stopped the fight in Miami.

"I think Liston's problem in the fight was that he swung and missed, severely stretching or rupturing his arm four or five inches below the shoulder," the doctor said. "In our post-fight examination, we could see the swelling and the blood."

Bennet was Joe Louis's doctor. When Joe had a dope seizure in New York in 1969, it was Bennet who helped to protect the fighter's image by covering the details of his emergency hospitalization. Bennet was also the physician for the Michigan State Boxing Commission. When I discovered this obscure circumstance, I could not but recall Truman Gibson's story about his encounter long ago at the offices of the Michigan commission, a story that also involved Joe Louis, as well as many other things.

Where were the doctors before the fight, and where were the doctors during the fight? Why would a man who had gone the distance in agony with a busted jaw in an insignificant fight – why would such a man fold in a world championship title match from a pain or a numbness in his arm? Why would a man with the most devastating right in boxing, a man impervious to punches, allow an injured left arm to move him to such passive and compliant surrender?

There are stories of the immense losses Ash Resnick incurred in Miami by betting on his friend. There are other stories of suitcases of money being sent by Ash to New York, where other, less ostentatious bets were made.

The night after Bennet's disclosure, Sonny was arrested back home in Denver. Doing over seventy-five in a thirty-mile-per-hour residential zone, he was carrying a seven-shot .22 revolver in his right-hand coat pocket, along with six cartridges and one spent shell. The arresting officer, Patrolman James Snider, asked him about the pistol.

"It's mine. I shot at my girlfriend."

He was in his Cadillac. There was a girl in the car with him. The cop told her to get the Cadillac out of there. He could barely force the handcuff around Sonny's wrists. Another cop arrived, and together they got him cuffed.

Sonny was drunk – he told the cop he'd had half a bottle of vodka – and he got belligerent during the ride downtown, asking the cop if he wanted to "mix it up" or "go round and round" and once trying to escape when the car slowed for a stop sign.

"I really didn't know who I had," Snider said, "until I got to headquarters and another patrolman said, 'Hi, Sonny.'"

Sonny refused to take a Breathalyzer test. He was charged with speeding, driving without a valid Colorado license, and reckless and careless driving. He was let off easy on the pistol. Under Colorado law, it was a felony for an ex-convict to be in possession of a concealed weapon, but it was charged against Sonny only as a misdemeanor.

On the following day, Sonny was served by federal marshals with a notice of a $115,000 lawsuit that Ben Bentley had filed against him the previous Friday in US District Court in Chicago. The suit claimed fifteen grand in overdue wages and a hundred grand in lost income pursuant to Inter-Continental's failure to honor its commitment to grant him Chicago closed circuit rights.

On March 23, State Attorney General Richard E. Gerstein of Florida announced that, after a month's investigation of the Liston-Clay fight, it had been decided that there was no evidence of foul play. However, he said, several other circumstances surrounding the fight were "questionable." He spoke of "a well-known gambler and bookmaker" – he did not name him, but he was talking about Ash Resnick – who "enjoyed the full run of the training camp and was present in Liston's dressing room prior to the fight." Gerstein also said he wondered why Liston would pay fifty thousand dollars for the right to choose Clay's next opponent and promote his next fight "unless he or his managers knew the outcome of the fight in advance."

Kefauver was dead, but his spirit lived. On March 24, the day after Gerstein's guarded announcement, Senate investigators in Washington questioned Sonny's partners in Inter-Continental Promotions. The first called to answer was Garland Cherry, the Pennsylvania lawyer who held five percent of the corporation. He revealed that Liston had signed over more than half of his stock in December to Sam Margolis.

Sam was a big heavy guy, fifty-one, who smoked and chewed on a cigar as he sat before the committee.

SENATOR PHILIP HART: Mr Margolis, what is your business?

SAM: I am in the vending-machine business.

SENATOR HART: Are you or did you have a partnership in a restaurant in or near Philadelphia in recent years?

SAM: That is, prior to the vending business?

SENATOR HART: Prior to your entering the vending business. What was the name of the restaurant?

SAM: Sansom Restaurant.

SENATOR HART: All right, who were your partners in that restaurant?

SAM: My partners was my wife, Carlo Musciano, and Frank Palermo.

SENATOR HART: What discussions, if any, did you have with Frank Palermo concerning Liston in either a fight or the promotion of it?

SAM: I don't know if we ever discussed it or not.

Sam was asked by committee counsel if he knew Angelo Bruno, the criminal overlord of Philadelphia:

"Do you know Mr Bruno?"

"Yes."

"Did you have any conversations with Mr Bruno about Sonny Liston?"

"I don't recall having any conversations with Mr Bruno about Sonny Liston."

Under questioning by Senator Keating of New York, Sam said that he and Sonny had an agreement whereby Sam would receive half of whatever he could get for Sonny from the Nilon brothers in negotiating his position during the formation of Inter-Continental.

Keating asked if steps had been taken to put the agreement in writing.

SAM: No. I trusted Sonny.
SENATOR KEATING: Were you his manager?
SAM: No.
SENATOR KEATING: What was your title?
SAM: Friend.

Sonny had endorsed the shares before they were filled in with Sam's, or anyone's, name. The shares were now worth about a hundred thousand dollars after taxes. Sam had given fifty of the two hundred and seventy-five shares to his lawyer Salvatore J. Avena, who was one of two attorneys serving as counsel to him before the committee.

Keating brought up a meeting at Goldie Ahearn's Restaurant in Washington, DC, on March 19, 1958, the night of a local middleweight fight between Jimmy Beacham and Willie Vaughn. Present were Frankie Carbo, Blinky Palermo, and Sam.

SAM: We did not have a meeting. We went there to eat.
SENATOR KEATING: Was Sonny Liston's name brought into the conversation?
SAM: I never heard Sonny Liston's name mentioned there at that time, Senator.

When Jack Nilon came before the committee, he was asked about the 1962 manager's contract with Liston that entitled him to a third of Liston's purses.

> SENATOR HART: When did the change from thirty-three and a third percent to fifty percent occur?
>
> NILON: I would say after the Clay fight, after it was signed.
>
> SENATOR HART: Are you a licensed manager?
>
> NILON: No.
>
> SENATOR HART: How do you act as the manager in the Clay fight if you weren't licensed to be manager?
>
> NILON: I wasn't the manager in the Clay fight.
>
> SENATOR HART: Who was?
>
> NILON: I had a second's license.
>
> SENATOR HART: Who was the manager?
>
> NILON: Actually, there was no manager.

At one point, Nilon expressed the feeling that he did not really "feel that I want to be a fight manager," upon which Senator Hart asked him, "As the manager of Liston under this-fifty-percent agreement, what compensation would you receive, based on the Miami Beach Clay-Liston fight?"

> NILON: I would receive – the gross sum estimated is probably four hundred thousand.
>
> SENATOR HART: But you don't want to be a manager, none-theless?
>
> NILON: There is more to life than bread alone.

For years, Sonny had alluded to the inevitable. It was as if his fate were writ on a crumpled piece of paper, like those slips they had found on him in St. Louis in the summer of '59: an old and faded and irrevocable haruspicy folded away and sometimes forgotten amid those other slips, amid the lint and the nickels and the thousand-dollar bills.

"He told me, he said, 'Foneda, I'm gonna tell you. I've got to lose one, and when I do, I'm gonna tell you.'"

Though Foneda went most everywhere with Sonny, it was strongly suggested that he remain in Denver and not come to

Miami for the fight. "They said, 'Well, you ought to stay here with your business.' And I said, 'No, I ain't worried about that. I got a cousin here that can run my business.'" But Foneda did not go.

"So, this is the only thing that I hold against Sonny, is that he did not tell me when he was actually going to lose. And I'm back here betting."

When Sonny returned to Denver, he seemed to Foneda somewhat distant but not unhappy. "He wasn't really upset." But, as Foneda saw it. Sonny had let him down, gone back on his word to him. "In fact," he said, "after that, I didn't go with him anymore." Though they continued to spar and hang out together once in a while, the old days were over.

Sonny's bodyguard, Lowell Powell, was there on that stingy-brim night in Miami Beach, February 25, 1964, that night the unvanquishable Liston was vanquished by Cassius Clay.

When Liston failed to come out of his corner in round seven, the man in the stingy-brim hat knew what others did not know.

"I had bet a lot of money on Sonny. What we called a lot of money. Three or four thousand dollars was a lot of money, as far as I'm concerned. I was given odds that he would take Clay in so many rounds. I said, 'Sonny, I'm gonna put some more money on you.'

"He said, 'Don't put any more money on me, man. Two heavyweights out there, you can't ever tell who will win.' He said, 'You've got enough money bet.' That's as far as he would go with me.

"So, later on, after it all happened and he lost the fight, I said, 'Sonny, why would you let me lose my last penny on a fight and you knew you were gonna lose it? You could've at least pulled my coat.'

"He said, 'With your big mouth, we'd both be wearing concrete suits.'"

Myrl Taylor had been in Algoa with Sam Eveland in the old days and later on had gotten involved with the unions in St. Louis. Later, after another three-year stretch, he "wound up over all the laborers in the eastern half of St. Louis." He retired in 1993.

John Vitale, said Myrl, "liked to be around people. He always came to the fights." Not long before the Miami fight, Taylor approached Vitale. "I smell a rat here," he said to Vitale.

Vitale, one friend of the Teamsters to another, told Myrl: "Let me give you some advice. When there's two niggers and a million dollars involved, all you better bet on is that a nigger's gonna win."

"In other words," as Myrl said, "he's telling me, you know, get the fuck out of it."

As for Myrl's estimation of Vitale: "Well, he was supposed to be a big-time gangster, but he was actually a fucking informer for the fuckin' police. He had a code name and everything. But the Italians here, it was a different thing. People up in Chicago and shit like that, all the Mafia people, they killed somebody, they *killed* somebody. These people here, they never – they always just set 'em up and snitched on 'em. It was a different ballgame."

Sonny's mother, Helen, and eldest brother, E. B. Ward, put in a long-distance call to Sonny from Forrest City after the fight. As E. B. Ward recalled, it took the operator about thirty minutes to get him on the hotel phone. Ward asked him what happened.

"He said, 'I did what they told me to do.'"

Patsy Anthony Lepera was a gangster from Reading, Pennsylvania. "In those years," he said,

I was still making money through connections in Reading. One day, I got a call from Sammy to come down to his club. "We got something going." I walk in – there's Jimmy Peters the bookie and his brother Louis the Lug, the fight promoter – their real name is Lucchese. Joe Pastore is running the meeting.

Joe Pastore and me were good friends. When something was on, I used to get a piece of it. Now Joe tells us they got everything straightened out in the Liston-Clay fight. Liston is a seven-to-one favorite ... he's going off the board. Philadelphia is sending up a hundred grand to bet, and Reading got to come up with a hundred grand, too. That's what the meeting is for. Okay, I'll go for twenty-five.

In a few days, we got the hundred together, and Jimmy Peters is working the money. He's laying it all through the coal region. Lots of bets were laid off with the Mob in Cleveland and Vegas. These guys took the other mobs.

Lepera watched the broadcast of the fight.

It's the seventh round, Liston stays in his corner, his arm hurts, he doesn't feel like fighting anymore, he sits there on the stool. It's a TKO. This guy didn't just take a dive – he did a one and a half off the high board. It was so bad, I figured we blew everything. It worried me – I already spent my end. But no, everybody got paid off. We had to give up forty percent for the information. I come out with seventy-five thousand.

Bernie Glickman, who had handled Sonny in his transition from St. Louis control, had come down from Chicago and was around the fighters' camps before the fight.

"Right before the fight, he called me up," his son Joel told me. "He knew I liked to gamble and he knew I loved Liston. He said, 'Don't bet. There's something wrong. I don't know what it is.' I'll never forget that. I didn't listen."

A Chicago bookmaker remembered that night, too.

The biggest key to it, the biggest key was the odds. The fight was five-and-a-half-to-one here, and by fight time it was down to about two-to-one. One guy, he called me up from Vegas, he wanted to bet five grand on Clay. He was looking for four or five to one; but I'd already heard they were down to three-to-one, so I think I said I'd give him three-to-one. But for a fight to have dropped down like that. And if you knew anything about boxing, there was no way Clay could hurt Liston.

The oddsmaker Bob Martin:

I tried to lay eight-to-one, and I couldn't play around Vegas, and a friend of mine in Miami called me and got me out for five hundred. So I lost four thousand. I would have landed for ten thousand, so I would've lost eighty thousand. I couldn't get on, so I don't know where the line moved.

Martin did not believe that Sonny took a dive. "No," he said, "no chance." He tempered that somewhat: "In my mind, no chance. If a guy takes a dive, there's gotta be a motive."

When the Man says move, you got to move.

Somebody told me to look to the east, to Mecca, for the answer.

Liston had his crew down there in Miami. Pep Barone and the Nilon brothers were there. Ash Resnick from Vegas was there. Sam Margolis, an old friend and partner of Blinky's who had brokered Sonny's deal with the Nilons, was there. His hero Joe Louis was there.

And Clay had his. Among that crew was Malcolm X. The two had met in 1962, and, although Clay's interest in Islam had already blossomed by then, it was Malcolm who cultivated, and, in Miami, completed, Clay's conversion. Malcolm at the time was fallen from grace with the Nation of Islam leaders in Chicago, and he had already begun to fear violence against him. He saw in Clay a means of reinstating himself and offered to deliver the flamboyant fighter, and his embrace of Islam, to the Savior's Day convention in Chicago on the very day after the big fight. The Chicago leaders were not impressed: they believed that Liston would win. But the thought of the power and publicity a Black Muslim heavyweight champion might bring cannot have been lost on them.

"They were rough people," Truman Gibson mused when I broached the subject. They were murderously rough, as Malcolm X knew long before assassins from the Newark Temple No. 25 did their work in the cold early days of 1965.

Perhaps, in a world that was no longer Carbo's, a threat of Muslim violence might have worked against Liston. He had long been apprehensive of the Black Muslims, as he was of all he deemed to be estranged from their rightful minds. But any involvement by the Nation of Islam would have been more likely part of a straightforward business deal. Clay was the first great fighter to emerge in boxing's post-Carbo age. He had, so to speak, been born to freedom. True, he was owned in part by the Louisville consortium, but he was virgin meat as far as Mob leeching was concerned. Soon, when his contract with the

Louisville Group expired, he signed with a Muslim manager, Herbert Muhammad, a son of the Black Muslim leader Elijah Muhammad. Exalted as the Messenger of the Prophet Allah, Muhammad was a reformed alky born in Georgia of an itinerant Baptist preacher named Poole.

In the days preceding the fight, Clay had evaded questions concerning his reputed conversion to the Nation of Islam. On the day after the fight, he was ebullient with the profession of that conversion.

"I go to a Black Muslim meeting and what do I see? I see there's no smoking and no drinking and their women wear dresses down to the floor." (Not only a clean-cut young man, but one who knew that the gam was the devil's meat.) "And then I come out on the street and you tell me I shouldn't go in there. Well, there must be something in there if you don't want me to go in there." The separatist way was the way of nature, he said. "In the jungle, lions are with lions and tigers are with tigers, and redbirds stay with redbirds and bluebirds with bluebirds. That's human nature, too, to be with your own kind."

On that morning after the fight, proclaiming his conversion and announcing in victory his new name, Clay's jubilation was real. Knowing nothing of what Sonny knew, and having been a party to no conspiracy other than that of his own fear and bravery, he had no reason at all to disbelieve that he was, as he said, the greatest.

"White people wanted Liston to beat up and possibly kill poor little Clay," said Elijah Muhammad at that Savior's Day rally. "But Allah and myself said no. This assured his victory."

What a great title for a song, what a great title for a poem: "But Allah and Myself Said No."

Islam was a religion of slavery from its beginnings in the seventh century. The holy Koran looked upon slaves as the gifts of God, as those "whom God has given you as booty"; and the early, trans-Saharan slave trade in Africa was dominated by the Muslims. What a fine and fitting heritage, no matter how skewed and misknown, from which to enter the fight racket.

A tithe for Islam surely would not be too much to ask of a man of the faith so blessed as the champion now known as Ali. And from that tithe might be drawn a portion for Sonny. Clay was young, with a long future ahead of him. To a man who felt rather than knew his age, a cut of that future, a piece of every, increasing purse, might seem not a bad deal at all. But if the Nation of Islam had somehow got to Sonny, the unknowing Ali would have been sent into the ring praising the divinity and the blessing and the all-conquering power of Allah, rather than been constrained to not publicize his faith before the fight. To the Black Muslims, Clay's publicity value as a champion would be great, but were he to lose, having been known as a Black Muslim beforehand, his loss would be a loss for the power and image of the faith. The Prophet had not shared the future with the Messenger; and the Muslims, like just about everybody else, expected Sonny to bury Clay in the open night.

On February 16, 1963, a year before the Miami fight, the Court of Appeals in San Francisco had handed down its decision in a seventy-five-page opinion that confirmed the 1961 convictions of Frankie Carbo, Blinky Palermo, and the others. Alcatraz had been shut down, and Carbo was moved to another prison. Blinky lingered a while more on the outside, and was unincarcerated still the night Liston lost to Clay. It was not until June 5, 1964, that United States marshals took him from Philadelphia to begin his fifteen-year term in the federal penitentiary at Lewisburg.

The Devil gave, and the Devil took away. For Sonny, had the Devil not given to him in the first place, there would never have been anything to take away: because you could be the best, toughest, killingest motherfucking fighter in the world, but without the Devil it did not much matter a good goddamn, because it was the Devil's ring. There was no one left for Sonny to turn to; except to the Devil in himself.

"He who is by nature not his own but another's man, is by nature a slave."
Nature. Destiny. Fate. Guys like Frankie Carbo.

The writer Mark Kram recalls being with Ali many years later, in 1983, as they sat and talked by the trancing hushed-crackling flames of the fireplace in Ali's Los Angeles mansion. Ali became lost in silence, and, in that silence, he looked into the fire for quite some time. He turned to Kram and whispered to him: "Liston was the Devil."

In court on May 29, Sonny was let off gently on the speeding and gun possession charges brought against him in March. Municipal Judge Dan D. Diamond handed down fines totaling six hundred dollars. "You have been an idol of mine," said the judge. "God love you and bless you in your future. I'm sorry this had to happen." On an FBI memorandum reporting the judge's words, the Director, accenting those words with his pen, wrote, "Disgusting!"

On Christmas Day, Sonny was stopped for drunken driving and hauled to jail in a patrol wagon after becoming involved in "a shoving match" with the ten Denver policemen who had answered the arresting officer's call. He was wrestled into a cell, where he spent five hours of his Christmas. Counting a penny-ante speeding pinch that took place two weeks after the concealed-weapon rap in March, it was his third arrest in the months since the Clay fight.

He was sporting a close-razored moustache tight above his lip these days. He looked bloated some days, drawn on others. What little light had shone in those dead man's eyes could now hardly be discerned. He was described as "haggard" at the time of his arrest. While he now claimed to be either thirty – his date of birth as set forth in his license application for the Miami fight would have rendered him at that time a bit more than two months shy of his thirtieth birthday, though on the same application, he specifically stated his age as thirty – or his more customary thirty-two – a photograph taken of him early in November showed a man who appeared to have at least forty hard years behind him.

On January 30, 1965, a Denver jury found Liston innocent of the drunk-driving charges. When confronted with the police report that he had been staggering and stumbling while entering his car in front of a restaurant, Sonny explained that he had merely been just jive dancing to the music of his fine new 1965 Cadillac's fine new stereo tape player.

The suspicions and trouble stirred by the Miami fight were such that no state with a reputation for boxing would sanction the rematch. Art Laurie, who at that time was the chairman of the Nevada State Boxing Commission, told me that Senators Hart and Keating spoke to him personally about the prospect of holding the fight in Las Vegas. "They told me not to have anything to do with that fight, because our industry here was gaming, and that fight was going to stink out the place." They also told him that Sonny "only owned ten percent of himself." Laurie recalled that Ash Resnick, along with the promoters Mel Greb and Jack Doyle "came to my office and asked me for a date." (Greb and Doyle would later co-promote the Las Vegas Ali-Patterson fight with Inter-Continental.) "I said, 'That fight's not going to take place here.'" The governor of Nevada, Grant Sawyer, involved himself, and in the end, he told Laurie to use his judgment.

Laurie knew and liked Sonny. He had seen a lot of fighters in his time – born in 1918, he had been a heavyweight champion of the navy boxing team under Gene Tunney, and he later had refereed more title fights than any other official – but he had never seen a fighter with the brute force of Liston. Laurie was watching him work out on a sandbag one day in Vegas, and he saw something he never forgot: Sonny threw a left hook that carried such force that he blew the sandbag loose and sent it crashing to the floor. Furthermore, that force had wrenched open, straightened, and sent flying the S-hook by which the sandbag had been suspended.

Laurie said that "they" – and this, I now see, is what we truly need: a Gibbon, a full and glorious and detailed history of *them* – went for the money. "They got three hundred thousand dollars for the fight, and they bet it at seven-to-one. They got two-point-one million."

"The money was bet through Cleveland," Laurie said. "That's where they placed the money. That's what I understand."

Las Vegas was not alone in wanting nothing to do with this most suspect of sequels to the most suspect and infamous of heavyweight championship fights; and it came to be held, on May 25, 1965, before a sparse crowd at the Central Maine Youth Center, a schoolboys' hockey arena in Lewiston, Maine.

One thing is certain: in that rematch – it was Liston-Ali then, not Liston-Clay – when Sonny lay down in the first, he showed less acting ability than in the episode of *Love American Style* in which he later bizarrely appeared. That fight was not merely a fix – a fix that common lore attributes to physical intimidation by the legion of Black Muslims reportedly gathered there. These Muslims were, in fact, fewer than legion and were present to protect Ali from reprisal by the followers of the late Malcolm X, whose apostasy in breaking with Elijah Muhammad had been loudly denounced by Clay in his ever-increasing role as party-line mouthpiece – it was a flaunted fix.

When fights were tampered with, for the benefit of a fighter's career or the benefit of select few gamblers' pockets, or both, they were most usually rigged rather than fixed. Rigging was a simple and not illegal procedure whereby one fighter of greater capability – whether or not that capability was yet known to the general population of suckers – was pitted against another of lesser capability, who indeed might have been made to look better than he was in previous rigged fights. It was a straightforward matter, known as mismatching. (The 1954 *Boxing Reference Dictionary* of F. C. Avis offers the following definition of the noun *mismatch*: "a contest between two boxers of very different standards of ability." Sometimes mismatches occur unforeseeably, by nature, as it were; sometimes they occur by design.) As Truman Gibson said, all-out fixes were rare: when the same interests profited equally from a fight, no matter who won, what did it matter? Only when an extraordinary gambling payoff presented itself was a debt of fate called in. And only the designated loser knew. The preordained winner was never told, for the main burden of making the fix look real rested on him: for him, the fight must *be* real, and he must fight naturally and in ignorance. As a knowing accomplice, he would be not only a potential danger to the success of the fix, but also potentially nothing more than an unneeded and unwanted expense. Thus, the winner of a good fixed fight never knows that he is a party to the fix. It has been said that it is harder to throw a good fight than to fight one. But human vanity on the part of a victor does much to compensate in his heart and mind for any suspicion of inauthenticity on the part of his foredoomed opponent. The performance in Lewiston, however, was so bad that even Ali must have known.

Sonny – the eight-to-five favorite, despite the prior loss – could not repeat his Miami Beach routine of merely slouching on a stool while Jack Nilon announced his woeful incapacitation. For one thing, the physician at the prefight examination found no evidence of shoulder injury and declared him to be "the fittest man I have ever examined": for another the most willing suspension of disbelief would not countenance it. And so, in the first round, when Ali hit him, he went down. Sonny, who had been knocked down only once before – by a fighter whom the risen Sonny then had proceeded to give the most ferocious beating of his life – here was felled by a blow so slight that few could see it: a short right that seemed intended only to fluster and to fend off, a short right followed by a left hook that missed.

"Liston collapsed slowly, like a falling building, piece by piece, rolling onto his back, then flat on his stomach, his face pressed against the canvas." This account, from a front-page story in the next day's *New York Times,* describes the halting, unnatural, and awkward amateur choreography of a man who is performing a fall rather than the sundering spontaneity of a man knocked down unawares.

It was a shambles. The referee, Jersey Joe Walcott, the Camden, New Jersey, assistant director of public safety and promotional shill of Inter-Continental, lost control of the goings-on after the knockdown. While maneuvering Ali into a neutral corner, Walcott failed to follow the knockdown count of the timekeepers at ringside. After the fight was declared over upon the count of twelve, Sonny rose only to find out that the fight, which was over, was still going on as far as Jersey Joe was concerned. Confused, he squared off, like Ali, as if to fight again, while Walcott simultaneously and belatedly became aware of the timekeepers' twelve-count. "Twelve? You counted to twelve?" he asked.

"Yes, twelve. The fight's over," they replied – whereupon Joe rushed across the ring and raised Ali's arm in victory.

The crowd stood and chanted, "Fake, fake, fake," again and again, until the last of them dwindled and dispersed in disgust. "Fake, fake, fake." Some of them rushed the cordon of state troopers that surrounded the ring, yelling. "Fix, fix, fix," as Ali yelled back telling them to shut up, telling them that his was a righteous victory, a triumph of the "righteous life."

In reality, Ali seemed to have noticed the winning punch no

more than anyone else. He would describe it after the fight as the "anchor punch," the secret weapon of Jack Johnson as passed on to Ali by Stepin Fetchit, the elderly comedian and old-time movie player who was now a part of Ali's ever stranger retinue. In time, it became known in legend as the "phantom punch." Studied frame by frame, the film of the only camera that captured it showed what those who saw it that night in Lewiston saw – among the many who saw nothing – a punch that seemed too ineffectual to knock down, or even to ruffle, the leviathan that was Charles Sonny Liston.

"I overtrained for that fight," Sonny would say.

Maybe it said something, too, that he trained no longer to the nasty horns and pistol rhythms of "Night Train," but to "Railroad Train No. 1" by Lionel Hampton, who was from Ali's hometown of Louisville. It was as if that song, "Night Train," which was the beat and synesthesia of his deepest pulse, had now been taken utterly and without outward sound into the secret part of him, that secret part that was indeed becoming the whole of him.

But it was the damnedest thing: for once, finally, he had been cheered going into that ring in Maine. What a hell of a time to have it all taken from you.

Six months later, in November, he was talking about recruiting Cus D'Amato to manage him in a comeback. D'Amato called Sonny "a challenge" and said there was "a distinct possibility that I could make Liston the heavyweight champion again if he divests himself of the people around him." When told of D'Amato's statement, Sonny said. "It's the onliest way." And that was that.

By Christmas, his home in Denver was up for sale. On March 29, 1966. Sonny bought Kirk Kerkorian's place in Vegas for sixty-four grand: split-level, pastel green, with a swimming pool and a backyard that looked out over the sixteenth fairway of the Stardust Country Club. The address was 2058 Ottawa Drive, in the exclusive area of Paradise Township, less than a mile from where his hero and buddy, Joe Louis, lived, at 3333 Seminole Circle, in a house bought from Johnny Carson.

The tie between Vegas and St. Louis was not a tenuous one. Later, during Sonny's final days, one casino owner was known to associate with Charles "the Blade" Tourine, who in turn was implicated in dealings with John Vitale in St. Louis. Still later, it would be said by police intelligence sources that between one and two million dollars in gambling revenues were "illegally diverted from the Aladdin Hotel's casino in Las Vegas" and "channeled to underworld figures in St. Louis." This report of November 1980, said: "as much as $50,000 was brought to St. Louis each month by couriers, often businessmen who went to Las Vegas ostensibly to gamble. The sources said that both these couriers and Aladdin employees delivered the money to John J. Vitale, an alleged underworld boss.

"Until last month, the gambling resort was owned largely by St. Louis interests. Wayne Newton, the entertainer, bought the casino for about $85 million."

Sonny's first fight after the downfall in Lewiston came more than a year later. In Stockholm, on June 29, he knocked out Gerhard Zech of Germany in the seventh round.

"Blood streamed from Zech's eyes and mouth in the sixth round," said a wire service report, "and the flow continued in the seventh until Liston mercifully knocked him out."

His next three fights were in Sweden as well: a third-round knockout in Gothenburg of Amos Johnson, on August 19; a first-round knockout against Dave Bailey in Gothenburg on March 30, 1967; a sixth-round knockout of Elmer Rush in Stockholm on April 28, 1967.

"This fighting is for the bird," he wrote to a friend in January 1967. From Sweden, in May of 1967, the Listons returned with a three-year-old boy, Daniell, who lived with them as an adopted son.

"I'm my own manager now," he declared in the summer of 1967. "When they try you for murder, they got to produce a body. But nobody can produce anybody who is managing me except me." Later, within the breadth of that same day, he said, "All I need is a manager. Somebody with a nice, clean record."

He talked about leaving Vegas, buying a farm somewhere, maybe Colorado.

*   *   *

In the fall of 1967, it was rumored and reported that Sammy Davis, Jr., was to be Liston's new manager. "Why would Sammy want to get involved with managing a guy nobody wants any part of?" asked Dick Young in his *New York Daily News* column of November 18.

A guy nobody wants any part of. "Liston, the bum of bums" – yeah, that's what some other columnist called him – "the nothing of all nothings."

For the first time, as if uncaring, he indirectly admitted to his control by Carbo and Blinky. Applying for a license to fight in California, a member of the boxing commission in Sacramento asked him about his history of managers.

"One's doin' fifteen years," Sonny said, "and another's doin' twenty-five."

The California commission turned down his application, but in February 1968, a California license was granted him.

In the spring of 1968, *Sports Illustrated* published an article called "What's Become of the Big Bear?" The author, Jack Olsen, described his attempts to draw words from the once infamous man who was now all but forgotten:

"Sonny lounged on a long window seat and tried his best to stay awake. 'Been huntin' rabbits,' he said with great effort, 'and when we hunts rabbits, we don't get much sleep. We leave at two o'clock in the morning." Olsen spends much of the time talking with Geraldine, then finally there is a question that Sonny rouses himself to answer. Olsen asked him if he lost any friends after the Clay fights. Sonny looked dead straight at him and dead straight said: "No. I had my friends in my pocket."

PART 3
ALI VS THE USA

The Young Radical

Jack Olsen

Drama was piled on drama the night Cassius Clay won the world's heavyweight championship from Sonny Liston, and not all of it was in the ring. Dr Ferdie Pacheco, Clay's personal physician, was sitting at ring-side in the middle of a group of men with names like Omar and Abdul and X, Black Muslims who were there to cheer their number-one showpiece on to victory.

"You remember what happened after round four?" Pacheco said. "Cassius got something in his eyes and he wanted to quit? He came back to the corner with his eyes full of tears and Angelo Dundee did the natural thing: he soaked a sponge in water and wiped Clay's eyes with it. Well, when he did that these shock troops around me started saying horrible things. One of 'em said, 'I knew a white man was gonna screw us!' The white man being Angelo. And they said all these horrible words because they thought Angelo had put something on the sponge and *that's* what was making Clay's eyes hurt. These Muslims were saying that they were gonna get Angelo after the fight and beat him up and so forth. So I hollered to Angelo, 'Wipe your own eyes with that sponge! Wipe your eyes so they'll see there's nothing in it!' So finally Angelo wiped his own eyes to show them the sponge was okay. Can you imagine? He didn't have *enough* to do in the ring: he had to put on an act for the shock troops. He *had* to. Those guys don't kid around. They'd already warned Angie before the fight: 'Nothing bad better happen to Cassius.' They gave Angelo an awful time."

The Black Muslims, or "the Nation of Islam", as they want to be known, profess to be non-violent, especially about wars, but their textbooks reek of violence. They forbid the carrying of weapons, but they have perpetrated at least one bloody assassination and almost certainly more. They reckon adultery one of the two worst sins, but their leader has been the subject of paternity suits brought by his teenage "secretaries" and has been accused publicly of fathering eight children out of wedlock. And not the least of the Black Muslims' long list of contradictions is their acceptance of the heavyweight champion and their bestowal upon him of the super-duper holy name, Muhammad Ali. One would have presumed from the available literature that Clay would be near the top of the Muslims' white list. Elijah Muhammad has publicly gone on record against sport, calling it a "filthy temptation" which causes everything from theft to murder.

How does a religion which regards sport as a "filthy temptation" manage to embrace the world's best-known athletic figure? Elijah Muhammad does not condescend to answer such rude questions. Like his disciple Cassius Clay, he does not make conversation; he makes pronouncements. Clay himself offered this explanation of his acceptance in the inner circles of the Nation of Islam:

"When I first joined the Islamic religion and became a member I was already an established ranked pro. And this is the onliest way I have of making my livelihood. And some of our leaders mentioned that it would be bad for the public to be able to say that my religion caused me to be financially hurt and stopped from boxing."

The Muslims soon went a step beyond this kindly tolerance. Herbert Muhammad, son of the leader, became Clay's business manager and later his ring manager as well. "I can't do nothing without Herbert's okay," Cassius began telling business associates. "See Herbert. He'll tell you yes or no." Main Bout, Inc., was formed to handle Clay's theatre television rights, the biggest slice of the fight melon, with Herbert Muhammad as president and John Ali, national Muslim secretary, as treasurer. On the face of it, the move appeared irreconcilable with Elijah Muhammad's philosophy about sport.

"The truth is that the Black Muslim religion is about the most bendable religion in the world," said a relative of young Clay. "When they have got to choose between accounts receivable and the scriptures, they vote for accounts receivable every time. They thought sports was a mortal sin till Cassius came along. Now they're all running around in jock straps. They act like Cassius is Saint John or Saint Luke or somebody, but according to the Muslim beliefs, he ain't even a very good Muslim! Sometimes he talks foul, which is against their religion. He eats more than once a day, which is against their religion, and he makes his living from sport; shame! shame! They're getting a lot of mileage out of him now, but they'll drop him like a hot potato when he's outlived his usefulness to them. They're using Cassius, and he's too dumb to know it."

"Look at it this way," said Ferdie Pacheco. "Before Cassius came along, the Muslims were a lunatic fringe type of idiots. They were running around saying things like 'Kill Whitey!' and 'Take 'em with you!' And none of the coloured people were paying any attention. The Muslims'd put up a sign that said 'Mosque 29' and people laughed like hell and never went in. People were out looking for the action and the music and the chicks on Friday night; they weren't looking for Mosque 29 featuring women wearing dresses down to their ankles and nobody drinking or smoking or anything. That might make it in the Bible Belt in Ohio or someplace like that, but not in the coloured part of town. Now here comes the world champion and he's preaching the Black Muslim religion. And he's making it a big thing. Before he came along, you never even hears the Black Muslims mentioned."

"There's only one reason why they don't throw him out," said the champion's mother, Odessa Grady Clay. "They want him for his money and his popularity."

"That is correct," said her husband. "Muhammad using my boy and all the other people he's got. He preaches the whites are no good. Ummmmmmmmmmm. You take me. I know a lot of bad things the white man's doing, but I know a lot of good things he's doing, too. Now listen now! Ummmmmmmmmmm. Muhammad says the white man does all bad and he's got the solution. A separate land for Negroes. Like Marcus Garvey back in the Thirties and his Back-to-Africa campaign. That corresponds to the Black Muslims. It had the same motive: money. It's something that'll never come true, never gonna happen, it's impossible. Ummmmmmmmm. Whose material they gonna use, whose boats, whose money's gonna sail out? It's impossible. But they make a lot of money off it. Why don't these Muslims go down to Mississippi and do something? And fight! Now Martin Luther King went down there and faced those people, and the Muslims tried to give him sand, didn't they? How can you give a man like Martin Luther King sand? Why, he did something *I* wouldn't do! I wouldn't face those people down there, would you? The Muslims ain't going down there. They a money organisation. Muhammad's using my sons and he's using the black people, getting their money. You know what I'm talking about. He's got two mansions, boy!"

Cassius Sr, with his penchant for absolute statements, can satisfy himself that Elijah Muhammad is simply a money man working a grandiose con game on the American Negro, but a psychiatrist might take a different view of "The Messenger of Allah". Elijah said he was visited in the 1930s by a man named Wallace D. Fard, who turned out to be Allah, "not a spook God", said Elijah, "but a man." Fard stayed with Mr and Mrs Elijah Muhammad, then known as Mr and Mrs Elijah Poole, for nearly four years and never went to sleep. Elijah was fond of telling how he would spy on Allah through the keyhole and "Master Fard", without looking, would say, "Why don't you come in?"

Elijah learned from Fard that whites were descended from monkeys and that they were created about 4,000 BC by Mr Yakub, a biologist who came to be known as "the big head scientist" because he had been born with "an unusual size head". Yakub had been dabbling in evil experiments in his hometown of Mecca, according to Elijah Muhammad, and along with his sixty thousand followers was deported to an island in the Aegean, where he bred the white race. Elijah learned all this history from Master Wallace Fard. "I am the one that the world has been expecting for the past two thousand years," Fard told Elijah. "My name is Mahdi; I am God; I came to guide you into the right path that you may be successful and see the hereafter."

Such lessons in theology were restricted to the insides of the various Muslim "mosques" in Negro ghettos of Detroit and Chicago and Miami and other cities until Cassius came along and began trumpeting them to any reporter who would listen. A day before his fight with Floyd Patterson, Clay shocked the gentlemen of the press by quoting from Elijah's book, *Message to the Blackman*, about the Mother of Planes, that Negro-manned, bomb-laden satellite described by Elijah Muhammad. Cassius added in a respectful tone of voice: "On a clear night when you can see all the stars, look for the brightest. Watch it for a while. You'll see it shaking, that high up. Little white objects jump off it, make a circle, come back. Those are the bombers. On them are black men who never smile . . ."

Said Lawyer Gordon Davidson, "The father didn't even know about the Muslims when he was putting all his ideas into Clay's head. But the great portion of the Muslim philosophy is shared by the great majority of Negroes, sixty per cent anyway. Things like the desire to have pride in their race, the idea that they're black men and not just ex-slaves and Negroes. And when the father talked about things like this he created the base for Cassius to do something he never could foresee. The irony is fantastic. The father spouting all of this ancestral background and blah-blah. All the Muslims needed was to capitalise on it and they did. Very ironic!"

"And now Cassius's father says he hates the Muslims," said the fighter's Aunt Mary Clay Turner, "but if he'd have hated 'em at first, he coulda led Cassius right out. Instead, the father kept on trying to lead Cassius and me and everybody else right into that kind of thinking. He leaned toward Muslim thinking, even though he never would try to be one himself."

"The father set up the boy," said one of the original Louisville Eleven, the businessmen who backed the young boxer. "From the very beginning when we were dealing with the father a lot, when Cassius was still a minor, his father'd make statements that would be identical with those in *Muhammad Speaks*, the Muslim newspaper. In one of those early sessions, I think it was 1960, the father said to me, "We're not Negro, we're Arabs!" And when the money was divided up after each fight, he'd say things like, 'See, Cassius? I told you you'd never get a break from a white man in Kentucky!' Now the monster he created in this boy comes back to haunt him."

Early in 1964, before Clay won the championship, his father began to realise what was happening to his sons Cassius and Rudolph, and immediately he issued a blast against the Muslims. "They have been hammering at him and brainwashing him ever since he was eighteen. He's so confused he doesn't even know where he's at. They've ruined my two boys. They should run those Black Muslims out of the country before they ruin other fine young people . . . The Muslims taught my boys to hate white people, to hate women, to hate their mother." It especially galled the father that he would get collect calls from "Rudolph X". "I don't know no Rudolph X," he would tell the operator, and refuse to accept charges. Later his sons became Rahman Ali and Muhammad Ali, but the father did not know them under those names, either.

According to Muhammad Ali himself, he first heard the truth and saw the light at a Muslim meeting in Miami or New York or Chicago when he was eighteen. Not that Christianity had any too strong a hold on him at the time. Those who listened closely to his early pronouncements about religion might have detected that potentially he was a backslider, as children of dogmatic religionists so often are. As a teenager, his attitude about Heaven and Hell, for example, was revealing. "Last Sunday some cats I know said, 'Cassius, Cassius, come on now and let's go to church; otherwise you won't get to Heaven,'" he said. "'Hold on a minute,' I said to them, 'and let me tell you something else. When I've got me a hundred-thousand-dollar house, another quarter million stuck in the bank and the world title latched on to my name, then I'll *be* in Heaven. Walking around making twenty-five dollars a week, with four children crying at home 'cause they're hungry, *that's* my idea of Hell." I ain't studying about either one of them catching up with me in the graveyard."

Cassius has given three different versions of his first indoctrination into Islamism, and the sceptic might be tempted to discard them all and go back to a statement made by Aunt Mary: "He was brainwashed just like the Communists worked on our turncoats, and it started a long time ago, when he was sixteen. He came back from the Golden Gloves in Chicago and he had a Black Muslim phonograph record with him, and he used to play it over and over and over and over and over again. And sometimes I'd believe they'd hypnotised him. They had that boy hypnotised. He'd look at you funny, and I'd say to myself, 'They musta fed him something before he came back this way!' "

Cassius told one reporter early in his pro career: "I was at the corner of 125th Street and Lenox Avenue when I first heard the message. I didn't know who that Muslim speaker was, but everything he said made sense. The man made me think about many things I had wondered about. But I didn't join right away. I went to CORE, Urban League and NAACP meetings. I studied the Catholics, the Jehovah's Witnesses, Seventh-day Adventists, Baptists and Methodists in a search for knowledge. The most concrete thing I found in churches was segregation. Well, now I have learned to accept my own and be myself. I know we are original man and that we are the greatest people on the planet earth and our women the queens thereof."

Later Cassius told me: "My first contact with Islam was in Miami, Florida, about 1960 or early 1961. One of the brothers invited me to a meeting and I heard the truth and the facts about life and history and right away it hit me. It is not true that Malcolm X converted me when he visited me in Miami. It was the truth, the word itself, that converted me, what I heard when I first walked into that meeting in Miami. I heard the minister saying, 'Why are we called Negroes? Chinese are named after Chinamen, Cubans are named after Cubans, Indians are named after Indians . . . !" Cassius kept the list going for about two minutes, or one minute and fifty-five seconds longer than required to make his point. His habit of sticking on a list like a broken record passes for erudition in his intimate circles. " 'Hawaiians are named after Hawaiians,' " he went on, quoting the preacher. " 'Germans are named after Germans. Australians . . . Mexicans . . . Egyptians . . . Italians . . . Puerto Ricans . . . Indonesians . . .' " Then he paused for emphasis, like his father, and loudly quoted the preacher's punchline: " 'BUT WHAT COUNTRY'S NAMED AFTER NEGROES?' " Another pause. "And I said to myself, 'That's something to think about.' "

And still later he told me, "The first meeting I went to was in Chicago. All the writers heard I was going and they went there to catch me, in a Muslim Temple in South Chicago. Inside I saw nothing but six hundred, seven hundred people, all the women in their white robes, just like Mary in all the pictures with Jesus. Men all had on dark suits and bow ties and white shirts, neat haircuts. And I said, 'Why all these FBI men and newsmen out here?' Then I stopped to think. Hell, I'm supposed to be free. I'm not downtown integrating and marching. I'm not trying to marry a white woman or cause race trouble or running white people out of their suburbs. I'm in my own neighbourhood. I'm not smoking. I'm not drinking. Everybody in here's praying. There's no winking, no flirting, no adultery. I said, 'What's wrong, this must be right, this must be the real programme of God.' So I went to the door and I called out, 'Yeh, I'm here! Why?'

"They said, 'Are you a Muslim?' and I said, 'No, I'm not, not now. But the way you keep pressing me I just might be.' I said, 'They're the cleanest people next to God.' And later on I met Elijah Muhammad. He's the Messenger of God. You won't see no power on earth no greater. *The Messenger of Allah.* If he tells me to do something, I do it, real fast, before he gets it out of his mouth. And when I found out his programme, that we're not Negroes, we're Asiatic black people, gods of the universe and fathers of all civilisation, and the queen of the planet earth, I knew truth when I heard it. I said, 'That's God's truth, that's what I been looking for.' "

As long ago as 1962 the Louisville Sponsoring Group was aware that the Black Muslims were romancing Clay, but the group's position was that religious matters were private. "One of our first inklings came from the Louisville chapter of the NAACP," said a spokesman. "Clay had made some public statements about protest demonstrations to the effect that he didn't want dogs biting him, he wasn't a politician, things like that. The NAACP here had asked him to do some things that he turned down. And he told them, 'I don't go where I'm not wanted.' The NAACP didn't like the sound of this and they called us and met with us. And they said they'd found out the boy apparently was running with Black Muslims. We'd already begun to suspect. Rudy was converted before Cassius, and he'd sit at our meetings with his arms folded, eyes looking straight ahead, and he'd never say a word. We knew something was going on."

The official announcement of Clay's conversion to Islam came three days after he defeated Sonny Liston in Miami Beach to become world heavyweight champion. "A rooster crows only when it sees the light," said Cassius at a press conference February 27, 1964. "Put him in the dark and he'll never crow. I have seen the light and I'm crowing." He had not intended to crow, but a reporter told him that Elijah Muhammad had let the news out at a meeting in Chicago. "That is true, and I am proud of it," Clay said. "But what's all the commotion about? Nobody asks other people about their religion. But now I am the champion, I am the king; so it seems the world is all shook up about what I believe. You call it Black Muslims. I don't. This is a press word. It is not a legitimate name. Islam is a religion and there are seven hundred and fifty million people all over the world who believe in it, and I am one of them. Islam means peace. Yet people brand us as a hate group. They say we want to take over the country. They say we're Communists. That is not true. Followers of Allah are the sweetest people in the world. They don't carry knives. They don't tote weapons. They pray five times a day. The women wear dresses that come all the way to the floor and they don't commit adultery. The men don't marry white women. All they want to do is live in peace with the world. They don't hate anybody. They don't want to stir up any kind of trouble. All the meetings are held in secret, without any fuss or hate-mongering."

Cassius raved on and on about his new religion, and hundreds of newspapers, including *The New York Times*, quoted him at length the next day, as though they were quoting a world-renowned theologian. "Elijah Muhammad never had it so good," said one of Clay's annoyed stablemates. "Here he's been trying to peddle that screwy religion of his and getting no place, which is where he belongs, and then along comes this simple-minded kid falling for all the baloney and getting the Muslims the kind of publicity you couldn't buy. No wonder they broke their neck to get Cassius."

"I get telephone calls every day," the newspaper stories quoted the champion. "They want to me carry signs. They want me to picket. They tell me it would be a wonderful thing if I married a white woman because this would be good for brotherhood. I don't want to be blown up. I don't want to be washed down sewers. I just want to be happy with my own kind." He launched into his well-worn separation speech: "Animals in the jungle flock together. Mexicans, Puerto Ricans, Chinese and Japanese all live better if they are together. I don't like hot Mexican food and I would be unhappy if somebody made me eat it. At the same time, you may not like what I like – turnip greens and hominy grits or country music. If you don't like it you shouldn't have to accept it."

Clay finished with a personal vote of confidence in himself. "I am a good boy," he said. "I never have done anything wrong. I have never been in jail. I have never been in court. I don't join any integration marches. I don't pay any attention to all those white women who wink at me. I don't carry signs. I don't impose myself on people who don't want me. If I go in somebody's house where I'm not welcome, I am uncomfortable. So I stay away. I like white people. I like my own people. They can live together in peace."

Later he said: "I used to be confused like most American black men. I used to want to be anything but black. I'd smoke once in a while, take a beer, pour whisky in my Coke and I was about to try out reefers when I listened to our leader, the Honourable Elijah Muhammad, that itty-bitty man."

Odessa Grady Clay had the friendliest feelings toward the eleven wealthy men of the Louisville Sponsoring Group, but she charged them with one error of judgment when they failed to shield Cassius from the Muslims. "The big mistake was when they sent him to train at Miami all by himself," said Mrs Clay. "That's when the Muslims got him. That's how Sam Saxon got him and talked that Muslim stuff to him every day. 'cause I went there one year with Cassius and this old Sam, the Muslim man, was in Cassius's room every night, brainwashing him. If somebody'd been with Cassius, they'd never have got to him."

Later a variant of Mrs Clay's theory was worked up by Joe Louis, the former heavyweight champion, who travelled briefly with Cassius before quitting with the announcement, "I was born a Baptist and I'll die a Baptist." Said Louis: "He got off on the wrong foot. He got no help from his Louisville management. They stayed on one side of town and him on the other. He ran wild. Nobody told him to talk to people. Now nobody can stop him."

To the impartial observer of Clay's history, it is difficult to see how any measure short of house arrest could have kept the young fighter out of the Black Muslim movement. The religion did not have to seek out the man. Christianity, with its preachments of loving neighbours and the brotherhood of mankind, could not satisfy a mystical, unsettled Negro youth who was weaned on stories about lynching and rape and the lying, deceitful white man, plus the moon and the stars and the flickering mysteries of the East. "He was an absolutely perfect prospect for the Black Muslims," said William Faversham, the member of the group who was closest to Clay during the early professional years. "He's a boy for whom this sort of Alice-in-Wonderland religion would hold an appeal. He's a mystic himself. The universe fascinates him. Early in the game he used to have visions. He likes that sort of thing."

One can imagine how the Black Muslim penchant for prognostication must have hit the ears of the young Clay, who had lived on prophecies for years ("I will be the world's heavyweight champion") and who was the son of a man who lived on prophecies ("And I'll have a factory called Clay's Enterprises and I'll employ all my relatives").

"You have to understand the role of prophecy," explained a Louisville schoolteacher, himself a Negro. "If you can't stand the world you live in, and you can't change it, you've got to believe in magic, in predictions. That's Cassius when he was growing up, living with that wild father and all that crazy talk around the house. You've got to believe that things are gonna change. So predictions have a great charm and appeal. 'Next year the white man's gonna lose his power.' '1966'll be a bad year for the white man.' That's great news to some people dumb enough to believe it. Believing in predictions is a way of warding off evil in the present when you can't ward it off any other way. You can bear living miserable if you believe a prediction that tomorrow will be better. That's why you get so much predicting and prophecy in the Negro churches. That's why you get so much predicting and prophecy from Cassius Clay, too."

Clay himself analysed the phenomenon of forecasting the future. "What do all these people sitting there in Madison Square Garden think?" he once told a reporter. "They ask, 'Can I do it again?' They want to know. They want to see that *round*. People are superstitious. It's the *round* that gets them. They don't come to see me win. They come to see that *round*. People run to priests. They pray and shout in church. People is spooky-minded. They look at the moon. They wonder about numbers. Preachers say Jesus called them but they got no proof. I got proof. The round I call is the round they must fall."

A reporter once dared Clay to predict a knock-out to the very second. "Seconds are gimmick talk," Cassius said angrily. "There's nothing spooky or ghostly about calling the round – it's all science. I go into a conference with myself and then I prophesy. You start with the thought and then you turn it into reality, like the scientist figured out how to make the jet before he built it."

Later Clay's former assistant trainer, Drew "Bundini" Brown, said, "When I first met the champ, I told him he was a phony, doing all that predicting. He said to me, 'Every time I call the round, I'm scared to death.' There were tears in both of our eyes."

Young Clay was always obsessed by prophecy, and Elijah Muhammad did not fail to satisfy his appetite. "Look what he say here," Cassius told me one morning, pointing to a chapter title in *Message to the Blackman*: AMERICA IS FALLING HER DOOM IS SEALED. "And he teaches that before the year's over all Negroes in America are gonna be Muslims, before 1966 is over," Clay went on. "And he is teaching that this year all Negroes will rise into the knowledge of the truth, and he don't hide it. And the press can tell by the end of the year if he was right. And he says that things are getting close to the fulfilment of the Bible, where the Bible says you can tell when the end of time is coming because there will be wars and rumours of wars, men flying like a bird, horseless carriages, buildings being teared down like mad, daughters against mothers and mothers against daughters, men taking the place of women . . ."

"See, I read my Bible," the fighter's father had told me a few days earlier, "and we right on the time for Judgment Day now. Saint John asked God how will we know when it's the time, and God said people will be riding horseless carriages, people'll be flying like birds, and man will be loving man, and there'll be more tearing down and destroying and building up than ever before. Am I right? Ummmmmmmmmm. God said when the time comes there'll be wars and rumours of wars. Are they that? Ummmmmmmmmm. God's gonna come down and the devil's gonna try to tackle him, but God's gonna destroy the devil, take the key away from him and lock him up. And then God'll come down and rise nothing but the Christians! People like Elijah Muhammad's people, they will not be in the first resurrection. They're false prophets. God says beware of false prophets who come to you dressed as sheep but are raging wolves beneath."

"The old man is something else," said a family friend. "He sits there quoting the Bible and attacking the Black Muslims and if you listen closely you can hardly tell 'em apart!"

After relations with Cassius the elder had come almost to an end, young Cassius installed Elijah Muhammad in a parental role in his life, and sometimes in a supernatural role. "Look at the nation today," Cassius said. "The sit-ins didn't work; the swim-ins didn't work, the walk-ins, roll-ins, none of 'em worked. Thirty, forty was shot down in Los Angeles like animals, children who had mothers who were crying; children who wanted to live and breathe the fresh air God gave 'em are now daid and in the grave just because they were trying to get justice. So there's nothing for the nation but destruction. God himself must come, and he's here! *Elijah Muhammad is the man to fill the need.* If you don't believe it, just listen to what he says and watch it."

And yet Clay's subservience to the god-like leader, like most of his personality traits, appears to be part real and part pretence or self-delusion. One afternoon he told me how the wispy little Muhammad, like an angry father, had taken his driver's licence away. "Muhammad ain't playing, man!" Cassius said. "He makes you live clean and righteous. When he catch you, boy, you caught! I can't drive no more. I got to have a driver. I had that police trouble about my driving, those tickets, and Muhammad say he don't want to read about me in no more

trouble; so he said, 'You just quit driving!' and I had to quit.
He's *that* powerful! Anything he say, we do, man! The whole
country's scared of him, they don't even bother him." Cassius
forgot that he had arrived at our rendezvous minutes before
behind the wheel of his big black Cadillac. The Muslim hierarchy is indulgent toward the champion in such matters, and in
general treats him like a rich old uncle with a heart condition.
Thus he is not punished for occasional violations of Elijah's
specific orders, and for eating more than once a day, and for
minor offences which might get another member of the sect
suspended for as long as five years, as was one of Cassius's
friends ("for getting caught with a woman, you know what I
mean, man," Clay explained).

The champion may buddy up to one or another of Elijah's
trusted lieutenants, but his ultimate allegiance is to the big boss
and to the philosophy the big boss has spelled out in the three
decades since Allah appeared to him. Anyone who fell out with
Muhammad fell out with Cassius, as the late Malcolm X, once a
close friend of Cassius, quickly learned. Malcolm broke with
Muhammad over some of the leader's personal habits, and
immediately Malcolm found that Cassius was no longer his best
disciple. The last word between them was a message to Cassius
on his arrival in Ghana for a triumphant swing through Africa.
"Because a billion of our people in Africa, Arabia and Asia love
you blindly," Malcolm wired, "you must now be forever aware of
your tremendous responsibilities to them. You must never say or
do anything that will permit your enemies to distort the beautiful
image you have here among our people."

Holding the wire in his hand, Clay told Herbert Muhammad,
the leader's son, that he had seen Malcolm in his robes the day
before "and he didn't look very responsible to me." Said Cassius:
"Man, did you get a look at him? Dressed in that funny white
robe and wearing a beard and walking with that cane that looked
like a prophet's stick? Man, he's gone! He's gone so far out he's
out completely. Doesn't that just go to show, Herbert, that
Elijah is the most powerful? Nobody listens to that Malcolm any
more."

When a Muslim terror squad assassinated Malcolm in front of
hundreds of witnesses, Cassius said: "Malcolm X was my friend

and he was the friend of everybody *as long as he was a member of Islam*. Now I don't want to talk about him. All of us were shocked at the way he was killed. Elijah Muhammad has denied that the Muslims were responsible. We are not a violent people. We don't carry guns." When it was established later that Muslims had undeniably perpetrated the murder, Cassius refused to discuss Malcolm X any further.

Another of Clay's close friends was beaten up by Black Muslims in Boston, and again Cassius immediately showed where his fealty lay. "He's nothing to me," he said. "He was welcome as a friend as long as he was a registered Muslim. But not any more . . ." The friend had recommended that Clay quit the Muslims because he might be roughed up himself, to which the champion replied: "I will never leave the Muslims. If it weren't for the Muslims, I'd be nothing."

Despite a certain air of capriciousness, which creeps into almost everything Clay does, he seems to be in earnest about his religion. Asking him the simplest question about the Nation of Islam can be an exhausting process unless one has time on one's hands. On a television discussion programme, someone made the mistake of asking Clay the significance of the name Muhammad Ali. The answer was in perfect Stengelese: "Our religious leader the Muslims of the believers in the religion of Islam here in America – that's taught by Elijah Muhammad – honourable Elijah Muhammad – he named this great, honourable name – Muhammad Ali – after my victory over Liston. And I would like to explain to you that he teaches us that many people – that is a good question you asked – he teaches us that most people, all people from certain countries have names that have meanings. Like Mr Cassius Marcellus Clay was a slave fighter, the white man – I should say Caucasian. Way back they used to write about this, way back even before I joined the Islamic religion and got my name changed. They used to talk about this great man named Cassius Clay who was a white. Now he named my great-great-grand-daddy after him. Which means that this was not the name of a black man, but the name of a white man. And like for an example if I told you here comes Mr Chang Chong you would picture a yellow man from China. If I told you here come Mr Krushchev, you would picture a Russian. If I say here come Mr Castro, you would picture a Cuban. If I say here come Mr Lumumba or Mr Nkrumah or Kenyatta, Africans, right? Here come Mr White Cloud, Morning Trees, Tall Star or Silver Moon, you would picture Indians. But if I said here come Mr Smith, Mr Robinson, Mr Clay, Mr Tree, Mr Fish, Mr Bird, you would not know what colour he is until you saw him. He could be Negro or white because the people put at two million Negroes as the Honourable Elijah Muhammad teaches us here are named after the masters when we were freed a hundred years ago. But we were not given our names back. So therefore we who follow the honourable Elijah Muhammad it is indeed an honour for him to give us a name such as Muhammad Ali and the name Muhammad means one who is worthy of praises and one who is praiseworthy. And Ali means the most high. Clay only meant dirt with no ingredients."

While Cassius paused for air, somebody said, "It would be awful nice if one of these days the people who are white quit being so proud of being white and the people who are black quit being so proud of being black and maybe it would be better if we all had names like tree and bush and things like that."

Said Cassius: "Men should not be named after fishes; man should not be named after horses; man should not be named after birds and trees and woods and man should be named, men are supreme over all animals and he look like he kind of silly naming himself after a horse. Man is the most high. So Ali means the most high. Muhammad means worthy of praises and praiseworthy. So I think I have two names that really just stand up and hold its own against anyone on the planet earth."

A few minutes later he was launched on a sales talk about his leader: "I want to be a Muslim because after seeing the teachings that the honourable Elijah Muhammad is teaching these so-called Negroes in America, the onliest man who has black people sticking together, not begging, not on their hands and knees, forcing themselves on people that don't want him. He's the onliest man that have following teaching the so-called Negroes unity among their own, mainly respect of the black woman which he has never gotten from four hundred years out of black men. He is the onliest man teaching us the knowledge of our true language. This is Arabic. He is the onliest man teaching us the knowledge of our history, our culture, names and our true God whose proper name is Allah before we were brought to the shores of North America. He's the onliest man who is connecting us with all of the people in Africa, Asia, Egypt, Arabia, Sudan, Indonesia, Pakistan, who has never recognised American Negroes, and he is the onliest man who have followers that the white Americans really respect."

Cassius professes to believe without reservation in Muhammad, even in the outermost reaches of the leader's message. To Clay, the dietary prohibitions of the Islamic religion, as spelled out by Elijah Muhammad, have the force of divine law (even though he sometimes honours them in the breach), and he speaks of food restrictions like a Christian reciting a Sunday School lesson. "Our beans are crushed and mashed and cooked. We eat only whole wheat bread and whole wheat muffins. Cabbages and greens and green beans are cooked without fattenings and pork. We don't eat any sweet potatoes because they're not good for the digestive system. We eat squash cooked like sweet potatoes. We don't eat lima beans and collard greens; these are hard, animal foods. We don't eat shrimp, catfish, crabs, lobsters, all swine of the sea, and we don't eat garbage eaters like the hog on the land and the buzzard in the sky. We have a knowledge of these things, and once we start eating Egyptian cooked rice and Arabian baked string beans, carrot pies, squash pies, buttermilk pies, we're not at home with what you whites eat."

He was asked how it happens that some of the Black Muslims' dietary rules conflict with those of the world's 750 million Muslims, to whom the Black Muslims claim a spiritual kinship. "Well, Allah taught our leader more than he taught those African Muslims," Clay explained. "The African Muslims aren't as wise as us. The proof is all the African leaders have white wives, or a lot of 'em do. They're not as wise as us."

Like a child who learned his catechism, Cassius has all the answers. Do the Muslims teach hate? "In a way, we do. But are we wrong to hate the murders and the unjust treatment that we're getting? Sure, we hate that. But we're righteous people. We rely on Allah, and we don't bother nobody." What about Elijah

Muhammad's constant refrain that all white men are devils? "Elijah Muhammad teaches us that he didn't know about that hisself till thirty-five, forty years ago when God, in the person of Master Wallace Fard, came to America and he, Allah in the person of Master Wallace Fard, taught Elijah Muhammad. And Elijah Muhammad teaches us that this is not his own, it's just the truth that God taught him. And if God taught him that all white men are devils, and we believe that Muhammad is from God, then we have to believe it. And no white man has ever yet in the thirty-five years of Muhammad's teaching, no white man have took Elijah Muhammad to court about it. No white man has stood up and debated or challenged him to prove they wasn't devils, or invited him to a duel or a discussion, or fined him. Not one white man in America has stood up and said, "We are not devils, prove it, what's this false charge?" And this teaching is now all over America."

Until the religious issue all but severed relations between them, the Clays, Junior and Senior, used to engage in wild arguments about such matters. "The Muslims know I could bring him back to the church," the father said with sublime faith in his own rhetoric, " 'cause I drilled him all the time. I drilled him hard!"

There were long debates when young Cassius accepted his new name of Muhammad Ali. "Cassius Marcellus Clay was the most beautiful name," said Odessa, as though the name were now dead and buried. "It was from the Romans. It was a warrior's name."

Another who argued with young Clay was his plain-spoken "auntie", Mary Clay Turner. "He'd pick certain things out of the Bible to prove his points," Aunt Mary recalled, "and I'd say to him, 'Well, why don't you read something else in this good book besides those things you have underlined? You read on this page and then you flip ahead fifty pages for your next point and then maybe a hundred more and you point to something else.' I said, 'Read the whole thing! Don't let nobody dictate to you and tell you what to read!'"

"If Cassius had been reading like I been reading he wouldn't have been caught in that Muslim mess," Aunt Mary went on. "Right now if a man comes up to my boys and tells 'em to sign their name with an X, like a Muslim, my boys'll tell 'em, 'Why, that's the way my oldest great-grandmother was taught to write, sign her name with an X to keep from learning how to write,' I been over these things with Cassius so often, but now I give up. I don't even say nothing any more. Why, you have to be almost totally illiterate to be sold that Muslim bill of goods! I'll just plain old give you the facts. *You have to be illiterate!* Cassius is about the cleanest thing in the whole confounded Muslim organisation. All the rest of them have scars and smears on their names. If they haven't once been hustlers, well, they're hustling now! If they haven't been robbers, they're robbing now! This is it, you know I'm not lying! Practically every one of 'em's been in prison. Cassius falls for all that business about no drinking and no smoking, but he didn't know they drink behind the doors, and cuss, and whip their mamas and do everything. And they'd kill you just as quick as they'd kill me, and don't you forget it!"

Aunt Mary talks like someone who has abandoned all hope for her nephew, but Cassius Sr, with his perpetual ebullience, still grasps for straws. "I just can't believe Cassius hates white people. It's not in his blood to be like that. We might bring him back. Lemme explain something to you. Ummmmmmmmmmm. Suppose you're going from here to 12th and Broadway. You don't know how to get there and you ask somebody and he points the opposite way of the right way, and you start off. Now you can only go so far till you come to Florida and the ocean when you're looking for 12th and Broadway. Right? And you turn around and get on the right road. Ummmmmmmmm. That's deep, isn't it? You might think you hate, you might be taught to hate, but you don't *really* hate. You know why? Now hold on now! Because you a man, and I'm a man, and we both from God. We all have one father: God in Heaven. And the world's founded on love, and man was saved on love, and redeemed on love. Ummmmmmmmm. How long was Cassius here the other day, Peaches?"

"About twenty-five minutes," Mrs Clay answered.

"They keep him away from me," the father said. "They know I could bring him back. They tell him he can't stay around his parents."

"They don't like me 'cause I'm light-skinned," the mother said. "I can't help what I am. They hard on me. Yeh, they *hard* on me."

"Yeh," said Cassius the elder. "They hard on all of us."

Certainly the Muslims were hard on Sonji Roi, the beautiful Chicago entertainer who married Clay with the blessings of the Muslims and lost him to their insistent pressure on her husband. "They've stolen my man's mind," Sonji said when Cassius filed for divorce. But as in so many other matters, Clay's attitude toward women was distorted long before the Muslim influence came into his life. Just as the religion did not have to seek out the man, so the religion did not have to mould the man's attitude toward women, which seems to be that they are an inferior type of human: sinful, evil and temptingly corrupt. "When he was real small," Odessa Grady Clay said in a revealing memory about her older son, "he loved to chase chickens and dogs. When we took him out to his uncle's in the country the first thing he would do would be chase the chickens and ducks. And when he grew up you know what he used to do when he come home from grade school? He always liked to run girls with switches! We'd say, 'You don't run pretty girls!' He was always chasing girls, when he was eight, nine, ten years old. Every day after school he did it." She began to laugh almost hysterically. "And he always would bring me flowers when he was real small. Oh, he is such a kind-hearted, sympathetic person, just as good as gold!"

Later, in the middle of a lengthy interview, I suddenly asked Cassius: "Why did you used to chase girls with switches?"

After a long pause, he said, "'cause they was always wrong and they needed a whuppin'."

On one level or another of his thinking, Cassius appears to have made the decision to handle the woman problem by staying away from them. He treats them with elaborate courtesy, but steers clear of any personal relationships. When he was on one of his trips, the Clay bus stopped in Fredericksburg, Va., and six young and pretty Negro girls rushed up to talk to the champion. When one asked for a souvenir, Cassius said, "I'd give you my shirt, but I can't get out a fresh one. Lord knows I need one."

One of the passionate young men in Clay's party jumped up and said, "That's all right. Take mine, sweet thing!"

"Hush!" Clay said. "These little foxes wants to talk to the champ." After a polite conversation, he escorted them out of the bus and bade them a courteous farewell. "O . . . OOO," he said when the girls were gone. "Sometimes it's *so* hard to be righteous."

"This you can quote," said Solomon McTier, one of Clay's handlers. "He lives clean. He waves at the girls and keep right on walking!"

"I've never seen anybody train or keep his body in shape the way this man does, and it's hard to understand," said another member of Clay's camp. "Here he is a beautiful fighter, a beautiful human being, and at the age of twenty-four years old, he renews himself with the women like a man of sixty. Why, after he won the title against Liston, Sam Cooke, you remember Sam, the singer? Sam Cooke had three beautiful young ladies come over to Cassius's house in Miami. And these three women grabbed the heavyweight champion of the world and they said we're gonna go out and celebrate. But he would not go out and celebrate. At exactly quarter to one he told the three girls, 'I'm sorry, ladies, you are gonna have to leave. I'm gonna go to bed.' Now can you imagine that? Whether he was tired or not, here's a fellow that's just won the championship of the world, made his dreams come true, and he isn't gonna have some fun with these ladies? A young beautiful guy like this? And a very normal guy at that? You figure a guy like this is gonna go somewhere and get lost with the chicks after training so hard and sacrificing so hard to get the title. And at this very moment I can't understand it. I still see girls call this guy and want to come over and he'll say, 'I'm sorry, I got to get my rest.'"

Before Sonji came along, Cassius engaged in a few minor flirtations, but for the most part all his normal desires appeared to be sublimated into boxing. "He did have a crush on Wilma Rudolph, the Olympic sprinter," said Clarence "Slick" Royalty, a prominent sports figure from Louisville, "but nothing came of it. When she was here, Cassius was trying to hold her hand all the time, but she wasn't interested in him at all. Every time she'd get up to go some place he'd jump up beside her and hold her hand, but she wouldn't respond. She finally went back to Tennessee A&I and got married, and I think it bothered Cassius a little bit." Later he was linked romantically with a Sudanese girl named Rechima, whom he met on his trip to Africa. "She wears this wrap-around dress and has a gem in her forehead," Clay told reporters. "And she's beautiful just like me." But after a few months of separation, he stopped talking about her, and later denied that he had ever thought of Rechima as anything but a friend.

And suddenly Cassius was married. To the amazement of his friends and to the complete surprise of his biographers of the press, Clay drove to Gary, Indiana with Sonji Roi and was married in a closely guarded civil ceremony. After the wedding, he submitted to a short press conference. He said Sonji was twenty-two, a model and editor on various magazines, a Muslim like himself, and a woman who would fade into the background and keep her mouth shut, like a good Muslim wife. He said he and Sonji would go to Egypt and "when my children are born they won't be born in America. They'll be born in the hereafter."

He was asked where the hereafter was. "Somewhere near Arabia," said Cassius. He added that the "wicked world" was on the verge of being destroyed; "the way things are shaping up it won't be but about ten years." He said he and Sonji were not members of the wicked race; they were both "Asiatic".

Sonji Roi was not, in fact, the twenty-two-year-old editor of various magazines but the twenty-seven-year-old once-married mother of one child. For five years she had worked as barmaid at the Archway Supper Club on Chicago's South Side, and during that time she had been the girl friend of various star Negro athletes. Then Herbert Muhammad, the rotund son of "The Messenger of Allah", spotted her and put her to work in the office of his newspaper, *Muhammad Speaks*. Before her first week was over, Sonji met Cassius and struck sparks. "You never saw two people fall for each other so fast in your life," said a Clay confidante. "It was *bang!* Just like the movies." Sonji was regarded as an odd choice by some of the people around Cassius. "You figure it out," said Dr Pacheco. "Here is a man who spends all his time talking about women who paint their faces, women who drink, and what the hell does he fall for? A woman who paints her face, wears short dresses, drinks and smokes. Is that childish innocence on his part, or is there a little Elmer Gantry in him? I tell you: behind this superguy, there are many contradictions!"

Clay's own version of the affair with Sonji had them meeting on July 3, 1964, and beginning a common-law marriage three weeks later in Miami. "I said I would like to take her with me and would she marry me? This was in Miami. 'Would you marry me common-law to justify our driving to Los Angeles and checking into hotels on the way out and checking in the largest, biggest hotel in Los Angeles as my wife and taking you to religious meetings as my wife? I cannot be seen to commit adultery. It just cannot be in my name. I am the heavyweight champion of the world. You must marry as common-law to travel with me and check in hotels with me.' She did marry me common-law. That justified my sleeping with her in the bed and cohabit with her all the way on my trip to Los Angeles and back to Chicago."

According to Cassius, Sonji also agreed to become a Muslim. "That was the onliest reason I married her, because she agreed to do everything I wanted her to do." She became a Muslim by writing a letter to National Secretary John Ali proclaiming her belief in the Nation of Islam and promising to register as a Muslim. "Once that letter is accepted and you get lessons, you're a member," Cassius explained. "She was accepted even to the extent of teaching the girls and all of the ladies in Boston, Massachusetts, on her experiences and her life, at the time we were training, and she also had the honour of eating dinner with her leader twice with me. He accepted her as his daughter. He offered his home to show he accepted her . . . But I told her to be my wife she must wear her dresses at least three inches below her knees, she must take off lipstick, she must quit drinking and smoking in order to be seen with me, going to our religious meetings which was due to come up."

After their civil marriage in Indiana, Cassius kept Sonji in almost complete isolation from the press. Reporters who approached her in training camp were sharply admonished by Cassius himself to stay away, "if you ever want to have another interview with me." Anyone who asked Sonji about the marriage received only a cold glance in reply. The pretty ex-barmaid was trying dutifully to live her role as a Muslim wife. One day Chris Dundee, brother of Angelo and a close friend of Cassius, had a short conversation with Sonji in the Fifth Street Gym in Miami Beach. Chris talks with his hands, like the warm, friendly South Philadelphia Italian he is, and he has difficulty keeping them off whomever he is conversing with. To talk to Chris Dundee is to get your back slapped, your shoulders pommelled and your arms squeezed. After Chris spoke to Sonji, Cassius called him to one side and said, "You know you're not supposed to touch a Muslim woman? Now I know you didn't mean no harm, but you got to remember. Don't touch any Muslim woman!"

Said Chris Dundee later: "It gave me a creepy feeling to be talked to like that."

Six months went by before Clay allowed a reporter to talk to Sonji, and then it was only a short interview. "I kept her away from the press until I could coach her," Cassius explained. "Didn't want my baby to say the wrong things." He explained that the Islamic religion called for women to remain in the back-ground. "It's pretty demanding," said Sonji in her first meeting with the press. Behind the scenes, she was getting a neckful of the Islamic faith. "They were on him night and day," she said later. "Pestering him, pestering him, never gave him a minute's peace."

Occasionally the two would have a minor public spat, indicative of the smouldering resentment underneath. One day Cassius rushed into the house in Miami after training and poured himself a tall glass of orange juice. "You ain't cooled off yet, and you already had two glasses of orange when you left the gym," Sonji said.

"Who you, a fighter?" Cassius exclaimed hotly. "You a fighter?" He swallowed the juice in one gulp.

A few months later Cassius asked a Miami court for an annulment. His suit complained: "Prior to and at the time of the marriage and for the purpose of inducing plaintiff to consent to marriage she falsely and fraudulently represented and promised that on the pronouncement of the marital vows she would adopt the Islamic faith as her own and would without deviation adhere to its tenets and requirements, [but] she knew at the time the promises were false and fraudulent and secretly intended not to convert or adhere to these tenets. On June 11 an incident occurred when she told him she would not convert or adhere to the tenets and never intended to."

Said Sonji: "We've always had our little arguments about clothes. I told him that if I were embarrassing him I would stay out of the picture. I just want to be his wife and I won't let them take him away from me just like that." She said she had tried to adhere to the rule of Muslimism, that she had quit drinking and smoking and ate only the foods prescribed by Elijah Muhammad.

At pre-trial hearings, Cassius testified that he was in training for his second fight with Sonny Liston when he realised that his wife did not intend to comply with the tenets of Islam. "With all the world there, the Associated Press, the *Boston Globe*, African, Asian, European newspapers," Clay said, "she walked into the press conference with a blue jean, tight tight skin-tight blue jean suit on . . . This was about three or four days before my fight in Lewison, Maine, May 25, 1965 . . . Then after the fight in Maine we drove to Chicopee, Massachusetts, stayed there about a day and a half. She put on a short short short tight dress with no sleeves or nothing, contrary to everything that she had been wearing, and she walked into the lobby in this dress, went into the dining room in it, and I pulled her to the room and I asked her, 'Why would you walk into the lobby around the world embarrassing me in these type sexual designed clothes showing all parts or many parts of your body?' and she says, 'You have won your fight. I no longer have to pretend with you. I have never wanted to be a Muslim. I never will be a Muslim.' Unquote. Excuse the expression, 'To hell with all of you Muslims. You give me some money and I won't embarrass you in front of all these reporters, and I will catch a plane and will leave here and go to Chicago.'"

Clay was asked if he had loved Sonji when he married her. "I would like to say that I loved her only if she would follow me in my way of life and if she would take my name and everything else that I could give her and be what I wanted her to be. That's the onliest reason I would love her."

When the case came to trial, it developed that Cassius had no genuine grounds for a divorce, beyond the testimony of one

"Samuel X. Saxon" to the effect that in his earshot Sonji had promised "to comply with the Muslim faith." Cap'n Sam was cast in a familiar role: seconding Cassius.

"Cassius had no real grounds at all," said one of Sonji's advisors, "so we just sat down and worked out a divorce. We asked him how much he'd pay to get out of the marriage and it developed he would pay a hundred and fifty thousand dollars to her and twenty-two thousand five hundred for legal fees. So that was the end of that."

Slowly the wounds of the divorce healed, and Cassius began talking about getting married again. "I have no one in mind," he said one day, "but I'll tell you this: the next time I marry it'll be a girl of seventeen or eighteen – one that I can raise to my way of thinking."

The People's Champion Takes On Canada

John Cottrell

After the fiasco of the rematch with Liston, Ali accepted a challenge from Floyd Patterson, who had taken on the role of the representative of all that was good and wholesome and American. In a lengthy article in Sports Illustrated, *11 October 1965, Patterson had sworn to depose the new champion for the sake of the country. "I say it, and I say it flatly, that the image of a Black Muslim as the world heavyweight champion disgraces the sport and the nation. Cassius Clay must be beaten and the Black Muslims' scourge removed from boxing," declared Patterson. His reward for such rashness was a merciless beating from Ali that only ended in the twelfth round. The fight was so lopsided that Ali was slammed in the press for dragging the match out rather than putting Patterson out of his misery sooner. The victory did nothing to silence Ali's many critics and the man who had been briefly hailed as the saviour of boxing now had to look outside of the US to attract an audience. For his next four title defences, Ali took his championship to the world, beginning in Canada with George Chuvalo.*

Conscious of the financial advantages of making himself the boxer everyone wanted to see beaten, Clay once used to ask whether people hated him enough. In 1966 he found for the first time that it was possible to be hated too much. It was a great year for petty persecutions. Just as the Beatles were to lose a fortune because John Lennon indiscreetly said they were "more popular than Jesus", so Clay was to lose multi-million-dollar fighting engagements as a result of his honest statement that he had "no quarrel with those Viet Congs". Both the Beatles and the boxer were pilloried to a degree out of all proportion to their misdemeanours, but there was one basic difference between them. Lennon was prepared to "eat crow", as the Americans say; Clay stubbornly refused to apologise and was hounded out of his own country.

In many ways, 1966 was a grim, unhappy year for the world champion. His worst experience came in the first week when he had to appear in a Miami divorce court and explain what was wrong with his sixteen-month-old marriage. In his evidence he spoke for two hours about the way he considered his wife had failed to live up to her pre-wedding promises to be a good Muslim.

He said, "I talked to her seven or eight hours a day before we were married and told her all the things that would be required before I could marry her, and she agreed. For one thing she was supposed to dress modestly, but when I was in training for the Sonny Liston fight I came home one day and found her wearing tight pants." Clay further explained how his wife had attended a press conference in May, 1965, wearing a skin-tight, blue denim suit. "You could see all of her – the seams of her underwear. Tight pants with all those men around was wrong." Sonji's lawyers asked Clay if he approved of the dress she was wearing in court. He said he did not. "All her arms are out and her knees are showing, and it's too tight." This, tragically, was the basic dispute between two people who had formerly seemed a devoted couple. It was a seemingly trivial matter, this question of dress, but for a strict Muslim like Clay a fundamental principle was involved.

The Clays were separated in May, 1965, almost immediately after the champion's sixty-second defeat of Liston. "Everything was fine until the fight," Sonji said. "We were going to buy a house somewhere. First we were going to go away for a while, and then all this happened." It blew up with a quarrel over Sonji's choice of clothes and the following month Clay announced that he was seeking an annulment of his marriage because she was not a good Muslim by dressing immodestly and using cosmetics. The champion declared, "It is up to her to accept my way of life, but apparently she does not want to." Sonji countered that she had pleaded with him by telephone not to take this action and that now she would fight it "with everything I possess". According to her, all their marital troubles stemmed entirely from his membership of the Muslim movement. "Cassius said that Elijah Muhammad told him I was embarrassing the entire Muslim nation by not wearing the long white dresses the Muslim women are supposed to wear. I don't drink, don't smoke. I attend meetings and services and observe the dietary laws. I was baptised in his religion. All except the dress. I never joined that part. I am not accustomed to wearing stuff like that. I'm normal like other women. I don't like to wear that stuff."

They had been married just ten months when Clay filed papers seeking an annulment. Sonji then told reporters, "All I know is that I love my husband and he loves me. I want to live with him, but I can't if he won't let me . . . It's just this religion. I have tried to accept it and I have explained this to him, but I just don't understand it." The following day, when visiting friends in Chicago, she was still wearing "gear" that would shock Muslims – bright turquoise slacks, a jet black wig, false eyelashes and face make-up. For the attractive young woman who had once been a night club barmaid the change to Muslim dress was too much to accept.

At the end of June, 1965, Sonji won a court award of £120 a week in temporary payments from her husband. She had asked the Miami judge for £375 a week (her expenses included £100–£140 a week for hotel bills and £5 a week to keep her wigs in repair) and she had told the judge that she wanted a reconciliation. But there was never a hint of reconciliation and when the case finally came to the divorce court Clay told the court that he had excommunicated his wife for her lack of modesty and other offences against the Muslim faith. After the all-day hearing in Miami he was granted the divorce, but at huge expense – 15,000 dollars a year in alimony. Soon the champion would have difficulty in raising the payments, even though it had been revealed in court that he earned nearly half a million dollars the previous year.

The year was also beset with troubles for Clay in his career. It opened with rumours that he would soon meet the logical contender for his crown – Ernie Terrell, holder of the W.B.A.'s version of the heavyweight championship. Considering that Terrell was endeavouring to sue Clay for one and a half million dollars for having billed himself as "world champion" in his fight against Patterson, it was remarkable that they managed to agree to meet on March 29th. But then a fantastic series of unforeseen obstacles arose.

It was hoped to hold the "clash of champions" in Madison Square Garden. This plan was immediately killed, however, by the New York State Athletic Commission's decision to refuse Terrell a licence because of his alleged association with boxing's underworld. On the face of it, this seemed a harsh decision. Terrell testified at the hearing that he was no longer associated with a gentleman called Bernie Glickman,* who was an old friend of Frankie Carbo, Blinky Palermo and other shady characters. Legally, the commission had no proof to the contrary. On the other hand, it was a fact that Glickman had been in Terrell's corner for his fight against Chuvalo, and the most damning disclosure at the hearing was that Glickman had recently accompanied Terrell on a flight from Chicago to New York.

The next move was to stage the fight in Chicago. The Illinois Atheletic Commission was not so sensitive about Big Ernie's alleged associations and granted him a licence after an interview lasting thirty seconds. Plans went forward smoothly for a few days until a new obstacle unexpectedly appeared: a letter from the US Army draft board which informed Clay that he was being considered for reclassification and requested him to fill in some forms. "I don't know what happens now," said the champion. "I just roll with the punches." In fact, he did not "roll" with them but stood firm and took them squarely on the chin.

The big punch came a week later: Clay's original Army qualification of I-Y in 1964 had been raised to I-A. It was all fully in order with the recent decision of Defence Department and Selective Service officials to accept anyone who had completed high school and scored more than a certain number of points in the Army intelligence test. The Army had lowered its sights and Clay came legitimately into full view . . . He, and thousands of

---

* Glickman, described as a Chicago fight promoter, placed himself in protective custody in March, 1965, when a Chicago grand jury began to investigate alleged gangster influence on the proposed Clay-Terrell fight. Glickman claimed he had been beaten up by gangsters, and it was suggested that the Cosa Nostra crime syndicate had tried in January to take over control of the fight, threatening to kill Terrell if he did not consent to fight Clay in New York.

others who had previously failed, were now eligible for call-up. As the official Russian news agency chose to put it: "The escalation of the dirty war which the United States is waging in Vietnam is demanding even more cannon fodder. The American army has become less demanding in its choice of cannon fodder." The classification review was beginning with men nearest the age of twenty-six and working down to nineteen-year-olds; Clay, at twenty-three, was therefore high on the list. His call-up was not expected to interfere with fight plans for March 29th; a draft board official felt certain he could gain deferment if he appealed.

Clay had every intention of appealing, and not just for a deferment. He was furious at the decision. He said that he did not want to scare anybody, but it was a fact that millions of Muslims around the world were watching what happened to him. "Maybe they'll be angry about this." He argued that he was too valuable to the country for the Government to call him to arms, that he was making millions for the taxman every year with his fists. He claimed that his religious principles made him exempt from service. Worst of all, though he could never have imagined the repercussions at the time, he told newspapermen, "I don't have no personal quarrel with those Viet Cong. We don't bear weapons. We don't fight wars unless it's a war declared by Allah himself."

When the Clay–Terrell contest was first planned it was envisaged as a potential six-million-dollar promotion. Clay's single statement on the Vietnam war changed all that; it caused most of the original 280 interested theatres to cancel bookings for closed circuit television. The influential *Chicago Tribune* accused him of treason, and a resolution condemning Clay for his reluctance to serve in the armed forces was approved by the Kentucky State Senate. It described his attitude as "repugnant" and said, "it brings discredit to all loyal Kentuckians and to the names of the thousands of them who gave their lives for this country during his lifetime."

These were just the first ripples in a great tide of anti-Clay feeling which would engulf the whole country. Of all the millions of words he had spoken, none earned him a fraction of the hatred he inspired by that single sentence about the Viet Cong. It brought down on his head the wrath of politicians, housewives' leagues, newspaper, television and radio opinion-makers. Even his favourite aunt (Louisville schoolteacher Mary Turner) expressed her horror at that remark.

At this stage he might easily have stemmed the tide by apologising for having made a "hasty" remark; instead he resolutely stood by his words. Called before the Illinois State Athletic Commission to explain his "unpatriotic statement", the champion worsened the situation by saying, "I apologise for saying the things to newspapermen. I should have said them to my draft board and Government officials." At the interview he also made a point of insisting that chairman Joe Triner should address him as Muhammad Ali.

There was no surprise at the outcome. Illinois State Attorney William Clark announced that Clay's fight with Terrell could not take place in Chicago because of "contract irregularities". The precise objections were not explained, but it was no secret that the State Governor and the Mayor of Chicago had called for the contest to be banned. Thereafter the fight was on the run and Clay was to discover just how effectively political pressures, backed by the opinion of pompous patriots, could ostracise a citizen who had become *persona non grata*.

Miami was approached as a possible venue, but this hope soon faded under pressure from the American Legion, the Veterans of Foreign Wars and various politicians. The pattern was to be repeated in various parts of the country – from Pittsburg and Louisville to the little township of Huron, South Dakota. Clay could not be forgiven for his derogatory comment on the US role in Vietnam. Equally, he found it impossible to withdraw a remark he knew to be true. Clay fairly argued, "Politicians have said the same as me, and worse. So why punish me? Why crucify me before the world? I ain't no coward. I'm the heavyweight champion of the world." But it changed nothing. Clay was not a politician; he was the world champion, and as a king among common citizens he was expected to set the appropriate example to American youth.

Forced out of the United States, the fight moved across the 49th parallel to the Montreal Forum. Angelo Dundee described this venue as "solid, definite, sure and certain". But this was rejected and so was the next plan to hold the bout in the Montreal suburb of Verdun. The situation was so grim that Clay had a dummy "passport to the moon" made up. Flourishing it, he joked: "Looks like we're going to have to go to the moon to fight, because no place on earth wants us. We'll just go up there and fight it out and the one that wins will get to take the spaceship and come back." At this point, with the fight date only three weeks away, a home for the unwanted match was found at Maple Leaf Gardens, Toronto. The arena authorities saw it as a great opportunity to replace Madison Square Garden as the site of major bouts and they said they would stage it provided there was no disapproval from the Ontario Government. It was optimistically estimated that the live gate could total 270,000 dollars and ancillary rights, including closed circuit television, up to three million dollars.

In Miami, while tucking into a typical Muslim meal of cabbage, mashed potatoes, broccoli and kosher steak, Clay shot a publicity line about being worried about this title defence. He moaned, "I got problems and pressures – now more pressures than I ever had. I am mentally low. I don't feel good. If fans want to see me beat they ought to come to Toronto. Terrell has a better chance of beating me than Sonny Liston or Floyd Patterson had. I don't say he will, but he's catching me at a low ebb." Then he flew to Toronto to sign the contract. The fight was due to be held in two and a half weeks' time.

But this match was doomed from start to finish. All the weeks of frantic effort to find a site were now wasted owing to a new and unexpected obstacle: Terrell refused to sign because of the terms laid down in the new contract offered by Maple Leaf Gardens, the promoters. He objected to the removal of the original agreement of a guarantee of 150,000 dollars from the live gate and television and cinema receipts and 12,500 dollars expenses. He also objected to a clause stipulating that should he defeat Clay he must defend the title against Canadian champion George Chuvalo whom he had beaten by a unanimous points decision in a W.B.A. title fight the previous November. This clause, argued Terrell, would put him under the control of the Maple Leaf Gardens promoters.

Ernie stated, "I would give anything to fight Clay to clear up the heavyweight muddle, because if he's barred from fighting anywhere in the world there will always be boxing fans who feel Clay is still the champion. For that reason I would fight Clay anywhere in the world for thirty cents. But this new condition makes it impossible to go through with the fight." It was not a very convincing argument. Mike Malitz, executive vice-president of Main Bout Inc., described his demands as "exorbitant", and certainly there had been so many cancellations for closed circuit television that the guarantee was unlikely to be met. Possibly Terrell declined because he realised that he had little to gain financially by fighting when, if he bided his time, he might become the No. 1 heavyweight attraction while Clay was hauled into the Army for two years. In any event, Terrell's backing down does not suggest that he was confident of beating Clay, for he had no reason on past performances to fear a second meeting with Chuvalo.

At this opportune moment, Irving Ungerman, manager of Chuvalo and a millionaire in the kosher chicken business, promptly stepped in with an offer for his "white hope" to meet the champion. Clay immediately agreed and remarked, "I think it would be a better fight." And so a world championship match was made with less than three weeks' advance warning. It was the second time a Clay–Chuvalo meeting had been proposed and the second time Chuvalo had substituted for Terrell. In September, 1963, when Terrell was indisposed with a stomach ailment, the Canadian came out of semi-retirement to take his place against Mike DeJohn in Louisville. Clay then said he would fight the winner but later backed down after Chuvalo had won on a split decision. "I don't like the way he fights," he explained. "I don't want to fight that man. He can cut you. He butts and does everything else. He's too rough." At that time there was no point in Clay endangering the prospect of a million-dollar purse for fighting Liston for the sake of meeting an "alley fighter". By 1966, however, he felt confident enough to face any heavyweight in the world.

It was a curious promotion. The W.B.A. naturally refused to recognise it as a world title fight; in their reckoning Clay and Chuvalo were ranked first and tenth respectively among championship contenders. As a W.B.A. official, Merv Mackenzie took a similar view, and yet as boss of the Ontario Boxing

Commission he was in charge of the fight in Toronto. At one time he advocated that it should be a fourteen- or sixteen-round contest so that it would not conform with championship regulations. In any event, the fight was not to be billed as a world title contest – even though all the world's Press regarded it as such. Under the new arrangements, Clay was to receive fifty per cent of the live gate and fifty per cent of the ancillary rights. Chuvalo was in line for twenty per cent of all receipts, while the remaining thirty per cent of gate money went to Maple Leaf Gardens and the thirty per cent of ancillary rights to Main Bout Inc. Considering his recent fighting record, Chuvalo could count himself extremely fortunate to be given such a deal with the added possibility of winning the world title.

George Chuvalo, born in Toronto of Croatian parents, made a sensational professional boxing debut in 1956. In a heavy-weight novice tournament he knocked out all four of his opponents in a total of twelve minutes, thirty-six seconds. Since then, in a career of strangely fluctuating fortunes, this raw Canadian scrapper had suffered eleven defeats in forty-seven bouts. His successes included a technical knock-out in October, 1964, against Doug Jones, the man who had almost defeated Clay, but more recently he had lost on points to both Terrell and Patterson and had given two miserable performances in Britain. In December, 1965, he had taken ten rounds to outpoint veteran Jamaican Joe Bygraves, the former British Empire champion, who had come out of retirement, and then he had been badly out-pointed by the then unranked young Argentinian Eduardo Corletti, who had once been knocked out by Floyd Patterson's younger brother. It was no wonder that the announcement of a Clay–Chuvalo fight was greeted with apathy. Clay was made an overwhelming favourite against a no-hoper and the betting was virtually nil.

As March 29th drew near, the match began to stimulate considerable interest. Canadians fondly dreamed that by some miracle a native son might at last hold the world title for the first time since Tommy Burns lost it to Jack Johnson in Sydney on Boxing Day, 1908. Clay, who stayed in Toronto at a motel with the inappropriate name of the West Point Motor Inn, made every effort to encourage this wishful thinking. He called Chuvalo "a nice man who has a chance to beat me because my training has been interrupted so much". He played up the angle that his training had been geared to prepare him to meet a 6 ft. 6 in. "giraffe", not a stocky Canadian bear; also that he was in bad mental shape owing to the stress of so much adverse personal publicity. He called himself "a warrior on the battleground of freedom".

All Clay's pessimistic talk and humility, plus flat-footed sparring displays, was so much propaganda designed to persuade Canadian patriots to part with their money at the turnstiles. It was true that Clay was not in peak condition. He had broken training five times in the confusion over the fight arrangements and two weeks before the fight he weighed 220 lb., a ten-pound increase on his weight against Patterson. But otherwise there was little reason to suppose that his title was in jeopardy. Chuvalo was simply not in the same class as the champion. The Canadian, a good-natured family man with four children, was strictly a brawler when he entered the ring. He had a plodding, pedestrian style, invariably and stubbornly moving forward, disregarding defensive measures in his determination to get in close and attack the body. He also had a reputation for not being too concerned with the finer points of the noble art, for being a dangerous kidney puncher and head-butter. While utterly lacking in fighting finesse, Chuvalo did possess three valuable qualities – tremendous guts, strength and stamina. He had never been knocked out in ten years of professional boxing and described himself with some justification as the world's most durable heavyweight.

After training work-outs for the Clay fight – four miles of interval running each morning and four rounds of sparring each afternoon – George had long tactical talks with Joe Louis. The Canadian made no secret of his strategy and his reasoning seemed perfectly sound: "I shall be depending on my strength and my punching on the inside. Clay will attempt to fight at long range. His speed is his greatest asset and his left jab is his main weapon. My aim is to wear him down, whether it takes fifteen rounds or shorter." There was no doubt that in terms of sheer physical strength he was a match for the champion. His wife Lynne also thought that he was in the right mental condition – "he's moody and difficult – and that's great. If he was too nice I would be worried. It shows he is getting in exactly the right frame of mind for the fight. It shows he knows this time it is do or die." Only Chuvalo's skill was in question; so much so that the fight was generally regarded as another gross mismatch, an illogical, one-sided bout as absurd as Patterson's title defences against Rademacher, Harris and McNeeley (also in Toronto). Fans and critics alike were due for an astonishing but welcome surprise.

Clay's third defence of his title in two years was discreetly billed as Muhammad Ali, the People's Champion, versus George Chuvalo, the Canadian champion. At the beginning it did not promise to be more than another opportunity for the king of heavyweights to show off his fancy footwork and lightning jabs and make his opponent appear a fumbling novice. Clay immediately went into his customary dancing routine, snaking out those taunting lefts to the head, while Chuvalo crudely plodded after him, fully prepared to take a series of jabs in exchange for the privilege of belting a few blows to the body. The champion appeared quite happy to do business with him on this head-blow-for-body-blow exchange basis. Indeed, on one occasion he allowed himself to be cornered, stood stock still and contemptuously laid a hand on top of the Canadian's head while Chuvalo swung more than twenty hefty clouts to the ribs and kidneys. Clay just grinned and invited George to hit him some more.

The champion took so many punches around the waist that his trunks were pushed down to reveal the top of his red protector. Angelo Dundee reproved him for taking unnecessary risks and it was not long before Clay himself realised that he was getting nowhere by clowning and trying to discourage an opponent with the stubbornness of a mule. In the third and fourth rounds, he still toyed with the Canadian, but every now and again a fighting-mad challenger blasted his way through the wall of jabbing lefts. Possibly Chuvalo was given an added incentive by the news that his seven-year-old son Mitchell had arrived; manager Ungerman shouted out, "Mitchell's here, George. Make him proud of you." Whatever his driving force, he refused to retreat and fought as though his life depended upon it.

In the fifth round, after being made to miss many times, Chuvalo steamrollered forward so relentlessly that he succeeded in rocking Clay with solid blows that caused the fans to rise to their feet and scream encouragement. He landed a right to the jaw (his highest punch so far) and scored more heavily when they traded punches in a corner. This was not the Chuvalo who had stumbled to defeat against inexperienced Corletti two months before; this was an entirely different man, a challenger who recognised his chance of a lifetime and who would readily give his last ounce of strength in seeking to exploit it.

Chuvalo, two inches shorter than his opponent, concentrated almost exclusively on a body attack. Occasionally his punches thudded into illegal kidney regions, but sportingly the champion never made a great show of protest and afterwards referee Jack Silvers, a clothing salesman, would explain that he took no action against low blows since the punches were unintentional, Clay was not complaining, and he did not want to spoil "the fastest heavyweight fight I or anyone else has seen for years." Angelo Dundee took a different view; at times he screamed out his disgust at the low punching and called the referee "a creep". He also instructed the champion to finish the fight before he ran into trouble. Clay apparently took no notice since he continued to punish his rival without ever committing himself to all-out aggression.

In round six Chuvalo caught Clay on the mouth with a wild left hook and 13,000 Canadians roared their approval. But the champion was well in control at this stage, boxing with superb artistry and an infinite variety of skill as though he wanted to show that he was a master craftsman who would never descend to the brawling "style" of his opponent. By round ten, however, he did not look quite so supremely confident; crude though it was, Chuvalo's bulldozing attack was breaking through and landing some thundering blows to the body. For once, Clay really knew how it felt to be hurt by body-punching and it stung him into renewed effort. Throughout the eleventh round, he scientifically tortured Chuvalo with an awesome mixture of jabs and hooks, and yet there seemed no limit to the punishment this brave Canadian could absorb. His face was reddened and swollen from a hundred jabs, but he fought on so gallantly that a brilliant champion was forced to abandon his gimmicks and reveal his full range of boxing skills.

Though he was so often made to look foolish and clumsy, Chuvalo never quite became Clay's whipping boy. Here was one opponent who never despaired, a man of granite whose spirit could not be broken by a far superior force. In the thirteenth round, he kept his pre-fight promise to finish strongly by storming back to belt the astonished champion with an avalanche of lefts and rights. Clay, who had never before been taken beyond twelve rounds, looked a little weary and concerned. Chuvalo's face was a mass of bruises and yet he still came forward and was actually hurting the champion. Under pressure, Clay called on hidden reserves of energy to launch an all-out attack in the fourteenth. He boxed beautifully, scored so heavily that there was no longer the faintest possibility of his title being lost on points. But could the Canadian score a knock-out? It was a remote possibility and, with absolutely nothing to lose, he recklessly and savagely stormed into Clay, hammering him about the head and body in what was a fantastically fast final round.

Clay was now made to wince in rare moments of pain, and the fans, solidly behind the Toronto boy, became delirious with excitement as they roared for Chuvalo to finish him off. Clay's advisers shouted for him to run, but he did not slip out of range before more blows had thudded into his body and caused him to buckle at the knees. At last, critics were getting an answer to that often asked question: can Clay take punishment as well as hand it out? The champion proved that he could. He survived this last desperate onslaught, kept sinking jabs into Chuvalo's puffed ball of a face, and at the final bell he was undisputably the well-deserved winner. Chuvalo had won the last round, but his damaging attack had come too late. Class had conquered. The scoring by Canadian judges was in Clay's favour as follows – referee Silvers 73–65; Judge Tony Canzano, 74–63, Judge Jack Johnston, 74–62. They gave George only two of the fifteen rounds.

Ironically, this fight which provided fifteen action-packed rounds was a financial flop compared with the 1963 second

Liston–Patterson fiasco which lasted less than one round and grossed four and a half million dollars. Clay's fifty per cent of the gate, television and film receipts netted him only 340,000 dollars – less than when he was challenging for the title. Chuvalo collected over 100,000 dollars; in addition, seven-year-old Mitchell Chuvalo won twenty dollars in betting his friends that his daddy would not be knocked out. The receipts prompted a Main Bout Inc. official to comment, "Clay in the US is a dead piece of merchandise. He's through as far as big money closed circuit is concerned . . . The money we made on this one certainly wasn't worth the effort."

As far as the paying customers were concerned, the effort in promoting a fight was never more worthwhile. Forget the statistics; the most important fact about this match is that it was an honest, hard-fought contest without the remotest hint of skulduggery behind the scenes, a fight altogether worthy of the best traditions of the world championship. There were no cries of "fix" on this occasion; for once the fans were given full value for their money by two boxers free of underworld connections. A breeze as fresh as the icy wind blowing off nearby Lake Ontario had swept away the smell that hung over the championship and brought back an air of sanity to the fight game. Clay had defended his title with dignity and given a highly polished display of the true boxing artist; Chuvalo's contribution was courage and a never-say-die spirit, the like of which had not been seen for many a year in a heavyweight title fight. No one could ask for more.

Clay called it his hardest fight and some critics rated it the best heavyweight contest since 1954 when Ezzard Charles bravely went the full distance with Rocky Marciano. This was perhaps putting it rather high; it was a very entertaining fight but not a truly great one since the outcome was never in serious doubt. Among recent championship bouts it was certainly outstanding and richly deserved a far greater financial return. Some critics argued that Clay lacked a lethal punch because he failed to knock out Chuvalo, but this does not necessarily follow since in forty-seven fights no opponent had succeeded in that. Facts can be misleading when considered separately. For example, Clay only twice managed to make the resolute Canadian back up in fifteen rounds – a detail which scarcely suggests that he dominated the fight as he did.

The stirring Toronto tussle left Chuvalo with a swollen distortion of a face. Clay, in contrast, emerged from his dressing room as handsome as ever, immaculately groomed and wearing a smart tuxedo. Close inspection, however, revealed slight puffing around the champion's eyes; his hands were swollen and he was sore around the left side after receiving so many low swinging rights. For the first time in his professional career one could visibly detect that Clay had been in a fight.

Intimate Look at the Champ

Isaac Sutton

Ebony Magazine, November 1966

From Canada, Ali returned to London where he stopped Henry Cooper for the second time on a cut, avoiding the indignity of being dropped by Cooper's lethal left hook on this occasion. That was followed by a demolition of the over-matched Brian London in three rounds on 6 August. Finally, it was on to Germany and southpaw Karl Mildenberger.

Like a bullet aimed at distant Germany, the giant Lufthansa jet airliner nosed its way up through the clouds, leaving Chicago far below. Across from me sat the heavyweight boxing champion of the world. As the light played on his handsome face, it was difficult to believe that this was the same Muhammad Ali who had slugged, boxed, danced and talked his way to the top of the boxing world under the name of Cassius Clay. He looked far more like a clean-cut young boy than a ferocious fighter as he slouched down in his seat, his short-sleeved shirt unbuttoned at the neck while he gazed silently out of the window.

The newspapers had let just about everybody know his reason for making the trip – to defend his title against Karl Mildenberger, top-rated heavyweight of the German ring. My reason for tagging along was not to get a story. Ali had invited me as a friend who had known him long before 1964 when he had won the title from Sonny Liston. Several times before, the champ had asked me to come with him and he would show me the world, but I had turned him down, not being a lover of flying. This time, as I had watched him pack his bags, he looked at me and said, "Well, looks like you're being left again, huh?"

I had shot back a sharp "No! I'm going with my buddy. You need someone to look out for you over there."

Imagine me protecting the heavyweight champion of the world. Then I remembered the time his mother, Mrs Odessa

Clay, had told me of his childhood days in Louisville, KY., when his older brother used to whip the boys who'd pick on young Cassius. Now his brother had gotten married and wasn't going on the trip, so I would be big brother to him.

The champ had dozed off to sleep and his trainer, Angelo Dundee, was pacing the plane to make certain that everyone in our party was relaxed, occasionally breaking the silence with witty cracks about some boxer with muscles between his toes. About three hours after take-off, the champ's mother – the lone woman in our group – awakened her son with kisses on his fore-head. "Is my baby okay?" she cooed.

"Yes, Mama, I'm fine," was the soft reply. "I'll bet you're nervous, huh, Mom – 35,000 feet up?"

"No baby. As long as I'm with you, Mama's just fine." She kissed him again and asked him to go back to sleep.

In the quiet hours of flight, I thought back to the way I had anticipated this trip, not just because it was my first trip out of the country, but for the chance it would give me to study a man about whom people had so many unanswered questions. I wanted answers myself.

I had met Ali a few years ago through a fellow photographer, Herbert Muhammad, who today is the champ's personal manager. At that time, Ali was still known as Cassius and was curious as a kid. He would come up to the office and watch me work in the photo lab and go on assignments with me. He seemed to like me and enjoyed watching me take pictures. Then came his chance to get a crack at the heavyweight title and all the publicity that went with it. Whenever he was before the public, he would come on with this slogan "I'm the Greatest." He bragged, mugged, stretched his mouth and became known as the big mouth of the boxing world. I found it difficult to connect this loud-mouthed figure the public saw with the likable young man who had been so sweet and quiet around me. He became famous for talking down his boxing opponents and saying things like "I can plainly see, this man will go in three," predicting the round in which the other man would be taken out. The public began to put him down and this disturbed me, because I didn't like to hear people talking about my friend.

But on the other hand, I, too, didn't like to hear him brag.
Finally I called Ali up one day and told him I had to have a talk
with him.

"I read the papers, I watch you on TV," I said to him. "I hear
you, but I know this is not you. Why?"

"Well," he answered slowly, "I wondered when you were
going to get around to asking me."

"People don't like you when you brag so much."

"Have I lost your friendship?" he asked.

"No," I assured him, "but I want people to like you."

He was quiet for a moment, then said, "Boxing is almost dead.
I've got to do something to stimulate it. This will save boxing."

"But why must it be *you*? Why can't someone else save it?"

He shut me up with a question of his own: "Can you think of
any way in the world to just talk and not cause any harm to
anyone, but make people so mad they want to see you get beat
up? This way they pay thousands of dollars to see my fights,
hoping I might get beat, and this money in turn goes to me."

I didn't question him after that. I just watched while he proved
himself to be not only the greatest boxer around, but also the
greatest salesman. I also watched when he toned down his brash
image, more recently, after victory upon victory had put across
his point – without his having to say it.

Shortly before we had set out on the trip to Germany, I spent
a few days at the gym and at home with him, trying to get ideas
as to the type of pictures I would want. As he quietly sat reading
some religious material, I shot his facial expressions. Then I
asked him to give me that famous one – with his mouth open. He
smiled and said, "You know I don't do that anymore."

This was when it first dawned on me that he was a changed
man – no more phony press shots. "Why?" I asked.

I was happy to hear him say. "No more make-believe. Back
then I was campaigning for the championship. Now I'm just
settling down to being myself. You see, in the beginning, you
didn't like me when I was witty and exciting. Now you don't like
me being quiet." He shook his head and added, "You just can't
please people, can you?"

Maybe the champ had been unable to please people in his own
country, but there was no hint of those difficulties in Germany.

When we landed in Frankfurt, where the title bout was to take place, about 2,000 people converged on the plane to greet him and I got stampeded in the crowd. Ali had to rescue me. As he did, he looked at me and smiled, saying, "Thanks, big brother, for protecting me." About 500 photographers penned us in a corner for more than an hour. Finally the police escort arrived to help transport all of us to the hotel where another 3,000 people lined the street and jammed the lobby. After the initial interviews and TV shots, the newspapers came out the next day, all carrying his picture on the front page and rating him a ten to one favorite over the undefeated Mildenberger. This we had not expected, for we had thought sentiment would be heavily on the side of the German. But the people praised the champ and seemed grateful that he had come to give Germany its first heavyweight title fight.

A king couldn't have been received with more honor than Ali was accorded and the people seemed to love him. Limousines were supplied for his convenience and at the hotel, three of them were lined up for him and his party. A uniformed chauffeur awaited the champ at the lead car, an expensive job that was said to be worth $12,000. But in a display of the modesty which I had noticed in him before, Ali went instead to the last and smallest car. When it was suggested that he ride in the other car, he shrugged it off with a casual "I'm fine, I'm fine," and had to be coaxed to move.

Unlike the earlier days when he would go to any lengths for publicity, Ali shied away from the press as much as possible and left promotion of the fight in the hands of the promoters. It was only after the requests for interviews became so demanding that he could not refuse that he consented to have an hour-long press conference at his hotel each afternoon. During the interviews he conducted himself with a restraint and dignity that shocked those who had expected to meet a bully of a kid with a big mouth. In fact, he was *so* quiet that he frequently had to be asked to speak up because he couldn't be heard.

Though the German people seemed to take to him greatly, one thing puzzled them about this man of whom they'd heard so much. He didn't smile. During his one personal appearance at the Hetti department store, where 10,000 people converged to get autographs, one woman offered me 500 marks ($178) to get him to smile, but he stayed on the quiet side until ten American MPs came up to him to say hello. Only then did he warm up, shouting out to the crowd, "Those are *my* guys," and inviting them onto the stage. He joked with them and later he and the MPs went marching down the street, arm-in-arm.

In spite of the remarks that have been made about Ali's attitude toward the military, it was with the servicemen that he spent most of his time when not training. They visited him each day at the gym to watch him work out and he reciprocated by inviting them to bull sessions at his hotel and spending many evenings at their bases.

Since his training for what was expected to be a tough fight was most important to him, Muhammad, who does not smoke, drink or gamble, lived like a monk during his days abroad, not even indulging in the sight-seeing trips that delighted his mother. All of the countless calls from girls wanting to date him or marry him were ordered to either my room or Angelo's. The champ was unimpressed. He would just sit there in his room like a little boy, doodling on a piece of paper or doing his fancy footwork to a James Brown record. One evening when the champ, his mother and I were seated in the hotel lobby, a big name Negro entertainer came in a little tipsy, with his blond girl friend.

"Hello, champion," he shouted in a loud voice.

"Hello, sir," Ali said, nodding to him. Then he leaned over to his mother and said, "You see, Mom, that's the bag they want to see me in— partying every night, drinking, going around here with a process and a white woman on each arm. Never, thanks to Allah." He was so angry he dashed upstairs, leaving us in the lobby. I ran after him, urging him not to let things like that upset him. "I'm okay. I'm okay," he insisted. "Just don't let him come upstairs."

Aside from his visits to GI camps, Ali spent most of his free time at the Amadiyya Missions Des Islam mosque where he would preach and pray. There he was greeted as a brother by Muslims from many countries, including friends he had made on a previous trip to Egypt. Of that trip he had once said: "There I was just a poor Negro from Kentucky and over there I was treated as a brother. No big I's and little you's." It also reminded me of his explanation of why he had become a Muslim: "When I was a little kid, I always knew something was wrong. Everything good was supposed to be white. And I'd ask my Mama, why is Santa Claus white? Why is Jesus white? Everything was *white*. Miss America was white. The good cowboy always rode a white horse. Angel food cake is white and devil's food cake black. When you got to heaven you had to be cleansed till your soul was pearly white. Mary had a little lamb it's fleece was *white* as snow. Snow *White*, the *white* tornado and even the President lived in a *white* house. So any man who came along and told me *black* is the *best*, I'd have to be a fool not to accept it!"

I have always known that he has very good reasons for believing what he does and that this should be his privilege. And, regardless of public criticism, I have believed him to be sincere in it, for, as he once said: "I'd give up everything I have for what I believe." If he were not sincere, I doubt very much that he would be considering devoting his full time to the Muslim ministry after he retires ("When I get whipped"). However, I have never witnessed the hatred of white people credited to him, nor do I believe that he hates them.

While the champ was busy training, his mother was busy, too, receiving about 16 letters a day and answering them through an interpreter. The German people opened their arms to her and she visited in seven homes and attended two big fashion shows. One night she broke into tears and cried out to me, "Why can't I be treated like this at home?"

I found the German people a little cold – slow in warming up to you. But once they did begin to respond to you, I found them to be the warmest people in the world. One thing I noticed was that there were no racial tensions. Everyone was treated the same. With thoughts of the way it was back home – of picket signs, riots and swastikas – I went to several department stores to see if I could buy a souvenir swastika or Nazi emblem. Clerks would stare at me as though I were a nut. One irate woman told me that if I wanted to buy some swastikas or Nazi materials, I'd do better to return to my "free America" where they would supply me with all I needed, but please leave them in peace.

Meanwhile, the day of the fight was drawing near and the champ was cutting down trees, running, jumping rope, doing everything to get into top shape and always pushing a bit harder than was necessary, as though trying to prove to himself in everything he did that he really was the greatest. As for his ability as a fighter and his punching power that people are always questioning, I have no way of evaluating him. But I did spend a lot of time watching his two sparring partners, Willie Johnson and James Ellis, flipping coins to see who would be the last to face him. A few days before the main bout, he sent to England for the highly-rated heavyweight, Jack Bodell. He wanted to work out with the tough Britisher. The first day the champ let Bodell bang away at him, hitting him each time. Afterwards, I asked the Englishman how it had gone.

"Not bad a'tall," he said.

Ali told him to get some good rest and be prepared for the next day, because he wanted a good work out. That next day the champ whipped him to a pulp in three rounds.

"How did it go today?" I asked Bodell again.

"Man, I tell you," he replied, "there is no man alive as fast and who can hit as hard as the champ. I say he must be the fastest heavyweight in the world."

Tension was high by the time the big night rolled around. Two American writers had gone to press with a phony story that the Muslims had made a deal with the Germans to sell out America by letting Germany win the title, since there was no return bout clause in the contract. I know that the only advice the champ received was to put Mildenberger away and not to take any chances with him. They kept reminding him, "Remember Max Schmeling." The only German ever to hold the heavyweight title, Schmeling had knocked out Joe Louis in 1936, though Louis later achieved a dazzling one-round knock-out of Schmeling in 1938. Ali's fight hadn't been intended as a test of power between nations, but many people, and particularly some of Ali's GI buddies, saw it that way. The champ knew it was important that he win.

That night Ali watched from his dressing room window as his friend James Ellis won by a TKO in the sixth round of the preliminary bout. He waited anxiously to congratulate Ellis, then called for prayer to be held by himself, Herbert, John Ali, the Muslims' national secretary, and Elijah Muhammad II, Herbert's oldest son.

Things went well in the ring, but around the fifth round, someone broke through the police lines carrying a box. He tried to get it up to the champ but was subdued by Herbert. The box contained only a holy prayer book. The man was a Muslim from East Germany.

By the sixth round, Mildenberger was bleeding badly and his guard was down. I was standing next to the champ's corner and heard Angelo crying out "Put him away with that left hook." I asked Herbert, "What's stopping him, the blood?"

Herbert said, "Yes. You know he doesn't like to hurt anyone. Seeing all that blood slows him down a bit."

In the twelfth round as the fighters were standing over us battling it out, I heard Herbert's voice clearly. "Brother, listen to me. He is not hurt. Put him away – NOW!" Then Ali let go with the lefts and rights that found their mark so well that the referee had to stop the fight.

Pursued by thousands of people, the champ made his way to his dressing room. The first thing he did was to rush to a large mirror on the wall and to stare into it for a long time, turning his head from left to right. Then he began to smile as though he were saying "And not a scar on my face."

After about an hour, newsmen were admitted. They came in, surrounded him and began pumping him with questions. It took another two hours for enough of the crowd to leave so that we could get him out of the auditorium. Police lined the hallways, but the champ called for his MPs, saying, "Where are my GIs?" They came to escort him, but the crowd was still waiting, knocking down doors and screaming, "We love you, Ali!"

Finally we made it back to the hotel by a back entrance and the champ spent the night celebrating by watching television. They were showing a new dance craze called the Muhammad Ali that's sweeping Europe. It's based on his dance-like footwork and fancy jabbing. His GI friends were still with him, so he asked me to order food for all of them. His victory feast consisted of six beefburgers, mashed potatoes, chocolate ice cream and soda pop. After dinner he said good-bye to his new-found GI friends and called Herbert in for prayer. He went to bed that night still heavyweight champion of the world, having done his part to prove that he really *was* the greatest.

Kicking the Cat

John Cottrell

Shortly after midnight on November 29th, 1964, Cleveland (The Cat) Williams, a big, gold-toothed Seminole-Cherokee-Negro was bowling down a dark, lonely highway in Harris County, Texas. He had had a few beers and was feeling pretty pleased with life as he drove home with three friends, two of them women. For years he had been frustrated in his greatest ambition as a professional boxer, but now the future looked bright. At last a world heavyweight championship seemed to be within his reach. He had been named to meet Ernie Terrell in the W.B.A. elimination tournament for the world title.

Suddenly, Williams's Saturday outing was turned into a nightmare. State Highway Patrolman Dale Witten flagged him down and began asking questions. The boxer, suspected of drunken driving, begged the patrolman not to arrest him. He explained that he had an important fight with Amos Lincoln coming up and then maybe a world title bout which would be in jeopardy if he ran into trouble with the law. Witten was not to be persuaded. There are different stories about what happened next. According to Witten, the boxer with a 50-pound weight advantage resisted arrest and a struggle ensued. According to Williams, the cop pulled out a gun to arrest him. However it started, the result was the same – Witten's gun exploded at point-blank range. The boxer felt as though his stomach had caught fire. With blood gushing from the wound, he collapsed face down on the road, rolled over and over in agony, moaning and leaving a crimson trail behind him.

It was nearly an hour before Williams was brought into a Houston hospital. He was unconscious, his stomach swollen. A blood transfusion was urgently needed and three boxers, Tod Herring, Mark Tessman and Dave Birch, were among the donors. No one gave The Cat much chance of survival. The bullet, entering from the left side, had ploughed through the colon and the small bowel, damaged nerves controlling leg movement and fractured part of the hip joint. The first operation lasted five and a half hours. Half an hour later, more surgery was necessary because he had started to bleed internally.

For days Williams hovered between life and death. Tubes were connected to his nose, a vein (for intravenous feeding), the right kidney, and to the bladder. Finally, after a third major operation, he was off the danger list. His survival was credited partly to his magnificent muscles, particularly in the abdomen. But while the man lived, the boxer was considered to be finished. The six feet three inch tall fighter with a classic physique now shrunk from a beautifully proportioned 215 pounds to a mere 155. For weeks he suffered continual pain in his stomach. To complete his misery he had to face charges which included assault on a policeman, carrying a pistol and drunken driving. The Texas court was apparently not wholly satisfied with the case against him for he was sentenced to only thirty days' imprisonment, and twelve of those days had already been spent under arrest in hospital.

When Williams had finished his sentence, he was still in pain and losing weight. Yet he was determined to fight again and sought the opinion of a specialist. He was advised that there was just a chance that he would box again if he had his damaged kidney removed, and the heavyweight from Griffin, Georgia, who knew no other business but boxing, insisted that it was done. The fourth operation put The Cat back on his fighting feet. In two weeks he gained fifteen pounds. He remarried, and then he began the long and lonely struggle back to fitness.

At dawn every morning, he left his home in the small, isolated township of Yoakum, Texas, and did roadwork on the huge cattle ranch belonging to his manager, oil millionaire Hugh Benhow. He built up his muscles by shifting 75-pound bales of cut grass, digging ditches, and hammering in fence posts. Then he turned to gym training in Houston. In February, 1966, fourteen months after his life had seemed ended, Williams was back in the ring – with one kidney missing, a 357 magnum slug still lodged somewhere up against his right hip bone, and his trunks hitched high to cover the ugly scars of four operations.

In his first come-back fight, against a young heavyweight called Big Ben Black, a savage attack smashed Williams down in round one – and caused his wife Irene to faint at the ringside. But The Cat with nine lives immediately sprang back to club his opponent to the floor and reach his half-century of victories within the distance. He continued his come-back by beating Mel Turnbow and Sonny Moore; then, on June 28th, he met Tod Herring, one of the fighters who had given him his blood. The main event that night in Houston's Coliseum was a W.B.A. world heavyweight championship bout in which Terrell retained his title with a points win over Doug Jones. But the crowd was far more pleased by Williams who finished his opponent in the third round with a vicious left hook to the belly. "We want The Cat," chanted the fans when Terrell came out to defend his title. Five months later they were to have their wish. On November 14th, in his fifth come-back fight of the year, Cleveland Williams was to fight for the heavyweight championship of the world.

The matching of this patched-up veteran of seventy-one prizefights with the mighty Muhammad Ali was not only a triumph for the courage of Williams but also for the faith of his manager. With oil millionaire Bud Adams, Benbow had bought Williams's contract in 1960 after he had seen him shake Sonny Liston with a tremendous hook to the jaw and then fail to follow up his advantage. They built a gymnasium in Houston and there Benbow spent months trying to reshape the style of his fighter, adding finesse to fantastic strength, teaching the Georgia strong-boy to set up his opponent with left jabs before unleashing his sledge-hammer right. Benbow was one man who still believed Williams could become a champion after he had been shot up on a Texas highway. He took over the whole contract of this ruin of a heavyweight. He put up a 25,000 dollar gymnasium on his ranch, and by the time Williams was matched with Clay, Benbow had invested at least 100,000 dollars in his great heavyweight hope. Benbow, a tough extrovert who claimed to be descended from the old sea-dog who once ruled the Spanish Main, had built his million-dollar ranch on land he left at the age of fourteen with only thirty-five dollars to his name, and he was now planning to start a boarding school for heavyweights there. He was a man who believed you get anything if you wanted it badly enough – even the world boxing championship.

Undoubtedly there was a time when Williams fully merited a world title bout. Over fifteen years he had had seventy-one fights, won sixty-five, lost five and drawn one. He had stopped fifty-one opponents – more than any other still active heavyweight. He was the last man to defeat Terrell – in 1962 at the South Houston Coliseum when referee Sonny Liston stopped the fight in his favour in the seventh round. He had been beaten within the distance only three times – by Bob Satterfield in 1954 and Liston in 1959 and 1960 respectively. Liston, a great friend of Williams, always insisted that he was the hardest hitting heavyweight in the business, and there was plenty of evidence for this. His big punch once anaesthetised a fighter called Johnny Holman for half an hour, and after taking one punch from The Cat, one Curley Lee never fought again. But all this was ancient history. Terrell had reversed his defeat in 1963 by a split decision and Cleve's four modest victories since his four operations did not prove that he was still the formidable knock-out specialist he had once been.

Nevertheless, Williams's sensational history gave the publicists plenty of material to work on. Automatically, the fight was projected as a battle royal and subjected to a spate of superlatives. After all, it was not only being held in Texas, where everything is the biggest and the best, but it was being staged in the largest indoor arena on earth – the breathtaking Houston Astrodome. No venue could have been so far removed from the little community hall at Lewiston, Maine, where Clay made his first title defence. Billy Graham reasonably named it the Eighth Wonder of the World and now it proudly proclaimed that title in giant lights. Inspired by the Roman Colosseum, Judge Roy Hofheinz, president of the Houston Sports Association, dreamed up the scheme for an even bigger arena and raised 45 million dollars to turn his vision into reality. The Astrodome was opened in April, 1965 – an air-conditioned, 66,000-seater palace of entertainment, with a two million dollars electronically operated scoreboard, ten thousand electrically movable front seats, luxury £10,000 a year apartments, and a staff of two thousand for capacity crowd events. Here, under a honey-combed dome rising 218 ft. and in a regulated temperature of 72 degrees, have been staged baseball and football matches, rodeo shows, circuses, a Billy Graham Bible-thumping crusade and a Judy Garland concert. It had never before staged a world heavyweight championship, but it was an ideal venue for a match designed to test public reaction, to see whether Clay, so modest and gentlemanly in Europe, could come back from self-imposed exile and still draw the crowds at home.

The pre-fight publicity on this occasion was far greater than that before Clay's European defences, but this was largely a case of each country getting the kind of ballyhoo it deserves. American boxing thrives on high-powered showmanship which is why such a character as Cassius Clay was projected as he was in the first place. Now it was back to normal, with all the usual stunts and loud talk. There was the medical examination staged absurdly in the grand ballroom of a swank hotel, with Williams dressing up in cowboy gear and the two boxers growling and glaring at each other. There was the champion telling the challenger, "I beat the bear and the hare, and I'll beat the pussycat." There was the challenger telling the champion, "I just hope you're as brave on Monday night as you are now. You're going to find this cat has claws." The actual examination lasted less than half a minute. Then Joe Louis performed with a tape measure and found both men to be 6 ft. 3 in. tall, with expanded chests of 44½ in. and waists of 34 in. Williams had the bigger fists and an inch-longer reach.

The publicity angles were limitless. When reporters tired of the old clichés from "the cat and the canary", they could always turn for comments to the W.B.A. world champion Ernie Terrell who was performing at a local dance hall open to white folk only – singing and strumming the lead guitar twice nightly for frenzied teenagers with his family group The Heavyweights, composed of five brothers and sisters. Above all, there were sensational quotes provided daily by the eccentric, larger-than-life Benbow who was continually hurling offensive, near libellous, insults at the champion. Even Clay, in his meaner moments, never subjected a boxer to such a relentless and nauseating barrage of jibes and sneers as those which flowed from the agile tongue of Williams's manager. Day after day, Benbow heaped verbal scorn on "that yellow dawg Clay". He even screeched in

the champion's face, "You'll need two big men in your corner –
to carry you back. You know you're scared because this is the
first honest fight you've had." Mostly, the champion ignored
these rantings with remarkable restraint. Unruffled by Benbow's
attack at the preliminary medical inspection, he concentrated on
staring out The Cat and quietly whispering menaces. He told
Williams, "That Benbow's too old and stupid to fight, so I'm
going to take it out on you . . . I give you till noon to ride out of
Texas."

Considering the wild atmosphere that prevailed in Houston,
Clay was comparatively courteous before the fight – certainly
more relaxed than when he last fought in the United States. He
publicly told Louis, "Lucky for you you're not in your prime,"
and he explained how he had developed "The Ali Shuffle" to
mesmerise the Big Cat – "After the shuffle you lead with your
right; and keep on dancing till the referee stops the fight." But
this was good humoured stuff. The champion was rarely malicious and while he was in Houston he fulfilled a round of highly
respectable engagements which would have exhausted ordinary
mortals. He addressed a local Law Society over lunch, talked to
students at the University of Texas, toured the Houston medical
centre, auctioned the gloves with which he beat Mildenberger to
raise 1,100 dollars at a high society charity ball, paid several
visits to a local integrated school for delinquent boys and donated
to the boys the dollar a head paid by spectators at his training
sessions.

In between the clowning and public engagements, the champion displayed masterly form when sparring with his superb trial
horse Jimmy Ellis. To prepare himself for any mauling with
Williams, he also wrestled in the gymnasium and hotel room
with his friend, Jimmy Brown, a Sampson of a man who had
recently retired after becoming one of the all-time greats of
American football. Finally, to leave no doubt that he was taking
this latest challenge seriously, he knocked down a sparring partner for the first time. The victim: one Mel Turnbow who nine
months before had twice put Williams on the floor before losing
on points over ten rounds.

As usual, there was no shortage of arguments from the challenger's camp to explain why Clay would be beaten. Like so

many heavyweights before him, Williams aimed to benefit from
the mistakes of his predecessors and could explain why this time
would be different. His plan was simple. Unlike the "suckers"
before him, he would not chase the dancing master all around
the ring, wasting energy and looking foolish. He would stubbornly anchor himself to the centre of the ring and put all the
onus of attacking on the champion, taunting him to come to him
and fight. "Me and Cleve have it all figured out," said Benbow.
"We ain't gonna fight Clay's kind of fight. For the first time in his
life Clay is gonna have a big, strong, two-handed fighter in there
with him. He's gonna be knocked out first time Cleve gets to him
and the world will be well rid of the biggest mouth in
boxing. . . . Cleve don't fool around. He crushes their bones
with either hand. He's knocked fifty guys deader than cow meat,
and he broke one poor feller's back – put him on crutches for the
rest of his life . . . I also want you to know that Cleve's a fine
clean-living boy, goes to church on Sundays, don't drink, has the
priest in his dressing room and is married to a preacher's daughter. He's gonna be a great champion – but that Clay won't be
around to know about it."

Benbow, never known to be reticent, spoke tens of thousands
of words about what his great heavyweight would do to the
champion – "A pro against an amateur – that's what it will be."
For his part, Williams was comparatively quiet. A man who really
preferred fishing to fighting, he simply said that he was now a
much-improved boxer and that he thought he could win. "I'm
going in there to fight, not to play games. It'll be do or die – and
I ain't ready to die." He kept out of any controversies arising
from Clay's beliefs and simply argued, "A man has to go his own
way. The Muslims asked me to join and I said no. The N.A.A.C.P.
asked me to join and I said no. I can't be bitter. I'm alive. I fight.
It's my way."

Highway patrolman Dale Witten was on hand in Houston to
give his opinion that Williams must have a chance – "if he hits
Clay like he hit me. That guy's got guts. I'll say that for him."
But for all the arguments in Williams's favour there were far
more solid ones against him succeeding. He was thirty-three
years old, inevitably beyond peak physical condition. In shape
and weight (212 lb.) he looked impressive enough, but according

to one medical expert, his loss of one kidney would prevent him from producing the full quota of adrenalin when he needed added inspiration at a critical stage of the fight. More important, the challenger who had been physically wrecked two years earlier was no longer as fast and as lithe as his nickname suggested. This was apparent when he sparred with Big Ben Black and Jefferson Davis before crowds of stetson-hatted Texans and their expensively dressed wives, and it was the most disturbing factor in assessing his prospects against a champion of prodigious speed. The bookmakers agreed. The odds were 6 to 1 on Clay, 4 to 1 against Williams.

Williams was an unusual man. In 1958 he withdrew from a return bout in Porthcawl with Welshman Dick Richardson only seven hours before the fight was due to start – because "a message from heaven" had advised him not to go into the ring. He refused to repay the air fare of himself and his trainer and was permanently suspended by the British Boxing Board of Control. Unfortunately, he received no such tip-off from the gods before tackling the man who was introduced in the Houston ring as "the heavyweight champion of all the world, Muhammad Ali."

At the start, it seemed that all the 35,460 fans (a record indoor crowd) in the Houston Astrodome were booing the champion, but within ten minutes those jeers were to be turned to cheers. Clay opened in his usual style. He spent the full first minute of the fight just prancing around with his fists below his hips, while Williams shuffled forward, carrying his hands high in strictly orthodox style. Not a single serious blow was exchanged. The Cat was quite unable to catch his prey and the champion took the opportunity to display his "Ali shuffle", a quick scissors step that only renewed the crowd's jeering. At last the challenger touched him with a long, harmless left to the head, and briefly Williams had the champion against the ropes. But Clay, still disdaining to use his fists, slipped out by brilliant footwork alone, and then he began to set about his skilful demolition work. In rare but superb flurries of lefts and rights, he hammered Williams with fantastically fast combinations, produced every kind of punch in copybook fashion. Blood began to trickle from the challenger's nose.

Early in the second round, when dancing away from the ropes,

Clay very nearly took a hard right to his completely unguarded jaw. Otherwise he never looked in the slightest danger. With a left and a right to the face, he sent more blood gushing from Williams's nose. The challenger lunged forward, but he never succeeded in landing a worthwhile blow. Briefly he achieved the comparative glory of getting into a clinch with the fastest heavyweight on earth, but as he moved forward he only ran into greater trouble. Now his nightmare began. Following a left feint, a superbly timed straight right to the jaw sent Williams crashing to the floor. The Cat wobbled to his feet at six and leaned against the ropes until referee Harry Kessler of New York had completed the compulsory eight-count. Told to box on, the champion sailed directly into the attack again, and another left and a right exploded with deadly accuracy on his opponent's face. Down went Williams again – this time for three seconds. After a five-second breather, he was exposed to more punishing blows. Every lightning punch seemed to land with uncanny precision and as Williams slumped to the boards for a third time Clay stretched his arms in a great "V" for victory. His rejoicing was premature. The bell denied a finish at this stage and Williams got off his back to be helped back to his corner.

The champion was not to prolong this affair as he had done against Mildenberger. When Williams pushed his weary body forward to enter the breach once more, Clay tore into him and within a few seconds the challenger had been laid flat on his back by another quick-fire burst of lefts and rights. Clay towered over his victim, looking down and shaking his head as though despairing for his utterly beaten opponent. Williams, the man renowned for his stubborn courage, forced himself up yet again and staggered back with his arms shielding his aching head. Even the tough Texans were now screaming for the massacre to be ended, and a few seconds later, when Clay was landing punches as he pleased, the fight was mercifully stopped. It was all over after one minute eight seconds of the third round. In seven minutes of action the challenger had not landed a single punch of consequence.

This was a classical Clay back with the speed that no heavyweight in the world could approach. The champion who had been booed at the start was given fully deserved cheers for a savage but technically superb exhibition of the boxing arts. For the time being, all the non-sporting controversies surrounding him were forgotten. True greatness had been seen that night and suddenly the promoters were clamouring for the champion no one had wanted a year before. Now only Ezzard Charles (eight), Tommy Burns (eleven) and Joe Louis (twenty-five) had more successful heavyweight title defences to their credit, and plenty of critics were prepared to compare Clay with the immortal Brown Bomber. Of course, people could say that he had merely beaten an ageing, one-kidney opponent who was a shadow of his former self. What could not be denied was the faultless manner in which he executed his task of destruction; this was the complete professional, a classy champion boxing with controlled aggression.

The man who had the ill-luck to meet Clay in such devastating form and mood afterwards remarked that he would rather face a cop with a revolver than meet a champion "with two fists that carry bullets in each hand". He then announced his retirement from boxing and complained that his manager had harassed him so much before the fight that he had been mentally unfit to enter the ring. Poor Williams. Nothing went right for him. He did not even automatically collect his purse for his painful efforts. His share of the gate was withheld pending legal proceedings in which millionaire oilman Bud Adams, who formerly owned half Williams's contract, claimed the boxer owed him 67,000 dollars advanced for living and hospital expenses. As for Clay, it was estimated that he had now grossed a total sum of 1,800,000 dollars for his five fights in 1966.

Was there any heavyweight who could live in the same ring as Clay? After publicly attributing his success to the Muslim faith, the champion talked confidently of the future, of possibly defending his title against Zora Folley and then perhaps the promising young Thad Spencer. There was talk of staging a world title fight in Japan or the Middle East. But this was looking far ahead. For the moment there was the long-awaited matter of a summit meeting with the W.B.A. world champion, Ernie Terrell. If anyone might worry Clay, it was said this could be the man. It was time for the moment of truth.

Negroes and the War

The Times, Thursday, 22 June 1967

The war in Vietnam has meant two quite different things to American Negroes. On the one hand many individual Negroes have fought bravely and well in Vietnam and have found there the status, the promotion, the sense of purpose and the money that they have been denied at home. Having experienced this temporary equality in the service of their country they will be all the more unwilling to accept inequality when they return home. On the other hand the mainstream of organized Negro opinion, encouraged by leaders as far apart as Dr Martin Luther King and Mr Stokely Carmichael, has strongly opposed the war, partly because it is seen as a white man's war against people of another colour, and partly because it diverts money and attention from the needs of the Negroes at home.

The maximum sentence imposed on Tuesday on Muhammad Ali (or Cassius Clay) for refusing military service may, if it is ever carried out, do something to strengthen Negro opposition to the war. It could also harden white opinion against the civil rights movement by reinforcing racial prejudice with outraged patriotism. So far, it is true, Muhammad Ali has won no great following as a Negro leader. He lacks the necessary magnetism and oratorical skill, and has staked too much of his reputation on buffoonery. But when a black heavyweight boxing champion is punished for his principles by a white court his personal failings can easily get overlooked. The symbol obscures the person.

Strictly in law, Muhammad Ali does not appear to have suffered any special discrimination. Originally he applied for the status of a conscientious objector but could not satisfy the draft board that he personally, or the Black Muslim organization to which he belongs, were against all wars on principle – particularly since other Black Muslims were already fighting in Vietnam.

He was granted a special appeal to a national board with a Negro member, but the verdict was the same. He also sought exemption as a minister of religion but failed – hardly surprisingly – to persuade the authorities that he was a full-time bona fide minister under the terms of the law. All that was left for the federal district court to decide this week was whether he had in fact refused call-up.

The judge, however, had some discretion in deciding the sentence, and he chose the maximum. He may have argued to himself that the danger of being accused of racial prejudice, or of creating a Negro martyr, was less than the danger of opening the door to a flood of cases brought by Negroes seeking to avoid service in Vietnam. At any rate he rejected the idea that there were wider issues in the case that called for mitigation.

For most people it is these wider issues that will seem most important. The essence of Muhammad Ali's attitude is that he sees the Vietnam war primarily as a white man's colonial war against people of another colour with whom he has some instinctive sympathy. Like many other Negroes he is also aware of the bitter irony that the United States is willing to spend so much money fighting a rather dubious battle in the name of freedom and democracy for a distant country while spending so little on the same cause at home. To this extent the war is at the expense of the American Negro, and it is a war that makes the Negro more acutely aware of his separate identity, his separate interests and his alienation from white society. In the court of public opinion it is reasonable to accept this as a mitigating factor in judging the conduct of one man.

Beyond the Confines of America

Mike Marqusee

On 23 August, as a result of Ali's appeals, a special judicial hearing was held to review his draft status. Ali's legal team submitted a twenty-one-page statement on his behalf, but the champion also appeared in person to testify in his own words:

> It would be no trouble for me to go into the armed services, boxing exhibitions in Vietnam and traveling the country at the expense of the government or living the easy life and not having to get out in the mud and fight and shoot. If it wasn't against my conscience to do it, I would easily do it. I wouldn't raise all this court stuff and I wouldn't go through all of this and lose the millions that I gave up and my image with the American public that I would say is completely dead and ruined because of us in here now.

Much to the dismay of the federal government, and the surprise of mainstream commentators, Judge Lawrence Grauman ruled that Ali was "sincere in his objection on religious grounds to participation in war in any form." Two days later, L. Mendel Rivers, the right-wing chair of the House Armed Services Committee, denounced Grauman's ruling to a meeting of the Veterans of Foreign Wars and threatened to raise hell on Capitol Hill if Ali was deferred. The Justice Department, insisting that Ali's objection to the war was "racial and political," convinced the Kentucky appeal board to ignore Grauman's recommendation and uphold the 1-A classification. The case then proceeded to the national Selective Service Appeals Board, where the Justice Department again opposed Ali's claim, using information obtained by the FBI to show that Ali's motivations were primarily political.

"*I ain't got no quarrel with them Vietcong.*" It sounds so modest, yet it struck people as terrifyingly outlandish. It could be the plaint of any ordinary soldier-citizen. Just how is it that the ostensible enemies of the nation-state to which one is assigned become one's personal enemies? This is a magical process which national establishments have managed with great care and ingenuity since the dawn of the modern era. The counter-process through which Ali broke free of its mystic grip, and defined his own loyalties, is an exemplary voyage of the sixties.

The "I" who had no quarrel with the Vietcong was, first, the highly personal "I" of a young man wondering why he was supposed to kill or be killed by people he didn't know. It was also the "I" of a boxer who wanted to be left alone to be a boxer, a man who had made great efforts to free himself of the burden of representation, a man who only wanted to be an "I." But because of his conversion to the Nation of Islam, and his travels in Africa, this "I" assumed other, collective attributes: black, Muslim, African. Ultimately, it became the "I" of all those who felt they had no quarrel with the Vietcong – and all those who felt they did have a quarrel with America.

Ironically, Ali's reclamation of his selfhood had given his "I" new representative burdens. In retrospect, "I ain't got no quarrel with them Vietcong" seems a characteristic Sixties declaration, highly personal yet charged with political import. In it, the various vectors of the Sixties – individualist and collectivist, particularist and universal – intersected.

Muhammad Ali refused complicity in one of the atrocities of the twentieth century. Against this, the fact that he didn't know Le Duc Tho from Nguyen Kao Ky, Haiphong from Hué, is nothing. After all, there were many bright and well-informed people who could list every strategic hamlet, but who remained blind or indifferent to the welfare of the human beings who occupied those hamlets. Jeremiah Shabazz emphasizes that Ali made up his own mind, without pressure from the Nation of Islam. "He never studied day-to-day current events like the thousands of white kids who opposed the war. But even though he was unsophisticated in his thinking, he knew it was a senseless, unjust war." In opposing the draft and the war, and paying the price for that opposition, he reached beyond America and "Americanism," beyond blackness and Islam. Ali's stand against the draft was one of the most piquant expressions of that broadening of human sympathies that was the best of his era.

*   *   *

When he finally fought Terrell in Houston in early 1967, Ali's ferocity shocked the pundits. Terrell, a powerful hitter, probably Ali's most dangerous opponent since Liston, had made the mistake of calling him "Clay" during a pre-fight press conference. "What's my name?" Ali roared again and again as he pummeled Terrell. "Uncle Tom! What's my name?" The *New York Daily News* called the fight "a disgusting exhibition of calculating cruelty, an open defiance of decency, sportsmanship and all the tenets of right versus wrong." Jimmy Cannon called it "a kind of lynching." Arthur Daley called Ali "a mean and malicious man whose facade has crumbled as he gets deeper into the Black Muslim movement." Another veteran boxing correspondent, Milton Gross, confessed: "One almost yearns for the return of Frankie Carbo and his mobster ilk."

Rarely has the hideous hierarchy of boxing's values been made so explicit. Ali's violence in the ring (and within the rules) was declared reprehensible by the very people who condemned him for not engaging in much more deadly violence in Vietnam. Even the violence of organized crime was considered less discrediting to the sport of boxing than Ali's crime of conscience. As in the Patterson fight, it was argued that somehow Ali had stepped over the ill-defined line demarcating the permissible limits of aggression in the ring. When Mike Tyson bit Evander Holyfield's ear, he was clearly breaking the rules and making a mockery of a sporting contest. But what exactly was Ali's offense? That he allowed his anger to become visible? That he was in uncompromising mood? Even one of his admirers has described the Patterson and Terrell fights as the "only times he deliberately inflicted pain" in the ring. Surely Ali, like every other boxer, deliberately inflicted pain every time he stepped into the ring. In both these fights Ali had hyped the symbolic character of the contest; in each one he was fighting more than his opponent. His critics saw these fights through this lens as much as Ali did. It's hard to resist the conclusion that what really rankled was the spectacle of an uncompromising Ali glorying in his opposition to – and momentary triumph over – "the American way." Neither Patterson nor Terrell ever complained about Ali's treatment of them in the ring.

*   *   *

On a rare holiday in the first week of January 1967, Martin Luther King contemplated photographs of napalm-scorched Vietnamese children published in the latest issue of the radical journal *Ramparts*. Over the last year, he had grown increasingly distressed by American violence in Vietnam, but his sense of responsibility to the civil rights movement had caused him to refrain from outright opposition. Now he resolved to break what he was later to call "the betrayal of my own silences." On his return from holiday, he informed SCLC colleagues of his determination to make anti-war activity his priority. Some were uneasy with their leader's new course, and feared it would alienate both the government and white liberal supporters. On 25 February, in a speech in Beverly Hills, King argued that "the promises of the Great Society have been shot down on the battlefield of Vietnam." Yet more controversially, he claimed that US policy in Vietnam "seeks to turn the clock of history back and perpetuate white colonialism."

On 6 March 1967, the national Selective Service Appeal Board unanimously upheld Muhammad Ali's 1-A classification. That same day, President Johnson told Congress, "The knowledge that military service must sometimes be born by – and imposed on – free men so their freedom may be preserved is woven deeply into the fabric of the American experience." On 14 March, Ali received his induction notice. Thanks to the rapid intervention of his lawyers, the call-up was postponed until 28 April so that he could fight Zora Folley at Madison Square Garden on 22 March. In his last appearance in the ring for more than three and a half years, Ali was at his most dazzling and dominant, finishing off the challenger with a knockout in the seventh round. That month's issue of *Ring* magazine declined for the first time to designate a fighter of the year because "Cassius Clay," the obvious candidate for the award, "is most emphatically not to be held up as an example to the youngsters of the United States." That week saw 274 US deaths in combat, the highest tally since the war began.

On 29 March, a federal judge rejected Ali's three draft appeals, including his objection to Louisville's all-white draft board. Induction became inevitable. Only now did Elijah Muhammad come to his disciple's support in the pages of *Muhammad Speaks*.

All Ali wanted, Muhammad insisted, was to "go his own way . . . but he is being blown up as one of the greatest criminals in America, a country in which he does not even belong." More significantly, on that same day, Martin Luther King arrived in Louisville for an SCLC board meeting. Following the meeting, the board issued a statement condemning the "morally and politically unjust" war and the draft which "discriminates against the poor and places Negroes in the front lines in disproportionate numbers and from there to racially segregated cemetery plots in the deep south."

While in Louisville, King took time out to meet privately with Ali, who was visiting his home town. Afterwards, the two men met the press, and King praised the boxer's stance against the draft. "As Muhammad Ali has said, we are all victims of the same system of oppression," King told the newsmen. Ali nodded, gave the older, shorter man's rounded shoulders an affectionate squeeze and called him "brother." In private, King's humor was as irrepressible as Ali's and the two men seem to have hit it off. More importantly, Ali's stand gave King a focus for his appeal to young men caught in the draft, and King's increasingly vocal critique of the war and direct support for Ali reduced the champion's isolation.

The SCLC had chosen to meet in Louisville, where King's brother, A. D. King, was a leading pastor, partly in order to support the bitter and protracted open-housing campaign waged by local blacks. Marchers through segregated white residential areas were greeted by white mobs throwing rocks and bottles, while police stood passively to one side. After meeting with King, Ali toured the city's black neighborhoods. "In your struggle for freedom, justice and equality, I am with you," he told the protesters. "I came to Louisville because I could not remain silent in Chicago while my own people – many of whom I grew up with, went to school with and some of whom are my blood relatives – were being beaten, stomped and kicked in the streets simply because they want freedom, justice and equality in housing." It was an extraordinary statement from the man who had told the world he didn't want to "carry a sign" or live in a white neighborhood, who only three years before had publicly renounced both the integrationist program and political methods of the civil rights movement. Revealingly, hardly anyone seemed to notice the shift; supporters and opponents alike saw Ali's increasingly political explanation of his attitude to the war as a logical extension of the man's personality, and in keeping with the changing temper of the times. Both Ali's turn to the Nation and his support for the integration struggle in Louisville had their roots in his personal identification with a larger constituency. It was his abiding sense of responsibility to that constituency that compelled him to re-define again and again the parameters of the role model, to reconstruct who and what he represented, independently of the powers that be, even as he exploited their media in order to do it.

In Louisville, Ali visited churches and schools and was dogged by reporters. Later that day, he made his most explicitly political statement yet about the war and his refusal to participate in it:

> Why should they ask me to put on a uniform and go ten thousand miles from home and drop bombs and bullets on brown people in Vietnam while so-called Negro people in Louisville are treated like dogs and denied simple human rights? No, I am not going ten thousand miles from home to help murder and burn another poor nation simply to continue the domination of white slavemasters of the darker people the world over. This is the day when such evils must come to an end. I have been warned that to take such a stand would put my prestige in jeopardy and could cause me to lose millions of dollars which should accrue to me as the champion. But I have said it once and I will say it again. The real enemy of my people is right here. I will not disgrace my religion, my people or myself by becoming a tool to enslave those who are fighting for their own justice, freedom and equality. . . . If I thought the war was going to bring freedom and equality to twenty-two million of my people, they wouldn't have to draft me, I'd join tomorrow. But I either have to obey the laws of the land or the laws of Allah. I have nothing to lose by standing up for my beliefs. So I'll go to jail. We've been in jail for four hundred years.

The confused young fighter who merely wanted to avoid the unpleasantness of military service had matured into a hero of global solidarity. In Louisville, Ali testified to the transformative power of the experience of struggle, one of the keynotes of the sixties. Circumstances, personal and historical, had locked him in conflict with authority; in the fire of that conflict, new and powerful links between the inner self and a broader community were forged. Undoubtedly, Ali received help in drawing up statements such as the one he issued in Louisville, though probably more from Chauncey Eskridge than from the Nation of Islam. Nonetheless, however shaky his grasp of geography, his understanding of the moral dimension of the choice before him was now deeply informed. Significantly, much of the rhetoric and many of the arguments he deployed derived from Malcolm X, whose shadow, unacknowledged, seems to have hovered over Ali during these years of challenge and change.

The resistance to open housing in Louisville was one of several events in 1966 and 1967 which fed King's growing pessimism about the prospects for peaceful social change. Returning to Louisville in July, he told a crowd, "The vast majority of white Americans are racists" – he had arrived at a position little different from that held by Malcolm in the last year of his life. Five days after meeting Ali, and exactly one year before his assassination, on 4 April 1967, King delivered his magnificent oration at the Riverside Church in New York. In this speech, his most uncompromising indictment of the war to date, he wove together the themes of racism, war, poverty and America's global role. Responding to those who pressed him to condemn ghetto rioters, he explained, "I could never raise my voice against the violence of the oppressed without first having spoken clearly to the greatest purveyor of violence in the world today" – the American government. "Every man of humane convictions must decide on the protest that best suits his convictions," he declared, "but we must all protest." Describing himself as "bound by allegiances and loyalties which are broader and deeper than nationalism," he recommended conscientious objection to "all who find the American course in Vietnam a dishonorable and unjust one.'

Only three years before, when he received the Nobel Peace Prize, King had been fêted by the media and acknowledged as the preeminent leader of black Americans. But his militant turn against the Vietnam War infuriated many former allies. Roy Wilkins, Whitney Young, A. Philip Randolph and Bayard Rustin all publicly distanced themselves from King, as they had from

Robeson twenty years before. "Dr King has done a grave injury to those who are his natural allies," lectured the *Washington Post*. "He has diminished his usefulness to his cause, his country and his people." The *New York Times* rebuked his "reckless" attacks on America and described his opposition to the war as "wasteful and self-defeating." *Life* magazine characterized the Riverside speech as "a demagogic slander that sounded like a script for Radio Hanoi." Hoover wrote to Johnson: "He is an instrument in the hands of the subversive forces seeking to undermine our nation." The NAACP board described King's attempt to link Vietnam and civil rights as "a serious tactical mistake."

Alarmed at the growth of anti-war sentiment among blacks, the government and the military launched a counter-offensive. General Westmoreland told reporters in Saigon, "I have an intuitive feeling that the Negro servicemen have a better understanding than whites of what the war is about." Westmoreland also repeated his racial view of the conflict: Orientals valued human lives, including their own, less than Americans, and were therefore harder to beat on the field of battle. Briefed by the military, the *New York Times* reported, "In Vietnam the Negro for the first time has been given the chance to do his share of fighting for his country" and concluded, "The Negro's performance in battle is in every way the equal of his white comrades." But among black youths such assurances rang hollow. At a Senate hearing on the draft, the editor of the Howard University newspaper told the politicians that black people saw little reason to risk their lives. "Those people who benefit most from the society should be those people who will lay down their lives for it." On 5 April, the day after King's Riverside speech, an anti-draft caravan toured New York City schools; the *Times* reported with some bemusement that interest in the caravan's message was keenest among young blacks and Puerto Ricans. The next day, a draft-card burner was sentenced to two and a half years in prison for refusing to accept a replacement card.

On 11 April, Ali was ordered to report for induction. On 15 April, Manhattan witnessed the largest anti-war demonstration yet staged in the United States. One hundred and twenty-five thousand gathered in Central Park and later heard speeches from King, CORE's Floyd McKissick and Stokely Carmichael (who described Selective Service as "white people sending black people to make war on yellow people in order to defend land they stole from red people"). A columnist in the *New York Times* complained that the protesters smelled bad and dismissed them as frustrated misfits, but the unprecedented size of the demonstration made it clear that the misfits were becoming a force in the land.

On 25 April, Ali's lawyers filed a petition in federal court stating that their client would not agree to induction and requesting exemption on religious grounds. The Justice Department contested the petition; a spokesman argued, "If he wins, all the Muslims will refuse to take the oath, and where will we get the soldiers?" The next day, Johnson intensified the bombing of North Vietnam. His supporters argued that domestic criticism was undermining the war effort and accused dissenters of disloyalty. A letter to Secretary of Defense Robert MacNamara from one thousand seminarians urged an extension of the conscientious objection criteria to include moral objection to a particular war, thus "easing the coming confrontation between the demands of law and those whose conscience will not permit them to fight in Vietnam." Neither the government nor the judiciary was prepared to contemplate such a concession to the anti-war movement. The federal court rejected Ali's petition and he was ordered to report for induction.

On 28 April, Westmoreland assured a joint session of Congress that the war was just, necessary and winnable. That morning, Ali reported, as ordered, to the Federal Customs House in Houston. Outside, a small group of demonstrators, including SNCC's notorious Rap Brown, cheered the champion. Students from Texas Southern University appeared with a banner reading "Stay Home Muhammad Ali." Others held placards urging "Draft Beer – Not Ali." The heavyweight champion, along with twenty-five others called for induction that day, spent the morning filling out forms and undergoing routine examinations. The induction ceremony took place at 1:05 p.m. Three times the sergeant in charge called the name, "Cassius Marcellus Clay," and three times Ali refused to step over the yellow line marked on the floor. After being formally advised by a Navy lieutenant that his refusal was a felony offense and made him liable to imprisonment, Ali submitted a written declaration claiming exemption as a minister of Islam. He then issued a four-page statement to the media:

I am proud of the title "World Heavyweight Champion" which I won in the ring in Miami on February 25, 1964. The holder of it should at all times have the courage of his convictions and carry out those convictions, not only in the ring but throughout all phases of his life. It is in light of my own personal convictions that I take my stand in rejecting the call to be inducted into the armed services. I do so with full realization of its implications and possible consequences. I have searched my conscience and I find I cannot be true to my belief in my religion by accepting such a call. My decision is a private and individual one. In taking it I am dependent solely upon Allah as the final judge of these actions brought about by my own conscience.

Although Ali still claimed the right to act and speak as an unrepresentative individual, he also now appealed explicitly to his obligations as a role model, which he had radically re-defined. To the boxing authorities, his use of the heavyweight title as a platform for protest was an intolerable affront. One hour later, before Ali had been charged with any offense, the powerful New York State Athletic Commission suspended his boxing license and stripped him of his title. Within a month, other state commissions had followed suit, as had the WBA, Madison Square Garden, the British Boxing Board of Control (at this time, Harold Wilson's Labour government was still backing Johnson in Vietnam) and the European Boxing Union. It was the beginning of his three-and-a-half-year exile from the ring.

Boxing promoters welcomed his removal from the scene, and quickly announced plans to stage an elimination contest for the "vacant" title among a wide array of contenders. "There is more money to be made in a tournament among these men than in a continuation of Clay's one-sided fights," reported Robert Lipsyte. When asked about the champ who had made him a fortune, Bob Arum, who was promoting the eight-man eliminator, responded jokingly, "Cassius who?"

Ali's refusal to cross the yellow line was front-page news, not only in America, but around the world. In Guyana, Cheddi Jagan led a picket of the US embassy. In Karachi, a young Pakistani fasted outside the US consulate. There was a demonstration in Cairo. An editorial in the *Ghana Pioneer* deplored what it called the "concerted efforts" to strip Ali of his championship. During the first major British demonstrations against the war in April 1967, among the host of leaflets handed out in Grosvenor Square was one reading "LBJ Don't Send Muhammad Ali to War." Bertrand Russell congratulated Ali on his courage and assured him, "The air will change. I sense it." Incensed by the hypocrisy of the American government, an Irish boxing fan named Paddy Monaghan, a hod carrier who lived on a council estate in Abingdon, began a long and lonely picket of the US embassy in London. Over the next three years, he would collect more than twenty thousand signatures on a petition calling for the restoration of Muhammad Ali's heavyweight title.

Lionized abroad, Ali found himself a prisoner in a society increasingly polarized over the issues he stood for. In an editorial entitled "Clay v. the Army," the *New York Times* argued that to exempt "Clay" would "chip away the foundation of universally shared obligation on which the Selective Service system rests. Citizens cannot pick and choose which wars they wish to fight any more than they can pick and choose which laws they wish to obey. Moreover, if Cassius Clay and other draft-age objectors believe the war in Vietnam is unjust, they have the option of going to prison on behalf of their beliefs." The latter argument was one which Ali refused to accept: "If justice prevails, if my constitutional rights are upheld, I will be forced to go neither to the army nor jail."

Black opinion on Ali remained divided. An editorial in the *Amsterdam News*, headed "American Tragedy," linked Ali's draft defiance to King's Riverside protest. It noted that Ali's objections to military service "stem ultimately from our centuries of racial injustices" but was careful not to endorse his stand. A survey of Harlem opinion in the same paper revealed contrasting perceptions. A black Rockefeller aid declared, "It's a tragedy. It is being blown up out of all proportion. He's not Ralph Bunche or Roy Wilkins, whose views on foreign policy would carry weight as far as Negro opinion is concerned." But a community activist in a local youth project disagreed: "It should encourage every black man in the new generation to follow in his footsteps." In his syndicated column, Jackie Robinson criticized King's statements on the war and in particular his support for Ali. "I admire this man as a fighting champion and a man who speaks his mind. I can't help feeling he wants to have his cake and eat it too. I can't help wondering how he can expect to make millions of dollars in this country and then refuse to fight for it." He asked King: "What values do you have in mind when you praise him [Ali] and say he has given up so much? I think all he has given up is his citizenship. I think his advisers have given him a bum steer. I think the only persons who will come out well in this situation are his lawyers."

Robinson's views, however, no longer carried great weight among younger blacks, and among the most politically conscious it was Ali and not Robinson who now epitomized black aspirations. Those who had placed the burden of symbolic representation on black sports stars now found the tables turned. A writer in *The Liberator* relished their discomfort:

By refusing to obey, Ali poses a problem of disastrous potential. How can the government overcome? Can "responsible negro leaders" be called upon to quell the redoubtable Muhammad Ali's influence over black youth? But Messrs Roy Wilkins, Whitney Young, A. Philip Randolph, and Ralph Bunche are scorned as paid buffoons of white liberalism! And the Reverend Dr Martin Luther King has defected to the peace movement! In short, Muhammad Ali has become the establishment's domestic Vietcong: his impact far outweighs his size.

Two days after Ali refused induction, King preached a sermon in his Ebenezer Baptist Church in Atlanta. With the atheist Stokely Carmichael sitting ostentatiously in the congregation, King urged "every man in this country who believes that this war is abominable and unjust" to take the path of conscientious objection. And once again he singled out Ali for praise. "He is giving up even fame. He is giving up millions of dollars in order to stand up for what his conscience tells him is right." The following day, 1 May, Ali's lawyers moved to politicize his conflict with the government by filing an appeal in federal court on the exclusion of blacks from draft boards. In the two states dealing with Ali's case, Kentucky and Texas, only 0.2 percent and 1.1 percent of draft board members were black, although blacks made up 7.1 percent and 12.4 percent of their respective populations. On Ali's behalf, the lawyers asked that all draft boards in Kentucky be restrained from functioning until more blacks were appointed. The appeal was denied.

A week later, a hitherto little-known group of Oakland militants calling themselves the Black Panther Party for Self-Defense burst on to the national scene when they invaded the California state legislature in a protest over what they saw as an attempt to restrict their constitutional right to carry arms. "As the aggression of the racist American government escalates in Vietnam," their press statement declared, "the police agencies of America escalate the repression of black people throughout the ghettos." Their analysis was echoed by an increasingly indignant James Baldwin, who argued, "A racist society can't but fight a racist war – this is the bitter truth. The assumptions acted on at home are the assumptions acted on abroad, and every American negro knows this, for he, after the American Indian, was the first 'Viet Cong' victim."

In Washington, DC, a week after refusing induction, Ali toured the ghetto and spoke to inmates at a federal penitentiary. At Howard University he was welcomed by a huge and enthusiastic crowd comprising the majority of the student body. At the invitation of the newly formed Black Power Committee, Ali spoke from the steps of Frederick Douglass Hall (university officials had denied the committee permission to hold the meeting inside). "We have been brainwashed," Ali told the crowd. "Even Tarzan, king of the jungle, in black Africa, is white." When a heckler offered to take his place in the army for $1000, Ali shot back, "Your life is worth more than a thousand dollars, brother." Unprotected, Ali immersed himself in the throng. According to local newspapers, a "carnival atmosphere" prevailed. Students said they were impressed by Ali's "lack of arrogance" and his "positively black" presence.

Days later, Ali addressed another student crowd at the University of Chicago's Stag Field. "I have lost nothing," he told the students, a mix of black and white. "I have gained the respect of thousands worldwide, I have gained peace of mind." In a call-and-response routine that was to become a stock-in-trade in the coming years, he bellowed, "Who is the heavyweight champion of the world?" and the packed stadium roared back the indisputable answer, "Ali! Ali! Ali!"

On 8 May 1967 Ali was indicted by a federal grand jury in Houston. Of the twenty-one citizens on the jury, one was black. Ali was photographed, fingerprinted and released on $5000 bail on condition he did not leave the US.

In early June, Herbert Muhammad brought together a number of black sports stars for a private meeting with Ali in Cleveland. Some observers were convinced Herbert wanted the stars to persuade Ali to make a deal with the government. If that was so, Herbert had seriously underestimated his fighter's determination. The stars, including football players Jim Brown and Willie Davis and basketball heroes Bill Russell and Lew Alcindor (who later converted to the Hanafi brand of Islam and changed his name to Kareem Abdul-Jabbar), found Ali in a mood of quiet determination. Many left the meeting deeply moved by Ali's sincerity and courage. "Ali didn't need our help," Jabbar recalled, "because as far as the black community was concerned, he already had everybody's heart. He gave so many people courage to test the system." For Bill Russell, Ali in 1967 was "a man accepting special responsibilities." He told *Sports Illustrated*:

> I'm not worried about Muhammad Ali. He is better equipped than anyone I know to withstand the trials in store for him. What I'm worried about is the rest of us.

Years later, Russell told Thomas Hauser, "Philosophically, Ali was a free man. Besides being probably the greatest boxer ever, he was free. And he was free at a time when historically it was very difficult to be free no matter who you were or what you were. Ali was one of the first truly free people in America." But at this moment this truly free man was facing not only the threat but the likelihood of jail. Gerald Early claims that Ali was no "martyr" because "he never went to jail." But this is to substitute hindsight for history. In 1967, and for the next three years, Ali had every reason to believe he would end up in prison and never fight again. After all, in those days there were few, if any, precedents for a black person defying federal authority and getting away with it. Robeson and Du Bois had been effectively silenced and forced into exile for merely articulating the ideas that Ali was now acting upon.

In Houston, on 19 June 1967, Ali was tried by an all-white jury. His attorneys raised a host of objections, including a protest against the all-white make-up of the draft board that had classified him, but the Justice Department and the judge insisted the only relevant factor was Ali's refusal to obey the induction order. The black attorney prosecuting the case for the government argued that if Ali escaped the draft, large numbers of black youths would be encouraged to join the Muslims. He also noted that, in the course of his dealings with the Selective Service, Ali had claimed exemption on a variety of grounds, and that therefore there was reason to suspect that his claim to conscientious objector status was insincere. (Under the law, sincerity was a crucial test for all CO applicants.) The illustrious defendant listened to the arguments in bored silence. After deliberating for twenty minutes, the jury found him guilty. Ali asked the judge to pass sentence quickly. "I'd appreciate it if the court will do it now, give me my sentence now, instead of waiting and stalling for time." The prosecution told the judge that "Clay" had a record of good conduct but "he got into trouble when he joined the Black Muslims, which are just as much in politics as religion." For the first time in the proceedings, Ali objected. "My religion isn't political in no way."

The judge handed down the maximum sentence of five years in prison and a $10,000 fine. The usual sentence in these cases at the time was eighteen months, and even the US attorney seemed surprised at the severity of the judgement. Ali was released on bail pending appeal. His passport was confiscated.

In Washington, on the day of Ali's conviction, the House passed a bill to extend the draft for another four years. The vote was 337 to 29. The House also passed a law – by 385 to 19 – making it a federal crime to "desecrate" the flag. The following week, on 23 June, Ali appeared at his first and only anti-war demonstration. Johnson was scheduled to speak at a $500-a-plate fund-raising dinner at the Century Plaza Hotel in Los Angeles. In response, local anti-war activists organized a rally at the Cheviot Hill

Playground. Twenty thousand turned out for the largest anti-war gathering yet held in southern California. The speakers included Benjamin Spock and Rap Brown. Ali arrived in a Rolls-Royce and mounted a garbage can to address the crowd. "Anything designed for peace and to stop the killing I'm for one hundred percent," he told them. "I'm not a leader. I'm not here to advise you. But I encourage you to express yourself." And he launched into his now familiar refrain, "Who's the champion of the world?" The *Los Angeles Times* noted suspiciously that the crowd replied with "Clay's Black Muslim name." The demonstrators then marched (without Ali) to the hotel, where the Supremes were performing for the president (their boss, Berry Gordy, regarded this as a sound commercial move). Governor Ronald Reagan had placed the National Guard on stand-by. When some of the demonstrators began a non-violent sit-in in front of the hotel, 1200 LAPD officers attacked the crowd with clubs. After an hour of mayhem, fifty demonstrators had been arrested and at least two hundred injured. A shocked (white) demonstrator commented, "I saw Mississippi in Los Angeles last night." The city council condemned the demonstrators and refused to hear the organizers' well-documented complaint about police misbehavior. It was to be several years before anti-war activists attempted to stage another mass demonstration in Los Angeles.

The violence outside the Century Plaza may have deterred Ali from future participation in large-scale anti-war protests. Certainly, from that moment on, without in the least diluting his anti-war stand, Ali preferred to speak as an individual, from his own plat-forms. Not that it made any difference to the forces of law and order. On 25 July, an FBI memorandum recommended intensi-fied surveillance of "Clay," who, the anonymous author complained, has "utilized his position as a nationally known figure in the sports world to promote through appearances at various gatherings an ideology completely foreign to the basic American ideals of equality and justice for all, love of God and country."

In August 1967, Ali's appeal against the confiscation of his pass-port was heard in Houston. Talking to Hugh McIlvanney before the hearing, Ali was at pains to distinguish himself from other black power figures and to assert his belief in non-violence:

Rap Brown and these boys can say what they like because they're nobody. Nobody gives a damn. With me it's different. If I went to a negro district they'd come runnin'. It would just take some young fool to throw something and that would be it. He don't care anything about race. He wants publicity. He wants to see a nice fire. I want to keep away from that stuff.

Ali's lawyers presented recordings of Ali's appearances on television to support their client's contention that he had said nothing anti-American or inflammatory. Ali himself promised to inform local police chiefs before he visited black areas. But this belated attempt to persuade the courts that Ali really was a role model of the old school came to nought. The judge decided that his presence at the Los Angeles peace rally revealed "a ready willingness to participate in anti-government and anti-war activities." He told Ali he should consider himself lucky not to be confined to one state or district.

The second half of 1967 witnessed an intensification of domestic anti-war protest, climaxing in the spectacular demonstration outside the Pentagon and militant anti-draft actions in Oakland. Yet as protests swelled, so did the ferocity of the war. By the end of the year, there were half a million US troops in Vietnam, who were, according to the Department of Defense, killing or seriously injuring one thousand non-combatants a week. In early 1968, the CIA launched Operation Phoenix, in the course of which tens of thousands of Vietnamese civilians were kidnapped and tortured. In March, US troops slaughtered 347 civilians in the hamlet of My Lai, an atrocity concealed from the American public until November 1969. The war was costing the US taxpayer some $2 billion a month and leaving some one hundred US troops dead each week. The Pentagon Papers reveal that one of MacNamara's assistants characterized US war aims at this stage as "70 percent to avoid a humiliating US defeat" and only 10 percent "to permit the people of South Vietnam to enjoy a better, freer way of life."

The Unconquerable Muhammad Ali

Hans J. Massaquoi

Ebony Magazine, April 1969

Noon rush hour pedestrians did a double take at the boyish looking, dapper brown giant who had just stepped out of a mid-Manhattan hotel lobby into the street. His mischievous eyes, set deeply into a broad, clean-cut face, seemed to challenge the crowd to recognize him. He was not to be disappointed. "Look over there! Isn't that Cassius Cl . . ., I mean Muhammad Ali?" a woman exclaimed, pointing toward the young man in a camel hair coat. Before her male companion could respond, the young man out in, "Yes ma'am; that's right. You are lookin' at Muhammad Ali, the heavyweight champion of the *whole* world." The woman was convinced, as was everyone else who had overheard the exchange.

Within minutes, "the *whole* world" – or so it seemed – was converging on its most controversial sports personality. It was a rare sight as jaded Manhattanites, reputedly unimpressed by celebrities, patiently waited in line to get Ali's autograph, shake his hand and to let him know that in their book he was still the champ.

There were murmurs of disappointment when Ali announced that he had to leave as a chauffeur-driven, silver-grey Cadillac limousine pulled up. "See my new limousine?" he asked like a little boy showing off a new toy. "Just bought it last week for $10,000 – I mean cash, baby. They think they can bring me to my knees by takin' away my title and by not lettin' me fight in this country, and by takin' my passport so I can't get to the $3 million worth of fight contracts that are waitin' for me overseas. Shoot! I ain't worked for two years and I ain't been Tommin' to nobody and here I'm buyin' limousines – the President of the United States ain't got no better one. Just look at it! Ain't it purty?" he asked rhetorically while giving the top of the sleek car an affectionate pat. "Y'all go and tell everybody that Muhammad

Ali ain't licked yet. I don't care if I never get another fight. I say, damn the fights and damn all the money. A man's got to stand up for what he believes, and I'm standin' up for my people, even if I have to go to jail."

"I know everything will turn out all right, Mr Ali," a mink-dripping white matron assured him. She was obviously referring to his pending appeal in the US Supreme Court of a five-year jail sentence and $10,000 fine for – as Ali puts it – "standin' up for what I believe," or – as Uncle Sam puts it – "violating the Selective Service Act." (Ali's lawyers have appealed the sentence on the grounds that their client is a conscientious objector; that he is a bonafide minister of the Muslim faith and that both the Louisville [Ky.] and Houston draft boards which ordered his induction have systematically barred black persons from membership.)

"I'm praying for you, son," an old black woman spoke up. "My whole family is praying for you."

"Thanks a lot ma'am. Y'all do that," the champ replied in a rare display of humility.

"May I have an autograph for my ten-year-old son?" a white man approached Ali. "He thinks you're still the greatest."

"You've got a smart son," Ali quipped and obliged. Suddenly, he let go with a barrage of sledgehammer blows that stopped only fractions of an inch short of the terrified father's chin.

"I know you can hit, champ," the man recovered from his shock.

"Then you're not as dumb as you look," Ali rejoined with characteristic irreverence.

"Hey champ! When ya gonna show dem bums again who's boss?" a burly cab driver hollered from the curb in unmistakable Brooklynese.

"As soon as they find somebody who's crazy enough to go in the ring with me," Muhammad hollered back, adding, "How about you?"

"My, is he cute!" came a gasp from a group of Afro-wearing college girls. They got no argument from Ali. Instead, he returned the compliment in his own familiar style: "Hi soul sisters! You're sho'nuff foxes – almost as purty as me." The girls giggled appreciatively.

At this point, the chauffeur broke in, reminding the champ that he was late for an appointment. "Okay, y'all take it easy now," Ali shouted to the crowd, then flung his 225-pound bulk into the back seat of his limousine which soon purred out of sight.

The wide-spread "we-love-Ali" sentiment which is much in evidence these days wherever he goes is a far cry from the hatred that engulfed the young champ when he first refused induction into the Army two years ago. Even more inflammatory than his refusal proved his off-hand remark, "I ain't mad at no Viet Congs," which was widely quoted (out of context, he insists) in the press. It did not matter that respected members of Congress and other persons in high places had made stronger anti-Vietnam War statements with impunity. The then twenty-five-year-old kid from Louisville, Ky., was singled out to bear the brunt of a white backlash from various organized and individual "patriots." While the guardians of America's cherished freedom of speech stood mute, and before his conviction by any court, Ali was summarily stripped of his title and barred from the ring. Black Americans got the message – as they did when Adam Clayton Powell was kicked out of the House of Representatives.

Throughout his ordeal, Ali never wavered in his refusal to bear arms, whatever the cost. "I don't believe in killin' nobody," he said time and again. "We Muslims don't believe this nation should force us black people to take part in no wars, for we have nothin' to gain from it unless America agrees to give us the necessary territory or land wherein we may have something to fight and die for."

Since his marriage on August 18, 1967, to statuesque, then seventeen-year-old Muslim beauty Belinda Boyd and the subsequent birth of their chubby daughter Maryum on June 18, 1968, Muhammad has done just about everything but settle down. More on the move than he ever was during his fighting days, he now is combining marriage and fatherhood with the triple careers of a visiting college lecturer, itinerant Muslim minister and high-powered business executive.

As far as his marriage is concerned, Ali – true to Muslim tradition – believes as much in the need for "honoring our women" as he does in their inferiority. "Allah," he insists, "made men to look down on women and women to look up to men; it don't matter if the two are standin' up or layin' down. It's just natural." Naturally, he doesn't "take any sass" from Mrs Ali, who quickly learned to humor her temperamental spouse. Naturally, also, he has no big ambitions for their daughter. "All I want her to become is a clean, righteous person, a good Muslim woman, a good sister, maybe a teacher of black children," he says. "If I ever have a boy, I would want him to be a 101 per cent believer in Elijah Muhammad and make up his own mind as to what he wants to be in the world."

His numerous troubles notwithstanding, Ali may yet wind up a multi-millionaire without ever laying another glove on an opponent's jaw. Moreover, he may achieve that feat while serving his jail sentence in a federal prison. Expectations of a future windfall for Ali and a small, integrated group of business partners are literally being fed by thousands of saucer-size hamburgers that are currently outselling the proverbial hot cakes in a black ghetto on Miami's Northwest Side. Billed as "Champburgers" along with the strangely reminiscent claim, "We Are The Greatest!," they are the staple of a quick-service restaurant franchise business that is expected to flourish throughout the nation's black communities. At the insistence of Champburger tycoon-to-be Muhammad Ali, future franchise restaurants – like the experimental one in Miami – will be built exclusively in black neighborhoods and run and staffed by "indigenous franchisees," meaning by blacks. Another stipulation insisted upon by the champ is that "neither the company nor any of its franchisees may sell any food product containing pork or shellfish," two important dietary restrictions of the Muslim faith.

Ali, who received six per cent of the million-dollar Champburger Corporation's stock (later sold publically at $5 a share) for lending his well-known, if somewhat controversial "name and image" to the venture, will receive royalties of one per cent of the firm's annual net sales. As a member of the board of directors and a vice-president, he is contractually charged with the duties of promoting Champburgers through public appearances, provided he manages to stay out of jail.

Opinions are divided over whether Ali knows more about fighting than about promoting or whether it's the other way around. But it is generally agreed that it was the one-time Louisville Lip who single-handedly revived the dying sport of boxing with some of the most bizarre promotional gimmicks fight fans had ever seen. They included Ali's famous – now largely defunct – poetry, and his near-accurate predictions of the rounds in which his opponents would fall. On one occasion, he appeared in public decked out in hunting togs, ostensibly while tracking down "that big, ugly bear." Everybody, including Sonny Liston, knew whom he meant by that. People who recall some of these highlights in Ali's career warn that if Muhammad Ali can do for Champburgers only a fraction of what Cassius Clay did for boxing – McDonald's, White Castle, Kingburger, Big Boy and Kentucky's Chicken Colonel had better watch out.

Ali sees no conflict between his Black Muslim view of whites as "devils" and his association with whites in a business venture (the only other black on the five-member Champburger Board of Directors is Chicago Atty Chauncey Eskridge). "We Muslims do business with the white man every day," he explained. "But we don't depend on him and we don't Uncle Tom. They (whites) know who we are when they come to do business with us. We do not compromise or weaken our faith in doin' business with them. They know that I believe that they are devils and I don't deny it when they ask me.

"We fly their (whites') airplanes," he continued, "because we don't have no airport and airplanes. We wear their shoes and clothes that come from their factories because we don't have no land to build our own factories. We use their toothpaste and toothbrushes because we are twenty-two million educated people who don't have enough sense to make our own toothbrushes. So, in the meanwhile, who else is there to do business with besides our own selves?"

While Ali is waiting for his Champburger "eggs" to hatch, the bulk of his income derives from his lectures before black, white and integrated student groups. Last year, for an average $1,000 honorarium, "prof" Ali lectured on thirty campuses, including Princeton, Rutgers, MIT, Howard, UCLA and Notre Dame. Whenever possible, he combines business with pleasure by visiting local mosques where he never fails to inspire his Muslim brothers with his fiery oratory.

Another source of revenue for Ali are public appearances on a variety of major TV shows (Johnny Carson, Merv Griffin, etc.) and exclusive interviews with representatives of foreign television stations and the foreign press. Recently, he picked up a quick $10,000 for participating in the filming of a staged bout with retired champion Rocky Marciano in which a computer is to determine the winner after the film has been edited. The novelty film is earmarked for national television.

"All this ain't no big money, the kind I used to make as a fighter," says Ali, "but it takes care of me and my family."

Ali is visibly irked by persistent rumors that the Black Muslims have taken him for a ride. "Many people," he fumes, "both black and white, have said in the white newspapers that I am only bein' used by the Muslims, that all they want from me is my money and that as soon as I would stop fightin', they would drop me like a hot potato. Now I hear nothin' anymore from those people. The white man has stopped me from boxing and I have more Muslim brothers than I could ever dream of havin'. Every city I go to, the Muslims are waitin' with open arms and offer to share what little they have with me.

"I tell you where my money went," he suddenly shouts angrily. "The white man took it! Uncle Sam took it! What the white press and the Negro Uncle Toms will not mention is that not the Hon. Elijah Muhammad, but the white man made a special law, just for me, to take 80 per cent of all my fight money (he grossed an estimated total of $3,820,212) before I was paid after each fight, leaving me only 20 per cent. With that, I could barely take care of myself, let alone hundreds of thousands of Muslims and their families.

"But I tell you what I did with my 20 per cent. I bought my father and mother a $40,000 home in Louisville and furnished it. In 1967, I bought my mother a brand-new Cadillac convertible for takin' care of me all of my life. And I bought my father two nice automobiles for his sign-paintin' work. I myself have a well-equipped, paid-for home in Chicago, valued at $65,000. My first wife (sometime model and now singer Sonji, whom he divorced in 1966 for refusing to adhere to his Muslim beliefs and customs – ankle-length dresses, no make-up, no alcohol, no nicotine, etc.) was awarded $50,000 cash security bond and $1,200 a month alimony for ten years. I have paid at least $60,000 of my money for draft lawyers, not countin' many thousands of dollars of airplane bills, hotel bills and my various Eldorado Cadillacs and limousines (he estimates he has owned "about ten or eleven"). All of this I managed out of my 20 per cent. Elijah never asked me for no money, and if he had, I couldn't have given him none because the government left me none. Some day, though, I still hope to be able to help him with his black education centers throughout America and his buyin' of farmland throughout the country to help feed and educate our people."

There isn't a waking moment in Ali's life that isn't somehow tinged by his fanatical, all-consuming faith in Elijah Muhammad's message of a black man's Allah. He still is disgusted with the press which would run long columns on his punches but ignore the motivating power behind them. "It was the Islamic religion that got me to the title, that made me fearless enough to stand up and shout, 'I'm the greatest!' And it was the Hon. Elijah Muhammad who got me to the Islamic religion," he insists. "When I first went to that little storefront mosque in Miami in 1960, that changed my whole life.

"Look how happy I am. And I have more problems than anybody here. If the average man had my problems, he'd be jumpin' out of the window. Don't nothin' and nobody worry me. If the FBI would pick me up now and tell me I lost my appeal and that I would have to go to jail, I'll just go and get adjusted to that kind of life. The reason I can still be happy is because the Hon. Elijah Muhammad has taught me the truth. When they wanted me to denounce him and asked me, 'Which do you want – the Muslim or $20 million, all kinds of white women and a big home in Hollywood?' I said, 'Give me the Muslims,' and I haven't regretted it yet."

Ali regards the current shift from integration to black power as a total vindication of his mentor. "When Elijah Muhammad first set up his little bitty schools and taught black children about black history because white teachers and Uncle Tom Negro teachers weren't teachin' the kids properly," he reminds his listeners, "everybody – even black folks – laughed at him. Look around you now! Now all blacks say they want black teachers and black history. A few years ago, the so-called Negroes would have cut you if you called them black; now they cut you if you *don't* call them black. Who you think taught them? Ain't nobody but the Hon. Elijah Muhammad.

"I'm glad that my people are beginnin' to wake up. But it still bothers me to see a black brother with an Afro hair style, African robe and African shoes and beard and if you ask him his name, he says, 'George Washington.' I feel the same about black girls who wear naturals and mini-skirts. They look like proud Africans from the chin up and like Twiggy from the neck down. But I'm not knockin' any of them. At least they are beginnin' to move toward our own kind and not toward integration."

Ali's compulsive urge to lecture incessantly on "the truth as taught to me by the Hon. Elijah Muhammad" has never depended on the size of his audiences. A packed college auditorium is great, but a ghetto barbershop with a few "souls" standing around will do just fine. All of Ali's lectures and sermons hew a rock-hard Black Muslim line, though each bears his inimical personal touch. Thus, an Ali "argument" against interracial marriage – a cardinal no-no in the Black Muslim faith – goes like this: "No intelligent black man or black woman in his or her right black mind wants white boys and white girls comin' to their homes, schools and churches to marry their black sons and daughters to produce little pale, half-white, green-eyed, blond-headed Negroes. And no intelligent white man or white woman in his or her right white mind wants black boys and black girls comin' around their homes, schools and churches to marry their white sons and daughters and in return introducin' their grandchildren as little mixed-up kinky-headed, half-black niggers."

If the foregoing assertion fails to impress, Ali will follow up with this dizzying excursion into nonsequiturs: "Black and white are two opposites, right? Okay, if the white man is your opposite, he is your opposition. If he's your opposition, he's your opposer. If he's your opposer, that makes him your opponent. And if he's your opponent, he's your enemy."

As far as Ali is concerned there is only one thing more harmful to the black man than the white man: the white woman. "White women," he warns, "are the most dangerous; they smile at you and the next thing you know, you let your guard down. But that'll never happen to me.

"What hurts me more than anything," he continues, "is when I pick up the newspaper or turn on television or go to the movies and see black men huggin', kissin' and makin' love with white women, pretendin' to be in love with our four-hundred-year-old enemy and brainwashin' black boys and girls into believin' that white women are prettier and better than our beautiful black sisters."

Ali is quick to point out that he doesn't hate whites. "I don't hate nobody and I ain't lynched nobody. We Muslims don't hate the white man. It's like we don't hate a tiger; but we know that a tiger's nature is not compatible with people's nature since tigers love to eat people. So we don't want to live with tigers. It's the same with the white man. We know from all he has done to black people that he is the devil; so we don't want to live with him."

Nothing can shake Muhammad's belief in the Black Muslim assertion that the black man is the "original man" who predated the white man by "trillions of years." Consequently, he regards as anti-climactic any white achievement – including the recent orbiting of the moon. "Black men put the moon up sixty-six trillion years ago," he lectures with grave sincerity. "There weren't no white people on this planet then. White people are just now learnin' about gravity. The Hon. Elijah Muhammad teaches us that black men drilled into the earth and with high explosives caused a piece to go into space. That piece is now the moon. Can't nobody live on it 'cause it got no water on it. If anybody lands on it, his eyes will pop out, or sumptn." Then he adds as a closing clincher, "God Himself is a black man."

"I never said I was the smartest; I said I was the greatest," Ali once quipped after the Army rejected him twice because of a 1-Y classification (he subsequently was re-classified 1-A after the Army lowered its standards). That quick-witted rejoiner should have served as cue for those who condescendingly dismiss the champion as an intellectual featherweight or mere buffoon. Many of them should wish they were as "dumb" as Ali. At age eighteen, he was "dumb" enough to have himself signed to the most lucrative (50–50) contract ever negotiated by a beginning professional in boxing's history. It was a contract he signed with the Louisville Sponsoring Group consisting of twelve business-wise millionaires. Later, "dumb" Muhammad loud-mouthed himself into contention for the coveted title shot at a time when, by his own admission, he was No. 9 on the contender list.

Today, he displays the amazing memory of a Malcolm X for storing and recalling at will volumes of Muslim rhetoric. Although he clearly lacks the slain leader's command of English, polish, general knowledge and intellectual depth, Ali can be a formidable opponent in a verbal exchange.

To assess the champ's intelligence is to apply standardized measuring tools to a totally unstandardizable quantity – something akin to gauging happiness or anger with a measuring cup. Chances are that an IQ test capable of accurately calibrating Muhammad's strange blend of nimble-wittedness on the one hand and dogmatic one-track-mindedness on the other will never be devised.

What is true for Muhammad's intelligence can be said for his entire personality – it simply can't be pegged. Realizing this, a sportswriter once compared the mercurial pugilist's personality with "a jigsaw puzzle whose pieces were cut out by a drunken carpenter, a jumbled collection of moods and attitudes that do not seem to interlock." There is little doubt in the minds of those who have close contact with him that he is one of the most enigmatic, most difficult-to-define personages in the public limelight today. No opposites, it appears, are too far apart or too contradictory to be comfortably housed within the expansive psyche of Muhammad Ali. Thus he finds no difficulty in blending an almost ascetic frugality (some of his friends call it stinginess) with an Arabian oil sheik's extravagance. (Sample: He will have himself limousined to a cut rate Harlem restaurant decked out in a $300 suit to dine on a couple of $1.89 steaks.) An unrelenting, sometimes vicious bully in the ring (ask Floyd Patterson), he is all tenderness and affection whenever he meets little black slum children toward whom he seems irresistibly drawn. Ali will brag about his popularity, his importance in the world scheme of things, then efface himself, insisting that he would be nothing without "the Hon. Elijah Muhammad." Although his fierce militancy serves as model and inspiration for his fellow Black Muslims, Ali numbers among his close associates retired film actor Steppin Fetchit who earned millions with his deft portrayal of cringing, shuffling and dim-witted black stereotypes. Ali is a kidder who doesn't like to be kidded; a prissy Puritan with a roving eye for "foxes;" contemptuous of alcohol, he displays infinite compassion for drunks. He can be amusing or a monumental bore, super polite or super rude, boisterous or brooding and sullen. The contradictions go on and on *ad infinitum.*

Essentially, all of Ali's current problems have grown out of his stubborn refusal to fit himself into the role prescribed traditionally for a black heavyweight champion of the world. That role – eagerly sought and accepted by most of his predecessors – requires that the champ work tirelessly at being "a credit to his race" as defined by whites and white-washed blacks. It expects him to confine his opinions to matters of the ring, except when paying tribute to the system that allowed a kid from the slums to rise to prominence. In return for the proper enactment of his role, he is entitled to certain privileges and emoluments, including status, wealth, women (even white ones if that's what the champ prefers) and – above all – the unreserved adulation of white America.

The bitter disappointment of the boxing establishment with its wayward champ, who not only thinks for himself but has the temerity to say what he thinks is vented by Nat Fleischer, publisher of The Ring magazine and veteran boxing sage. Fleischer wonders why, despite the "magnificent and munificent return for his labors as a professional boxer, Clay (he refuses to refer to the champion by his Muslim name) saw fit to turn his back on Selective Service, on the Army, on defense of the nation which made him a rich man and a world champion, on boxing, which had made him a world figure." Hinting at some sinister "mystery" surrounding Ali, Fleischer predicts that in due time there will be an airing of what he calls "the strange story of the conversion of a fine, straight-forward, winning personality into an attacker of the Establishment of the United States of America."

The Nat Fleischers of America need not venture far for an answer to their "mystery." They will find it in the black slums of Louisville, Chicago, Kalamazoo, New Orleans, Houston, Cleveland, Los Angeles, Miami *ad nauseum.* They will find it in the eyes of little black slum boys – in the sullen looks which one day are bound to erupt in other shouts of defiance: "Damn all the money! A man's got to stand up for what he believes, even if he has to go to jail."

The Great Fixed Fight

Neil Allen

The Times, Thursday, 22 January 1970

Neil Allen looks at last night's computer match

They got to him in the end. Cassius Clay – Muhammad Ali, self-proclaimed "the greatest", and still undefeated heavyweight boxing champion of the world – was beaten by a computer on BBC television screens last night in the most unarguably fixed fight of all time.

In a dream contest brought to an uncanny kind of reality Ali was knocked out in fifty-seven seconds of the thirteenth round by Rocky Marciano, another undefeated heavyweight champion, at the end of a forty-five-minute programme which seemingly brought much of the excitement of a major occasion in sport to millions of British homes.

A few hours before Muhammad Ali had sat in one of the 1,000 theatres in the United States which were also showing the bout supposed to end all argument about who was the best ever. In down-town Philadelphia the big, brown young man, who can no longer get a match anywhere in the United States because of his refusal to serve in the Army, saw Marciano go down in the sixth round and then himself suffer knockdowns in the tenth and twelfth before the finish came from a sweeping left to the head.

Ali, like the public and all but three people connected with the film, did not know how the bout would end. He disagreed loudly when the computer made the eleventh round even and shouted: "If I lose, that computer was in Alabama."

Afterwards he said: "It takes a good champion to lose like that. Sure it upsets me. But it's just a fiction, a make-believe fight. People have seen me in the ring for the last time tonight. I will never fight again. The people would like to see me fight but the boxing officials and the politicians haven't got the guts."

Sadly he recalled that Marciano, who gave up the title in 1955, was killed in a plane crash last year, three weeks after the two men had completed their acting stint in Miami. "Rocky was my buddy and he really wanted to see the film," he added. Marciano is reputed to have received $50,000 for his part but Ali, through a guarantee and a percentage of the receipts, may earn more than $100,000.

The staged contest was the idea of Murry Woroner, aged forty-four, a sports enthusiast and communications expert who had already made a huge success of "all time" heavyweight and middleweight boxing eliminations on the radio.

The meeting of Ali and Marciano in the film studio was the result of the radio heavyweight series in which Ali was outpointed by Jim Jeffries and Marciano won the final from Jack Dempsey. Ali sued Woroner Productions for $1m. but the suit was settled for a dollar when Ali was promised a filmed bout with Marciano.

Marciano, by then forty-five, had to shed 40 pounds in weight before, wearing a toupée, he met Ali, aged twenty-seven, for rehearsals in Studio City, Florida, last year. The boxers filmed seventy-five one-minute action sequences covering a variety of possible situations and then the sections were put together as rounds. Evaluations of the undefeated careers of the two men, chiefly gathered from reports of their bouts and opinions of sports writers, were fed into a National Cash Register 315 computer.

I had felt cynical about what seemed a piece of gimmickry totally irrelevant to sport. But when I saw the BBC's film yesterday it was sometimes difficult to remember that it was not all real. Marciano looked much trimmer than seemed possible at his age and even if most of the blows to the head must obviously have been pulled the body attacks of both men carried conviction – even if I remain convinced that in real life Ali would have stayed away and won on points.

The knockdown punches were clearly identifiable. Ali is caught by the left hook with which the British champion Henry Cooper floored him, and Marciano is briefly toppled by a typically sharp right from Ali. The end, with Ali clutching desperately at the ropes as he tries to beat the count, reminded me clearly of the last seconds of Archie Moore against Marciano.

Of course when Marciano bleeds on the colour screen it is by permission of Heinz. Of course this "fight of the century" is not going to settle the endless saloon-bar debates traditional in the sport. But last night's entertainment, hailed by the BBC as "the most sensational fight of this electronic age", is certainly more engrossing than the first filmed boxing match. On that occasion, at the Edison Laboratories in 1894, champion Jim Corbett conveniently knocked out Peter Courtney "just before the film ran out".

PART 4
ONCE MORE
UNTO THE BREACH

Mr Anonymous is Angry,
But Not With Cassius Clay

Neil Allen

The Times, Saturday, 24 October 1970

After Beating Zora Folley on 22nd March, 1967 in New York, Ali would not box again professionally for three years while tangling with the draft board, the US government and boxing commissions across the country. He was stripped of his title and the undefeated champion was left in the boxing wilderness. In his absence, Joe Frazier became heavyweight champ with his fifth round knockout of Ali's former sparring Jimmy Ellis on February 16th, 1970.

On 26th October, Ali's exile from the ring was scheduled to come to an end when he was booked to step between the ropes to face Jerry Quarry in Atlanta, Georgia. Neil Allen, of The Times, *met with Quarry ahead of the hotly anticipated encounter.*

Mr Anonymous could normally be the nickname of Jerry Quarry the tough twenty-five-year-old Irish-American heavyweight who boxes Cassius Clay here on Monday over fifteen rounds for £68,000, glory and every status short of the official world title.

It has been uncharacteristic of Quarry that in the past few hours he should twice have become angered. First, over the statement by Governor Lester Maddox that the day of the bout should be a day of mourning in Georgia because the governor regards Clay as a draft dodger. Second, at the suggestion that the ringside doctor might be black because, said Quarry, he is worried about a facial cut stopping the contest.

The chunkily-built, thick-necked Quarry has a professionally dented nose and a small mouth which lets out words so quietly during television interviews that he seems a diffident, almost negative, personality. But after five hours of the humid gymnasium I found him relaxed and talkative as the final drops of sweat stained the wooden floor.

Now that Quarry had ended all his sparring with three rumbustious rounds of left hooking against a rapidly weakening opponent, I asked him: "What can you say in Clay's favour?"

Quarry said shortly: "He's a good boxer – very fast of foot."

"What about his limitations?"

Quarry, equally swiftly, responded: "He's a man, just like me. When he gets up in the morning he puts one leg into his pants and then the other."

If that sounds straightforward to the point of simplicity it still sums up the attitude of Quarry. In some ways he is just like the character in Simon and Garfunkel's song, "The Boxer", for he has known hard times and hard beatings. He is a fight fan's fighter, just as Cassius Clay is likely to appeal to the *New Statesman* reader who has never been to a boxing match in his life.

Quarry, whose great-great-grandparents came from Ireland, but who is also about one eighth Cherokee Indian, is regarded as one of the four best heavyweights in the world. But he does not disguise the fact that boxing is much more than a living for him.

"Yeah, I love to fight. Why? I guess I just like beating on people's heads. Maybe that's my way of getting out of myself."

On the other side of the gymnasium, Quarry's nineteen-year-old brother, Mike, unbeaten in twenty-three bouts as a professional light-heavyweight, had said: "Looking at Jerry today, I'm reminded of what the manager of your British champion, Eddie Avoth, said when I beat him over here. The manager said: 'I don't think you or your brother are afraid of anyone.' And we're not, you know."

Jerry Quarry is not a sadist, nor an unthinking animal. In the gymnasium, his two children and his attractive sister were always close to him while he sparred, skipped rope and shadow-boxed. If he ever raises his voice at all, it is with a preliminary warning cough. But for all his mild manners it is in the ring that he is happiest. Once he has started talking about boxing, it is hard to get him to stop:

"Well, I've boxed over a hundred and thirty rounds for this fight. I've got a fair kick in both hands and I've always fancied my chances against Clay. I've got very quick hands . . . and he knows it. I think I can get him in close and pin him around the body. I'm going to fight like an Irishman should, pressing him all the time and belting, him around the belly. I'm gambling his legs will go."

For a man who is feeling the tension more every hour now, he was generous about Clay's controversial position in American society. "What he's done or said outside the ring is his affair. My only beef with him concerns boxing matters, and that will be settled on Monday. I felt that it was unjust that he should have had his licence taken away. I've always said that a man should only lose his title in the ring, and not for his convictions. I think he should have joined the Services, myself, but I've got to respect his beliefs."

Quarry knows there is a great deal against him. But in turn, he says he is not worried about lack of inches ("I've often been shorter than my opponents"), claims he prefers being the underdog ("that puts the pressure on him and takes it off me"), and candidly admits he would rather box someone with the straightforward style of the heavyweight champion, Joe Frazier, than the elusive Clay.

"Frazier beat me and I learned that I should always fight my fight and not theirs. I went out to prove something to the people and tried to be strong and trade punches with Frazier. He hurt me. But you know, in the last round, before they stopped it, he wasn't punching hard any more. He'd almost punched himself out. But they stopped it because my right eye was closed.

"Frazier was the cleverest dirty fighter I ever met. He had the most talented elbows and head. But Floyd Patterson was the dirtiest of all. Mr Congenial, he seemed. But in the ring he was always trying something. He cut me with a lace, and I remember in our second fight that I had him down during a round and clearly after the bell he hit me with a good right hand.

"I've suffered four cuts, two by Patterson, and three knockdowns. One of those came from Patterson; but when they showed the film they couldn't detect the punch. I slipped."

Quarry finishes at last, thanks you for the interview, and the gym is suddenly empty.

Two hours before, the exit of Clay has been very different.

"Say, you still got Thad Spencer?" he shouted to the veteran manager Willie Ketchum. When Ketchum, a man not handicapped by sentimentality, replied: "No, but I got a guy who's going to fight him", Clay whooped incredulously.

"You're a crook," he yelled delightedly. "Soon as you's finished with one racehorse, you gets another. I'd love to be a manager, with a big belly and cigar and driving those fast cars."

Then, looking down at his brown body, he sighed. "Trouble is, they's nearly all Jewish." Everybody roared. For quick Jerry Quarry, the punchline would have been totally out of character. But then genius makes it own rules.

Sting Like a Bee

José Torres

The reference to cuts in Allen's interview was prophetic – Ali stopped the game and bitterly disappointed Quaryy on a cut at the end of the third round. Less than two months later he squared off opposite Oscar Bonavena in New York on 7th December. What follows comes from José Torres's Sting Like A Bee. *Those of a nervous disposition, be warned – the story contains scenes of violence and strong language from the outset.*

Oscar Bonavena is big and tough and has two words of English. They are "motherfucker" and "cocksucker". He is a white Argentinean and he is so strong he would probably argue that power is the only ingredient necessary to make good prize-fighters. While not as big and powerful as that other Argentinean, Luis Angel Firpo, el Toro de las Pampas, who once hit Jack Dempsey so hard that Dempsey landed in a sportswriter's lap, Bonavena is still a good puncher, who can always take a man out with one of his wild cannonball shots.

Two things these two paisanos had in common: they were both tremendously powerful with over-developed physiques and both possessed brains suitable for weightlifters. Their action in the ring depended entirely upon their physical mechanism. Whether training or in competition their brains lacked for use. That important muscle was always out of shape. But Bonavena had one thing that Firpo never had: balls. Bonavena was not an easy man to put down. Bonavena would put anybody into the most grueling test of them all: the test of wills.

Naturally, I felt Ali shouldn't be put into this kind of test so soon after Quarry. After all, Ali had gone only a total of three rounds in forty-three months; forty-three months of doing everything but boxing; for forty-three-months Ali's mind had been diverted. As a matter of fact, his restlessness seemed to be caused as much by what he wanted for blacks in America as for what he wanted of his own boxing career. Consequently, for all that time, Ali learned more about other problems, about the real problems confronting the Muslims of his country. His boxing thoughts; his fistic concentration was distracted.

Given his performance against Quarry, it would have been more logical, I thought, to match Ali with an older fighter like Floyd Patterson who probably couldn't offer any serious danger to Ali any more, or even a rematch with George Chuvalo who might sweat out some of Ali's present weaknesses without the risk (in my opinion) of a Chuvalo victory. But not Bonavena. Bonavena scared me.

I had boxed Bonavena a few years back in the gym. I knew a little about him, and his attitude inside the ring. And if what I knew was correct, Ali was in trouble. Let me analyze Bonavena a little.

You hit Bonavena and it's like giving food to a hungry man or electricity to a bulb. A punch to any part of Bonavena's body generates his desire to go on charging, punching, and asking for more, and that is, believe me, discouraging. This mule of a man violates in his own peculiar way, the basic of boxing. He doesn't follow at all the "I-hit-you-you-don't-hit-me" rationale. His philosophy seems to be, "You hit me and I hit you. Let's see who falls first."

The trouble with Bonavena is that getting hit doesn't concern him at all, to the contrary it appears as if your punches give him energy. So his theory is more: "Hit me and you generate my power, then I give *you* pain."

When I was in the ring with Bonavena, he assured me that he wasn't going to hurt me. "I'm much heavier," he had said, "and I know I shouldn't use my power on you."

"Use it," I remember answering, "but if you see that I'm hurt, then lay off." My ego began working. "If I hurt you," I continued, "I'll do the same."

After three rough rounds in which we went at each other with more than we normally thought to use in the gym the other boxers stopped their workout to watch this Torres-Bonavena war and gave us a tremendous applause at the end.

"I didn't hurt you, did I?" Oscar asked me.

"No, you didn't," I said. "Did I hurt you?"

He smiled. "You are not a bad fighter," he said. Puerto Rican kids in the gym came up to me to whisper what a beating I had given the Argentinean heavyweight. Of course it was not a beating. I hit him plenty in the body. Bonavena missed every left hook or straight right he used to my head. A couple of times if he had hit me with one of them, he would have killed me. I was really watching for his big weapons.

I had a lot of confidence in myself then and I thought that a Torres-Ali fight would be a most interesting fight. I thought I had a formula to beat Ali. But being honest with myself I knew it would not be easy. Now, years after, that Torres-Ali fight out of my mind, and me retired, I still thought that Bonavena was nonetheless too dangerous for Ali, and this even though I once thought I could have beaten Bonavena. A question of style. A question of soul. Because Bonavena had a hell of a big soul. You never knew if he was an angel or a devil. I didn't think of most fighters this way, I tried to keep them where they were – problems for me to solve. But Bonavena was the real stuff you could not give a name to.

For style is another of the intricacies of boxing. I always knew it, but I learned it again the hard way. A Cuban named Florentino Fernandez once won over me by a technical knock-out in the fifth. In turn, I beat my countryman José González. Yet González came back to knock out Fernandez. Yes, a question of style.

Besides – for Ali – Bonavena had an unhappy style. Besides being indestructible, Bonavena had a habit of throwing punches from every angle. He was a tropical storm that took unpredictable directions. Yes, I thought, no one knows where the next punch is going to come from. If you want to know how much will and heart your fighter has, and don't care too much about his looks, then match him against Bonavena.

But if you have doubt about your fighter's confidence and you love him, you don't put him in with Oscar. For Bonavena is a fighter who can't be discouraged or intimidated, nor can his will be destroyed. If you hit a man with your best shot, and he doesn't flinch, the thing to do is to keep hitting him until he falls. You have to keep doing it until the last second of the last round. Even if he still is not flinching, you might still have won the fight. But usually, when a man is hitting another man hard and continuously and the other man simply smiles and keeps coming at him, the man throwing the punches suffers. He can get discouraged, his will easily can leave him. And you have a loser. Besides, the ability to take punches as if he were a heavy bag and come bouncing back, is not the only thing Bonavena has. Bonavena also throws a lot of leather in those unexpected punches.

He punches hard. Very hard. I can refer to Joe Frazier. They had two encounters. In the first, on September 21, 1966, ten rounds, Bonavena dropped Frazier with a left hook in the fourth round. When the count reached eight and the referee waved them together, Bonavena hit him again, this time a straight right. Frazier went to the canvas again.

Two different punches had connected on Frazier's chin, each hard enough to send him to the canvas. Of course, he got up both times – he, too, had a will of iron – and, in fact, at the end of an unyielding, unruly, brutal fight, Frazier outpointed Bonavena. It had been close. Luckily for Frazier the fight was held in New York where scoring is by rounds. The two knockdowns only cost Frazier the loss of the round in which they occurred.

In California the story could have been reversed, for California scoring is by points and such a fight could, conceivably, have gone to Bonavena.

When they fought the second time, twenty-seven months later, Frazier had already won a version of the world's heavyweight crown. Pennsylvania was one of the few states in America which recognized Frazier as a champ. So Philadelphia, the champ's hometown became the site for his second defense of the title. The first had been against another Spanish fighter, Mexico's Manuel Ramos, who hadn't been able to take Frazier's savage attack past the second round.

The fight began with Frazier putting on his ever-present pressure. For ten rounds it looked as if Bonavena was going to be knocked out. But from the eleventh round on, Bonavena came back, became the dominant presence and made the fight. For the first time in all those rounds Frazier concentrated on defense. It had been the first time since the night he knocked out Buster Mathis in eleven rounds – for the world championship of New York, Pennsylvania and Massachusetts – that Frazier had gone over ten rounds.

So, for the second time, Bonavena threatened to beat Frazier. Yet, again at the end, with Frazier at the point of exhaustion, Bonavena had lost. His only consolation was that he had been the first to go the distance with Joe and had done it again, almost won again, not a poor showing when you consider that Frazier had a record of nineteen K.O.'s in twenty-two fights.

So it was likely that while Bonavena's unique style was hardly the kind of tune-up Ali needed, Bonavena had been the man who had given Frazier the most trouble, Ali and Dundee were probably looking to set up Ali's magic again. Ali is happy if, when he enters the ring to fight one man, he's actually fighting two – if he is also taking on his next opponent. If the opponent who comes after the opponent you're fighting has a lot of respect for your present opponent, then you're hitting the second man psychologically every time you hit the first one physically. And that builds confidence.

When a man has this kind of confidence, when he can look into future fights, then this man has a certain control over fear. Of course, no fighters admit fear. They call it butterflies or nervousness, or feeling shaky. Still, the kind of pressures fighters get are almost unbearable. But Ali went into a match with positive thinking. He was able to sleep well a week or two before fights, for Ali *knew* he was going to win and nothing can be better than that for a fighter's confidence. It seems true that the more fights you win, the more you're likely to win.

When one's confidence gets really solid, you begin to believe that you can only be defeated by accident.

So I used to worry about the possible accidents in a fight: a butt, a broken hand, and quickly my mind began eliminating them. A butt? My peek-a-boo style prevented the other man from using his head on my face. A broken hand? I could beat any man alive with the other working hand. That was confidence at its peak.

Ali and Dundee had this kind of confidence, or did they know?

I was wondering if their confidence was now built on a belief in Ali's magic rather than on the skill of his comeback technique.

December 7, 1970: It is the day of the Ali-Bonavena fight. At twelve Muhammad Ali and Oscar Bonavena are expected to be here. Three hundred people are moving around and they all want to observe the weigh-in. If you don't know that this is part of boxing's long routine, you could think that we are here waiting for the arrival of the President. There at the Felt Forum, a small arena situated to one end of Madison Square Garden, the majority of the crowd is from the press and the media. Every American radio, television, magazine and newspaper seems to have its representative here today. This is the time when both fighters come face to face in boxing trunks knowing that very soon they'll be throwing leather at each other; the moment when you see the other fighter bigger and stronger than you. And if the other guy shadowboxes and at the end throws a left hook to the air, you see him in better condition than you; and you see the punch he threw harder and faster than any one punch you ever threw. It's painful how your mind amplifies these situations. A fighter suffers in weigh-ins. Some can't even control themselves.

It happened to my last opponent. Minutes before the fight he was substituted for by a friend of mine (who happened to be there wishing me luck at the time the news came my opponent couldn't go on).

The problem had started at the weigh-in ceremony. My rival, after first taking a good look at me, complained of a bad right arm. Then he said it was his left one. The closer I got to him, the more pains and illnesses were uncovered. I knew what was going on. I had often felt the same way when younger, but had had control over my feelings. By fight time my rival had a bad case of diarrhea. I hadn't intended to go that far, but I had literally scared the shit out of him. Believe me, this is a common story and not an isolated case. A fighter on the day of a weigh-in and a fight goes through more than an actor on opening night.

Seeing boxing leeches everywhere I think about these things and I get angry the leeches are here. I can smell them miles away. Can they talk! Sometimes they persuade fighters. They start getting free tickets, then a couple of bucks. By the time you become a top contender you might just as well be addicted to this man. You find yourself asking funny questions, like: "Why am I giving this man two hundred bucks? What is he doing for me?" Yes, these men are here.

Now they talk with each other and with the kind of men that you see only at big fights because they have friends at the Commission's office and at Madison Square Garden; the ones with hangover written on their faces. These are the people with the cigars in their mouths and black hats. They spit on the floor while talking to you. They are the ones who get free loads at the Annual Boxing Writers' Dinner, at fight announcement luncheons, weigh-ins, victory celebrations and bars. These are the types that movie actors like to play in fight films. Well, here they are. Present.

Boxing writers, as usual, are sharing with each other their predictions. And making jokes. Just before fighters show up at weigh-ins the atmosphere is dull, with old boxing people, old boxing commissioners, repeating the same old stories. A retired fighter comes to these weigh-ins and often finds boxing writers asking the same old question: "How do you feel?"

What do they expect one to answer? That you don't feel good? That you are not in shape to return to the ring tomorrow?

Former champions are around. I see Gene Fullmer. A tough man. He was the world's middleweight champ with a style similar to Bonavena's. "Wow!" Gene says, "there are more people here than I saw in all my fights."

Yes, there are many people here. That's why the weigh-in is held here at this large place and not at the Commissioner's office, where most fighters have their weigh-in ceremony in New York. But this is a big one, and Ali is in it. Ali brings action into every phase of his fights: medical examination, weigh-ins, press conferences, the signing of fights, the announcements of fights. There is excitement wherever Ali is.

New York Boxing Commissioner Edwin Dooley is coming in. Only a few notice his presence. He says hello to some of the writers. He is whispering something to John Condon, Garden Publicist. You don't see the chairman at every weigh-in, he's saved for the big ones.

There is some commotion. Writers are walking toward the north side entrance of the Forum. One of the fighters is coming. I can't see. Someone says it's Bonavena. Another group of people are running toward the other side of the ring. I can see both fighters now. Ali is followed by Bundini Brown and Dundee and also a few Black Muslims who keep the crowd at a distance from Ali. Bonavena has two men with him. Both are Spanish, Puerto Ricans. Bonavena had signed with them and these two Puerto Ricans have been the last managers for Bonavena, who seems to have a manager for each of his fights. He doesn't get along with managers.

Just before the fighters' entrance, I was wondering if the Garden people or the commissioners were going to let them be near each other. At the Ali-Quarry weigh-in, the promoters didn't let the fighters be together. They were afraid that Ali, who always puts on a show at weigh-ins, could make a bad scene and spoil the fight.

Of course, promoters and commissioners remember that afternoon in Miami when Cassius Clay came in to the weigh-in and shocked everyone present by staging one of the most emotional put-ons ever done to boxing. At that time, Clay, who had talked himself into the championship bout with Sonny Liston, was the underdog in every betting parlor and in every newspaperman's head. At that time Ali did an incomparable job on Sonny Liston's arrogance. Liston was reduced to saying, "That boy is crazy."

They don't want none of that here. Here is New York, a respectable town engaged in serious business. Of course, here nobody expects a similar confrontation to the one in Miami, Bonavena can't understand too much English and as he told me in Spanish, "Ali talks too fast for me anyhow."

"Chi, chi, chi, chi," Bonavena screams at Ali now that they can see each other. Bonavena extends his right hand and rubs the thumb with a finger and keeps repeating "chi, chi." Now he surprises the audience. "Chicken," he says clearly in English. "Chi, chi, chi."

Everyone seems amazed. But I know what he is doing. Chi, chi is a way to call chicken in Spanish. His extended hand with the rubbing of the fingers means that he has corn in his hand for the chicken. "Chicken," Bonavena repeats, and Ali can't keep from smiling. In a few years, Bonavena has gotten a new word for his English vocabulary. Chicken. But he speaks good Spanish. "Tu eres *maricon*," he says now to Ali who knows what maricon means – queer. His ego, his machismo seems hurt, but he's a pro. He won't show it to us.

Bonavena pinches Ali and repeats the word maricon. Then he calls him "puta" and says, "Black! You stink!" Ali makes unhappy gestures as if Bonavena is crazy. Even through his cool, I can see he's angry.

Ali's traditional script has been tarnished. He was not expecting this kind of competition from Oscar. Ali, whose pre-fight programs always had worked with blacks doesn't seem to know what to do with white fighters. Not with this one, anyway. Bonavena, unlike many of Ali's past black competitors, does not behave in accordance with Ali's script. Bonavena is not taking the supporting actor bit as Ali always expects when he writes his scripts. It could mean trouble.

Nevertheless, Ali, who always sets the stage and tells his actors what particular part to take, had not been able in the past to penetrate white boxers. He didn't even try. He appeared to be standoffish whenever he met a white man inside the ring. I have a feeling now looking at him smiling at Oscar's remarks, that Ali is aware of his trouble with white fighters. He seems to accept that it is more difficult to psych out a white boxer.

Of course, Ali doesn't necessarily understand his own magic. He said on several occasions that Allah provides him with victories. But one thing is clear when he fights black fighters, he doesn't let Allah do all the work. For Muhammad Ali understands the black man in this country. That's why he psychs them. Ali goes to the root of his people, their culture, their customs, their suffering, their superstitions. It is a profound knowledge of many things that have to do with blacks. Because he understands them and can penetrate their thoughts, they become easier to defeat.

While his latest struggle has been to convince blacks that "black is beautiful," he always knew where to hit black opponents before fights. Some new variant of "black is ugly" is where he would hit them. "White fighters always give me more trouble than 'niggers,'" Ali told me many times.

Looking over the record books I can't find a heavyweight champion who in his first professional fight allowed his first opponent to go the limit. That is with the exception of Muhammad Ali who fought a white ex-cop from West Virginia, a washed-up fighter, who went the full six rounds with Ali. For a time, there seemed little difference in his subjection of white or black fighters, but after becoming champion, Ali again had more trouble with whites than blacks.

In his first defense, he had no difficulty in knocking out Liston in one. Against Patterson, people begged the referee to stop the one-sided match. After the opening round Floyd was fighting with a painful back. It was Canadian George Chuvalo who first gave Ali some trouble. After receiving hard shots to the body, Ali only won the fight by going fifteen tough rounds. Then came England's Henry Cooper who gave Ali trouble until the fight was stopped as a result of an ugly gash over Cooper's eye.

Against Brian London, a live punching bag, Ali had no trouble and knocked him out in three. But against unknown German fighter Karl Mildenberger, Ali had to wait until the seventh round before solving the German's awkward left-handed stance and even then, Ali seemed to keep having trouble until round twelve when Mildenberger fell under a continuous attack from Ali.

Ernie Terrell and Zora Folley, both black, were no contest for the young champion.

These results were not the work of a man who knew the style of these men; their faults or their strong points. He knew something that goes beyond the speed of the punches, beyond one's ability to avoid punches.

But here facing Oscar, Ali seems passive, he doesn't have the witty remarks, the outraged outburst. He is very quiet. Perhaps he smells trouble, perhaps he's not worried, perhaps he's saving his energy for tonight.

I think that the three-and-a-half years he was off made a different man out of him. His behavior is similar to that shown in Atlanta. Is it because he has fallen in another bag, or is it because the Black Muslims warn him off from psyching white devils?

Well, he probably doesn't want to waste words and witty remarks on a man who wouldn't understand them. For his part, Bonavena doesn't care. He talks Spanish to Ali as if Ali understands him . . . or the reporters, who with the exception of three of us, don't understand Spanish either.

This weigh-in ceremony is nothing in comparison with Ali's previous ones in Miami with Liston, in Las Vegas with Floyd or in Houston with Terrell. Condon announces Ali's weight as 212; Bonavena's as 204.

The ceremony is over and both fighters are leaving Felt Forum. They are going back to their respective hotels to pretend they are going to rest.

Now the thinking, the real thinking begins. Now the fighters will picture how the fight is going to go. Bonavena, the proud Argentinean, full of machismo, will probably picture his victory with Argentina going crazy. It is really something to dream about a victory over Ali. He is the most important athlete since Joe Louis.

Ali will have people in his room and he'll be talking and demonstrating, against an invisible opponent, how Bonavena is going to fall. That's the way Ali releases his tension.

Will he start the fight by doing the same thing he did with Quarry? Go all out in the first?

Muhammad Ali has done it again. You can't get one more soul in this place. And when Madison Square Garden is full of people, the excitement is outrageous. And then, Ali brings a special crowd to his fights. There are more blacks here dressed with fancy clothes than there were in Atlanta, but somehow they look less conspicuous. New York changes scenes.

If you go by the ringside seats and begin to ask people what's a jab, a right cross, or an uppercut, they might think you are talking about drinks. Many ringside people come here to show off. Others to pretend. Seventy-five dollars for a ringside seat! The place is full of people, people who can afford to be here and people who will not eat for the next few days, and people who pawned their best jewelry just to be here tonight.

Argentineans living in New York seem to be all here and they are chanting from two different sections. They are sitting a few rows back of the ringside seats.

Oddly enough, this crowd reminds me of the people who only come to Golden Gloves; a special crowd. They can name you any of the Golden Gloves champions in any given year.

I won the New York Golden Gloves in 1958 and I went to the 1966 Golden Gloves finals in the old Madison Square Garden, and people began to remind me about that wonderful year when I won the tournament. Then they would ask, "What ever happened to you? Did you quit the game?" Not knowing that I'd just won the *world's* light heavyweight crown a few months before.

Something like that characterizes the crowd we have here now. They only come to big events, and as in the Golden Gloves where whites root for whites, and blacks for black fighters rather than dividing on which side they bet their money, so, tonight, you can tell whites will be rooting for Oscar.

I'm sitting in the fifth row, behind the press row and Ali looks good from here. Bonavena walks around and waves to some of his countrymen who come toward the ring to tell him in Spanish how to beat Ali. "Ringo," one of them screams at Bonavena, "keep on top of him and throw punches. You're too strong for him." Bonavena shakes his head yes. Smiles. Many people call Bonavena Ringo, because his hairdo is similar to the Beatles' Ringo. And Bonavena, like a few other fighters, Muhammad Ali included, has joined the music world and has made some recordings in Argentina.

Here the music is different; if you are to play good music, you have to maintain the rhythm yourself and spoil the other man's rhythm. I bet that Ali won't be able to keep his rhythm. Bonavena won't let him. As referee Mark Conn gives the instructions, Ali's lips move. Maybe Angelo taught Ali some Spanish. Bonavena smiles through the mouthpiece. I look at both fighters' stomachs and like with every other fighter, they tremble. Both fighters move their bodies as if to keep warm, but as they listen to the referee's instructions, they move to relieve the pressure. Now they walk back to their respective corners.

Ali stops, faces his corner, extends both hands, palms up. Now he closes his eyes and begins to pray. The man with the bell seems to be waiting for Ali to end his Black Muslim ritual. As Ali's hands move down and his body turns toward the ring, the bell rings. Again, I feel that funny feeling in my stomach.

Ali walks to the middle of the ring, now slides to his left and feints. Bonavena's body moves down to evade the punch that never came. Now Ali slides to his right. He is moving good and seems in control. Everyone is quiet.

Bonavena rushes Ali. Ali moves back and makes a swift move to his left and feints again. Bonavena's short arms move to block the punch that should have gone to his face. There was no punch to block. Ali smiles. Bonavena rushes again and throws a wild left hook. Ali steps back.

Ali seems in control. And he looks good while moving with class, sometimes by the book. Bonavena now runs toward Ali like a bull attacking the bullfighter. Ali, just like a banderillero, moves to one side and instead of putting in the sticks simply pushes Bonavena against the ropes and heaves Bonavena's head between the third and fourth ropes. Ali is signaling the Argentinean that the ring is here, not there.

Bonavena comes back. He is mad. People laugh and the Argentineans chant in Spanish: "Rin – go. Rin – go."

Bonavena charges Ali again. This time Ali gets hit with punches that appear to have hit him below the belt. Ali stops to complain. The referee signals Bonavena to bring his punches up. Bonavena shakes his head and walks toward Ali who moves continuously. I didn't like Ali's complaint to the referee. That's lack of professionalism. A boxer is there to do the fighting. It's the referee's job to restrain any man he sees who accidentally or purposely breaks the rules.

As the bell ends the first round, Ali makes a military about-face and Bonavena walks sloppily toward his corner.

I'm getting ready to walk toward the press row to give my friend Pete Hamill some of my quick impressions of the first round and I hear a man saying: "That fuckin' Argentinean looks like a fire hydrant. And walks like one."

Many writers bang at their typewriters as I kneel to whisper to Hamill that perhaps the six to one odds in favor of Ali are justi-fied. Obviously, I had thought that the ones responsible for those odds were crazy.

I discussed the fight with Pete many times before tonight, and now Pete seems to have a question mark on his face. "The old Ali is back," Pete says. I nod yes.

The ten-second whistle sends me back to my seat. Angelo is now leaning against the ropes and whispers instructions to Ali. In the other corner Oscar says yes with his head at everything his trainer says.

The bell. Audience is more relaxed now. You can hear some noises. Everyone is analyzing the fight. My two younger brothers just came down from their cheap seats to kneel in the aisle beside me. Both are amateur fighters. One, Rambert, is rooting for Ali. The other, Tony, wants Bonavena to win. The Spanish blood, he had explained. I have two brothers here. One thinks like a white tonight the other like a black.

In the ring Ali maintains his posture. He is the king. Bonavena keeps trying to penetrate Ali who moves as in the previous round, and presents a difficult target.

A jab. Another one. Now he moves back. Ali is good tonight. Was I wrong! Ali throws a one-two combination and both punches land on Oscar's head. Rambert jumps up to applaud. I look at some white faces ringside and they seem to be resigned to another victory for the "loud mouth."

The bell catches Ali evading a wild left hook and a round-house right hand.

Whites are quiet and so is my brother Tony. Ali is handling Bonavena like a baby. The old moves have come back to Ali and he's going to be a tough man to defeat tonight. True, Oscar has landed a few shots that would never have hit Ali at his best, but still in comparison with the Quarry fight, Ali seems to be ready for Frazier, the other man in the ring tonight. Ali is probably looking at Frazier in his mind instead of at Oscar.

At the bell, Pete looks back and gives me the victory sign. We are pulling for Ali.

Now it is the third round and Ali begins to do exactly as he did in the previous two rounds. He moves and flicks left jabs. Oscar also does exactly as he did in rounds one and two, he charges, sometimes with control, most times with anger. One thing he does which I think many of us so-called smart fighters never do: he misses and keeps trying. He misses some more and keeps trying. He doesn't get frustrated. Any change in Ali's pattern and then we would see why Bonavena tries and tries and tries.

Oscar keeps up the pressure. He swings stiff punches like a mad man. What patience! Bonavena seems to be saying to himself: "Don't worry, we'll catch up." And he charges again. The elusive Ali still moves like in the first. He pushes Oscar around. Oscar charges, Ali steps to the side and pushes Oscar again. Pressure doesn't seem to bother Ali as I had expected, although he himself is not punching much.

Of course I expect Ali to be a little slower in later rounds, but I expect the same from Oscar. So their deterioration will be relative. Which means that Ali will win this fight going away. I see no reason why Ali should change his pattern.

Ali misses a good right. Very seldom does Ali lead with a right, but he did. It looked good, even missing. A left jab hits Oscar. Ali backs off. Ali throws two fast jabs. Oscar bends and hits Ali in the belly. Ali moves away toward his corner and now turns his back to Oscar and walks two steps to his corner with the sound of the bell.

"There is no way for Bonavena to beat Ali," Rambert says to me and Tony. "He's something tonight. Better than ever." Tony doesn't answer. I make believe I can't hear. "I told you," Rambert continues, "Ali is Ali."

There is not much excitement. The fight is going as expected. Ali is playing with Oscar and blacks are relaxed. They are winning too. So they simply enjoy the evening. Ali's victories win more than simple fights in side rings. Blacks are conspicuously quiet. No words are necessary when their man is doing it with his fists a few feet away. So the lack of excitement is a combination of the disappointment of Bonavena's followers and the comfortable acceptance of Ali's crowd.

We can all hear the bell to start the fourth. Again; there goes Oscar. He wants to hit and be hit. His hands are lower than before. Ali jabs and crosses with a right. The jab hits. The right cross misses. Oscar walks in. A left hook is blocked by Ali. Oscar throws another hook, again Ali blocks it. Ali is not moving like before. He is no longer on his toes. Now they are both in the middle, of the ring, and for the first time they get inside. Man-to-man. They in-fight. Ali has changed.

Rambert looks at Tony. Tony looks straight into the ring. Ali is being hit in the body. He remains inside. Bonavena is happy.

The movable target has stopped. Bonavena smiles. His man is right in there with him. The latter part of the Quarry second round is back with Ali.

He is now against the ropes and Bonavena pounds away. The crowd is on their feet. This action is Bonavena's first threat to Ali's dominance. The sleeping crowd has awakened. The white man is hitting the nigger.

However, Bonavena's punches don't make contact with Ali's vulnerable spots. Not yet.

Ali has given up something under the continuous pressure. I think it's a matter of confidence. Hamill turns his head to look at me. Rambert jumps up and shouts instructions at Ali. Tony smiles while he fixes his glasses. Happy white faces surround us. The Argentineans come alive. In fact, they are running around with the special cops pushing them back to their seats. Now the Argentineans chant again. Some of the whites chant with them.

Bonavena is banging Ali. Ali blocks a wicked left hook to his right side with his elbow. Bonavena connects with a looping right to Ali's face. You don't see this too often. Ali's face touched? Another right lands on his face. Ali now tries to move out of the ropes and Bonavena pushes him back. Bonavena punches furiously. Bonavena the unorthodox is throwing crazy punches. He punches down. He pulls one hand back and punches with the other. He extends his left for measurement and shoots the wildest uppercut I've ever seen. Bonavena uses his peculiar, strange style. It is not that he is unpredictable; we know that he is going to throw these types of punches. The trouble is that fighters are not used to standing in front of awkward swings.

Ali throws a flurry of punches. Not hard, just to distract Oscar who seems impossible to distract. Oscar has his chin down, against his chest, and keeps punching at Ali. Some of the punches miss, some don't. The bell. People applaud the fighters. "The people liked this round," Tony mumbles to Rambert. "Bullshit," Rambert says, "these whiteys want Ali to get killed." Tony laughs and I go to see Pete.

"He's tired," Pete tells me. "I think he's in trouble."

"He is not tired. He is losing confidence," I say.

An English writer in the next seat agrees with Pete. "No doubt," the English writer says, "Ali is tired."

For a man supposedly in top physical condition, Ali should not be tired. He has no reason to be tired. He is an old pro, and old pros don't succumb to pressures and that's all Bonavena is giving. Ali's confidence is what is affected. He is disconcerted because Bonavena has not been paying attention to Ali's punches. Oscar comes right back. Only one thing is pushing Ali to the ropes and that's frustration. For three rounds, Ali pulled and pushed and kept himself away from the ropes. Why now?

It is not that Bonavena is getting better. Oscar is unchangeable. He does the same thing over and over, he just waits for his rival to "get tired" or waits until his man gives up. You check Bonavena's record and you can understand why thirty-seven of his forty-five opponents have not been able to finish on their feet. Bonavena's refusal to step back is a good formula; a good compensation for the stillness of his brain.

One thing is sure, Bonavena no longer looks like the six-to-one underdog. Don't forget, if Bonavena connects good he might finish this fight. It was not for kicks that he knocked George Chuvalo down. In fact, he has been the only man to drop the Canadian.

Forty seconds have passed in the fifth round. It is a copy of round four. Ali is now against the ropes again. Oscar is striking everything; arms and gloves, body and head. A tremendous right chop misses Ali by an inch. People make sounds of amazement. Bonavena stands square in front of Ali, his body pushing forward, his hands moving from every angle toward no particular spot. Bonavena just wants to make contact with any part of Ali's body. Ali seems to look for a rest. Oscar doesn't let him.

Ali throws a soft flurry of punches, each one hits Bonavena around his head. It provokes no change. Bonavena keeps coming. Ali remains against the ropes. A right by Bonavena hits Ali flush on the mouth. There is the bell and Oscar throws one more right that misses.

Rambert is shouting instructions to Ali who is now sitting on his stool, breathing hard. Angelo doesn't stop talking. Bundini Brown is massaging Ali's back with a wet sponge. They are obviously worried. Bonavena has probably won the last two rounds.

In the Garden, the sense of commotion is building. I can feel it in the seats. There is no longer the quietness of the first three rounds. I feel the commotion. Round six begins. Silence.

Bonavena comes to Ali. Ali waits for him with a jab. A right. Another jab. Ali is close to the ropes again. Ali says something to Oscar. Oscar smiles. Ali throws one, two, three jabs. Now a left hook and a right. The right hits Bonavena on the forehead. I couldn't see if the left hook made contact. Bonavena chases Ali, who moves backward and to the side. Ali has become again, as in the first three rounds, a moving target. Hard to connect. Oscar keeps walking in patiently waiting for Ali to stop.

But now Ali stops only to throw punches. Oscar tries to counter, but Ali is not there. Oscar keeps up the pressure. Ali moves, not as fast as he once did, but moving fast enough to prevent Oscar from coming close. Ali punches and moves. He is doing it beautifully.

When a boxer punches, the other one concentrates on evading the punches. If you punch and move, by the time your opponent gets set you are not there. Ali is doing that now.

Tony complains. I don't know why but people are booing Ali. "This Bonavena is dumb," Tony says. "He's following Ali around. He should cut the ring short." Ten seconds to go and Bonavena charges. Ali is too far from Bonavena to hit him or to be hit. Ali throws a one-two combination which misses over Oscar's head. Both fighters get inside for the first time in this round. The bell catches the referee as he separates the fighters.

Not many punches were thrown in the last round. I score for Ali. It was a dull round, the dullest so far, but I thought Ali was coming back to being himself. He's probably doing what he did to Mildenberger. Took his time to figure the German out. He might be doing the same with Oscar.

If he does, it would be impressive. With Bonavena you have to content yourself with hitting him once in a while and keeping away from his attacks. You can't waste time working out a plan for Oscar. This man is impossible!

That was the bell for round seven. Bonavena comes out slowly. Ali meets him. A right, a hard one, hits Oscar just below his forehead. Ali throws a left hook, another right, steps back and comes in again with a jab – right cross combination. Oscar tries to counter but Ali returns a hard left hook, and a right uppercut that catches Bonavena on the chin. Bonavena's mouthpiece flies in the air. Ali hits and his punches seem fast and hard. Ali steps back, as if to watch Oscar falling down.

Oscar smiles again. He maintains the same pace. Nothing has happened. Indestructible Oscar keeps coming in. Ali moves. I look straight at Ali and he seems worried. Bonavena is charging and the clock says that there are forty seconds left to the end of the round. Ali is against the ropes. Bonavena forgets about Ali's face, and throws every punch to Ali's body.

Many times when a fighter gets hit on any part of the face there is no pain. But if you want to give pain to your rival, the thing to do is to hit him in the body: in the hanging ribs, in the solar plexus, in the liver. It is painful and many times scary.

I've hit fighters in their bodies with so much force that they couldn't help but let out an involuntary groan like a wounded wolf. Usually the man who connects will jump at the hurt fighter with more punches. I never attacked after such a punch. I used to step back and let my rival savor every second of pain. I was not only a sadist but a technician; I know how discouraging those punches were to the body. I became world's champion by throwing one. A left hook to the liver.

So, that's probably what Bonavena is doing now. He seems desperate as he pounds in all kinds of punches to Ali's body. Ali is leaning on the ropes, making every effort to diminish the force of the punches. His elbows block many, but some of Bonavena's uppercuts are getting through.

I run toward Pete. "He's in trouble," I say. Pete watches closely and nods his head. "He can't figure this guy out," Pete answers as he looks at the action in the ring. A wild Bonavena hook lands in Ali's hanging ribs at the bell. Close round but I think Ali won it.

Tony stays in my seat while Rambert comes to the press row to analyze the fight with Pete, the English writer, and me.

The only trouble with analyzing fights is that I have to do all the talking. "Ali is in serious danger of losing," I begin. "Tricks don't work with Bonavena and the more tricks Ali tries, the more frustrated he gets. He has to stop that. The only thing he can do is move and punch; punch and move. If he wants to trick him, that's the trick to use. The only trick." I look at my pad. I have Ali winning rounds one, two, three, six and seven. But Oscar's pressure is starting to pay off.

"Move, Ali," I shout. Bundini signals me not to worry.

While we wait for round eight, I'm thinking this is a very important round. Ali had predicted on a television show, that Oscar was going to fall in nine. So he'll probably come out throwing more leather to soften Oscar. If he's going for the kill in round nine, he has to do some mollifying in the eighth. My thoughts are disturbed by the bell. Round eight.

Surprisingly, Bonavena is the one who increases the attack. Ali tries to move back. He can't. Bonavena is swinging terriffic shots to Ali's body. The crowd stands. Oscar is punching with fury. He pushes Ali. He has Ali against the ropes again. Once more, Ali is in trouble. A special cop is pulling me and my brother from the press row. No one is allowed to scream from the press rows and we are going wild shouting instructions to Ali and yelling at him to move. I want Ali to do the same thing he did in the first couple of rounds; to move to the side and to push Oscar toward the ropes. Tony screams that Ali is too tired. "Bonavena has the victory in his pocket," Tony says.

Bonavena pounds on Ali. Ali becomes the stationary target again. He is there for Bonavena to swing at him. Fifteen seconds to go and Bonavena is having a party with Ali. Oscar throws a flurry. The bell. Big round for Bonavena.

"This is the round," Rambert says. "Ali will knock this guy's brains out."

"What fight are you watching?" asks Tony.

One thing we should all expect. Ali is going to try to fulfill his prediction. The first time he had been embarrassed was in New York, in the old Madison Square Garden. The night he predicted he was going to knock Doug Jones out in six. He failed and won a very close decision. He might try harder this time. But so far, Ali is getting the worst of the exchanges. And we all know that Ali doesn't like to get hit.

The bell for the ninth.

Blacks stand up. No one dares to complain. If a black is blocking your view, get up too. Can't complain.

Ali charges. A right hits Oscar. Ali is flat-footed. He's looking for power. A jab and a right hit Oscar again on his face. Oscar misses. Ali connects with a tremendous right to Oscar's chin. Bonavena is stunned. Ali is really trying to end the fight now.

Perfect shots like the one that just hit Oscar tend to give one a feeling of thousands of ants running through one's body. One loses control over legs and hands momentarily. This feeling lasts for perhaps one to three seconds. We call it being shook up.

Ali goes for the kill. His perceptive eyes have seen what many of us saw. Wow! Bonavena just hit Ali coming in. Bonavena is throwing rights and lefts to Ali who seems hurt by Oscar's right. Ali fights back now. An exchange. Both fighters are connecting. They are swapping terrific punches. Strangely, Bonavena is against the ropes. They are still swinging. Oh! Indestructible Bonavena is down. Half of his stocky body is outside the ropes. Referee Conn says there was no knockdown. It was a slip. Oscar's gloves are being cleaned by Conn. Ali comes. The trade continues. A wild left by Oscar. Ali is almost down, and the crowd is up on their feet.

What a round! The fighters are still in there and they are punching savagely at each other. It's hard to describe every punch, but Ali has never been hit like this before. Oscar and Ali both seem tired. Oscar connects. Now Ali comes back with a left hook-right cross combination. Not too much power. There is the bell. Both fighters are swinging. Referee Conn breaks them apart. About six punches are thrown after the bell. It was an even round. No, I think Ali won it. Close.

Ali is wrong again. People boo. Argentineans chant again. Bonavena had one little victory. Ali's predicted round is over and *he* was the one who almost got knocked out. I've never seen Ali hurt this much. He was in bad shape. He showed guts. All those so-called experts who always said that Ali had no balls have just been proven wrong. Of course, I think Ali was wrong in trying to accomplish his prediction. Amateurs do that. But perhaps he had his reasons.

My two brothers are happy. They both predict that their favorite is going to win. And they're saying that the other man was at the edge of being knocked out. They are both right.

Believe me, four years ago this would have never happened. Ali's head is not right. How can this happen? How can a fighter like Bonavena, whose only major ingredient is toughness, give Ali so much trouble? Something must be wrong with Ali.

Round ten just started. Bonavena is pressing but not with the same drive as before. Ali is backing up flat-footed. A turtle follows a turtle. Twenty-five seconds have passed and not a single punch has been thrown. Both fighters are showing the effect of the blows they traded in the previous round. They are saving energy. Ali throws a lazy jab. Bonavena slowly increases the attack. Ali is tired. The crowd is now pulling for Bonavena again. But Oscar seems weary. They are both coasting trying to recover. Four hundred and sixteen pounds struggling together, looking to recover every muscle and nerve. Having been pounded over and over, it is not an easy thing to recover in one minute.

People boo Ali who moves back slowly with Oscar chasing him drowsily. No style now. Ali just walks backward. When Bonavena makes a move, Ali extends both his arms. This round is much worse than the sixth. Ali keeps walking sloppily back. Oscar follows like a drunken bear.

Physical tiredness has a limit. When a fighter is in good physical condition he tends to breathe fast the first minute he encounters physical effort. Then he reaches a balance and can punch and move and punch and even get hit, but his level of tiredness is not affected. For Oscar that seems to be the case. He can't get more tired than he is now. I have my doubts about Ali, however, because Ali's confidence is involved here. When confidence is affected the level of tiredness starts being determined by the mind, not the body.

Of course, one is exhausted after a fight is over. That's to be expected. A fighter can enter the ring at ten one night, and knock his opponent out in one round. At twelve, the winner is going to be "dead tired" and not because of the energy he used in the ring, but because the tension of two or three months training is leaving his head and body.

But the assumption here is that if this fight keeps going on the way it is now, Ali will be more tired than Oscar.

In the ring there is no action. People boo Ali. He's causing the dullness of the fight. He is also preventing Oscar from connecting solid blows. Professional Ali doesn't let the crowd bother him. He should be well ahead on the score cards.

There is the bell and people boo. I think the judges might give the round to Oscar. But it was about even.

Round eleven finds Ali leaning against the ropes. Oscar is throwing awkward punches to Ali's body. Ali tries to push Bonavena but as far as Ali is concerned, Bonavena now weighs two tons. Bonavena, this far along in the fight is one heavy mass. Oscar is shoving his body through Ali's extended arms. Not a punch has been thrown by Ali. He is tired.

Bonavena is doing the pushing now. He sneaks a left to the body. Bonavena takes a look at the clock. Twenty seconds are left until the end of this dull round. Bonavena opens up with lefts and rights to Ali's still body. The bell. And people applaud. Another Bonavena round.

It goes on like that. The thirteenth is like the twelfth and the fourteenth like the thirteenth.

Three rounds have passed: I'm looking at my pad, and it makes me nervous. I have Ali ahead seven to six, with round ten even. Of the last five rounds I have given Ali only one, the thirteenth and that one was close. Ali seems to be hanging there. His magic is not working.

Rounds twelve and fourteen were easily Oscar's rounds. Similar to the eleventh. A big fifteenth round for Oscar could provide a tremendous upset, as far as boxing experts are concerned.

At the bell, both fighters walk slowly toward the center of the ring. Conn makes them touch gloves. It is a tradition. The touch of the gloves for the last round.

Bonavena charges, Ali moves back. They both seem a little fresher. They know it's the last round. They're probably prepared to go all out. Bonavena throws a wild hook, then launches a right, and Ali steps back and jabs. Bonavena keeps the pressure on. He feels he can win this fight if he can capture this round convincingly. He throws another right that lands on Ali's left shoulder. Bonavena is hunting. The round is one minute old. Ali tries to move on his toes. Bonavena presses. Bonavena jabs. Bonavena walks menacingly to Ali. He throws another of his awkward left hooks. Ali pulls back. Bonavena prepares to shoot a right. Ali waits. Bonavena telegraphs his right. Ali steps in with a wicked left hook. It beats Oscar's right. Oscar's legs wobble. Indestructible Bonavena is going down! His eyes stare at the ring lights. His body falls. Bonavena is badly hurt. He is up, his eyes are glassy. He's up, but his legs refuse to stay straight. Ali is coming. Ali hits. He doesn't seem tired now. Ali is connecting. Oscar's body is down again.

Referee Conn does not send Ali to a neutral corner and Ali happily remains close to Oscar, who is now struggling to get up. Oscar's body is rolling. He's walking like a wounded dog. Arms and legs move on the floor as he tries to stand up. Conn follows him counting with mouth and with fingers.

A towel is thrown into the ring. It came from the direction of Oscar's corner. Powerful Bonavena is finally up. I think Conn counted to nine. Ali is right on top. A left hook and a right hit Bonavena on the forehead. Bonavena is out on his feet. Another left by Ali. Bonavena is down. The fight is over. It's a technical knockout; three knockdowns in one round and the fight is automatically over.

The magic of Ali. The magic of Ali. Nothing else. Indestructible Oscar is looking, but not looking at Ali who moves with his hands high and now embraces Bundini. The fight is over. Just when every black in the place thought Ali was finished, he came back. To a dull, unexciting match, Ali provided a fantastic ending. It has to be the magic of Ali. What else?

One of the worst fights in which Ali has been involved became an interesting match in two minutes and three seconds of the last round.

That quick, unexpected left hook by Ali is going to convince many people to think that Frazier – who in fact is a hard guy to hit clean – will be easy to take out with that type of punch. Ali shouldn't listen to them. Ali should try to get his confidence back by fighting a couple of stiffs. But, of course, he is going on to Frazier next.

PART 5
SMOKIN' JOE

Soul Music in Frazier's Workshop

Rex Bellamy

The Times, Tuesday, 16 February 1971

"MARCIANO REINCARNATED IN BLACK" PREPARES TO FACE CLAY

The gymnasium, just the sort of place you could pass without noticing stands in the shadow of a railway bridge on a dingy stretch of Broad Street, which carves a 10-mile groove down the length of Philadelphia from Cheltenham in the north to the United States Navy Yard, the Delaware River, and Gloucester County in the south.

A small notice reads "Training headquarters for Joe Frazier, heavyweight champion". Another suggests "One dollar admission to training" if you want to get out of the rain. But no one bothers about the money. A dollar cannot mean much to the entourage of a man already guaranteed two and a half million of them (over £1m.) for his next fight – against Muhammad Ali, otherwise known as Cassius Clay, in New York on March 8.

Inside, all is drably, almost clinically, clean: unadorned brick walls, a newly panelled ceiling, and no furniture that is not essential to the function of the place. "It's the best gym in the east", says Yancey Durham, Frazier's manager. In addition to sparring partners and handlers, there are maybe forty onlookers, lined up silently against the wall, as though they think it unwise to be in the target area when things start happening. Everyone is waiting.

A thickset man, in a green dressing gown and black, monk-like cowl, bounces briskly down the bare staircase. Frazier is ready. He strips to a T-shirt and a pair of long, close-fitting, green woollen pants, and climbs into the ring. For the next hour he never stops moving. Sweat streams from every rippling muscle. He is only 5ft. 10in. tall, but built like a tank. In his younger days they said he was too short, and "bottom heavy". Now they talk about his neck, chest and thighs.

Ken Mugler, a public relations man and local boxing buff, says: "This guy is like Marciano reincarnated in black. He just keeps coming. He wouldn't know how to quit." They know Frazier here. He is a local man, his home just a few miles from the gymnasium. Clay, too, has been living in Philadelphia.

Frazier shadow boxes, then has a total of five rounds with three different partners: middleweight, light-heavyweight, and heavyweight. The men who are working with him include Willie "The Worm" Monroe and Pete "Moleman" Williams, who sound as if they came straight out of Runyon. Today Frazier is concentrating on speed. Durham, timing him to the second, tells him exactly when to land body punches. Frazier keeps coming forward, like a fidgety bulldozer without a reverse gear. In a confined space like a boxing ring he cannot be eluded for long.

More shadow boxing, then over to the speed ball. Durham makes him swing and duck his shoulders. Frazier's children come across to say hello. He stops and stoops to plant kisses on them. More shadow boxing, this time in front of a full-length mirror. Finally, out flat on a table, repeatedly sitting up fast and twisting his torso as he does so. His feet are held by a handler.

Other men are working around him and the *mélange* of noises is unique – recorded blues-rock soul music, jangling ceaselessly to match Frazier's own jump and verve ("He can't seem to do without it", said one observer); the slap of leather on leather from all round the gym as Frazier and the rest go about their work: and the grunts of hard physical effort. No voices, just the sounds of fighters in their workshop.

Frazier sings with a night club group, The Knockouts, who have a fast show of uninhibited soul music. He is said to have a genuine talent for the business. But how did "Try a Little Tenderness" get into the training repertory? Maybe he has to remind himself that his fast but light sparring partners are to be evaded rather than clobbered.

The man is all quivering, restless energy. "There's a certain frenzy about him in training that I don't think I've seen in any other fighter", says Bud Collins, of the *Boston Globe*. Frazier's intensity is frightening. This, you feel, is what men must have been like in the days when they had to catch and kill their dinner before eating. You remember that Frazier was cutting meat in a slaughterhouse when Durham spotted his potential as a fighter.

Every day the routine is the same. In the mornings he runs five miles in Fairmount Park, supposedly the largest park within city boundaries anywhere in the world. Later, the gymnasium. "The work don't get no easier", says Frazier. "I feel like I'm in top shape. But the more shape I get in, the harder I work." His words are difficult for British ears to follow.

Someone tells him Clay is boxing 10 to 15 rounds a day. "He's working unnecessary hard. What's he trying to do – kill himself already? Before he get out there, he may fall on his face. He don't need to train all that hard because the fight isn't going the distance.

"I'm pretty sure I'm a better fighter than he is. And I don't think he's going to be able to rough me up. I know all them tricks and I got a few tricks myself. I don't think I'll change my style. I just go out there and do my thing."

Inevitably, he is asked about Clay's role in the Black Power movement. "I don't believe in all that black stuff. I believe every man should think what he wants to think and do what he wants to do. If there's anything I can do to help black people, or help anybody, I'll do what I can. What we want today is that everyone should be together as one. Preachin' it don't mean a thing. Making a lot of noise and talking about what you do don't mean you're a good-hearted fellow or a good man. You got to go out and do.

"He talk about what a true brother is. Tell him to look at me. I'm a true brother. I'm for real. Right? You tell him to get ready. You give Clay a message: tell him to take it easy and don't get nervous. I'll be there on time."

Incidentally, the official measurements for the first time include "mouth normal" and "mouth expanded". In this department, Frazier finishes second.

This is an even-money match. Madison Square Garden is ready for a record live gate of $1,250,000 (£520,000) and nationwide theatre television may run from £4m. to twice that sum. At least one man is offering up to £1,650 for a ticket. The

New York Times says: "The fight mob and the smart money are picking Frazier, but Ali has such an appealing personality that his salesmanship has won him heavy support elsewhere."

Frazier says he could retire after this bout. "I got enough money to get out if I want to. But I just love money. It's so comfortable. It makes things so sweet for me. The only way to get it is to work hard – and I'm working hard. So tell Clay to watch out."

For God, for Country, and for Perenchio

Budd Schulberg

It is the Muslim mask . . . that they want beaten in. . . . They are the whites . . . who served in wars gone past and those with sons and nephews in this one . . . who root for Joe Frazier to do this thing for them . . .

DICK YOUNG, New York Daily News

I can't lose, 'cause I'm fightin' for people all over the world. If I win, people all over the world's gonna win. If I lose, they all gonna lose.

MUHAMMAD ALI, training for Frazier

What we have here is the Mona Lisa. You don't expect us to sell it for chopped liver. . . .

JERRY PERENCHIO, defending his closed-circuit theater prices
of ten to twenty dollars and his sixty-five-thirty-five split of
an estimated sixteen-million-dollar gross

When it was announced that two prize fighters, two black men, two heavyweight champions were to divide a purse of five million dollars to decide which was the one true champion, a special excitement ran through the country, the big money excitement, for this was an event as significant to the *Wall Street Journal* as it was to *Ring* magazine. How wonderfully American it seemed that a poor, rural Carolina colored boy (Joe Frazier), who only half a dozen years ago had been slaving in a Philadelphia slaughterhouse, was to earn – for guaranteeing his public one hour in the ring – eight times more than he would have earned in the slaughterhouse if he had worked at his old job for the next fifty years. America loves big statistics, and here was the all-time whopper. His manager was straight out of Horatio Alger too, Yank Durham, a white-haired, brown-skinned loser most of his life, whose Jeep accident in World War II had aborted his own dreams of boxing glory, and who had worked for years as a welder for the railroad while training a long line of failed fighters in dingy gyms. Until along came Joe, a fat tub of a teenager who wandered into the gym to try to lose a little weight. And for his lifetime of obscurity old Yank will now be compensated with 20 percent of that two and a half mil., maybe half a million green ones. Before taxes, that is, but let's not think about that yet. Even after taxes, the loyal gray fox won't have to go back to welding again. When you think about Joe Frazier and Yank Durham you think about America – Love-It-or-Leave-It, and Crown Thy Good with Brotherhood and all that jive.

And only in America, Harry Golden would tell you, would Cassius Clay, the most famous conscientious objector in America since Lew Ayres, be allowed to compete for the title it had confiscated from him, and offer him two and a half million dollars, and open to him its press and its airwaves and at least half its heart. The Fight was too big for the fight business. Madison Square Garden offered each fighter one and a half million dollars' guarantee against 30 percent of the live and closed-circuit gate. Houston was ready to go to four million. But Yank Durham hadn't poked around those dingy gyms all his life for nothing. Or rather, he had. He and Ali & Company got together, they were partners after all, and decided on six. If Dempsey and Tunney were good for a million apiece thirty-five years ago, this was a bargain. It wasn't a fight any more, it was a *happening*, a war between two undefeated kings that could outgross in a single night an all-time box office winner like *The Bridge on the River Kwai*.

So what was more natural than that a big Hollywood agent who handles big stars like Burt Lancaster and Andy Williams and services big musical spectaculars should move in and promote The Fight. Ten years ago if you had mentioned a name like Jerry Perenchio, guys like Jack LaMotta would have looked over their shoulder for fear you were dropping the name of a soldier for Frankie Carbo. But all of a sudden Hal Conrad and people who worked the fight beat all their lives are out and a slick Hollywood hustler who doesn't know a mouthpiece from a groin protector is the new Mr Big. Figures. If The Manly Art is social history ready to play to a closed-circuit audience of one and a half million and another three hundred million in San Juan, Mexico, London, Manila . . . then it is the time of the Jerry Perenchios who know how to count a house and to move a happening.

This is not to put Perenchio down – it is to put him up, really – for we are not talking about the man, but about the species. As the environment changes, dinosaurs die, and swifter, more adaptable animals take their place. Perenchios were bred in television, came of age with the medium, learned with McLuhan that the medium was the me$$age. Jerry Perenchio isn't a boxing man but that no longer matters, he's a hawker of happenings, and in Ali-Frazier he latched on to one the whole world would be watching. All he needed was the money, and he got that from the original Horatio Alger, a Canadian sports nut who happily has a way with a dollar, a man who gets his hockey highs from watching his lowly Kings outskate the Boston Bruins, who cries when his Los Angeles Lakers blow it to the Knicks, and who is so proud of his Forum (the plushier Madison Square Garden of the West) that we have seen him pick up a cigarette from the thick orange corridor carpet as if he were tending his own home – Jack Kent Cooke, who may yet restore vigor and respectability to the foundering game called capitalism.

The Lord of the Ring seems to have been working overtime in creating this matchup of opposites on half a dozen levels. Millions of people who feel that boxing is a brutal business that ought to be outlawed are going to make an exception and watch this fight, because they want to see Muhammad Ali Up the Establishment. Millions more want to see a no-nonsense champion who flaunts neither black pride nor antihonky prejudice but believes in sticking to his trade and piling up as much money as he can for the childhood sweetheart he married and their five kids. No Uncle Tom, he's just a hardworking boy who believes in getting up at dawn, running his six miles, and driving his body to its physical limits in pursuit of that pot of gold at the end of the great American rainbow. We have the law-abiding pragmatist against the quixotic black ideologist, an Afro-American version of the Lincoln-Douglas debate except that the pragmatist can hook you to death in the aggressive style of Marciano and the ideologist is as quick and telling with a jab as he is with his mouth.

Can a powerful slugger moving constantly forward lick a master boxer moving in and out and from side to side, firing rapid combinations from tricky angles? That has always been the perfect match, the irresistible contest between speed and power, each man confronted with the ultimate problem of solving the style of the other. For strange as it may seem to the uninitiated, *thinking* is the key to victory in the ring. Assuming that both men are physically primed, it will be the signals from the brain that make the difference, even to sluggers like Dempsey, Marciano, and Frazier, who look as if they are just heedlessly banging away. With his short arms, heavy legs, and lack of height, Marciano was resigned to taking six punches to get inside and drop his own bombs. But he would have been catching sixty punches if he simply banged in as he had when he was a crude beginner. His trainer, the dandy old bantamweight Charley Goldman, worked with that crude power as a sculptor works a great piece of marble, shaping it to his own design without trying to alter its essential impact.

We were reminded of this when we went down to Philadelphia to watch Joe Frazier training for his shoot-out with Muhammad Ali. Frazier and Durham have built their own modest and practical gymnasium in North Philadelphia, a two-story nondescript building in a neglected section of the city where nondescript is the name of the architecture. There is nothing to inform you that you are visiting the headquarters of the heavyweight champion of the world. The only sign in the window advertises: "Yank Durham – Manager of the Year." Yank is a throwback to the old school who speaks of his fighter in the first-person singular: "Quarry made the mistake of trying to punch with me and you saw what I did to him in seven rounds . . ." He has never had a champion before but he calls the signals and Joe Frazier is the same obedient citizen in the training quarters that he is in society. While from Angelo Dundee, a manager-trainer of many champions, Muhammad the rebel takes only what he chooses, setting his own rules in the training ring as he does in the world.

At the door of the gym, an ancient black man called "Unc," who turns out to be Joe's uncle from South Carolina, hesitates to let us in. Yank and Joe take a dim view of writers. They have their two and a half million dollars and couldn't care less about fielding questions from fight reporters whose interest in the titleholder has been something less than ardent. "Where were they when we needed them?" is the hard-boiled attitude. Unlike Ali, Joe is not enchanted by the sound of his own voice except when he is singing with his musical group. "Clay talks enough for both us us," Yank Durham says as his fighter, lean as a panther, goes through some awesome warming-up exercises. "He c'n do all the talking he wants. Talk's cheap. I'll do my talking in the ring." Silently, self-contained, Frazier goes to work on his sparring partners with grim efficiency. A tape recorder provides a loud musical background, Joe and his "Knockouts" rocking "You can make it – if you ca-an . . ." Some forty black spectators have drifted in, more out of curiosity than partisanship. In the ring the pattern of the actual fight to come is being projected. Moleman Williams is reaching Frazier with left jabs, more than one would consider healthy for any fighter to take on the head. But Frazier isn't any fighter, he has developed a style of shock absorbing, a contempt for pain, that enables him to shuffle through the bullets and close with the gun slinger. Fire away, fire away, his style seems to say, but if you can't stop me dead this has to wind up in hand-to-hand combat. A young, obviously frightened newcomer had come to replace a light-heavyweight contender whom Frazier had rendered *hors de combat* with a busted mouth. The lad could box, and as he peppered Frazier with timid jabs we could see what the faster and more authoritative jabs of Ali's would do to the handsome sculpture of Joe's face. Joe was trying to pull his punches, but he made the new boy wince as he walked through the jabs and slammed him to the body. "Under and over," Yank was calling from the corner, reminding his property to hook the left to the body and then double it up to the jaw.

On the street outside the gym there was a commotion, and we looked out to see about twenty pickets from the Southern Christian Leadership Conference. "Only the White Chauvinist Pigs Will Make Millions" read one of the signs. Some of the others: "Ali-Frazier, Yes! Chartwell, No!" "Lower Ticket Prices," "Give us Zack Clayton for Referee," "Get-Rich Fight Promoters Exploit Black Community."

Ever since Chartwell, the Hollywood agency, had announced
that it would be selling the closed-circuit rights on a sixty-five-
thirty-five basis with theater owners having to ante up stiff
advance guarantees, there had been protests from black communities across the country. If black fighters were the marquee
names selling this super-attraction, why shouldn't black promoters and black organisations have a chance to share in the returns?
It seemed a fair question, especially in these times when community control and power-to-the-people are the flags of an army
emergent. A veteran of hard times, Yank Durham took the
protest in stride. He went out, joshed with the protestors, and
told them he was ready to join their picket line himself. He was
all for the brothers getting as much out of this fight as they could.
But he and Joe had been on poor street too long to be willing to
sacrifice any money of their own. We watched with admiration
the humor and natural diplomacy with which Yank handled a
delicate and possibly explosive situation.

"We met with a black group before we dealt with Chartwell,"
Yank explained as we re-entered the gym. "I told 'em if they had
five million we were ready to sign. They said, 'Fine, fine, why
don't we talk about it?' We didn't want talk, we wanted money in
the bank. This fellow Perenchio, all I know about him is he came
up with the money – we got it in the bank right down the street.
We're not for white power or against black power – we're with
green power."

Yank Durham and Joe Frazier did their best to disavow the
roles of "white hope" and "spokesmen for white racists"
assigned to them in the morality play. Unfortunately the choice
was not theirs. The Fight has to have its hero and its heavy, and
must be rooted in its own soil of political pride and national
prejudice. In 1971, with its Calley trial, its "incursion" into
Laos, its soul-searching to the brink of collective nervous breakdown, America has to confront the black champion who thinks
for himself with another black champion who – even by his
silence, his noninvolvement – plays the game "the American
way." *Ring* magazine, the bible in its field, refused to name Ali
its "Fighter of The Year," insisting ". . . the winner should be a
model for the Growing American Boy . . ." So *Ring* honored
Frazier. The New York *Daily News* kept the morality pot

boiling, telling its readers, "It is the Muslim mask of Muhammad Ali that they (the "silent" majority) want beaten in. That is what they fear, that and his refusal to serve in the armed forces. They are the whites . . . who served in wars gone past and those with sons and nephews in this one . . . who root for Joe Frazier to do this thing for them . . ."

From the other side of the barricades, CORE hailed Ali as a black model and scolded Frazier for presenting an image insufficiently black. And a black writer for a weekly magazine of conscience teed off on Frazier for "refusing to grant SCLC the franchise rights to show the bout in the black ghettos, proceeds to help fight poverty." It is true that both Frazier and Ali, through their respective managers, might have helped black organisations if they had jointly insisted on this in their contract with Chartwell. But the demonstration outside Frazier's gym was not logical but allegorical. At this point Frazier had no more to say about franchise rights than Ali, which was nothing. But the symbols had to be Ali, the first "free" black champion vs Frazier, "the house nigger of the white chauvinist pigs."

In the private quarters of the gym, before Frazier could get to his shower, a nationally known columnist wanted to ask some questions. "No questions, I'm all through answerin' questions," Frazier said brusquely.

"But I drove down from New York just to talk to you," the columnist pressed him. "I've been two and a half hours on the road."

"Man, you must've got lost. Only takes me ninety minutes," Frazier said.

"I've got a column to file. It's in a lot of papers."

"Cool, man. Glad you're makin' it," he said, opening the door to his private dressing room.

The columnist had never been known for Christian patience, and his face was flushed. "Are you saying you're not going to talk to me?"

"You should have been here last month. I answered all the questions."

The columnist's fever line ran off the chart. "If I walk out of here I'm going to knock your brains out."

"Go ahead, be my guest."

Exit the columnist rushing back to New York to tell the world what a rat Joe Frazier was. If he had been able to stay a little longer he would have seen a different man. "Is he somebody important?" Frazier asked. A black sports writer from Washington identified him. "Well I still say frig him," Frazier held his ground. "I told the man I don't feel like talking. Just because he's got a lot of papers do I have to keep answering the same old questions?" He seemed to be asking rather than telling us, and behind the abrupt, edgy manner a likable human being began to peek through. "I don't want to hurt his feelings. I don't want to hurt anybody. I just don't have time for a lot of questions now. I've got a job to do and I want to take care of business."

"Joe, at the contract signing, Ali was up to his old tricks. He even tore your jacket and—"

"You're asking me about the weigh-in?" Frazier cut in. He seemed to have forgotten his mad on the columnist and was answering questions easily now. "Hell, if Clay wants to do this—" he stood on his toes, opened his mouth and his eyes wide, and gave a more than passable impersonation of "The Greatest," "let 'im go ahead. They fined him five thousand last time, and if that doesn't shut him up let them fine him ten – or whatever it takes to make him obey the rules. I got more important things to do with my money."

"They say he's going to bring an envelope into the ring and open it with his prediction five minutes before the bell?"

"He c'n predict anything he wants. I get enough mail. I'm not interested in reading his mail."

His disinterest in Ali's theatrical gamesmanship was utterly convincing. More sophisticated than Liston, tougher-minded than Patterson, he carried with him a cool unflappability that expressed itself in short, hard sentences that belted you like his hooks.

The Franklin Park Motor Inn, Frazier's hotel headquarters, presented a scene as unprepossessing as the gym. Except for ourselves and Jim Bethea, the talented black reporter for Washington's *Evening Star*, the hotel bar was empty. Yank was sitting in a corner with his small, playful son and a couple of the sparring partners. The talk was good-natured kidding as to who was the best crap shooter in the camp and about the stiff workout Ken Norton, a promising young heavyweight from California, had given the champ the day before. No reporters dropping in for last-minute stories. No fans waiting for the champion's autograph. Even the local Philadelphia papers seemed almost unaware that they had a champion in their midst. "No. 1" to *Ring* magazine, and the seven-to-five favorite on the morning line at Vegas, the official heavyweight champion of the world seemed to attract more pickets than supporters. Or maybe the cruel fact was that Joe's supporters were all out in the white suburbs and in the Polish, Irish, and Italian sections of our cities. "I stand up for the black man," Frazier had said. "But the most important thing is, I stand up for Joe Frazier." Oddly, if we must fall back on these plantation-day categories, the origins of Cassius are much closer to "house," while Joe is strictly "field." His father, the poorest kind of Carolina dirt farmer, scratched out a living of collard greens and chitlins for a family as large as Joe Louis's – and did it with one arm when he lost the left in a shotgun accident. When little Joe was born, the neighbors came around to see if the boy would be born with one arm. The father predicted that of all his sixteen children, Joe would become the famous one. The boy became his left hand in the field, set up a homemade punching bag in back of the shack when he was six, and sentimentalists in the Frazier camp wonder if he didn't develop that powerful left hook to compensate for his old man's deficiency. All good colorful stuff, human interest, with the makings of myth. And yet there is something about this thunderingly effective champion, that doesn't get through to anybody except the form players and the patriots.

While the official champion was concentrating on the hard job ahead of him, the people's champion was lighting up the skies of Miami. His living quarters – a brainstorm of Angelo's – had been the Octagon Towers, a prosperous Jewish retirement home near the beach. The most ecumenical of Black Muslims, he had quickly won over this unlikely following of elderly Jews, most of whom never had talked to a black man on equal social footing before. Indeed, Muhammad was the first black man ever admitted to the Octagon Towers. Now the guests had grown so fond of him that they decided to give him a farewell party, with a big cake decorated with a ring in which the triumphant Ali is standing over his fallen foe. An old lady who had never seen a fight made a *haemische* presentation talk in which she told him how much they were all going to miss him. Ali responded with a funny and touching talk of his own, cutting the cake and calling the people by name. "I can't believe it, a prize fighter, a *schwarze*, he's so sweet, he seems like a nice Jewish boy," a rounded *mamale* gave him the final accolade.

Next afternoon in Chris Dundee's Fifth Street Gym the place comes to life with the entrance of the star. Three hundred people have been waiting to watch him train, Miami vacationists, blacks, hippies, reporters from Germany, India, California. . . . The room is full of name fighters, Jimmy Ellis, Luis Rodriguez. . . . Ali's brother Rahaman a.k.a. Rudolph Valentino Clay is furiously skipping rope. All eyes watch Ali as he glides through his exercises, punching the light bag with the rhythm of a jazz drummer, whopping the heavy bag with effortless dance steps, shadow-boxing with dozens of punches in combinations quicker than the eye, refracted in the full-length mirror on the wall. As he swifts around the ring, a master of ceremonies asks the crowd to "please keep as quiet as possible. The champion will be concentrating. Please do nothing to distract him during this workout." This brings a cynical smile to the faces of old-timers in the gym. For weeks it has been Ali who was doing the distracting, pretending to collapse from light punches, clowning in the corners, and wise-cracking with his audience. For the first month he had worried his trainers and friends with his apparently frivolous attitude. He had paid for this inattention in the Bonavena fight. Now he was alarming his training family by tooling around the southern Florida countryside in one of his new cars, socialising with celebrities and their foxes passing through, telling one and all how easily he would handle Frazier – and yet not accepting the discipline of daily drudgery that would condition a boxer for the kind of superchallenge he faced. One would have thought Ali's messianic visions would have driven him to months of devoted preparation, the kind of almost religious self-denial that Marciano put into his regimen for long, lonely periods that conditioned the body and the mind. Perhaps Ali had come to believe in his own perfection instead of his perfectibility. Losing was simply not in his lexicon. The inborn cockiness of the young Louisville Lip was now hitched to the sky-wagon of Ali's religious-black nationalist conversation. His strength was as the strength of ten because his heart belonged to Allah and the Third World. Joe Frazier was not only too short and slow of foot, he was *on his own*, which appeared to Ali as much of a defect as a glass jaw or a nothing right hand like Ernie Terrell's.

Add to this a lively mind, a restless spirit not easily adapted to the daily grind, and you have some of the explanations for Ali's seemingly inexplicable reluctance to get down to the hard, serious work of training for The Fight of his tempestuous career.

For three weeks, though, he had been running his three miles each morning (while Frazier ran six), getting his rest, and working eight or ten rounds almost every day. Sometimes he would dance as he hoped to against Frazier, and sometimes, to the puzzlement of writers passing through, he would lie back on the ropes and let strong, squat sparmates pummel him in the body. He had already proved he could take hard shots to the body from Liston and Quarry, Chuvalo and Bonavena. If he had practiced sliding off those ropes and getting back to the center of the ring where he had dancing and punching room, these workouts would have made more sense. He would have to float more than he had against Bonavena, that he had learned from his fifteen rounds with the bully boy from Buenos Aires. "I'll be dancin', movin', jabbin', punchin' Joe and he won't be able to find me," Ali had been telling us. Yet against a heavy-muscled brawler from Jamaica he frequently stood flat-footed and let the hired hand flail away. He had done this in training for the Quarry fight, possibly show-boating for Petula Clark and a group of VIPs passing through, and had suffered a rib bruised so badly that Dr Pacheco had X-rayed it to make sure it was not broken. It was a well-kept secret, but Ali had carried that internal and unnecessary wound into the Quarry fight.

It would seem as if this quixotic champion is a dual personality, Muhammad Ali, the seer who has entrusted his fate to the hands of Almighty Allah; and Cassius Clay, the Huck Finn of the Golden Gloves, who still likes to see just how much he can get away with.

But during his rubdown in the bare cubicle partitioned with beaverboard from the rest of the gym, he was serious and spoke

without exuberance. Seeing him stretched out naked on the table
he looked far too big and solid for a dancer. He is so artistically
proportioned that one forgets he has the thighs of a pro football
player, his upper legs measuring more than two feet around, his
shoulders heavily developed, his biceps as large as a weight-
thrower's. Somehow this deceptive heft doesn't go with his style,
either in the ring or on the speaker's platform. Somehow you
expect a man with a nimble mind and nimble feet to be slight
and slender. Except for the freaks like Willard and Carnera, Ali
is the biggest heavyweight champion in boxing history. The only
thing freakish about him is that he seems to have been born with
a light-footed welterweight dancing in his mind. Now he lifted
his large, lean torso in a strenuous calisthenic, twisting his waist
from side to side without lowering his feet to the table. When he
lay back to rest a moment, he was asked, "You're getting a chance
to win or lose your title in the ring after four years of being
rejected. Don't you think those four years will hurt you? Don't
you think that kind of rejection is bad for an athlete?"

" 'Scuse me," he said. "Can't talk now." He lifted himself into
another exercise more strenuous than the last. Twenty-four
times. When he lay back again, he picked up the conversation.
He didn't seem impatient. In fact, he seemed to welcome the
verbal counterpoint to the physical routine – "Everything you go
through, all this mess you been goin' through, I think it makes
you stronger. You thrive on bein' rejected. Joe Frazier, everything
nice and easy for him, he don't know what pressure is."

"But . . . ?"

" 'Scuse me. Can't talk now." He threw himself into the most
strenuous exercise we have ever seen a fighter execute. Not Joe
Jouis, not Marciano, not Floyd Patterson. He raised his torso
and his legs at the same time, bicycled his legs rapidly a dozen
times, then lowered himself from the waist up but held his feet
above the table, then repeated the liftup from the waist and the
furious bicycle-motion. Sweat poured from his face and he
groaned with the effort. We counted twenty times. When he lay
back he was tired but he wasn't breathing hard. "I hate exerci-
sin'," he said. "It's so boring."

In a quiet voice before the next exercise, he told us why he felt
sure of winning. "When Frazier comes in he'll hear booing.

They'll all be cheering for me. All the blacks and the white hippies. This'll be a mismatch. No contest. Jerry Quarry felt the pressure in Atlanta. Joe Frazier will be feelin' it in New York. It'll be on me too, but I'm used to it. I thrive on it. I got more experience, I'm bigger an' faster – no contest!"

Angelo Dundee and Dr Pacheco came in and he hung on them one of those sneak punches they have learned to live with. They were handling Jimmy Ellis in his fight with Tony Doyle in the local arena that evening, and the plan was for all of them to fly up to New York early next morning for the physical exam in the Garden. "I'm gonna go right from here to the airport, catch the four-thirty," Ali told his white manager-trainer, who restrained his protests because this is the unique fighter who runs his own camp. "It makes sense. I'm finished with my work for the day. This way I get to the hotel around eight o'clock, have a nice dinner in the room, I'm in bed by ten, get my rest, I'm up early in the mornin' to do my runnin', back at the hotel for a nice breakfast – then the physical exam and back to the hotel and rest until I go on the Johnnie Carson show."

"Whatever you say, champ," says Angelo, who believes that fighter and trainer should travel together. "But Johnnie Carson? You really want to do the Carson show? All that excitement and people around you? I'd think you'd want to fly back to Miami right after the physical, avoid the crowds, you can always go on Carson after the fight."

"Know what Carson said? After I'm finished with boxin' I'll have to be thinkin' about my next career. He c'n do me a lot of good."

Angelo feels the Garden went behind his back to Herbert Muhammad to line Ali up for the Carson show and that too much is on the line to take a chance with a talk-show the champ can do any time he chooses, and especially if he licks Frazier. But he has lived this long with Mercury Mu by playing it cool, so he tells the champ to fly well, he'll meet him in New York in the morning.

We have breakfast with Dundee on the plane next morning, and of course Topic A is Ali. After twelve years he is used to Cassius's sudden whims. He accepts them as part of his champion's multilayered personality. Cassius was a skinny fifteen-year-old when he came to Angelo's hotel in Louisville in 1957. The lad had seen Dundee on television, handling Willie Pastrano against John Holman. "He was a student of boxing even then," Angelo reminisced. "He's been studying it since he was twelve years old. He understands the science of it and he knows the psychology. He's a born psychologist. That's why you can't bullshit him. Everybody asks me, is he difficult? He's the easiest fighter I have ever handled; Cassius is my friend. I liked the kid right from the start. So much talent, so intelligent. He's one in a million. Fascinating to be around him. Always makes things *happen*. There's that inner excitement. With most people, you can tell what they're thinking. But you can't second-guess Cassius. He stays one step ahead of you. I think he could have been anything he wanted to be. This goes beyond boxing. This is history. I was there at the beginning and I hope to stay to the end. There's no money in this for me. I've made twice – three times as much with other fighters. But I enjoy working with him. Being part of history."

In hours of talk with Angelo Dundee he is able to discuss Clay-Ali with honesty and passion without once alluding to his fighter's religious-political ties, legal status, or relationships to Herbert Muhammad and the Black Muslims. That Angelo is still in the corner of a champion who preaches separation of the races is a testimony to flexibility on both their parts.

At the New York Hilton we cooled our heels for twenty minutes. "The onliest champ," as he called himself, was in conference. When we reached the suite, we found Ali, Richard Durham, and C. B. Atkins, always identified as "Sarah Vaughan's ex-husband," winding up a meeting with a Hollywood film promoter to close a deal for a feature-length documentary on Ali's life. Jerry Perenchio claimed he already owned the rights to this as part of the package deal Ali and Herbert Muhammad had signed with Chartwell. A bitter disagreement had come to a head in Ali's cubicle at Dundee's gym only a week before when Perenchio had laid some strong language on Richard, and the black writer had handed it back to him: "This ain't no plantation deal, you don't get the house, the field hands, and all the cotton for that two and a half million."

"We got a contract for *this* . . ." Perenchio had insisted, point-ing to the chest of the inert Muhammad Ali stretched out waiting for his rubdown from the seemingly deaf-and-dumb Cuban masseur.

It had been a strange place for a discussion of the fine print in Ali's contract, and regardless of the merits in the case, the four-letter words flying around the silent Ali hardly seemed calculated to improve his concentration on the eve of The Fight. And as much as we would like to see Ali and Durham produce their own film-bio of a remarkable life, we wondered if protracted meetings with fast-talking Hollywood agent-types was the way to keep your mind focused on Frazier.

When the wheeler-dealers drifted off, the talk finally got around to business, fight business.

"You know, Angelo," Ali began, edging in from left field as he frequently does, "isn't there somethin' about comin' from hot weather to cold weather – the blood gets thinner or thicker or somethin'?"

Angelo and Dr Pacheco exchanged a look that said: Here it comes, and the doctor explained how blood thins in warm weather, etc. Ali nodded. "I thought so. I could feel it when I was runnin' this mornin'. Down there I was runnin' *good*. Today after a mile or so I could feel the difference. So I get to thinkin', what if that happens to me in the fight? Maybe I better stay up here and get adjusted to the climate."

Angelo paled. The plan had been for all of them to fly back to Miami right after the medical exam, the trainer hoping to keep his fighter away from crowd scenes and big-city distractions. "Okay, okay. I expected this. Even told my wife to leave my bag packed to come up or the next plane in case you wanted to stay up here. Of course you know what Frazier is doing. He's driving right back to Philly after his checkup. Staying away from crowds and reporters."

"Let 'im do what he wants. He's not used to pressure. All that *pressure*. He needs to go home. I'll be comfortable here. Go to the checkup and then come back here and rest. Do the Carson show tonight but after that I'll be in bed at ten o'clock every night, get my full night's rest, run hard every mornin', eat only the right foods, start taperin' off my workouts at the Garden . . ." He had fallen into that soft, sing-song cadence that was beguiling and hypnotic.

"I'm with you, champ," Angelo said, in a rather hollow voice. "Whatever you say. You really want to do the Carson show?"

"Well, I told 'em I would," Ali said. "Won't take too much out of me. Then right home to bed. Good night's sleep. Out runnin' early in the mornin'. Gettin' used to this climate . . ."

Angelo Dundee nodded in poker-faced agreement. Wheels within wheels were figuring how to get his giant problem-child safely home to Miami.

On our way over to the Garden, Ali was quiet and self-reflective, suggesting the mood we had seen when he was lying on the rubbing table muscle-sore and leg-weary after the Bonavena fight. "Angelo, I been lookin' at the film of the Frazier and Ellis. Jimmy was really doin' good those first few rounds, makin' 'im miss and movin' 'im around – he was way ahead until he got caught. And then he got up and tried to fight, which is dumb. He should of retreated and let his head clear. Now me, I'm bigger'n Jimmy, Angelo—?"

"Of couse, champ, a whole lot bigger."

"An' I'm even a better boxer, faster – don't you think so, Angelo?"

The tone was plaintive, like a small boy trying to talk himself into big dreams. His trainer assured him that he agreed. 'So if Jimmy can handle him for three rounds, I oughta be able to do a lot better, don't you think so, Angelo?"

Was he putting his anxious white trainer on? No, it sounded quietly for real. In the big limo, surrounded by a covey of retainers, for a few minutes he seemed to become that fifteen-year-old hopeful calling on the big-time manager back in Louisville fourteen years ago.

Arrival at the Garden was another story. From the quiet of the limousine he stepped out onto the stage of public life and *insto-change-o* he was ten feet tall, the eyes were flashing, and the mouth was working as a flying wedge of personal bodyguards and police moved him through the worshipers trying to touch him. Frazier had come and gone uneventfully, he and Yank pulled in tight and seeming to share a common spine like Siamese twins. Now five hundred reporters and photographers were waiting for the show to start and Ali, as we say in the business, "threw in both knees." If the fight game ever gave awards for the best performance of the year, Ali's mantel would be lined with Oscars. Introduced as the *"former* champion of the world," Ali takes the cue and becomes writer-director-star of "The Fall and Rise of Muhammad Ali." "*Former!* (He models the emblazoned championship belt.) I brought the belt along today to show you who's the true champ. All you fellows with your typewriters, drinkin' every night, pickin' against me, never learned ya lesson with Liston, did ya? Frazier says he's gonna come out smokin', smokin's bad for the lungs, gives you cancer, I'm gonna bring my fire extinguisher with me next Monday night, straighten this mess out once and for all."

The commissioners and their doctor are trying to shut him up long enough to get the examination under way. "Now let's be serious," the state physician pleads. "Have you had any headaches?" "Headaches!" Ali rolls his eyes like Stepin Fechit. "I don't get headaches, I give my opponents headaches." Whatever the doctor asks becomes a feed line for this heavyweight Groucho. "You want me to touch the floor twenty times! Let's see you do it first." And when he does execute the bending exercise, facing the doctor he fits dialogue to the occasion, "Yassuh boss, yassuh boss . . ." Told to extend his arms horizontally: "When I stretch out my arms I'm used to holding them up *this* way!" Up go his arms in the victory salute that has become as familiar as Eisenhower's double V. When the doctor takes out his tongue-depresser Ali drops another one-liner: 'Do I *have* to open my mouth?" Even stretched out on the examination table Ali keeps up the running monologue. He goes into his Frazier poem with new couplets for the occasion. Then the doctor thumps him on the chest. "Did you hit Frazier that hard? I hear he can't take a punch." Said a reporter at our shoulder, "If Frazier knocks him out, he can always get a job writing material for Flip Wilson."

The Frazier checkup had been a routine fifteen minutes. The stand-up comic champion of the world had been on for half an hour, and the Q. and A. period was only beginning. A Rumanian reporter asks a question in the form of a political speech ending with the presentation of a doll from his homeland. Ali takes it, turns it over, and straightfaces, "Where was this made – in Japan?" He catches the photogs moving in for their pictures – "Next thing they'll be sayin' the heavyweight champion's playin' with dolls," and tosses the toy to Bundini. He demonstrates his latest flurry of combination punches: "I call it the ghetto-whupper." He pretends angry scorn for Joe Frazier. "He's got some nerve announcin' a victory party. Duke Ellington an' his trio. He can't even dance. Ain't got no rhythm. They say Joe Frazzuh got lots of endurance/ but he better be takin' out life insurance." Is he going to stay in New York or fly back to Miami? "I'll leave it up to you. What would you like me to do?" The press has five days to fill the sports pages of the world with stories that will be like omelets without eggs if the master chef of this homecoming feast isn't on the scene. "Stay! Stay!" The exile returned happily acknowledges their need. John Condon, press officer for the Garden, nods in approval. Ali will complete his training here at the Garden. More one-liners for the press. As Ali goes, so goes the action. Angelo Dundee has them booked on the five o'clock plane to Miami.

The rest of the day was a surrealist jumble of images, impulses, happenings, as if Dali and Picasso had collaborated on a mural of madness in The Manly Art. Ali's dressing room, where a score of people would have made a crowd, looked like a less orderly Chicago Convention. Ali's own entourage was lost in a crush of old champions and one-eyed connollys, Muslims and movie stars, cops and commissioners, representatives of Chartwell, Burt Lancaster and his retinue, the press and the world at large. Bundini was there of course, with his entire family, and at one point in the confusion we overheard John Ali, an associate of Herbert Muhammad and the "black, adviser" to Chartwell, asking Bundini to set an example by moving out – "So the champ has room to breathe in here – we've got to help him, brother." Everybody seemed to be telling everybody else to leave – and the guards were pushing but nobody was leaving. People were pressing to get his autograph while Ali was struggling to get into his street clothes. "See what I mean?" Angelo was mumbling. "He'll get mobbed if we stay in New York. We've got to get back to the airport."

In the corridor outside the dressing room, edgy guards in brown uniforms were trying to clear a path for Ali's escape but they were outnumbered and resentful. "I was on the door when Ali brought that mob in last time," a beefy young guard was complaining. "If we gotta go through all this again they oughta put a special squad on and pay us a bonus."

"But you get to see the fight free," said a fan squirming toward the dressing room door.

"I'd rather spend my ten bucks at a moviehouse and get outa this mess!" said the angry guard, pushing him back.

Condon, Angelo, and bodyguards, official and self-appointed, held a feverish strategy meeting on how to extricate Ali from the loving fans who would be threatening to crush him to death. A limo was ordered to come down an inside ramp to a loading zone in the bowels of the Garden. Ali would be secreted to the landing platform via a service elevator and whisked away from the Garden before followers would realise what had happened. Another case of total breakdown between theory and practice; for as we headed toward the car, a thundering herd came pounding down the ramp. Montage: Eisenstein movie: the crowd berserk. Flash of fear. We'll be crushed between Cadillac and mob. We who survived a Waffen-SS ambush in Munster and the Rhine crossing. What a way to die. Implanted in the metal of a Detroit monster. Dr Pacheco's voice: "Jump in – quick!" Into the front seat as the first wave of Ali's army breaks against the side doors. Faces leering in and screaming their love, "*Aleee . . . Aleee!*" while they twist the door handles, beat on the glass, clamber over fenders and, as the besieged limo inches forward, somehow cling to the trunk compartment and pound on the roof.

Into rush-hour midtown traffic crawls the limo, carrying some fifteen passengers, at least half a dozen clinging to the outside and a full ball team inside, the magnet himself in the back seat, flanked by best friend Howie Bingham and a Muslim brother from Philadelphia, Bundini, Richie Durham, and Angelo on the jump seats. Doc Pacheco, the shaken driver, and your shaken observer in front. Behind us comes the army, able to keep up as foot power easily equals motor power in New York traffic. More pounding on the windows. A few city cowboys still seem to be riding the roof. "You seen all them big movie stars – you ever seen anything like this?" Ali calls softly as his fans reach out to touch him through the glass. No we never had, not Gable, or Cary Grant driving up to Grauman's Chinese. We stare into the faces of the frantic. Young blacks, old blacks, Puerto Ricans, hippies, but a sprinkling of older whiteys as well. An elderly Jew, red-faced from running through the chill March afternoon, is waving his arms and begging for us to lower the window so he can shake Ali's hand. Half a dozen red lights later a battalion of diehards is still running. One unlikely long-distance runner becomes the star of the chase. Long-haired, pimple-faced, in faded GI jacket and dirty sneakers, he keeps abreast of the car from Thirty-third Street to Fiftieth, from the West Side to the East Side, still with us at the twelfth stoplight, waving like a crazy and begging us to lower the window.

"He's gonna wind up at Kennedy with us and get on the plane," says Ferdie Pacheco.

"Lower the window," Ali said. "He deserves it."

There were demurrers. Opening the window to one, even this unlikely-looking marathoner, meant a horde of hands trying to open the door and climb in. But to Ali, white hippies were his people too; down went the window and in came the sweaty hand to slap resounding skin with the hero's. "Hey, champ, you're my man!" "And you're somethin' else!" Ali responded. The kid leaped in the air and uttered a profane oath of joy. At that moment he could have been run over by the oncoming traffic and died in ecstasy.

We were over the bridge and fighting the traffic to Kennedy Airport, but the drama wasn't over. Traveling with Muhammad Ali is like being caught up in an old Pearl White serial leaping from one cliff-hanger to the next. All that talk about a documentary – Ali was living his documentary, only the cameras weren't rolling. Halfway to Kennedy, Ali slid in sideways from left field again. "Is the airport on the way to Philadelphia?" No, he's assured, Philly is the opposite direction. "How much time we got – think we'll make the plane?" "We got thirty minutes – we'll make it easy," Angelo says. But Ali has Philly on his mind. The weather is socking in and he doesn't like to fly. The brother at his elbow is quietly pushing Philadelphia. Ali is thinking of going back to his new one-hundred-fifty-thousand-dollar home. And maybe also of pulling some of the old capers on Frazier. "How long would it take if we drove to Philly?" Each question comes softly from the back seat, provoking another cryptic chess game between Ali and Angelo. They reach the airport with just fifteen minutes to takeoff. Angelo rushes ahead to validate the tickets.

Storm clouds darken the sky. Ali asks the driver how much it would cost to drive back to Philly. Angelo is at the airline counter. Ali is in a huddle with his group. He's inviting Dr Pacheco to see his house in Cherry Hill. Angelo says they have less than ten minutes to get to the gate. Ali decides he's hungry. A group of black employees in the restaurant excitedly hover around him. He sits down at a big table and begins to order. Angelo says he can have a nice steak on the plane. Ali wonders if they shouldn't eat in the restaurant and take the next plane. Meanwhile the chauffeur is standing by to see if Ali will decide to make the drive to Philadelphia. The loudspeaker announces "Last call to Miami". Howie Bingham, phoning the stewardess to see if Ali can have steak on the plane, returns with the announcement that he can have *two* steaks on the plane and all the fresh vegetables he desires.

Five minutes to takeoff. We hear our name paged and go to the airline phone. From the Garden, John Condon wants to know if it's true that Ali is on his way back to Miami. And is he going to stand up Johnnie Carson? We say we don't know where Ali is going but he did ask us to make his apologies to Johnnie. Condon is unhappy. He has six hundred newspapermen on his neck wanting to interview Muhammad Ali. We hear ourselves saying that Ali's cutting out of New York is not an act of bad faith. Who (except Angelo) could have foreseen the intensity of the mob that came running down that ramp and chased him halfway across Manhattan? There had been a change in the chemistry of his crowds since the Bonavena fight. He had always had a gift for hotel lobbies and street corners but now, as The Fight came closer, adoration was turning into a frenzy that neither the Garden's nor the police security forces seemed able to control. Angelo's fears had been realistic. To face the crowds that would be waiting for him at the Carson show would be to risk serious injury. Hardhats were ready to flatten him in hate. But the real danger now seemed to be coming from the peace lovers ready to trample him with love.

Almost 75 percent of America was now agreeing with Ali that we had no moral justification for fighting in Vietnam. Only here was a young man whose protest march was a walkout on million-dollar purses, a walkout on the championship that is every boxer's dream, a walkout on the big Christmas tree of material goodies there for the asking of the talented conformist. To walk away from all that, stay out of jail, and finally make the world you had defied pay two and a half million dollars to watch you come back on your own terms – there was something outrageously American about the saga that attracted not only hippies and blacks but millions of middle-class citizens across a broad spectrum of political faiths who respond to boldness and originality backed up by ability. Muhammad Ali had become Lucky Lindy and the Brown Bomber, Bobby Kennedy and Joan Baez, all rolled up into one irrepressible folk hero hailed as our favorite defender of the truth and resister of authority. Anyone who had all that going for him had better get out of town if he wanted to stay in shape. The symbol of national dissent and anti-establishmentarianism also happened to be a professional pug with a hell of a fight on his hands.

With Ali a last-second passenger to Miami (Angelo winning the splittest of split decisions), the boxing reporters are reduced to interviewing each other. For days and nights, it seems, we stand manfully at the bar set up for the press in the Hotel New Yorker, drink deeply of Garden booze, and think deeply about The Fight that for these precious few days has driven from our minds the civic concerns and international furies. We welcome the escape to press room hospitality where an overwhelming majority of our American colleagues seem to agree with Frazier that he'll stop Clay in ten or less, while nearly all our English and European friends lean to Allegory and Ali. New York, that troubled giant of a city, is grateful for brief respites from daily anxiety. The Mets had given the city a reprieve from paranoia with their improbable victory over the Orioles in the early autumn of '69. That rare bird – almost as extinct as the dodo – had flown forth: civic pride. "We're No. 1!" New Yorkers had called to each other, and for a few days of euphoria they had been able to believe in the greatness they had taken for granted in the good old times, before drug addiction, race riots, pollution, traffic snarls, sit-ins and lockouts had mugged the city and fenced its grandeur. Now Muhammad Ali, with the cooperation of Joe Frazier, was giving old No. 1 a brief reminder of the glory years.

If At First . . .

Felix Dennis and Don Atyeo

"I'm not excited about fighting anymore. You people are the ones who're excited, not me. I've been fighting since I was twelve. It's just another night to jump up and down and beat up somebody."

Muhammad Ali

Joe Frazier was a master slugger, a throwback to the days when men fought each other with bare fists face-to-face across a chalk mark on the floor. His nickname "Black Marciano" was an apt description, for like "The Rock", any finesse Frazier possessed in his squat, chunky body was entirely eclipsed by his unshakeable determination to knock out his opponent.

Every day, Joe Frazier soaked his head in rock salt and water. "It makes me mean and toughens my skin," he would say, and indeed, whenever he was hit he would instinctively smile. He christened himself "Smokin' Joe", after his habit of steaming from his corner at the bell until he was crouched head to chest against his opponent. "I'll be so close to him they'll have to dig the hairs from my beard out of his chest before they pick him up," he had sworn before demolishing Jimmy Ellis in the fifth round of their championship bout.

In his autobiography, veteran British boxer Henry Cooper paired Frazier with Sonny Liston. "They were slugger-killers from the hard American school," he wrote. "You could hit Frazier with your Sunday punch and you could break your hand. He'd shake his head and come on after you. Those guys can also break your heart." By 1971, Frazier had consecutively broken twenty-six professional hearts – twenty-three by clean knockouts – and was the Heavyweight Champion of the World.

Joe Frazier should have been an All-American legend. Born in

the swamplands of South Carolina, his childhood as the son of
an impoverished dirt farmer was a running battle for survival.
Four of his twelve brothers and sisters died of worms, scurvy and
starvation. In the few spare moments he was allowed between
work and sleep, Joe slung a flour sack over a beam and trained to
become "the next Joe Louis". His favourite chapter in the Bible
he laboriously read a page at a time each night was the Book of
Judges "because it's about war, and fighting puts me in mind of
war."

Married at fifteen, Frazier headed north, first to New York
and then to Philadelphia and a job in a slaughterhouse (prompt-
ing one later critic to suggest he fought like he worked, "up to his
elbows in entrails and tripe"). In 1962 he dropped by a local gym
to lose weight and was persuaded to resume boxing. Although an
unlikely candidate for ring success with his sawn-off reach and
barrel-shaped legs, within two years he had reached the trials for
the Tokyo Olympics. In the final he was beaten by a 300-pound
Buster Mathis. As consolation he was offered a position on the
team as a sparring partner.

Frazier's Olympic hardships make Ali look by comparison as
if he won his gold medal in a raffle. Prior to Joe's departure for
Tokyo he fought an exhibition with Mathis in San Francisco.
Buster broke his finger on Joe's rugged skull and was dropped
from the team. Frazier became the American heavyweight hope
in a field stacked with Russians. In his qualifying fight it was he
who broke a thumb on his opponent's head, but mindful of
Buster's fate, stoically kept his injury to himself. As with all
legends, he went on to win the gold medal.

On his return to Philadelphia he was laid off from the slaughterhouse because of his thumb. For the next year he lived a
penniless existence as a janitor at the Bright Hope Baptist
Church. In 1965 his luck changed. Under the auspices of his
trainer Yank Durham, Frazier became a corporation – Cloverlay
Inc. – owned by forty respectable Philadelphians. After thirteen
consecutive victories – all knockouts barring a hard bout with
Oscar Bonavena – the press recognised him as a serious heavyweight contender. Durham shrewdly held his fighter back from
the scramble for the WBA title, vacated by Ali's exile. Instead he
matched Frazier with Mathis for the NYAC crown, which he

won in the eleventh. Later he picked off Jimmy Ellis, who had emerged as the WBA champion.

Frazier's life outside the ring was at once solidly respectable yet enviably glamorous. While continuing to read the Bible and worry publicly about preserving the reputation of his title, he became rich, bought a mansion in Philadelphia and drove a gold Cadillac. Occasionally he rode a large Harley Davidson motorcycle (with hand-tooled boxing gloves for handlebars), and wore tailored wet-look leather ensembles. Between fights he sang – albeit poorly – inoffensive rock and roll with his backing group, The Knockouts, at such desirable nightspots as Caesar's Palace. Affable enough for a man who had been hit as often and as hard as he had, his social image was a far cry from Sonny Liston's inarticulate chain-gang charisma.

Joe Frazier had it all – fame, fortune and the Heavyweight Championship of the World. And he had built it all himself out of nothing. He should have been a legend. But he was not.

The fly in Frazier's ointment was of course Muhammad Ali. In another time he would have been universally hailed as a boxing colossus. As it was, to all but serious students of the sport, he was either regarded as a second-stringer who had usurped the title, or overlooked entirely. Even his admiring biographer Phil Pepe subtitled his book *Come out Smokin'* with *Joe Frazier – The Champ Nobody Knew*.

At first Frazier bridled at his assigned role. "What do I have to do?" he wailed. "I've beaten everyone they've put in front of me!" After winning Ellis's WBA title he shouted ecstatically, "I'm free at last!" Nine months later, after eliminating Bob Foster, Ali was still at his shoulder in the shape of 1,000 chanting fans. It was then that Frazier realised if ever he was to be popularly recognised as Marciano's legitimate heir, he would first have to beat Muhammad Ali.

The biggest draw card in heavyweight boxing is a match between a consummate boxer and a master slugger. Jess Willard v Jack Johnson, Dempsey v Tunney, Joe Louis against Billy Conn, Marciano and Ezzard Charles . . . all of them results of what *Sports Illustrated* termed "the classic confrontation". On March 8th 1971, a fifth classic bout was nominated to the list

when Joe Frazier met Muhammad Ali at Madison Square
Garden in yet another Fight of the Century.

The Frazier v Ali promotion was almost as much a boxing
milestone as the fight itself. "Contrary to what some people say,
boxing isn't show business," snorted one disgruntled would-be
promoter who had been left by the wayside in the race to engi-
neer the match. A Beverley Hills celebrity agent named Jerry
Perenchio proved him wrong. Perenchio had met neither Ali
nor Frazier until he signed them. In fact, he had never even
seen Frazier throw a punch. "I really don't know the first thing
about boxing," he candidly told the press. What he did know
was show business, and under the very noses of the cigar-chew-
ing, smoky-backroom boxing barons, he stole the sport's
choicest plum.

"You've got to throw away the book on this fight," he said.
"It's potentially the greatest single grosser in the history of the
world. It's like *Gone With The Wind*. And that's why I'm involved.
I know how to book Andy Williams into Salt Lake City. Well,
this fight is like booking Andy Williams into five hundred Salt
Lake Cities all at once."

Perenchio backed his beliefs by offering the two fighters the
unprecedented sum of $2.5 million apiece. Both Frazier and Ali
– who had originally priced themselves at $3 million – accepted,
discarding tenders from Madison Square Garden and the
Houston Astrodome. Perenchio then set about stumping up the
cash. After scanning a list of some seventy potential backers, he
settled for a Los Angeles based sports buff who owned a basketball team, a hockey team and part of a football team as well as
the Inglewood Forum stadium. Jack Kent Cooke put up $4.5
million. Madison Square Garden, which agreed to stage the
fight, guaranteed the rest. As return on their money they hoped
to gross $20 million.

The publicity leading up to the fight was as one would expect
for such a massively financed venture. Both Ali and Frazier were
always on hand to growl the requisite threats for the press. But
there was little real venom on either side. In an unguarded
moment Frazier actually admitted to liking Ali, although he
reserved doubts about Ali's commitment to the black man when
"a lot of guys around him are white". Ali himself, as far back as

1970, had spoken warmly of his opponent, dreaming how one day they would both get together and discuss "freedom for black folks", visit the ghetto to help "the old wine head, sitting on a doorstep, drunk", and generally "wake up the black people".

"Me and Joe Frazier will be buddies," he had said. "I just want it to go down in history that I didn't sell out or Uncle Tom when I got famous, and I don't think Joe Frazier's going to do that, either. He ain't dumb."

Given these past statements, Ali's jibes about Frazier's wits, looks and awe of whites sounded slightly hollow. Even Ali seemed unconvinced and it was left to the public to provide the malice – the NAACP demonstrators who threw up a hostile picket line around Frazier's Cloverlay Gym; the New York cabbie who told Phil Pepe when he learned about the fight, "Good, Frazier will kill that draft dodger!" Just how emotionally charged an issue the fight had become was indicated by an incident during the Philadelphia screening of the Ali v Bonavena bout. A forty-year-old black crane operator named Leslie Scott became involved in a heated argument with a white man over who was superior – Ali or Frazier. According to police records, Scott pulled a knife on the white man, who then identified himself as a policeman. Scott fled and the policeman shot him dead. Ali visited the funeral parlour where Scott lay in his coffin. "I ain't worth dyin' for," he said, shaking his head.

Ali's pronouncements during training also sounded slightly off-key. "It's gonna be the champ and the tramp," he boasted to the sports writers. "I hit so much harder now. I hit Bonavena so hard it jarred his kinfolks all the way back in Argentina. Joe Frazier ain't a great fighter to me. He's a great fighter to the fans been reading his clippings. But to me he can't even dance. I'll be dancing on March 8th. I'll be dancing, moving and hitting, and Frazier won't be able to find me."

But Ali appeared to be taking his training lightly. Although he talked often of "dancing", he spent most of his ring time lying on the ropes, content to cover his face with his gloves and absorb punishment like a punching bag. Several critics wrote him off as lazy.

Privately, he confessed that training was now more of a job than enjoyment. "Ain't in my lungs – they all right," he gasped between breaths. "It's in my muscles. They get tired. Ain't like when I was a young man. Now I'm older, gonna be twenty-nine."

As the fight date drew nearer, Ali's thoughts seemed to stray further from the job in hand. A month away he had caused concern by saying he needed one more bout before Frazier, against Jimmy Ellis. However, as the weeks passed, he grew increasingly blasé about the World Champion. Almost every day he would cut short his training to mingle with the celebrities who dropped in to the gym. With a week to go, Ali flew to New York for the physical and was mobbed every time he set foot out of his hotel. He positively basked in the glut of multi-racial adoration, and it was only Angelo Dundee's subtle persuasion which managed to coax him back to the 5th Street Gym. Wrote Budd Schulberg of the challenger's apparent serenity: "Perhaps Ali had come to believe in his own perfection instead of his perfectibility. Losing was simply not in his lexicon."

While Ali was showboating, Frazier was holed up in his Cloverlay retreat, relentlessly pounding the big bag. He trained as if he had more to lose than Ali, and to him he had. The stakes were made painfully obvious when Frazier broke training to attend a fight in Philadelphia. As his name was announced from the ring, the hall echoed with boos . . . in his own hometown! While Ali fiddled, Frazier grew more sullen by the hour. "He's getting mean," said Yank Durham happily. "That means the fight's getting close. That means he's ready."

By 9pm on March 8th 1971, Seventh Avenue from 31st Street to 33rd Street was choked with the mandatory black limousines of boxing's newest and most exclusive fans. "I lost count of the number of famous legs I tripped over," reported one British writer. These legs belonged to luminaries such as New York Mayor John Lindsay, Frank Sinatra, Ed Sullivan, Hugh Hefner and Barbi Benton, Hubert Humphrey, George Raft, the Teddy Kennedys, Ethel Kennedy, Bernadette Devlin, astronaut Alan Shepherd and literally dozens more. If they were fortunate, these famous faces had snapped up their ringside seats at the official price of $150. If they had resorted to the black market, they may have paid $1,000.

As with the Bonavena fight, the question on everybody's lips was not, who do you think will win, but rather who do you hope will win. But unlike the Bonavena audience, which split on the issue of colour, the Frazier house was a house divided over ideals. If you were for Ali you were for ecology, women's liberation and peace in Vietnam. Conversely, if you were for Frazier, you supported Law and Order, Spiro Agnew and the status quo.

The Garden officials, fearful that Ali would be torn apart by his fans if he arrived outside the stadium on the night, had set up a makeshift apartment for him in a third-floor press room. At 9pm he awoke and wandered across the room to look down on his brother Rahaman lose a six-round preliminary against British fighter Danny McAlinden. At the bell, seemingly unperturbed, he caught the elevator for his dressing room. Several blocks away, Joe Frazier put down his guitar and made his way from his hotel room to the Garden.

Downstairs in his dressing room, Ali tore open an envelope and produced a scrap of paper on which he had written a week before his prediction: "FLASH. I predict first of all, that all the Frazier fans, and boxing experts, will be shocked at how easily I will beat Joe Frazier, who will look like an Amateur Boxer compared to Muhammad Ali, and they will admit I was the Real Champion of all time. FRAZIER FALLS IN SIX."

At 10.30pm, Frazier threaded his way through the crowd wearing a green and gold brocade robe emblazoned with the names of his five children. A moment later, Ali, resplendent in white satin, red velvet trunks and white "Ali-Shuffle Shoes" adorned with red tassles, also appeared. The two men reached the ropes almost simultaneously. The roar from 19,500 throats was overwhelming. In the ring, Ali immediately began shadow boxing – dancing and flicking at the air until he had edged his way into Frazier's corner. There he leaned over and patted Joe's head. "Chump," he said. At centre-ring, while referee Arthur Mercente ran through the rules. Ali continued his verbal cold-warfare. Frazier replied just once. Looking up into Ali's face he hissed, "I'm gonna kill you!"

For two rounds Ali managed to erase the doubts lingering in the minds of the critics who had witnessed the Bonavena marathon. Once again, the Ali who opened the match was the old Ali, dancing and jabbing as fast and as frequently as ever, the red tassels flying about his feet. Joe Frazier was, as always, Joe Frazier, a fighter with a seemingly boundless capacity for absorbing punches. Like Oscar Bonavena, his style was ugly and awkward, "a wild beast tangled in a thicket," as one magazine put it. Frazier depended on his pillar-box legs taking him in as close to his opponent as possible to land his leaden blows. (Frazier's reach measured just 71 ins, compared with Ali's 80ins.) But even when he managed to force Ali back against the ropes, his hooks swished by as Ali swayed from the waist like a cobra.

In the third round, the pattern began to go awry. At the bell, Ali slid from his corner and inexplicably backed onto the ropes before Frazier was anywhere near. It was a red rag to a bull, and the champion needed no further encouragement. Frazier was on his toes as he hurled his hooks at the immobile target. Ali snapped his head clear split seconds before each one could land, but the hooks and rights falling on his arms and body were no pulled punches. At one point Ali half turned towards the crowd and laughed, shaking his head in an elaborately mimed "no". But when he tried returning his own jabs, they skittered off Frazier's skull like so many ping pong balls thrown against a brick wall. It was Frazier's turn to smile. Crouched before Ali, pinning him like a butterfly in a display case, he took the round with ease.

Back in the corner, Dundee implored Ali to stay away from the ropes. For the first time in the fight, Ali accepted a stool.

After surviving two rounds of one-sided brutality, Ali regained sufficient composure in the sixth and seventh to partly rebuild his scorecard. He still favoured the ropes, but instead of merely ducking and absorbing Frazier's bullets, he fought back. Soon his jabs had begun drawing blood around Frazier's eyes and lips. By the end of the fight, the champion was to look like a butchered product of his former employment.

But although Ali was taking the points, he was nowhere near winning the fight. As emphasised by Bonavena three months before, points are of small value against a slugger with a sweet tooth for the grand knockout. It was only Ali's talent for avoiding the crucial Frazier punches to the jaw that kept him on his feet. How long this talent could continue was the vital question.

Round eight saw Ali promise, with a laugh in Frazier's face, that he would stand for ever. Dropping his hands to his sides, he haughtily disdained to make any attempt at defence. The promise held good for round nine, perhaps Ali's best ever. Back on his feet he circled and jabbed at his opponent's head. Frazier halted and, for the first time in the fight, stepped back. Ali's showboating vanished as he stood off the ropes, trading short, solid uppercuts with his opponent. Step by step, Frazier was driven back. *Ah-lee, Ah-lee,* chanted the crowd. Near the bell, Ali landed three consecutive right-left combinations. Frazier sagged, and as he walked back to his corner he was wobbling.

Round ten, Frazier charged from his corner, bunched up in fury, straight into Ali's glove. Ali worked on Frazier's raw face and then slid back onto the ropes. Frazier followed, but to ringsiders he seemed punched out, exhausted. Ali did not catch a single dangerous blow, while several times he visibly jolted Frazier. Ali shouted confidently to Dundee, Bundini and old Fred Stoner huddled in his corner, "He's out!"

But in the next round the tide turned again. At the bell, Ali moved from his corner straight to the ropes. Frazier pressed forward and swung a left. Ali dodged, slipped and fell. Referee Mercante ruled no knockdown, but Frazier closed in all the same as if to deliver the coup de grace. Pushing Ali back he landed two left hooks to the head. Ali countered with a right and Frazier stepped away. Ali remained with his back against the ropes and imperiously waved Frazier back. The champion moved forward a step and landed a perfect left hook to the jaw. The wild, wolfish look in Ali's eyes vanished; in its place appeared the fixed, glassy stare of a shell-shock victim. Ali's legs turned to jelly as he reeled around the ring avoiding Frazier's onslaught. Bundini sent an arc of water flying through the air, an act that earned him NYAC suspension. "Trying to revive my soldier," he explained later. Somehow, Ali survived.

For two rounds Ali hung on, avoiding as many shots as he could and smothering what he couldn't with desperate clinches. Frazier ignored exhaustion and tried his hardest to destroy the shadow which had haunted his entire championship career. In the final round he succeeded. With a long, grim left hook dredged up from the depths, the fighter with the autopsied face conjured the unthinkable on his opponent's immaculate features.

Ali was standing out from the ropes when the blow landed. Unsupported, his right leg buckled, his left leg shot out straight ahead and he fell spread-eagled to the canvas where he lay with his feet pointing to the roof. In the three seconds Ali was on the floor his cheek swelled obscenely. At three he had climbed up from the bottom of the pit and stood shaking the mist from his eyes. At the bell he was still standing. Whatever else his critics seized on gleefully after the fight, cowardice was not included.

When it had ended both fighters collapsed exhausted. Somebody at ringside shouted, "draw", and the chant was taken up *draw, draw*. But there was only one winner. The tears coursing down Bundini's cheeks told the story; the three judges merely provided the figures in the record book. Muhammad Ali was the fourth boxer in prizefighting's five classic bouts of skill against strength to have his talents sabotaged by a slugger.

In the dressing room, Joe Frazier sneered through his battered face at the reporters. "What can you say about me now?" he demanded. "I always felt like the champ. I fought everyone they put in front of me. God knows!" Softening, he paid Ali his dues. "You've got to give him credit," he said. "He takes one good punch. That shot I hit him with in the fifteenth round, I went way back to the country to throw. God, he can take it!" Afterwards Frazier slipped out the back door of the Garden into a waiting limousine. Only a handful of fans waited to see him off. Some weeks later, Frazier was admitted to a Philadelphia hospital. His biographer Phil Pepe attributed his three-week convalescence to emotional and physical exhaustion. Rumours circulated that Ali had effectively ended Frazier's fighting career.

Ali did not stay at the Garden for the press conference. Dr Ferdie Pacheco drove him to New York's Flower & Fifth Avenue Hospitals to have the grossly swollen jaw X-rayed. Ali slumped in the back seat exhausted during the long ride. At one point he focused and muttered, "Must have been a helluva fight 'cause I'm sure tired." The jaw was not broken; it was only a cheek haemorrhage. The injury did not surprise Dr Pacheco. What did astonish him were Ali's hip joints. Forced to bear the brunt of Frazier's blows, these joints – the toughest in the human frame – had swollen up to such a degree that they almost paralysed Ali.

Floyd Patterson considered losing to be the fighter's perennial dread. "We are not afraid of getting hurt but we are afraid of losing," he once told *Esquire*. "A prize-fighter who gets knocked out or is badly outclassed suffers in a way he will never forget. He is beaten under the bright lights in front of thousands of witnesses who curse him and spit at him, and he knows that he is being watched, too, by many thousands more on television and in the movies, and he knows that the tax agents will soon visit him – they always try and get their share before he winds up flat broke. The losing fighter loses more than just his pride and the fight; he loses part of his future, is one step closer to the slums he came from."

Floyd, who went into hiding for nearly a year after losing to Johansson, may have been overstating the ignominy of defeat. But other fighters also recall failure as a particularly bitter pill. Rocky Graziano: "They look at you different. How soon they forget. It's no longer hi ya, champ! It's hello . . . You feel self-conscious. You go to the old places, the old joints, and you walk in and it's completely different." After Joe Louis lost to Ezzard Charles, Louis arrived at the New York address where his post-fight parties were traditionally held. The only other guest turned up at 3 a.m. the next morning.

Defeat for Ali, the man who had proudly promised "If I lose, I will crawl across the ring on my hands and knees and tell him, Joe Frazier, you are the greatest," would seem to have almost certainly been an intolerable humiliation.

Shakespeare reserved tragedy for kings and princes, believing only they truly had the capacity to suffer the necessary fall from grace. Ali was unquestionably a latter-day king, and the press had no hesitation in ascribing tragic proportions to his failure.

But Ali appeared curiously unaffected by his misfortune.

"Oh, they all said about me that if I ever lose, he'll shoot himself, he'll die," he told reporter George Plimpton the day after the defeat. "But I'm human. I've lost one out of thirty-two, and it was a decision that could have gone another way. If

I'd gone down three times and got up and was beat real bad, really whupped, and the other fighter was so superior, then I'd look at myself and say I'm washed up." If defeat meant the end of all the reporters, cameras and crowds, he said, then he didn't mind. "I remember thinking that it would be more relaxing to be a loser."

Of course the press and its public had no intention of forgetting Ali, and despite his words to the contrary, he seemed relieved by the continuing attention. The next day he was eagerly guiding an army of fans through his still-unfinished $250,000 house in the New Jersey suburb of Cherry Hill. Later he bolstered his spirits with a conspicuous new $15,000 Oldsmobile trimmed with $7,500 worth of gold plating.

Defeat did have its compensations. For the first time in many people's eyes, Ali looked human, sitting propped up in bed telling the world's press "I'm not going to cry." Frazier's fists went a long way to defusing the frustration Ali's critics had suffered for almost a decade. Besides blotting his unblemished record book, the defeat marked the end of "Ali, the Man They Love To Hate." Coincidentally, three months after the fight, the eight judges of the Supreme Court voted unanimously to overturn Ali's draft conviction and five-year sentence.

Only a few months after his defeat, Ali began preparing for his second comeback. His choice of opponent hardly came as a surprise. Jimmy Ellis was definitely no "unrated duck". Although Joe Frazier had beaten him in five rounds, Ellis had won the WBA tournament and as he had matured as a fighter relatively late in life, at thirty he was not far from his prime. Under Angelo Dundee's tutelage, Ellis had developed into a hard-punching, stand-up boxer whose sneaky right hand had knocked out six opponents in the first round. "My guy," said Dundee, who elected to work in Ellis's corner against Ali (Ali adopting Sugar Ray Robinson's old trainer Harry Wiley), "is the best first-round banger in the heavyweight division."

Beating Ali had become almost an obsession for Ellis. "I don't care if I never win another fight as long as I live – if I win this one," he said. "I lived in the shadow of Ali too long." Ellis had grown up in Louisville with Ali and claimed to have beaten the former champion as an amateur. "Beat him with ease!" As Ali's long-term sparring partner, Ellis had had the benefit of 1,000 plus rounds with his opponent. The experts noted that if anyone knew Ali's faults and weaknesses, it was Jimmy Ellis.

But conversely, Ali had also come to know Ellis like the back of his glove. In selecting him, Ali knew that the fight might become gruelling, but would hold no dangerous surprises. Entering the ring, Ali was like a student who knew before an exam, if not the answers, at least what questions were on the paper.

Although he admitted to being "a little pulpy", Ali looked close to top form on the night. After surviving Ellis's promised scorching first round, he laid the foundation for his victory in the fourth. Jimmy Ellis: "It was a right hand in the fourth round hurt me so bad I couldn't really fight my best after that. I knew about that right hand. After all, I been seein' that right hand for a long time. When it came it sneaked up on me and it ruined me."

Ellis was reeling as the round ended and from then on the fight followed the unspectacular pattern of virtually every other Ali v Ellis sparring session. Ali moved easily, changing direction at will, a master instructing his prize student. "He wanted to prove he could go twelve rounds on his feet, and he did," said Dundee. In the twelfth, Ali caught his opponent with a fatal left uppercut and followed through with a combination, leaving the groggy Ellis sagging on the ropes. Ali did not attempt to finish him off and the referee stopped the fight. "Ain't no reason for me to kill nobody in the ring," explained Ali later in the dressing room.

After the Ellis bout, Ali began his own version of Joe Louis's Bum of the Month Club. Joe Frazier's old partner, Buster Mathis, was the first contender. Mathis, who was still desperately trying to live down a humiliating capitulation to Jerry Quarry two years before, was a great overweight whale of a man with a belly like Santa Claus. The day before the match, Ali did not even bother to train, although he himself weighed in at his heaviest fighting weight to date – 227 pounds.

The fight was broad farce. For ten rounds, Mathis floundered after the former champion, trying to land his "speciality", a wild left hook. Ali calmly avoided most of Buster's attempts, although at one point when he was trapped against the ropes, a fist did bounce off the top of his head. "He's hurt, Buster. He's hurt!" screamed Mathis's trainer, Joe Fariello. Ali turned to the frantic Fariello and shot him a wink before coolly gliding away.

In the eleventh, Ali loosed a short right to the side of his opponent's jaw and Mathis flopped down on to his hands and knees, shaking the floor with his weight. The bell saved him. During the break, Fariello considered throwing in the towel. He should have. It was only Ali's new merciful image which saved Mathis from a brutal beating. As it was, even Ali's half-hearted punches caused Buster to wobble and sent him to the floor three times. Despite Dundee's insistence that he "Take him out, damn it Ali! Take him out!", Ali preferred to coast to an easy points victory. The television networks passed over the opportunity of televising the fight, save for a ten minute edited clip which showed Ali and Mathis performing to a soundtrack composed of *Waltz Me Around Again* and *I Want To Hold Your Hand*.

Back in the dressing room, Ali defended his new pacifism. "I see a man in front of me, his eyes all glassy and his head rolling around," he said. "How do I know just how hard to hit him to knock him out and not hurt him? I don't care about looking good to the fans or to Angelo. I got to look good to God. I mean Allah." Somebody asked if he was in the wrong business. Yes, he agreed, there was enough killing and hurting in the world. After deposing Frazier he would retire. But wasn't his professed non-violence a triffle incompatible with past bouts, such as the Patterson and Terrell bloodbaths? "Them was the days of the draft thing and the religion thing and black against white, all that," was the reply. "Now them days have gone for ever. I don't need to do like I did then. I'm more educated and more civilised."

The Bum Club continued just days after Buster's embarrassing exit when Ali signed to fight a German heavyweight named Jurgen Blin on Boxing Day, 1971. Blin, a blond ex-butcher from Hamburg, appeared to make a reasonable showing in the early rounds until the fight degenerated into a dull series of clinches, with Ali resorting to the ropes much more than in his two previous bouts. In the seventh, Ali regained his composure and put Blin on the canvas. The German staggered to his feet, but it was obvious even in the cheap seats that he could barely stand. His corner threw in the towel. "It would have been easier for him to have been knocked out cold," said Ali. Such was the mis-match that even Ali's admiring Swiss fans could not be inspired to attend the fight in large enough numbers to provide the promoters with a profit.

On March 2nd an arrest warrant for Ali was issued in Chicago for his failure to comply with a court order directing him to deposit $44,000 guaranteeing Sonji her alimony. Ali paid up and then travelled to Tokyo to recoup his loss by outpointing big Mac Foster – another former sparring partner – on April Fool's Day.

Ali continued his international season by meeting George Chuvalo in Vancouver a month later, the same George Chuvalo he had easily outpointed six years before. In 1970, Chuvalo had been so badly beaten by boxing's rising star George Foreman that his wife had pleaded with the referee from ringside to stop the fight in the third. Ali could only manage a decision over fifteen rounds. Another month and he was in Las Vegas facing Jerry Quarry, the same Jerry Quarry he had beaten in three rounds in the first fight after his exile. This time the meeting lasted until the seventh.

Next Ali went to Dublin where he had agreed to fight a near-sixteen-stone Al "Blue" Lewis of Detroit. Only Ali's mother, whom he took along to see Ireland and the English crown jewels, seemed at all excited by the arrangement, apart from the Irish boxing fans who were to see their first major world heavyweight match in sixty-four years. Ali had a cold and confessed he had grown weary of too many fights in too many cities. The only time he cheered up was when Peter O'Toole knocked on his hotel door ("Hiya Lawrence, come on in").

But for a protracted "Irish Count" which annoyed Ali, "Blue" would have been back in his dressing room long before he actually was. After the fifth, Ali settled for punching practice until referee Lew Erskine stopped the fight in the eleventh. "Thank you," said the relieved Lewis. Ali collected his standard $250,000 pay-cheque (for exhibitions he charged $6,000, with opponents thrown in) and returned to New York to meet another old foe, Floyd Patterson.

Before he did so, Ali purchased a Pennsylvania hilltop, which, as "Fighter's Heaven" or "Muhammad's Mountain", came to exert a considerable influence on future events. Ali had heard about the mountain from Gene Kilroy, who persuaded him to drive the 30 miles from Reading, Pa., along Highway 61 to the township of Deer Lake. Ali camped in the open, breathing the country air, viewing the rolling Pennsylvania farmlands and dreaming of the spartan life of ancient fighters. When he returned to civilisation, he bought Fighter's Heaven for $200,000.

Angelo Dundee feared Ali would spend thousands clearing the land, putting up buildings and so on, only to lose interest in the project halfway. "And once Muhammad's lost interest, there's nothing you can do about it." But Ali had been well and truly seduced by the natural life. He cleared the land – chopping down hundreds of trees himself for the exercise – drew up the blueprints, built a collection of log cabins, and unearthed several huge boulders, which his father painted with the names of the boxing "greats". Swooping down on the surrounding farms, Ali bought up as many artefacts as he could from his phlegmatic Dutch-stock neighbours. One of his prize acquisitions was a massive iron bell, made in 1896 and costing $2,000. An antique ironclad quarry wagon stood in stark contrast to Ali's Rolls-Royces and Cadillacs. Long benches cut from whole tree trunks lined the courtyard. The gymnasium that he built, Angelo likes to think was modelled on his own spartan 5th Street establishment. "A real place," Ali would tell the visitors who flocked to the camp each weekend, "a valid place for fighters to come and work and sweat like fighters should, not like all those places with chandeliers and thick carpets and all those pretty girls around."

As much as the clean air, long country runs and the honest sweat helped Ali, Fighter's Heaven was equally important for Ali's psychological outlook. Since long before the Ellis fight he had been cutting a despondent figure in the gymnasium. "Used to be, before the Liston fights, all I thought about was fight, fight, fight, be the greatest, be the champion," he would tell the reporters. "Now it's like I go to work, put in eight hours a day, do my job. I got other things on my mind, heavy things." His "Uncle Tom's Cabin" at the new retreat afforded Ali the

THE MAMMOTH BOOK OF MUHAMMAD ALI

opportunity of collecting these "heavy" thoughts. His output of philosophic lectures increased and his poetry changed from boxing doggerel to odes extolling freedom, destiny and truth:

> *I am riding on my horse of hope,*
> *Holding in my hand the rein of courage.*
> *Dressed in the armour of patience,*
> *With the helmet of endurance on my head,*
> *I start out on my journey to the land of love.*

Welded together, these thoughts became what Ali and Bundini referred to as "The Mission", a rather hazy but implicitly believed philosophy of life for the black man. "We are both sons of God," said Bundini. "We feel we are on a mission to do good for all people, bringing people together through understanding. The black man is the onliest one can save this country. If the black man pack up and leave, this country will fall, because there's a sin on it already. We got to overcome this sin, forget it, straighten up from today on. The young people know this and the champ is their hero."

At thirty-seven, Floyd Patterson had made a profitable success out of failure. Since his Las Vegas massacre at the hands of an avenging Ali, he had made two abortive efforts to win another crown for the third time: first he was eliminated from the WBA tournament and then outpointed by title-holder Jimmy Ellis in Stockholm. Going in for a second time with Ali made no boxing logic at all, but with 17,378 people willing to pay $512,361 to watch him try, Floyd was not especially daunted by his impending humiliation. And as *Sports Illustrated* pointed out, he was decidedly more fortunate than many of his former colleagues – Sonny Liston, dead; Zora Folley, dead after striking his head in a swimming pool; Hurricane Jackson, last seen shining shoes in the Garden; Eddie Machen, dead after falling from his balcony.

For Ali, the bout was little more than Broadway show biz. As the two fighters performed pre-fight callisthenics in their respective corners, Joe Frazier was called up into the ring to be introduced to the crowd. Immediately Ali forgot all about Floyd and launched into a long harangue at his Nemesis. Frazier chuckled, avoided Ali's attempts to throw off his restraining cornerman, and sat down.

Surprisingly, Patterson put up a spirited performance before his exit. Ali, who had trained lightly, found himself losing the third, fourth and fifth rounds to his determined elder. With his opponent landing his famous combinations and, especially in the fifth, several snappy rights, Ali had difficulty penetrating Patterson's unique defence. In the sixth round, Ali opened up with uppercuts and chopping rights, one of which sliced open Floyd's left eyelid. Ali concentrated on the eye and within two rounds had worried it to an open wound. At the bell for round eight, Patterson did not leave his stool. After the fight, Ali praised Patterson for his grit, Floyd apologised for not doing better, and everyone tried to forget what had taken place.

Two months later, Ali's Bum of the Month Club reached a new nadir when he faced Light-heavyweight Champion Bob Foster. Although his record of forty-two knockouts in fifty-four fights indicated that Foster could perhaps be expected to provide some stronger opposition than Patterson, "Blue" Lewis and Blin, the mis-match was made obvious at the weigh-in where Foster surrendered 41 pounds to his opponent. What made the fight even more depressing was the venue, a nightclub in a gambling casino in Stateline, Nevada, the poor man's Las Vegas! The sign in the lobby of the Sahara Tahoe Hotel which read "Live November 21 Muhammad Ali v Bob Foster. Next Attraction November 23 Isaac Hayes's summed up Ali's situation. He had become a cabaret act, performing amidst slot machines, blackjack tables and waitresses in orange boots.

Ali himself was disgusted by the event. The day before the fight, Bundini and Dundee tried to wake him for training. Ali refused to get out of bed. "I'm not excited about fighting anymore," he said when he finally arrived for the weigh-in, twenty minutes late. "You people are the ones who're excited, not me. I've been fighting since I was twelve. It's just another night to jump up and down and beat up somebody."

Ali toyed with Foster at the beginning, obviously content to string out the mis-match until his dutifully predicted fifth round. A ringside spectator shouted "Phoney", and Bundini urged his man to stop playing. Ali turned fully away from Foster and snapped "Shut up!" The match glimmered in the fifth when Ali unseated Foster four times. Foster survived the round, in the process nicking Ali's left eyebrow, the first time he had ever been cut in his twelve year professional career. Foster went down twice more in the seventh, after jolting Ali several times with his right, before finally staying down forty seconds into the eighth round.

Ali had five stitches in his eyebrow. "Now people know he's got blood," cracked Dundee. "I don't know if the cut came from a butt, a thumb or a punch, but the important thing is Ali won and we can go home."

1972 had been a frankly uninspiring year for Ali. But at least he had kept busy, which was more than Frazier had accomplished. Indeed, compared with Smokin' Joe's performance as Heavyweight Champion, Ali's year looked positively interesting. Frazier's embarrassing slaughter of unknowns Terry Daniels and Ron Stander spoke volumes for his negative view of his role as champion.

Frazier also had a negative view of Ali. The promised rematch was delayed for months, firstly because of Frazier's hospitalisation and then by financial complications involving the rematch agreement held by Jack Kent Cooke. But as the months passed, it became obvious that Frazier was avoiding Ali. Five million dollars apiece had been discussed as the price of the rematch, but even this could not tempt Frazier. Instead, he signed to meet Olympic gold medallist George Foreman in Kingston, Jamaica, for less than a million.

On January 22nd 1973, Frazier charged across the ring at the bell and caught his challenger with several of his left-hook specialities. It was the only moment in this extraordinary fight that Frazier looked anything like the Heavyweight Champion of the World. Foreman's first counter-punch was a sickening body blow, which stopped the champion in his tracks. The second caught Frazier flush on the jaw and sent him skating across the canvas. Foreman hit him again on the jaw and Frazier resumed his position on the floor. He regained his feet and charged in; Foreman reached out and pushed him off as if he were an over-enthusiastic female fan. Another punch and

Frazier's head and shoulders shot under the bottom rope. Only the bell saved him.

Soon after the start of the second round, Foreman crashed yet another right into Frazier's jaw. When he staggered back up he was wobbling and the challenger lifted him clean off his feet. After the sixth knockdown, Foreman glanced inquiringly at the referee and when Frazier had recovered his feet he was led off to his corner. George Foreman was named the new Heavyweight Champion of the World one minute and thirty-five seconds into the second round.

Ali was asleep when Frazier surrendered his title. "They woke me up to tell me," he recalls. "I thought: My, my, there goes $5 million out of the window."

Frazier's savage defeat spurred Ali into the toughest training session he had undertaken for months. He contracted to fight British champion Joe Bugner and low-ranked Ken Norton a month later, but his eyes were set on higher stakes. "There's too much involved for me to lose," he said when questioned about his intensive workout. "We're too close to the big one. There's something around the corner. Wait and see."

At twenty-two, Bugner had already seen much of Ali, sparring with him on four occasions and appearing on the same card when Ali fought "Blue" Lewis. He was something of a black sheep in British boxing after having relieved Henry Cooper of his title, but Ali was a Bugner fan and had often predicted a glowing future for his young opponent. The fight, held in Caesar's Palace, lasted the full twelve rounds. Although Ali looked fresh and fit, he declined to despatch Bugner sooner. Several critics suggested he was baiting a hook for Foreman, whose management had shown a marked reluctance to consider Ali as a possible contender.

It was left to an unknown fighter whose last match was before an audience of seven hundred for a $300 purse to shatter Ali's careful plans. Ken Norton was ranked seventh in the heavyweight hierarchy but, as one magazine noted, he seemed to have sneaked into the listings. A former marine built like an hourglass ("He'll break in half," laughed Dundee), Norton had yet to meet even a reasonably rated heavyweight when he signed with Ali. Ali was Norton's big chance, and he was not about to pass it by. Assisted by a hypnotist (Dr Michael Dean), trainer Eddie

Futch – who had plotted Frazier's victory over Ali – worked to implant ring tactics in Norton's subconscious.

Dundee said he realised it in the first round; Ali said he knew in the second. Whichever round it occurred, by round three the dark red blood trickling from Ali's mouth confirmed that Ken Norton had broken Muhammad Ali's jaw, and with a punch no one had even seen. Dundee believes that the injury was a fluke; a one-in-a-million combination of two missing back teeth and Ali's opening his mouth at the precise moment Norton clipped him. "In the third round I asked him to let me stop the fight," remembers Angelo. " 'Let me stop it', I said. 'Your jaw's broke.' He says, 'No, I can beat this sucker . . . he won't touch my jaw.' What bigger thing can you have thrown in your face than a guy boxing with a broken jaw for twelve rounds?"

Norton's unrefined style paled beside Ali's experience, but his strength, and the broken jaw, compensated. At one point in the tenth, Norton darted up under Ali's guard and literally lifted him off the floor. Nevertheless, the match was a close-fought contest with the judges narrowly awarding it to Norton. As the doctor wired Ali's jaw later that night, he was amazed at Ali's courage. "There was a quarter-inch separation," he said. "The pain must have been unbelievable."

Sitting at home alone (Belinda was in hospital after trying to fight her way past three security guards to reach her injured husband in the ring), slurping ice-cream through his clamped jaw, Ali said he had nursed a twisted ankle during the fight, an injury which had forced him to abandon his training a week before the match. According to Ali he had suffered the sprain while revolutionising the game of golf. "I don't stand there an' look at the ball and wiggle the club like Arnold Palmer and Jack Nicklaus and them cats," he said straight-faced. "I was walkin' up to the ball and hittin' it while I was walkin' and knocking it three hundred . . . three hundred and fifty yards. Then I figured I'm gonna do even better. I was gonna run up and hit the ball. First time, I hit the grass. Second time I lost my balance and swung all the way round and fell down and twisted my ankle." The excuse was so outrageous that the listening press found it impossible to disbelieve.

Ali was philosophic about his broken jaw. "Funny, the jaw didn't hurt so much in the fight. Under all the heat and excitement, you don't feel it. Like a man in a street fight, he get cut in the stomach, fights on with his guts hangin' out and don't feel nothin' until he gets to the hospital." Resourcefully salvaging some capital from the disaster, he said the injury had been sent as a test from Allah. "What happened is Muhammad Ali ate a lot of ice-cream and cake," he confessed. "He didn't do his running, he didn't punch the heavy bag. I'm ashamed Ali let himself get into such shape. He won't do it again. Going back to the old Golden Glove days, I was too busy puttin' on a show, talkin', laughin', making jokes. When I start trainin' again all that is out. I'm gonna get up at five, say my prayers and run three miles. Train up at my camp in the Poconos, just me and my manager and a sweaty gym, like in the old days." After that, he said, he would "bump off" Norton in four, Frazier in six and then tackle Foreman. "But I won't knock him out. I'll beat him so bad they'll have to stop the fight."

Many critics were unwilling to give Ali a second chance, heralding once again the end of the legend. Recalled Bundini: "Some guy comes up to me in the hotel with two thousand Ali buttons, the ones with THE PEOPLE'S CHAMP written on them. He says, 'Well. I guess these aren't good anymore. He's had it.'"

Ali also revealed after the fight what the "something around the corner" that he had referred to while training for Bugner had been. He had, he said, cancelled himself out of a record $5 million payday.

When his jaw had healed, Ali barnstormed across the US drumming up ticket sales for the return match. Then he closeted himself away in Fighter's Heaven for a rigorous work-out. "He's never concentrated this hard on a fight," said Harold Conrad. When he emerged. Ali was a fit man. Even Dundee claimed to have lost ten pounds.

Ken Norton was also not about to rest on his laurels. His windfall (Ali referred to him as "The man who shot Liberty Valance") had rocketed him into the major league and he was already hungrily eyeing Foreman's silver belt. At his training camp in the ominously named Massacre Valley, 80 miles from Los Angeles, Norton worked to secure his overnight stardom.

Interest in the rematch ran high as the scheduled date approached – September 10th, five months after the first bout.

Indeed, Ali's spirited tub-thumping succeeded in eclipsing George Foreman's first title defence against Joe "King" Roman, a boxer even less well known than Ken Norton had been before his San Diego triumph. England, for example, readily agreed to closed circuit coverage of the rematch, but refused to touch the championship fight. "No interest," explained British impressario Jarvis Astaire. "Yes, yes," babbled Ali, delighted to be back at centre-stage, "they are all talking about Muhammad Ali like it's his life or death on the line. Is he through, or is he not? Is he still the fastest and most beautiful man in the world, or is he growing old or slow? It shows you what they think of Ali that this question would come up."

The rematch may have posed the question, but its result provided no answer. Before the fight, Ali promised to thrash Norton. "I took a nobody and created a monster," he said angrily after being told that Norton was maligning him. "I put him on *The Dating Game*. I gave him glory. Now I have to punish him bad." By the middle rounds Ali was clearly ahead and seemed set to administer his punishment. But then Norton's enormous strength and youth turned the tide. Ali continued to dance and jab, proving once again that the ropes were not necessary for him to survive twelve rounds, but as the final round approached he seemed less and less capable of remaining one step ahead. Also, Norton's style was unsuited to Ali's jabbing. Whereas a George Foreman left hook could remove the ex-marine from the ring in no time at all (and later did), Ali had difficulty in fathoming Norton's peculiar habit of leaning back off his splayed right foot.

In the twelfth Ali tried a desperate gamble. Coming down off his toes, he met Norton at ring centre and slugged it out, stopping the Californian's monotonous advance. Ali's last-round combinations proved sufficient to win him the nod from referee Dick Young, a decision that really could have gone either way.

Ali was so upset by the bout that a few seconds after the bell he turned and swung at Bundini, who in turn took a frustrated poke at camp photographer Howard Bingham. Ali's lawyer Bob Arum was equally disappointed. He was carrying a $10 million offer for a Foreman v Ali match from a British promoter as well as a rematch plan for Frazier in December. Ali's close shave against Norton cast a considerable shadow over both proposals.

While Arum resumed negotiations with the Frazier and Foreman camps, Ali wound up his minor league commitments by flying to Indonesia to meet Dutchman Rudi Lubbers on October 20th. Although Ali padded out the event to the full twelve rounds, the only remarkable aspect of the match was Ali's capacity to draw international crowds. Thirty-five thousand Indonesians showed up for the fight, and at an exhibition bout Ali charmed another 45,000 onlookers. "They never had a fight there before in Jakarta, yet he's adored there," said Dundee. "Places we would go that people you would think never heard of him, they heard of him!"

Ali returned to Fighter's Heaven nursing his hands. The old bursitis inflammation, which caused shooting pains up into his shoulders every time he landed a solid blow, had reappeared after the first Norton bout, restricting Ali's training programme. He compensated by sparring his snarling $2,000 German Shepherd, Shadow.

Joe Frazier was the opponent eventually chosen to replace Shadow, at a price of $850,000 (the same as Ali's purse). Locked away in the ghetto neighbourhood of North Philadelphia, Frazier sweated long hours honing his body to a high-tensile 210 pounds. He worked without the watchful eye of his "creator", Yank Durham, who had recently died in his fifties. The formidable Eddie Futch, fired by a wilfully confident Ken Norton, now presided over Frazier's former ballroom of a gym, with its secretary, wall-to-wall carpeting and baby-blue telephones.

Frazier, training under a giant photograph of the left hook which sent Ali to the canvas during the Fight of the Century, impressed the boxing writers with his determination. "He acts like a man who has lost something he thought he did not love, only to discover soon afterwards that he did truly care," reported *Sports Illustrated*. Frazier was also desperate to dispel suspicions that Ali had ruined him, that his kidneys were badly injured and that he had lost part of the sight in his right eye. "I can't remember when I been in better shape," he rounded angrily on doubting pressmen, "and I kin give a whole list of doctors who'll say the same thing." He talked little about the Foreman disaster ("That was in the past. That was yesterday. That is finished"), except to admit he had fought a dumb fight. His big mistake, he said, was in getting up immediately after the first knock-down instead of resting and clearing his head.

Once more the publicity machine was cranked into action as befitted a genuine "Superfight". Frazier, like Sonny Liston, was a perfect foil for Ali's caustic tongue. Everything about Smokin' Joe provided Ali with ammunition: his self-effacing Middle-American lifestyle; the ugly, awkward way he fought; the terrible punishment he masochistically soaked up (which made Ali recoil in horror and conclude Frazier was punchy before his time). But the litany had such a soggy familiarity about it that it served to remind the fans just how long the two had been at each other's throats.

Then, in finest Ali tradition, it all boiled over. Seated beside each other in front of the television cameras, the ritual mud slinging had almost run its course when Ali touched an unexpectedly exposed nerve. The two opponents had been bickering over who had come off worse after the first fight.

"You went to hospital," sniped Frazier.

"I went to hospital for ten minutes and you went to the hospital for ten months," retorted Ali.

Frazier: "Just for a rest. In and out."

Ali: "That shows how dumb you are . . . that shows how ignorant . . ."

With that Frazier snapped. Pulling out his studio earplug he leaped up and reached across to yank Ali from his seat. Both men grappled, heaved and eventually rolled off the stage into the audience where they were prised apart by alarmed spectators.

Ali, of course, had been separated from almost as many fights outside the ring as inside, and there was nothing to suggest that he regarded this particular piece of photogenic horseplay as anything special. Frazier was a different matter. When he issued his half-cocked challenge he was livid, as he was on most other occasions when Ali scorned his racial allegiances ("white man in a black skin", "Uncle Tom"), snapped personal insults ("soooo ugly") and slurred his intelligence. Such was the unassuming nature of the man that Frazier was unable to take Ali's act anywhere but to heart, and it consumed him to the extent that he was prepared to pay a $5,000 fine to button Ali's lip on the floor of a television studio. Once again Ali had succeeded in psyching an opponent into unreasoning hatred.

It was in this strained and bitter atmosphere of genuine enmity that Ali and Frazier climbed into the Garden ring before 20,788 witnesses on the edge of their chairs. From the word go it was Ali's fight, "ring generalship," as *Sports Illustrated* put it, "over a one-man army fighting a war of attrition."

Ali took the first round in arrogant, peacock fashion, dodging and slipping Frazier's best shots, bottling him up when he pressed too close. In the second, Frazier rediscovered his familiar two-fisted drumbeat rhythm, only to have it shattered by a stunning right – a slugger's punch – which visibly shivered him to his toes. The referee saved him by diving between the hunter and his kill in the mistaken belief that the bell had sounded.

Ali won the first six rounds with ease, his combinations and left jabs keeping "The Bull" at bay. He avoided the ropes like a disease and Frazier could not work his way close enough to land his short, heavy punches. But Ali failed to smother either Joe's juggernaught charges or remove his death's-head smile. Later he estimated he was throwing four times the number of punches Frazier could manage – a conservative estimate – yet his opponent never relented.

By the end of the seventh round, Frazier's grit appeared about to bear fruit. In the eighth, he strode across the ring into the opposing corner and unleashed a battery of left hooks at Ali's head. Ali stayed on the ropes, apparently arm-weary and capable only of looping his arm around his opponent's neck and dragging him down into a clinch. The ninth continued in the same vein until Ali dropped to his heels and moved forward to slug it out at Frazier's invitation, as he had done in the closing round of the Norton bout. Again the gamble paid off. Frazier never recovered and Ali never looked back.

Celebrating his twelve-round victory in his dressing room, Ali happily berated the press with, "I told so." The press's general pre-fight scenario had held that the match was to be a double-tragedy, a showdown between two fading, ageing gunslingers from which only one would emerge, badly shot up, but still able to announce his retirement with at least a modicum of dignity.

The press was perhaps half right. In his dressing room, Frazier was claiming he had won every round . . . in fact every minute of every round. The reporters crowding around appeared to be taking down his fuzzy logic. Actually they were writing his obituary.

The victor, gnawing a frozen lolly on a stick, was by no stretch of the imagination badly battered. "Can you see a mark on it?" he demanded, thrusting his face at the line of cameras and writers. "Can you believe that this is the face of a thirty-two-year-old man who has just fought Joe Frazier twelve rounds?" Then he sat back and smiled, content in the knowledge that once more he stood poised to enter his name in the boxing record.

PART 6
ON THE ROAD AGAIN

Before we get to the fateful meeting with Foreman in Zaire, let us take a moment to look at some of the steps along the road, starting with Ali's visit to Ireland, where he touched down in July 1972 to face Al "Blue" Lewis in a non-title bout. Lewis was a former sparring partner of Ali's. On the comeback trail since his loss to Frazier in their first meeting, Ali needed to rebuild his reputation. Before the fight, he was interviewed on Irish TV, as recounted in Dave Hannigan's The Big Fight. *From the same book comes a lively account of the contest itself, before Neil Allen of* The Times *looks at the first meeting between Ali and Joe Bugner. Finally, A. S. (Doc) Young ponders Ali's future after Ken Norton broke his jaw in their first meeting.*

The Big Fight Part 1 – In Living Colour

Dave Hannigan

On Monday evening, Ali and a few senior members of his retinue decamped to the RTE television studios in Donnybrook to record an extended interview with journalist Cathal O'Shannon. To be shown on Tuesday night at ten forty-five, immediately after an experimental colour broadcast of "Show-jumping from London", the promoters were fervently hoping it might have a positive impact on the size of Wednesday's wall-up crowd. Upon arriving, Ali's first port of call was the make-up department. Far from the cameras, he was already on the stage. Settling into the chair to be prepared for the spotlight by make-up lady Evelyn Lunny, he couldn't resist a warm-up performance before the main event.

"I took out my powder and started powdering him, holding my knees together to stop me falling," says Lunny. "And he turned to everybody in the place and he said: 'Isn't this just the prettiest face you've ever put powder on?' I was only in make-up about a year and I was very, very excited. Truly, I had never made up anybody who was coloured – Indian, Chinese or Black – up to that point. So I thought, what have we got in the department, and to be honest, we didn't have a lot. We had make-up to make white people look black or various shades. Then he turned around to everybody again and says: 'Look, she thinks she's going to hurt me with a powder puff and I'm about to face Al "Blue" Lewis!'"

It was a face that didn't need much enhancement.

The idea for the television programme came from John Condon, a director at RTE who realised that it wasn't too often that one of the world's most famous people hung around town for more than a week. He asked O'Shannon to get involved in the project even though the journalist knew very little about sport. What he lacked in specialist knowledge, O'Shannon made up for with interview technique and exhaustive research. As soon as he knew there was a chance he'd be sitting down with Ali, he read every article and book he could unearth. The extent of his homework comes through and three decades later "Muhammad Ali versus Cathal O'Shannon" remains a classic encounter. Getting Ali into the chair, however, wasn't without its little dramas.

"We went up to Opperman's place to meet him," says O'Shannon. "He'd already been there for two or three days and it seemed to me that every whore in Ireland had turned up there, including black whores from Manchester and London. God knows how they all got in. Within an hour of us arriving at the hotel, his mother arrived and she had with him his infant child Muhammad Junior. When she saw all these black whores, she chased them all out of it and then she gave out yards to him. She gave out stink and we all witnessed this right in front of the check-in desk. She followed him around he place, shouting 'Get rid of these bitches' and all sorts. Anyway, they were cleared out and he looked very sheepish at this time. Rahaman, a very smooth-looking fella with a little moustache who reminded me a lot of a black Errol Flynn, cooled the mother down. In the midst of all this stuff, we chatted to Ali for a few minutes about the possibility of an interview and he said: 'Yeah, I'll do it.'

"The question was what would we pay him? We knew that he had been to the BBC a year before and done a Michael Parkinson interview and they had flown over about twenty of his people with him especially and had to pay him 14,000 quid. We paid him one hundred pounds. A hundred pounds, imagine that, Christ almighty, you'd be amazed at the difficulty we had with that. When Angelo Dundee said he wanted the money in cash on the night, we had to go into the canteen in RTE to try and find cash because we had a cheque written. I haven't a clue why they wanted cash."

The search for used notes in the cash registers of the canteen wasn't even the worst part of the build-up. That happened inside the VIP room moments before taping began.

"The first thing Ali said to me in RTE was 'I hate this fucking place!'" says O'Shannon. "I thought, this is great, we're going on in twenty minutes to tape an hour-and-a-half programme. So

I said: 'How could you say that? You've only just got here.' He said: 'No, no, I mean the place I'm staying in.' He hated Opperman's because the previous night he had come into town, walked along O'Connell Street, gone into the Gresham Hotel, and of course he was followed by every kid and hanger-on walking around O'Connell Street. He loved the crowd, adored it actually and loved showing off, so he felt too isolated out in Opperman's. To be honest, I nearly crapped myself when he said: 'I hate this fucking place!' "

By the time O'Shannon was under the lights in the studio that normally housed the station's flagship programme, *The Late Late Show*, he had regained his professional demeanour. Apart from Dundee, Harold Conrad and a couple of others sitting in the front row, he and Condon had filled the seats by inviting family and friends, all of whom were suitably thrilled at the chance to spend an evening in Ali's company. Many of the exchanges are typical Ali at that time in his life, well-worn lines freshly delivered to a new and receptive audience. From the moment he strode across the stage in an open-necked shirt and a pair of slacks, he had them eating out of his hand. Settling back into the chair, he crossed his legs at the ankles and grew ever so slightly embarrassed when O'Shannon opened with a question to the audience.

O'SHANNON: Well, do you think he's the prettiest?
ALI (*SHAKING HIS HEAD*): I didn't say that, I don't know how that got out.

That was to be his last pretence of modesty for the duration.

O'SHANNON: You are doing a lot of fighting?
ALI: Well, yes, I think the boxing game should stay alive, I think every contender should get a shot at the title. The new tramp, I mean champ, Joe Frazier is not doing nothing, fighting once every seven months, fighting people you could beat and you can't fight.
O'SHANNON: You're so right about that.
ALI: I have to keep the game alive.
O'SHANNON: How do you feel about the fight with Al "Blue" Lewis?

ALI: I'm fighting Lewis for one reason, mainly because Frazier won't fight him, George Foreman won't fight him and Jerry Quarry won't fight him. To most boxers and managers, this is just a business and they figure they got a top contender and they don't want to take a chance and lose unless they are paid great. Top-notch fighters fighting "Blue" Lewis can't receive a proper payment because he's not famous and yet he has a chance of beating them. They have nothing to gain and everything to lose. I'm fighting him because everyone else is ducking him and he's a good fighter. Plus, it would be kinda hard to bring a top-notch fighter here because the price couldn't be put up.

O'SHANNON: What sort of a chance does he have with you?

ALI: Two chances . . . (*Pauses for effect.*)

O'SHANNON: What are they?

ALI: Slim and none (*He bows his head and puckers up his lips, satisfied with the gag.*)

O'SHANNON: I suppose I asked for that . . . Angelo Dundee has just handed me a piece of paper saying you hope to go to fight in Tehran in three weeks' time.

ALI: I – Ran in Tehran. Yes, we're going, just an exhibition, a government invitation. We're working on it now.

O'SHANNON: So your next big fight, I suppose, is against Floyd Patterson.

ALI: Patterson, right, the rabbit.

O'SHANNON: The rabbit?

ALI: I call him the rabbit.

O'SHANNON: Why's that?

ALI: The way he fights and he calls me Clay and my name is now Muhammad Ali but he insists on Clay so I call him the rabbit. Plus, I'm going to fight the rabbit in the garden.

O'SHANNON: Madison Square Garden, of course . . . You then go on to fight Frazier, I gather?

ALI: Yes, if he comes out of hiding. He bought a plantation down in South Carolina, some chicken plantation. I know he's a slave but he don't have to buy no plantation.

O'SHANNON: How do you really feel about him?

ALI: Well, he's a good slugger. He's not scientific. He's rough. Physically, I know I beat him. I won nine rounds. He's already ugly and I beat him so bad that night and he was so ugly that his face should have been donated to the bureau of wildlife. (*The most over-used line of the trip receives yet another airing and the crowd erupts.*)

O'SHANNON: He toured here with a show.

ALI: I heard. He flopped like he do everywhere else. He's got a singing group called the Knockouts and he thought just because they gave him my title he could go everywhere and draw people and get rich. I understand he draws eighty people or maybe a hundred people in a 20,000-seat arena. In London, in a 4,000-seat arena he drew twelve people and had the nerve to keep on with the show.

O'SHANNON: He did a little better here, he got eighty-seven at one actually and 1,041 at another.

ALI: I know I can beat him singing but I don't call myself a singer. I can come here and fill every place because the people know who the real champ is.

O'SHANNON: But you have been a singer too, you had a show called *Buck White*, didn't you?

ALI: I was in a play called *Big Time Buck White*, a black militant play about the problems we have in America. The play was a flop but I was a hit. The play lasted six days but the worst critics said my part was a hit. I want to get that straight.

O'SHANNON: Why is it you think that you draw the crowds? Of all the sportsmen in the world, you are a great crowd drawer.

ALI: Mainly personality has a lot to do with it. Like a salesman's business depends entirely on his personality. If he's rude and unsympathetic, the buyer will hope that he goes away and never comes back. But very often if the salesman is good he can make a person buy something he doesn't even intend to . . . Very few fighters, if you take the camera up close and see my nose and my face, I'm not ugly, I'm not ugly like most fighters. They've got noses like that (*presses in on the nose*) and ears like that (*pulls left ear forward*). "How you feeling, champ?" "Ugh, ugh, ugh . . ." I'm pretty, I'm a pretty fighter and I have a personality. I know how to talk to the wise heads. I had a talk with your great Mr Lynch in your parliament house and I know how to talk to men like you with less intelligence than myself . . .

There is a prolonged bout of laughter then that causes him to grow especially animated

. . . Just listen to the people laugh, just listen to them laugh. Very few comedians can do this and that's their job. It's personality that attracts. Like in America I stand up for black people and, regardless of what it costs me, I speak out for what I believe in. Just like in Ireland you got people fighting for what they believe. Then you have all the Muslims in Pakistan, Saudi Arabia, Syria, Lebanon, India, Abu Dhabi, all throughout Libya, Kuwait, they all recognise me and call the name Muhammad Ali. You add all of this up and all I represent and I AM THE GREATEST! (*Slapping the chair with his hands, his voice is at full pitch.*) I CANNOT LOSE! I'M PRETTY! Many want to say this but they fear it. They see this in myself and some hate me for it and some love me for it and add it all up and we got a large crowd. Joe Frazier is ugly. He's flat-footed, he can't sing, he can't fight and he has no personality.

O'SHANNON: He can't fight?

ALI: No, he's a slugger, a street fighter. Don't get me wrong. He's good but he's not skilful. He's known for taking a lot of punches. He's not like Floyd Patterson or Sugar Ray Robinson or Joe Louis or Jack Johnson or Jack Dempsey. These were great scientific fighters. Joe Frazier will take five punches to hit you once.

O'SHANNON: Why do you think he beat you the last time?

ALI: The reason he got the decision if you looked at my face and his face after the fight, both his eyes were closed, his lip was cut, his nose was bloodied, his head was swollen and he spent one month in the hospital. Did you all hear that? He spent thirty days in intensive care, no phone calls and no visitors. That's a terrible beating when you have to stay rested for thirty days. I'm not complaining. He got the decision but next time I'll get him. I played too much with him, plus I found out that three of the judges was on the local draft board.

With characteristic modesty, O'Shannon downplays in his part in the success of the show, feeling it was the kind of thing Ali had done "a thousand times before".

"It's strange but, you know, with Ali, there was no way you could go wrong from an interviewer's point of view," says O'Shannon. "You knew he would react properly because he was such a bloody showman. A total and absolute pro. If I had dropped myself in it, I felt he would have picked me up out of it. I was in the safest possible hands. I'd worked out the questions but didn't even go over them with him. I just said we're going to cover this sort of area and that was enough. I had interviewed John F. Kennedy before that but to tell you the God's honest truth, this was a much bigger thing."

There are certain occasions in the interview when astute questions play a vital role in provoking the subject and offering a glimpse of something more substantive than his practised put-downs of Frazier and pre-cooked punchlines.

o'shannon: How was it, Muhammad, anyway to be a Negro boy in the South?

ali: We say black now.

o'shannon: All right, black. Is it not the same thing?

ali: No, Negro is . . . we're talking about . . . all people are named after a country. The Chinese are named after China, the Cubans are named after Cuba, Irish people are named after Ireland, Indonesians named after Indonesia, Japanese are named after Japan, Australians are named after Australia, but there's no country named Negro!

o'shannon: All right, let me . . .

ali: Do you understand?

o'shannon: I understand.

ali: You're not as dumb as you look.

o'shannon: Do I look that dumb?

ali: Naah, only kidding.

o'shannon: What I really mean is did you feel that you were deprived, that you and your family and other blacks were second-class citizens?

ali: Did we feel it? We knew it! Not only second class! Add up all of the nationalities you have on earth – they come first. Right now, you can come to my home town and you're freer in America than I am. The Chinese, the Japanese that the black people helped America to fight or even the Germans are freer. The day after the war in Vietnam, the Vietcong will be more of a citizen than the American Negro. So we might be the fiftieth of sixtieth class if you break it down. If we were just second class we'd be all right.

O'SHANNON: This is something you feel strongly about?

ALI: Strongly? I know it's the truth, I live right there every day.

O'SHANNON: What attracted you to Islam in the first instance?

ALI: The Muslim religion is the true teachings of Elijah Muhammad right there in America and no power structure or nobody will challenge him. It is the history of ourselves, the history of our true religion, our nationality and our names. We don't have our names. I notice how proud you all are of your names. Chinese have names like Ching Chung, Lu Chin. Russians have names like Kosygin or Khrushchev. And you have names like O'Connor and Grady and Kennedy. [*How interesting that be should refer to the surname that crops up in his own family?*] Africans have names like Lomumba Nkroma. Jews have names like Weinstein and Goldberg. Italians got names like Dundee, Bienvenuti and Marciano. We have names like Grady [*one more reference to his ancestors*] and Clay and Hawkins and Smith and Jones and Johnson but we're black.

O'SHANNON: These are the slave names?

ALI: When I heard this I knew it was the truth because it's history. Muhammad Ali is a beautiful black name, name of our ancestors. When I heard this I just had to walk out of the Church of Christianity because they never taught us our true knowledge. Then they told me how we were brainwashed in America. We see Jesus, he's white with blond hair and blue eyes . . . We see the Lord's Supper, all white people . . . We see the angels in heaven, all white people. We look at Miss Universe, a white woman . . . Miss America, a white woman . . . Miss World, a white woman . . . Even Tarzan, the King of the Jungles in Africa, he was white. (*The audience find this so funny that obviously enthused by their reaction, he puts his hands over his mouth in the manner of Johnny Weissmuller's Tarzan.*) You see a white man swinging around Africa, ahhhhhyaaayaaaa, with a diaper on, ahhhyaaayaaaa . . . he beats up all the Africans and breaks the lion's jaw. The Africans been in Africa for centuries but can't yet talk to the animals! But Tarzan, all of a sudden some goat raised him up and he can talk to the animals. So I'm just showing you how the black man in America has been whitewashed in his mind. And then we look at the good cowboys, they rode the white horses . . . and the President lives in a white house. They got TV commericals for White House cigars, White Swan soap, King White soap, White tissue paper, White Rain hair rinse, White Tornado floor wax, White Plus toothpaste. The Angel fruit cake was the white cake but the devil fruit cake was the chocolate cake. Everything good is white! Our religion teaches us the knowledge of ourselves, the knowledge of our culture, the knowledge of our history. It makes us want to be with our own, marry our own, live with our own, clean up ourselves, do for ourselves, quit forcing ourselves on white neighbourhoods, clean up our own neighbourhoods, makes us proud and makes us identify with our own brothers around the world. Being an intelligent man, I'm not only winning in boxing or in my stand on the draft, I'm a winner also in the movement that I follow for my people whose leader is Elijah Muhammad who we believe was taught by Allah, God himself, to teach the so-called American Negro the truth that's been hidden from them for four hundred years, the truth which will free them!

O'SHANNON: Why is it do you think the black Muslims preach the separation of the races, rather than integration of the races, as indeed many American blacks do?

ALI: Well, when we say separation, we know that as of now, we always have to be trading with one another, living with one another. When we say separate, we mean mentally, mainly. We've tried integrating for four hundred years and we been kicked and shot and brutalised. I understand this is some of your problem in Ireland where people are tired of being dominated by certain groups, tired of being rude and being mean, and they want to do for themselves. The same way in all countries – people are just tired and they're revolutionising things. They want to be free. We been in America under white domination, lynched, killed, raped, castrated, shot down daily. No justice in the courts, deprived of freedom, justice and equality and we now just want to be free. We can't do it. We've found out that black and white are disagreeable in peace. They can't

get along together so we think we should just now quit fighting, quit being violent now that we're doctors, lawyers and
mechanics, now that we're educated and we don't need to
pick cotton any more. We got millions of blacks being born in
hospitals every day and there are no jobs. We think that we
should now go on some land and build and construct and do
for ourselves, that's all.

O'SHANNON: Do you mean in actual fact that there should be
separate parts of the United States only for Negroes and only
for whites?

ALI: The holy Elijah Muhammad teaches us that we've been there
four hundred years. We fought the Japanese, we fought the
Germans, we fought the Koreans. If America went to war with
Ireland tomorrow, the black people would be over here so fast
shooting you. All the black people would be over here shooting
you with the American flag. And we believe that since we been
fighting all of America's enemies, not our enemies, we've
worked four hundred years, sixteen hours a day, from sun up to
sun down, that we should now be repaid. Don't give us nothing
but repay us. You got fifty states and we make up 10 per cent of
the population. Then divide up 10 per cent of the land and let
us build our own stores, grow our own food, make our own
suits, be like other people, not always begging white people for
houses, begging for jobs, begging for a seat in your restaurant.
May I use your toilet? May I ride on your bus? Now that I'm
grown and educated and now we're no longer slaves and we
can't get along, just let me go and live by myself like other
people. There ain't nothing wrong with that.

O'SHANNON: Muslims don't believe in war. You certainly don't
and you demonstrated that by refusing to join the American
Army, but you've said on one occasion that you could believe
in a holy war.

ALI: The holy Koran teaches us that we declare ourselves righteous Muslims who take no part in wars, no way, fashion or
form, that take the lives of humans unless it's a holy war
declared by God, Allah himself. This hasn't happened. If it do
happen, we have a way of knowing because our religious leaders speak out. But we don't take no part in wars, not just the
Vietnam War, no war.

O'SHANNON: Would you fight in a holy war, a war of this sort? How would you know that you should fight?

ALI: That's what I'm trying to say. We have a leader who will speak, all countries have leaders, we have a leader. If we are attacked, and we are right, we believe in fighting, but not being the aggressor.

O'SHANNON: Elijah Muhammad has said something that perhaps us white people have misunderstood, perhaps you can explain it to me, he said: "White men are devils."

ALI: Yes, he means just what he says. The deeds and the works of the man, what the American devils did to us. All the lynching, the killing, cutting the black people's privates out and sticking it in the mouth. I got a book called *The Hundred Years of Lynching* written by a white man. They did this for years. They took black women who were four months pregnant, hung us up by the feet, stuck a dagger in the stomach and ripped it just to pull the unborn baby out. Just to put fear in other slaves. They tied up black people to two horses and two horses pulled their arms and legs out. Lemonade trains with white people and white children of America used to come and watch them tie up ten or fifteen black men and pour gasoline on them and watch them burn alive. They took us and hung us up on trees and shot us. They cut our heads off, took the logs off and gave them to little boys. This is worse than the devil. The preacher in the church told us that the devil was under the ground and he'd wait 'til we died before he'd burn us up. This white devil in America burned us while we was alive. He didn't wait 'til we died. What I'm trying to say is the deeds and the works. If Elijah Muhammad can stand up in America for forty-two years before my little black self was born and say that the American white man is the devil, then the white man should get up and say: "You are a liar!" and carry him to court and say: "We are not the devil." Not one American, not one government official, not one mayor, not one senator, none of them will stand up and say they are not devils and this man is lying. What am I to do? I believe it.

Throughout this speech, he had the index finger on his right hand at full extension, wagging it determinedly as he spoke the last line. Keeping a serious scowl on his face, he glared at the audience with his arms wide in exasperation. To his credit, O'Shannon didn't allow him to get away with such a widespread condemnation of an entire race.

O'SHANNON: Do you believe that every white man is the devil? Angelo Dundee? Harold Conrad?

ALI: Angelo Dundee is Italian, he's got a lot of black blood in him. (*Pause for laughter.*) And Harold Conrad is a Jew. What I'm saying to you is this (*staring into the camera*): Elijah Muhammad, our leader, teaches us this and I believe everything he says. It's not for me to prove. You must remember this. You have not lynched me. It wasn't the Germans who did this to us, it wasn't the white Canadians who was right on our border. He's putting the emphasis on the American devils. Let's say we got one white fella in America who has proved that he means right. Let's say that we got another one – white people have died in demonstrations for black people – now here's the position I'm in. Let's say ten thousand rattlesnakes coming to bite me and in that ten thousand, there was one thousand who didn't mean no harm, and I knew there was a good thousand snakes out there. They all look alike so what should I do? Keep the door open and let the ten thousand in, hoping that the thousand will unite and save me even though one bite will kill me. Should I just be safe and shut the door? We do have white people saying: "I mean right, I got a black husband, all my children are black, I love everybody." I really believe you but I'm sorry, ma'am, there's ten thousand behind you that don't feel that way. What am I going to do? I know. I bet my hand on my family's life that there are some white that mean right but they are so few. I can't forget all the lynchings, the murders because there are two that mean right. When America drops bombs on Vietnam, she drops them on babies and boys. When she dropped the bomb on Japan, they don't say some are innocent. They just at war. When a person in Belfast leaves a bomb, they don't say, well, there's a kid who's innocent in here, there's an old lady who's blind, they just boom, leave the bomb! What I'm saying is, we have a problem and maybe there's a few bosses mean right but there's so many that don't. We have to look at the problem as a whole. I want to make that plain, I know that there are whites that mean right.

There were times in this portion of the interview when Ali appeared to be straining to reconcile Nation of Islam dogma with the reality of his experience in Ireland. After almost a week in what was then one of the whitest countries in the world, a week where his every move had been greeted by uniform adulation and affection, he couldn't just parrot the standard lines about "white devils" without equivocation. In attempting to adhere to the doctrine of his religion while carefully avoiding causing offence to his hosts though, he was clever enough to get himself out of verbal jams – the question about Angelo Dundee, for instance – by leavening the tension of the moment with wit and humour.

At the remove of nearly thirty years, it is the radicalism of his beliefs that stand out. Anybody too young to have ever seen him fight or to have watched him perform on television in his pomp would find it hard to reconcile this outspoken (if still quite charming) extremist with the sedate figure who has over time become a benevolent, grandfatherly icon in our lives. The thirty-year-old angrily demanding that a separate black nation be established in America was the Muslim charged with the task of explaining to the Western world in September 2001 that his religion was all not about hate.

"Rivers, ponds, lakes and streams – they all have different names," said Ali on a visit to Ground Zero in New York just ten days after the World Trade Center had been attacked. "But they all contain water. Just as religions do – they all contain truths. Islam is peace."

Ali's transformation from the rabid segregationist of 1972 to the ecumenical beacon of 2002 can be traced back to the death of Elijah Muhammad in 1975. Elijah was succeeded by his son, Wallace D. Muhammad, who renamed the Nation of Islam the World Community of Al-Islam, renounced the theory of black superiority and ceased calling for segregation. Ali accepted these new policies wholeheartedly, changed his stances accordingly, and began telling interviewers that "actions and deeds" mattered

far more than somebody's colour. The new direction set him on
a journey that brought him to his current status as a UN
Messenger for Peace, a man of such standing that in January
2002 he publicly asked the kidnappers of *Wall Street Journal*
reporter Daniel Pearl in Pakistan to release him in the name of
Allah. What a difference from the man Cathal O'Shannon tussled
with all those years ago.

O'SHANNON: You yourself have some little white blood in you.

ALI: Yeah, what are you saying?

O'SHANNON: You feel totally Negro?

ALI: Black? Nobody's really totally, like Chinese are yellow they
say but they are not really yellow. You're white but you're not
totally white. Gimme something white. (*He picks up a notebook
with white pages from O'Shannon's desk.*) See, this is white, you
not white, you kinda pinkish. I'm not black but I'm considered black, as far as the blood is concerned. Some people say
you talk so bad about us here in America, you got some white
blood in you. Oh yeah, how did I get white blood in me? Way
back a hundred or something years ago, the old slave master's
wife used to get tired and he would sneak back into old gran-
ny's shack, and she had big hips, she was pretty, and had big
breasts and big legs. She was strong 'cause she worked all day
to clean up the white lady's house, raise the white lady's babies
and poor white lady was tired and weak, and old black slave
lady was strong. He would sneak back at night and close the
door and you know what he would do?

O'SHANNON: I can guess.

ALI: You can guess what he would do! And then here come me,
half-black! (*He laughs aloud at that as do the crowd.*) They
laughing 'cause they know what I'm talking about.

For all the laugher, that exchange was the one where O'Shannon
felt uncertain about what would happen next.

"I thought he was going to hit me," says O'Shannon. "I'm
thinking to myself: 'Christ, he's getting angry now!' He clenched
his fist and his fists oddly enough weren't that big. He was a huge
man, big broad shoulders and a tiny waist, but my Christ, he had
a pair of feet on him that were ginormous. He had bloody great

boots on these huge feet, yet the hands weren't all that big. But at that point, I began to think maybe I pushed it too far. But then he began to tell me the story of how the slave master snuck around and was full of fun again."

When O'Shannon brought up the topic of Harold Conrad telling reporters that Ali was a wizard, possessed with magical powers which included the ability to see into the future and put curses on people, he couldn't resist the opportunity to demonstrate his magic. Once O'Shannon had produced some suitable silver paper from his cigarette box, Ali was off and running.

ALI: I can take, for an example to show you my powers, some silver paper and wet it and fold it . . . I can take this right here, for example, and if it don't work, you tell the people the truth, I don't make no promises (*He licks the paper.*) . . . I can take this here and I can fold it up like this. (*He folds it over several times.*) Now, you can give me your hand and I can say just watch me. (*He places it on the back of O'Shannon's right hand.*) . . . And you concentrate, that paper is going to get warm, so warm until it will start smoking until it gets real hot, do you feel it?

O'SHANNON: Do I feel it? (*Uncomfortably shifting in the chair, his voice goes up a few decibles.*) Oh, do I feel it! (*He shakes it off and examines his hand.*) Can I just see it for a second?

ALI: (*Picking the paper off the ground and holding it for inspection.*) Somebody from the audience . . . lady, come here real fast. (*A woman walks nervously on stage holding her handbag.*) . . . Is that hot? (*She just nods her head before walking off again.*)

O'SHANNON: He's a wizard . . . that's not bad. (*The crowd applaud the feat.*)

ALI: The paper is actually red-hot.

O'SHANNON: Quite truthfully the paper is still quite warm, I don't know how that was done but it's not bad.

Shortly after that *coup de théâtre*, disaster struck. One of the recording machines broke down and there was a delay of about twenty minutes. As technicians scrambled to get it running again, O'Shannon quizzed Ali to no great avail about the technique he had used to burn his hand. In the front row, however,

Dundee grew increasingly irritated with the stoppage. Like any conscientious trainer, he didn't want an already sick [Ali had the flu] fighter spending too long under the hot studio lights less than forty-eight hours before the first bell. "Come on, get this thing finished!" he shouted more than once. "Get it done!" Eventually, the longest wait of O'Shannon's life was over and the cameras were back on.

Beforehand, it had been O'Shannon's intention to get Ali to read something from Jose Torres's celebrated study of him, *Sting Like a Bee*. Dundee scuppered that plan, warning him not to ask his fighter to read live on television. He didn't say exactly why but his tone brooked no argument. Instead, Ali was invited to rattle off one of his poems, and ended the show with the same sort of flourish he finished so many fights.

O'SHANNON: Most of your poems are funny, but you've written one about your own people, I think at the time of the Attica prison riot. [On 13 September 1971, a four-day revolt at the Attica Correctional Facility in upstate New York culminated in 1,500 state police and National Guardsmen storming the prison. Of the forty-two people killed in the ensuing violence, ten were hostages taken by the prisoners.] It's a serious poem. You certainly have some very serious moments, as you've shown us tonight. Could you, before you go, say that poem for us?

ALI: This poem explains the Attica prison riot. Did you hear about that over here? All the black prisoners were shot. Just before, they held some white hostages and they said they would cut throats if they didn't get what they wanted. And the word was, well, if the throats were cut, then shoot to kill everybody. They found out during the autopsy that throats were not cut, they just shot them for nothing, the trigger-happy policemen. That [Nelson] Rockefeller [the New York Governor at the time] gave word: "Ten minutes or so, if they don't give up, open fire." One black prisoner came out to speak to the warden and the warden said: "You've ten minutes to surrender or we are going to come in and shoot you, what's your reply? We're going to come in there and shoot!" The black prisoner came out with a poetic poem, this didn't happen but this is what I wrote:

Better far from all I see
To die fighting to be free
What more fitting end could be
Better sure than in some bed
Where in broken health I'm led
Lingering until I'm dead
Better than with prayers and pleas
Or in the clutch of some disease
Wasting slowly by degrees
Better than a heart attack
Or some dose of drug I lack
Let me die by being black
Better far that I should go
Standing here against the foe
Is there sweeter death to know
Better than the bloody stain
On some highway where I'm lain
Torn by flying glass and pain
Better call on death to come
Than to die another dumb
Muted victim in the slum
Better than of this prison rot
If there's any choice I got
Kill me here on this spot
Better far my fight to wage
Now while my blood boils with rage
Less it cool with ancient age
Better valour for us to die
Than to Uncle Tom and try
Making peace just to live a lie
Better now that I say my sooth
I'm going to die demanding truth
While I'm still akin to youth
Better now than later on
Knowing the fear of death is gone
Never mind another dawn.

Then they opened fire on them but they died telling it like it was.
(*At the end of a virtuoso performance, he mimics the sound of a*

machine gun going off. Having listened in perfect silence to his rendition, the audience applauds.) I've another thing to say, this is one thing, this is one thing I love and admire about the Irish people. I've studied a little history since I've been here, I found out that you been underdogs for years, hundreds of years. People dominating you and ruling you. You can identify with this freedom struggle, you understand, I just have my mind on the other side of the water. But we're all fighting for the same causes and ideas, we just have different reasons and approaches.

The Big Fight Part 2 – Ali vs Al Lewis

Dave Hannigan

The fight was being broadcast on closed-circuit television in the US as a joint venture by Bob Arum's Top Rank Inc and a company called Video Techniques in New York. Arum was at ringside working as co-commentator alongside Reg Gutteridge. Watching the Dubliners launch into "Amhran Na bhFiann" and the crowd taking up the singing with them, Gutteridge told his international audience: "Well, this is a very cute way of playing it."

Everybody in the ring was standing with their backs to Hill 16, the most storeyed terrace in the stadium. Before the musical interlude began, it was one more barren space. However, the playing of the Irish anthem appeared to be the signal for a mass influx of non-paying customers through the tunnels on the Hill. They were throwing themselves over the fences, sneaking through gates, doing what they had to do to get in.

"They didn't get the crowd they expected," says Elbaum. "When we stood up for our national anthem, I looked around and said to myself: 'This is an awesome venue for a fight, it would look great with thirty or forty thousand but they could have held this fight in a hall, we didn't need no stadium.' Then they played the Irish anthem and everybody was standing to attention and halfway through that song, I swear to you, it was like the scene in a western movie when the Indians appear over the horizon. Thousands of Irishmen came in over the walls and fences and nobody made a move to stop them. It seemed to happen on cue; sing the Irish anthem and everyone gets in free. Wherever the holes were, they found them, so the place filled up a bit. It seemed as though far more people came in free than paid."

An announcement came over the tannoy: "Security and stewards to Hill Sixteen, please." Maybe the sound quality wasn't great because apart from two uniformed Gardai who strolled towards the terrace before turning around halfway, the response of the organisers was non-existent. "Will people kindly go back to their seats?" went another desperate request. Later, Conrad would estimate that 7,000 got in free.

"All the fellas sitting up in the gods started to make their way towards the pitch then," says John McCormack. "There was a wire fence around the field to stop people getting in who hadn't paid for the ringside seats, but sure fellas just came down and started climbing over the fence. They were making announcements over the loudspeakers asking the stewards to go all over the place to stop people climbing over the gates. But they weren't going to stop the Dubs, the Dubs were bunking in and that was it. They didn't care who was there. You had all these young fellas in jeans sitting there with fellas in suits who'd forked out serious cash to be ringside."

The best seats in the house cost £15 while the most distant standing spot on the terrace went for £2. There were also decent locations available for £10 and £5. Not that the price scale mattered too much to those who had gained access through Hill 16.

"A couple of my friends were working as stewards for the night," says Mick Daly, who watched the drama unfold from a seat in the Hogan stand. "Once the fight was about to start, they took seats in the centre of the pitch. They heard the call go out for stewards to make themselves known and eject the Dubs who were getting into the expensive seats, but my friends were sensible enough: they discarded their stewards' badges and stayed in their seats to wait for the fight to start."

Meanwhile, O'Hehir ploughed on with the introductions and Lew Eskin, editor of *Boxing Illustrated* magazine, referee and sole judge of the contest made his first appearance. Summing up the informed views on what might transpire, Gutteridge mentioned to his audience that Eskin sometimes moonlighted as a firefighter and this could come in handy if Lewis ended up being seriously hurt. Delivering his instructions to both fighters in the centre of the ring, Eskin wiped excess grease from Lewis's forehead. Then Ali returned to his corner, bowed his head and adopted the familiar pose for one more moment of prayer to Allah.

The first round was predictably tentative; the only highlight came when Ali, responding to the exhortations of Dundee who shouted "Hook him, hook him" all through, connected with a powerful left hook that stunned Lewis. Towards the end of the round, he offered a few left jabs of his own by way of a response, but neither fighter seemed especially enthusiastic for the fray in those opening exchanges. Just before a barely audible bell sounded, a voice from the crowd urged: "Come on, Muhammad, send him back to the penitentiary." Despite the lackadaisical pace, Lewis was puffing hard on the way back to his corner and a cut inside his mouth was already leaking blood.

"Al could fight inside and that was the plan," says Elbaum. "That was our shot, with the idea that he might tire him out in the later rounds. The other thing was Al could punch, I don't care what kind of a chin you got, if you hit the guy right you can put him in trouble, and put him on the floor. I had told Al: 'You go the distance with this guy and we're sitting pretty from here on in. We can make some serious dough.' So we had him trying to get to the body early, but unfortunately, nobody could take body shots like Ali."

During the interval, the crowd were invigorated by the appearance of a short-skirted round-card girl. Betty McDermott, who worked in a local hotel, made a lap of the ring to resounding catcalls and cheers. The timekeeper must have been one of those most taken by her because nearly a minute and a half elapsed before he rung the bell for the start of round two.

Another staid three minutes ensued. Ali was warned for punching low by Eskin; Lewis brushed him back with a decent left hook and almost scored big with another right. Still, when Ali backed him into a corner at one stage, he curiously allowed him out again without landing a solitary punch. Recognising perhaps that he was feeling the ill-effects of his cold, Luther Burgess was manically shouting at Lewis: "Fire, fire, let punches go." His charge didn't respond and it was Ali who finished the stronger, unleashing a combination just before the bell.

The third round promised more entertainment. Ali began by dancing around the ring and the crowd rose to their feet to applaud. This was the fighter they had come to see. Lewis was rooted to a spot in the centre of the ring as Ali shuffled around him, clockwise, then anticlockwise, picking him off as he went. But again, Ali ran out of steam and slowed down the pace until he found himself in a corner taking some good body shots. They looked better than they were, because after Lewis had let fly, Ali waved his right hand, inviting him back to deliver a few more. In true pantomime style, Lewis waved his left at Ali in copycat fashion. That this was the extent of the drama sums up a round that ended with Ali shoving Lewis around in his corner.

"It looks like Ali wanted to pin him in his corner then to save himself the walk back," says Reg Gutteridge, commentating. "But Lewis is certainly doing a better job than Jerry Quarry did."

As had become the pattern, Ali was on his feet awaiting the start of hostilities long before the bell for the fourth, and he produced some more shuffling that appeased the small band of spectators who could be heard slow handclapping the lack of real action. The two men traded flurries when Lewis caught Ali in a corner, but it was the Detroit boxer who suffered most when a right visibly weakened his legs. The slight buckle in his knees prompted a shout from Dundee: "He's tired, he's tired. Use the hook." Belying the obvious signs of fatigue, Lewis actually ended the round in good fettle, landing a few body shots, the effects of which were negated by the way Ali had his arms tucked by his sides in defence.

"The promoters had put a wrestling mat on the floor of the ring instead of a boxing mat," says Pete Hamill, then a journalist with the *Village Voice*. "And as a result, Ali couldn't get up on his toes and dance as he liked to do. A wrestling mat being thicker, there is much less bounce than in a boxing mat. From that point of view, he showed me for the first time that night that he could fight inside, stand there flat-footed and really fight inside. It made for an interesting fight because it showed me he could mix it as a fighter without resorting to the classic Ali style."

At a press conference the previous day, Raymond Smith had mentioned to Ali that his editor wanted an estimate of when the fight might end, in order to plan the different editions of the *Irish Independent*.

"You go and tell your boss that I will knock the bum out in the fifth," said Ali. "Because he can only bring in enough money in advertising on television for that many rounds, I won't carry him any longer than that." For good measure, he then demonstrated the sort of punch that would end the contest.

Without quite replicating the exact punch, he did all he could to make good on the prediction. Having spent much of the fifth seemingly content to work his opponent's body, Ali had been winded by a right cross that was really the only major Lewis offensive in the round. With thirty seconds to go, Lewis extricated himself from a corner and appeared out of danger. He was right in the centre of the ring when Ali measured him up with a left and dropped him with a right.

"I was pretty short so I had to stand up on my chair to see over the edge of the ring," says Arlynne Eisner. "I'd been pretty bummed out that everyone was cheering against Al because I'd grown up around him. When Ali knocked Al down then, my dad could see I was upset. So he leaned over and shouted to me: 'Don't worry, he's just put his legs up and that's a signal, he's getting back up, that's our code. Don't worry, he's going to be OK.' And he did, he got back up from that one."

His recovery was assisted by a long count from Eskin that drew criticism from Ali's camp.

"The count lasted twenty-two to twenty-three seconds," claimed Angelo Dundee's brother Chris afterwards. "It would have been all over then if the count had been right."

The fight would certainly have ended there without complaint. Many spectators got up to leave as Lewis hit the floor and even Ali raised his arms tentatively in triumph. But Dundee's timing was off. Lewis was down for exactly fifteen seconds, long enough to lose the fight, short enough for Eskin to offer some respite.

"There was nothing wrong with the count at the end of the round," said Eskin later. "Some folk in Muhammad Ali's camp have been saying that it lasted more than twenty seconds instead of less then ten seconds but that is wrong. I did not begin to count until Ali moved away to a neutral corner. Not more than three seconds could have been lost between the time Lewis went to the canvas and Ali moved back to a corner."

The bell gave Lewis an immediate chance to catch his breath and rehabilitate further. He looked in poor shape, though, as Ali scored with left after left in the opening minute of the sixth. As soon as Ali began to employ his right too, it appeared only a matter of time before Lewis went down for good. More than once, the aftershocks of a punch travelled all the way to his knees, yet each time he stayed upright. Eventually, the bandages on Ali's right hand glove came loose and he eased off the pressure. Buoyed by this latest reprieve, Lewis summoned new reserves of strength, producing excellent combinations the delivery of which was abetted by Ali taking a breather on the ropes for the last thirty seconds of the round.

"I thought that it was a helluva performance by Ali, a man who should have been in bed fighting the flu," says Barney Eastwood. "He should have been in bed two or three days before the fight and I really thought for a time it wouldn't even go ahead. Watching him then fight the way he did, I said to myself: 'That's a great, great fighter there, you need a special quality of a man to go out and do that under those circumstances.' I think his people didn't want him to fight but he wanted to go in, get on with it and get out, and he probably thought Lewis was a soft enough thing anyway. As it turned out, Ali was carrying a big handicap into that ring and Lewis must have realised the other guy wasn't half his usual self."

The seventh was similar in style and content to the previous round. In between long periods of inertia, Ali punished Lewis whenever he caught him on the ropes or in a corner without ever exerting himself unduly. Then, as the clock ticked down, Lewis emerged from his hibernation to try and do something before the bell. With Ali significantly ahead on points, the storyline had become less about Lewis's chance of effecting a shock and more about his bravery in the face of a far superior fighter. Before the start of the eighth, Conrad made a circuit of the ring, stopped by the commentators' seats and whispered to Arum: "He just won't fall! He just won't fall!"

For the majority of the eighth, the most animated individual on view was Angelo Dundee. Conscious of the fact that no matter how tired or how far behind he was, a puncher like Lewis could produce something dangerous, Dundee kept on urging his man to "finish it, finish it". It was all in vain because Ali gave his left most of the round off and delivered nothing but rights for over a minute. The cumulative effect of that relentless assault can be gauged by the fact Lewis didn't even have the energy for his by now customary end-of-round flurry.

"There's nothing I admire more in a fighter than courage and this guy Lewis certainly has that," says Gutteridge, as the bell sounded for the start of the ninth.

The leisurely pace of the eighth must have worked wonders for the stamina of both fighters because the ninth was action-packed. A round that began to the soundtrack of more slow handclapping from a belligerent pocket of the Hogan Stand exploded into life. Ali upped the tempo and launched an all-out attack, spending thirty seconds working Lewis to the head and body without having to take a single jab in reply. The crowd were enthused by this but there was never any indication that Lewis was going down under this barrage. Even when battered against the ropes, his legs appeared steadier than before. Then he shocked everybody by going on the counter explosively. Using the ropes almost as a springboard, he went right back at Ali. After succeeding with three stinging rights to the head, the crowd raucously voiced their approval of his efforts. If staying in there with Ali was a genuine achievement, offering such robust resistance with almost nine rounds in the books was worthy of their highest praise. In his corner, they watched his revitalisation and for a moment, just one fleeting moment, fostered real hope that he could yet do something extraordinary.

"'Blue' hit Ali with one really terrific punch," says Steve Eisner. "And he armbarred him and I was screaming: ' "Blue", hit him with one more, for Chrissakes, one more.' And 'Blue' looked back at us and shouted: 'I ain't got one more. I ain't got one more.' Luther says to me: 'Shit, we got to put more brandy in the water.' If you look at the tapes of the fight, Luther and I put brandy in his water to help 'Blue' and he doesn't spit it out after the third round. We had him swallowing it from then on just to try to get him through."

Ali exacted quick revenge for the embarrassing cameo he'd endured at the end of the ninth. He opened the tenth with a couple of swift lefts to the head and soon Lewis's right eye was nearly swollen shut. Sensing his opponent had nothing left, Ali picked him off at will, wobbling his legs more than once as Lewis, his mouth agape, desperate for oxygen, struggled to land a solitary punch in reply. It had become only a matter of time.

In Ali's corner, however, there was some concern. When he sat on the stool, he emitted a loud groan that worried his trainer.

"Did he catch you in the balls?" said Dundee.

"No, no, my nuts are OK but, oh gee, I sure am bursting."

Now that Ali had finally subdued Lewis, nature was calling.

"What's the next round?" asked Ali.

"It's the eleventh," said Dundee.

"I'm gonna have to open up on him in this round because I'm just bursting."

At the start of the eleventh, Lewis lingered just a few moments longer on his stool, the body language of a beaten fighter. In contrast, Ali was already up and waiting, anxious to make good on his promise. He danced around his shattered opponent, scoring as he pleased, and Lewis, his hands down by his sides, managed just two feeble jabs in the course of a minute and fifteen seconds before Eskin stepped in. The concerned way the referee embraced him suggested he knew better than anybody that this fighter had earned every penny of his purse the hard way. Ali raised his hands in the familiar pose of triumph, the crowd roared its approval and in a fitting end to the proceedings, Lewis walked across to Ali's corner and lifted him in the air to the delight of the fans.

"The end came, not for any one blow, but from the effects of a great accumulation and variety of shots," wrote Val Dorgan in the *Cork Examiner*. "Lewis, a pathetic, groping figure, reeled away with his hands up to his eyes. The referee intervened and in a sport which often suffers from a lack of sportsmanship, the end was expected. The former bad guy, Lewis, gathered his remaining strength to rush to Clay's corner and lift him in the air in a sign of submission which was not lost on the crowd."

It was about then that the real fun started. Within thirty seconds of Eskin stepping in, the ring had filled up with bodies. Some were television people there for a reason, others were just people chancing their arms. With nobody there to stop them, dozens of fans seized a unique opportunity to get close to their idol. As the crowd around Ali's corner grew out of control, the only person battling to keep the ring clear was Harold Conrad.

Waving what looked like a rolled-up poster, he personally shoved and manhandled several interlopers back out through the ropes. His efforts took on a comic appearance in the face of the relentless tide. No sooner did he send one fan on his way than a ten-year-old came sidling through the ropes, shadow-boxed his way across the apron for the benefit of the cameras and was then subsumed by the throng.

Conrad was genuinely shocked by the mayhem that ensued. The sight of so many previously well-behaved patrons clambering over press benches and barging through the ringside where the Taoiseach, Jack Lynch, was sitting became one of his most enduring memories of the whole evening. Having grown up in Brooklyn, where the Irish cop was a uniquely respected figure, radiating authority and never ever suffering fools, he couldn't understand how badly prepared the Gardai were for the onslaught of punters who thought nothing of shoving a uniformed cop out of their way. While most of the action was around Ali's corner, over on the other side of the ring Lewis and his camp were battling against the increasing bedlam too.

"As I'm towelling 'Blue' off, this Irish guy is climbing up the ladder and is trying to muscle me out of the way," says Eisner. "I turn to him and say: 'Will you let me towel the fighter off, please? Give me a moment, I'm working with my fighter.' He mumbles something back at me – it could have been in Gaelic because I didn't understand it in all the noise. I turned around and said: 'Fuckit.' I hit him with a hell of a right hand and he landed right at the feet of an Irish cop who looked up at me. I'm thinking that I might as well put the manacles on because I'm going to the big house. Suddenly, the cop looks up at me and yells: 'That was a fine punch!'"

An announcement came over the tannoy requesting more Gardai and stewards to the ring area, but reaching the centre of the crowd became an impossible task. Nobody could get in or out as every passageway was blocked by people. In the ensuing crush, four children were injured.

"We couldn't believe they rushed the ring," says Angelo Dundee. "I suppose it was better that they wanted to see him rather than not wanting to see him. In the midst of it all, Muhammad turned to me and said: 'Hey, there sure is a lot of nice people here, they all want to shake my hand.' We didn't mind that too much and he certainly didn't, he enjoyed that kind of stuff. Ireland gave a different feeling to other places we'd been, we encountered a legitimate warmth everywhere we went in Ireland and that was just one more manifestation of it."

In the photographs of the incident, Ali looks, at various times, bemused, irritated and downright angry. The home-town press didn't spare the rod when assessing the tumult they had witnessed.

"The ringside was busier than Grand Central Station in its heyday, and when the big fight ended, it would have been safer in Vietnam," wrote Sean Diffley in the *Irish Press*. "They rushed in from all quarters, treading the seats into splinters and one woman used my shoulders and then my head on her hopeful way to join Muhammad and all the rest in the hectic mayhem inside the ring. What she and the rest hoped to do there was not clear – the mass hysterical stampede would be a more fitting field of study for a psychologist! Overall, this notable occasion, the appearance of one of the greatest athletes of our generation, was tarnished by the bad manners of the Irish public."

Even after a semblance of order was restored and enough uniformed Gardai were on hand to begin escorting Ali out of the ring, the crowd were reluctant to let him go.

"People who had been generally well behaved just wouldn't let him get through to the dressing rooms," says Peter Byrne, who covered the fight for the *Irish Times*. "He was going nowhere, until suddenly this little Dublin guy who was ready to take the moral high ground jumps up on the apron of the ring and addresses the multitude. 'The champion has given us a great night's entertainment,' he says. 'Now be fair, Muhammad wants to go to his dressing room.' A pregnant pause for a few seconds and then this voice comes back: 'Let the dressing room come to Muhammad, we're not moving!'"

Twenty-five minutes after Eskin had called a halt to the contest, Ali finally made it to the sanctuary of his dressing room. Outside the drama continued to play out.

"It was charmingly Irish, an Englishman said, as he picked himself up off the ground," wrote Nell McCafferty in the *Irish Times*. "We got caught up in a jam in the pitch-dark alley under the stand. Peter O'Toole managed to get his friends through and a tall Negro said to a policeman: 'Whaddya mean am I in Clay's team! Look at my face, will ya?' He lit a match and the crowd opened before him. A very nice police inspector took me through, all the way into the dressing room, where Angelo Dundee became apoplectic. 'He's naked, he's naked, we can't have a lady in here.' His loins were in fact covered with a towel, but modesty dictated that I leave at once. Would that the same decorum have applied to the ring where a young lady in short skirt and white knickers climbed through the ropes between rounds to display a placard announcing the number of each round."

After Ali had finally relieved himself in the toilet, he lay down on a couch and asked to be given a few moments respite before meeting reporters. Suitably rested, he was effusive in his praise of Lewis.

"I was never worried at any stage but this was much tougher than the Quarry fight," said Ali. "I am delighted that we now have shown how good Lewis is. That guy has some real guts, man, and I am not sure if the public here realise just how tough and how strong he is. I hit him with some of my best shots at different stages of the fight and still, he just stood there. There were times when I could not believe it. I would rate him number five in the world. I had a cold and apart from that affecting my breathing, I think I have been boxing too much and am getting stale. He hit me with a few tough ones. Cold or no cold, a couple of times, he hit me very hard and I'm glad I proved that he is worthy of a crack at the best."

There were close to fifty journalists crowded in there and when one of them mentioned the presence of the Taoiseach, Ali slipped smoothly from gracious victor to gentle braggart.

"If I had known Mr Lynch was here, I would have finished the contest in the third round," said Ali. "I am very honoured indeed to have the head of the government come along to enjoy seeing me win. I have fallen in love with this country and the first real break I get from the boxing game, I intend to accept the invitation of Mr Terry Rogers of the Boxing Commission to bring my family over to Galway in the west of Ireland for a holiday. After Patterson, I hope Joe Frazier will fight me and then I will relax in Galway."

Down the corridor, Lewis was trying to turn a gallant performance into his calling card for future business.

"I want to meet Ali again back at home in the States," said Lewis. "I know I can beat him after I've got a few more fights under my belt. When I went into the ring tonight, it was the first fight I had in eight months. I know I hurt him and I also know that I have the punch to floor him. I am also prepared to come back to Ireland for a fight with the Irishman Dan McAlinden."

As is always the case, the loser's dressing room was a more spacious venue.

"I thought Lewis was an extraordinary character so I decided to focus on him afterwards," says John O'Shea of the *Evening Press*. "At one stage, I was the only journalist in his dressing room after the fight and I witnessed this scene involving Lewis and this kid. I don't know what the relationship between Al and this kid were. All I recall is Al 'Blue' Lewis trying desperately to explain to this kid that it wasn't the end of the world that he lost. The child couldn't understand what he was trying to say and it was a very pathetic sight."

It wasn't the end of the world for Lewis, but as the estimated attendance figures were becoming available, the scenario was looking apocalyptic for some.

"We did not lose any money," said Sugrue when asked about the official attendance of 18,725. "However, there simply was no profit and unfortunately we have nothing left over for the charity. This fight did put Ireland on the boxing map of the world and we now have the experience to run further shows here. I was disappointed at the response of the leading Irish firms. Perhaps they will offer more sponsorship if we put on another show."

In truth, no area of the promotion had been left untouched by chaos and bad management.

"This will tell you about the kind of conmen that were around that night," says Joe Brereton. "A nephew of mine was selling programmes and this fella came up to him with a badge, pretending to be a steward, and asked him for his money. I don't know where he got the badge but he got away with a handy sum of money off poor Seamus. I don't think he was the only young fella to be ripped off by this guy either that night."

Those used to filling Croke Park to the rafters for hurling

and football matches had their own idea about what went wrong.

"I would hope that the promoters might have a better understanding of the kind of money Irish people are prepared to pay for a sporting fixture," said Sean O'Siochain, general secretary of the GAA. "If the Cusack Stand had been priced at £2, I think they would have filled it and made more money."

An argument for another day. That night, everybody who'd read the papers during the build-up knew that a crowd of under 20,000 meant the promotion had been an unmitigated financial disaster. The best Sugrue could offer the press was a hope that more countries would buy the tape of the fight and alleviate the losses. His partner wasn't even bothering to think that way.

"While the final figures are not yet available, I'm afraid that we are going to incur a substantial loss on the undertaking," said Conrad. "The weather was perfect, the best boxer in the world was on the bill, yet the crowds did not attend. It was an artistic success but at this stage I'm not interested in any further promotions in Ireland. If we couldn't make money with this show, what chance would there be?"

Unperturbed by the failure to bring the people in, Conrad did what Conrad liked to do best that night. He and Mara Lynn hosted an elaborate shindig in their suite in the Gresham that went on until early morning.

At one point, he found himself deep in conversation with a Dubliner who congratulated him on the promotion of the fight. This particular patron praised the manner in which Conrad had got the combatants to appear authentic and enthusiastic in the ring when the bout was so obviously staged. For the New Yorker who had seen and heard everything, this was another first.

Conrad's festivities were ending round about the time Ali's entourage were checking into Dublin airport on Thursday morning. An early flight to London would allow them to catch a connection to the States and journey back to normality. Ali never has made that return trip to Ireland. But aside from the tape of the fight itself, he bequeathed the country another unique memento of his visit. For Bord Failte, the Irish Tourism Board, he recorded a promotional video that was shown to American audiences before the fight. Over a montage of quintessentially

Irish images like whiskey-making, fly-fishing and thatched cottages, Ali delivered the following script.

"Here I am in Ireland where every visitor gets a thousand welcomes," said Ali. "They even gave me the Irish shillelagh to help me win my fight but I don't need it. They told me this was the Emerald Isle. Believe me, they're right. I've never seen such a green country in all my life, not even Kentucky. The Irish people, I have found, are very proud of their ancient history and culture, just like I am, and they preserve a lot of their old customs. They have kept up ancient skills here that have disappeared in most nations and countries. One thing especially about the Irish people that they kept boasting to me about was how good they are at making whiskey, of all things.

"They say that their whiskey takes a long, long time to make but the funny thing is it don't take long to drink. Whiskey is such a big thing here in Ireland that they even go as far as to call it the water of life. And that's crazy. Ireland is also famous for its horses and the Irish people are crazy about all kinds of sports. That's why I'm the greatest also here in Ireland. They even have their own special games called Irish football and Irish hurling. They look pretty rough to me, these football and hurling players, I think I'll stick to boxing. I've been training for my fight so I didn't get to see all of the beautiful country of Ireland this time, but I promise you, as soon as I destroy ugly Joe Frazier, I'm coming back to Ireland with my family and I'm going to have a real rest and a true holiday."

Bugner Loses a Gamble in Which Few Finish Ahead on the Tables

Neil Allen

The Times, Friday, 16 February 1973

And, lo, it all came to pass. Muhammad Ali taken the full twelve rounds to a points decision over a courageous Joe Bugner and then praising his opponent before saying he would be happy to have a return contest in London.

Mind you, I never thought I would hear Ali saying he believes Bugner could become the world heavyweight champion. But he did, he really did (just before concentrating on a plug for Sammy Davis, Jr), and we can expect that prediction to appear quite frequently in future Albert Hall and Wembley programmes in order to boost the slowly foundering sport.

If that seems a light-hearted way to write about the determined, if sometimes limited, battle by Bugner, it is certainly not meant to reflect upon on our European champion and his thoroughly dedicated manager, Andy Smith, who deserve at least six cheers for their determined approach, in and out of the ring, against Ali.

Strangely enough, one of the more memorable conversations I have had, during six days and nights in this monument to Mammon, was with the former British bantam-weight champion, Alan Rudkin, who has just started out as a boxing manager. Little Rudkin, who fought three times for the world title, looked round incredulously at the absorbed gamblers and began to discuss the need for a gym in his native Liverpool, "where I could encourage the kids we're going to need desperately in the future".

The future is that the bottom is dropping out of the pyramid of British boxing and that last night's battle could mean little more than a lot of money for a few deep pockets. Hysterical

laughter from those concerned would be the most likely reaction
to any suggestion that a donation should be made towards a gym
in Liverpool, or any other large British city, out of the gross
receipts from last night's promotion.

But it is impolite to Bugner to remain any longer with idealis-
tic dreams certainly unknown here to a taxi driver who whisked
me away from the half-empty Convention Centre, inquiring
politely. "Was there a track meet here?" before asking the Vegan's
usual question as to whether I had "finished ahead on the tables".

Joe Bugner did the best he could against Ali in spite of a cut
by his left eye from a right-hand punch which started to bleed in
the opening round and made his face a bloody mask in the tenth
before Danny Holland's agile fingers in the corner again stanched
the flow.

As Ali afterwards admitted, he was hurt once by a double
right to the head which "made me hear bells", and of which
Bugner said, "I caught him with a tremendous right cross and I
felt myself going right through him." Both boxers were suffi-
ciently undecided as to whether that happened in the sixth or
seventh round. I thought Bugner certainly made Ali wince from
two rights in the ninth round.

The scoring of the three ring-side judges suggested that Ali
had won rather narrowly. I gave Bugner a share of two rounds
and Ali all the other ten and agree with Ali's comment: "Anyone
who thinks it was that close knows nothing about boxing." But I
have the greatest admiration for the way Bugner fought back in
the seventh – the round in which Ali had predicted he would
win – and was nearly always able to score with at least one solid
punch just when it seemed Ali might be able to slash his way to
a blood-stained victory inside the distance.

It does not necessarily mean that Ali was really trying to finish
the bout off in the seventh just because he gave an exaggerated
shrug of disappointment at the end of the round. The man's
fighting mind is so complex that he is always ready to change his
tactics, shift his ground more skilfully, opt out when he finds that
things are not all going his way. But he did give Bugner a fearful
caning in the sixth, including two vicious uppercuts, and smashed
home eight succcessive blows to the head when Bugner was
caught on the ropes in the seventh.

Bugner, looking comparatively marked, said afterwards: "I tried to fight him instinctively because it's impossible to have a set plan against Ali." It is true that Bugner tried desperately to get out of his cramped "tramlines" style of one step forward and two back, and that he sometimes succeeded. His flurries forward several times made Ali back up and look briefly harassed.

But whether Ali was feeling his thity-one years, his basic lack of a big punch, or had, as the promoter, Harold Conrad, suggested, overtrained, Bugner could never capitalize on his opportunities. He said later: "I wasn't overwhelmed by the opponent, but a little by the occasion." I think his chief handicap was the solid in his style, his dangerous tendency to stand by the ropes, his frequent inability to double up or treble up with head blows while Ali's chief second, Bundini Brown, was screaming: "Ring the doorbell, champ, and go into the house."

Bugner has a big heart, as he proved here, but he is too often a one-paced boxer. He may be only twenty-two, as Smith constantly reminds us, but, with forty-nine professional bouts behind him, is it not too late to teach him how to hook off the jab or put combinations together? Surely the cement of his style has been laid long ago and has set, immovable.

So it was a good, hard bout, and I am delighted, as was Bugner, that he was not beaten through cuts. He carried himself throughout with pride and, ignoring Ali's interview hyperbole, at least made it what "The greatest" later described as "an awkward fight".

But what it all meant, apart from proof of Bugner's homespun determination and Ali's lack of explosive power, I leave to more instant-opinion-forming minds than mine. At least it all turned out exactly as I said it would – which is not at all typical of most of sporting life in Las Vegas.

Thousands of people braved a frosty night to give Bugner long-distance support. His bout was seen by an estimated 30,000 on closed circuit television at sixteen places in Britain. Like the British supporters at Las Vegas, the cinema crowds gave Bugner a better reception than he sometimes receives at home.

At the Odeon, Leicester Square, one of six cinemas in London at which the contest was screened, the end of round seven – in

which Ali had promised to send Bugner to "heaven" – brought
the biggest cheer of the night. As the seconds ticked away in the
twelfth round there could not have been more excitement in Las
Vegas than there was in London.

Is Muhammad Ali All Washed Up?

A. S. (Doc) Young

Ebony Magazine, July 1973

Losses To Joe Frazier, Ken Norton Could Presage End To Colorful Career

We're talking about something big here. A big surprise. A big upset. And an internationally big to-do which has yet to end.

The date (and it *is* one to remember): March 31, 1973.

The place: The San Diego Sports Arena.

The event: A fist fight between Muhammad Ali, the vociferous, colorful, controversial former heavyweight champion, a pugilist whom irreversible fans still call "The People's Champion;" and Ken Norton, a little-known, lightly-regarded aspirant who lives in Los Angeles-suburban Carson, Calif, but "fights out of" San Diego because that is where his financial backers reside.

Muhammad Ali is such a huge *overdog* that one of Norton's friendly, Carson neighbors quite frankly tells him, "You're going to get your tail whipped!"

If Howard Cosell is asked prior to the fight to comment on the flat-out, slightly-vulgar prediction, chances are he'll say "Amen" to that because Howard Cosell, famous and controversial sportscaster, is Muhammad Ali's No. 1 cheerleader in professional broadcast media circles. As soon as his telecast begins, he is going to prove it.

As Cosell begins his national telecast into America's Living Room Athletic Club, it becomes boringly obvious that he believes Muhammad Ali is invincible, especially on this night, in this ring, fighting this patsy.

Like a school kid playing hookey, Howard Cosell has not done his homework on Ken Norton.

As the fight begins, Cosell shills unashamedly for Ali while nit-picking over every alleged "flaw" in Norton's style, stance, and strategy. Cosell is the man who constantly brags, "I tell it like (or does he say, 'as'?) it is." But he is capable, too, of telling it like it ain't.

But, as the fight progresses from round to round, Cosell slowly begins to comprehend a contradictory fact: Norton is no patsy. He will not genuflect in the presence of "the holy one."

This guy, Norton, is tough and the dearly beloved Muhammad is in trouble all the way up to his jawbone. Slowly, it dawns on Cosell that Ali and Norton are fighting one fight and he is "calling" another.

When, finally, this horrific fact *slugs* Cosell smack-dab in his mind, he seems to panic. Screaming, he summons Muhammad Ali's trainer, Angelo Dundee, to his side and, in effect, *demands* to know: "WHAT'S WRONG WITH MUHAMMAD ALI?"

Dundee will not at this time admit that *anything* is wrong with Ali. On the coutrary, Dundee claims total confidence in his man. Ali, he says in effect, will emerge triumphant, never fear.

But fear is in order, babe. There's no script for this one.

Norton, a tall, lean, hard athlete, out-maneuvers Ali and out-boxes him and out-slugs him – hitting him under the heart, to the liver, on the arms, "up side" his head.

And, while he's doing all that, he taunts Ali: "*Whip it on me!*"

Ali can't whip it on him.

So, literally adding injury to insult, Norton breaks Ali's jaw and wins the fight, breathing easier at the end of it than a fan who has merely left his seat in his Living Room A.C. to fetch a beer from the kitchen refrigerator.

Ring officials vote Norton a split-decision. They can, more logically, vote him a unanimous decision, but probably don't know how.

The fight is over now, the fantastic upset is a matter of fact. Cosell, as meekly as is possible for one of his world-class ego, confesses: "I was wrong."

That is the under-statement of our generation!

As the news of Norton's victory breaks universally, multi-millions of Ali's disciples begin belting each other with questions.

The question which most eloquently reveals their worst fear is framed in five earthy words: "*Is Muhammad Ali washed up?*"

Ali isn't having much to say at the moment. He won't be saying much for several weeks because, shortly after the fight, a physician repairs the compound fracture of his jaw and "wires" his mouth, but not for sound.

Ali's legions of excuse-makers are not, however, similarly handicapped.

"Oh," they say, attempting to fight off horror with mere words, "Ali under-rated the guy . . . He partied all night before the fight . . . He was out of shape – but the defeat will wake him up. He'll beat Norton, easily, in the rematch . . . He's stale. He's been fighting too much. . . ."

Between March 8, 1971, when Joe Frazier beat him; and March 31, 1973, when Ken Norton beat him, Muhammad Ali fought ten times, doing business, and lucratively, too, with such underwhelming gladiators as Buster Mathis, Al Lewis, and Joe Bugner.

Bugner, with whom Ali fought on February 14 in Las Vegas, was a harbinger of doom. A fighter so *underwhelming* that he was rated no better than a 20 to 1 shot in his hometown, London, Bugner nevertheless went the twelve-round distance with Ali, was in command until the sixth round and rallied later, fighting strongly in the eighth and ninth rounds.

"Ali," said UPI Writer Jim Cour, "had predicted another St. Valentine's Day massacre and a seventh-round knockout, but he was lucky to escape with a victory."

Ali, following a career-long habit, was kinder to Bugner, a white opponent, than he is generally to black opponents. Repeatedly, he attempted to belittle Joe Frazier after Frazier had whipped him. There was almost no limit to his villification of Floyd Patterson. "But," he said, "give Joe Bugner two more years and he will be the world heavyweight champion." He said nothing of the kind about Ken Norton.

The fact that Ali was unable to knock Bugner out is vitally important in any attempted projection of his future. One may, in fact, ask: Was Muhammad Ali, at his best, a truly great knockout puncher?

Nat Fleischer, late publisher of *The Ring*, boxing's "bible," rated Ali's jab second to Joe Louis's. Fleischer rated Ali as the third-best combination puncher behind Benny Leonard and Sugar Ray Robinson. Fleischer rated Ali third, behind Gene Tunney and Tommy Loughran, for footwork and rated Ali second, behind Jack Johnson, as a defensive fighter.

But Fleischer did not rank Ali among the three best body punchers, most aggressive fighters, best in-fighters, most durable fighters, best counter-punchers, or fighters with the most killer instinct.

Ali gained a great deal of publicity from the line, "He floats like a butterfly, stings like a bee." But no one thinks of a bee as a great and efficient ring-killer. When one thinks of great ring-killers, he thinks of fighters, the Joe Louis, Jack Dempsey kind, who carried cannons in their fists.

Floyd Patterson was a fighter who tested canvas with his back-side in many rings. Even Pete Rademacher, in his first-ever professional fight, floored Patterson. Patterson may be remembered for his gentlemanly ways, his Rip Van Winkle lifestyle or his riches; but he never will be remembered for his granite chin.

Yet Patterson, though handicapped by a bad back, went twelve rounds with Ali in Las Vegas on November 22, 1965. Ali hit Joe Frazier with a swarming hive of bee stings but Frazier continued to walk on in, knocked Ali down, and won the fight. Of Ali, Norton says: "I knew he couldn't knock me out."

The prime-time Muhammad Ali could snap off punches that cut up fighters and earned him *technical* knockouts. Occasionally, he laid a guy out cold, but not often. He knocked Al (Blue) Lewis to the canvas in Dublin but couldn't keep him there.

The prime-time Ali was fast but he rarely lingered in the pits of inside fighting. His inside game, if any, was weak.

Aforesaid, Ali had ten fights between Frazier and Norton. Will ten fights in two years, all victories, make a pugilist stale? Was March 31 merely an off-night for a superstar? Or was it proof that, indeed, Ali is washed up?

"I thought he was washed up three years ago," says Al Abrams, the *Pittsburgh Post-Gazette*'s veteran sportswriter. "He has lost his punch."

"Well," says Joe Louis, truly one of the all-time-greats, "I don't think he'll be champion again. He can win some fights if he gets into shape. But that long lay-off (when Ali was 'fighting' the military) ruined his career. Three and a half years is an awfully long time. . . ."

One of Ali's close friends says, "When a man knows he's really good, he tends to take things for granted . . . I think that explains what happened to Ali with Norton."

Ali, himself, has attempted to explain his loss to Norton by saying, "I didn't live right, spiritually, like I should have, praying like I should have. I did the wrong things. . . ."

When Ali appeared in New York City to sign for the rematch with Norton in "The Fabulous Forum" near Los Angeles in Inglewood on September 10, he said he will work hard and get back into tip-top condition and predicted, "I will win 'my' title back."

That won't be easily done. Ali's going to need all the "spiritual" help he can get in *that* campaign. He's going to need a miracle!

Of all the heavyweights who have been champions, only one has lost the title and regained it. That was Floyd Patterson who lost the title to Ingemar Johansson on June 26, 1959, and regained it from Johansson on June 20, 1960.

Patterson, who had won the title when he was twenty-one years old (the youngest ever), was twenty-four when he lost it and twenty-five when he regained it. Ali, born January 17, 1942, is now thirty-one years old – seven years older than Patterson was when he lost the title, six years older than Patterson was when he regained it.

If Ali whips Norton convincingly in the rematch, he has, according to New York Boxing Writer John Ort, "a good shot of beating George Foreman. First, however, he has to get by Norton. By losing to Norton, he's given the guy confidence and the second bout could be a tough one for him."

Dave Anderson, the noted *New York Times* sports columnist, believes "we'll find out (whether or not Ali is through) in the fight in September. I think he has lost his punch. If Norton beats him again, he is through."

But Bud Furillo, Sports Editor of the *Los Angeles Herald-Examiner*, makes a strong case for Ali.

"I don't think he's washed up," Furillo says. "What happened in San Diego probably was a case of Ali not being in top condition. I think he can win the title back. I think a fighter like George Foreman is made to order for Ali. Ali's a young thirty-one. He hasn't abused his body. He's a remarkable physical specimen. I've learned to be an Ali man. We're lost without him. He makes the sport of boxing. He's so refreshing. I recall that when Jerry Perenchio and Jack Kent Cooke were promoting the Ali-Frazier fight, Perenchio said, 'Ali is the biggest star in the entertainment business in the world.' It would be just great if he won the title again. We need this guy."

No one is a greater expert on comebacks than Sugar Ray Robinson, the former welterweight and middleweight champion who, in all probability, was the best fighter, pound-for-pound, in boxing history.

"I think the (Norton) defeat was the greatest thing that could ever happen to Clay (Ali)," Robinson says. "I fought Jake La-Motta once when I was not in good condition and got beat (February 5, 1943). The reason I got beat was that I was going into the Army in two weeks and I didn't train properly. But that set me straight. My personal opinion of Clay is that he's still the best man around. But he's got to learn or have someone educate him to what condition is all about. . . ."

But is Ali, at thirty-one, actually willing to return to school? Is he too old to be taught "new tricks?" A Gorgeous George sort of flake, always a super ego, having been a star for years, is Ali, at this stage in his career, coachable?

Ali's broken jaw is the factor most often mentioned when boxing auditors attempt to predict the outcome of the rematch.

What effect will it have on Ali in the rematch? Will it make him gunshy? Behind that serious injury, has Ali, public utterances notwithstanding, actually lost his confidence?

Two or three days before Muhammad Ali fought Sonny Liston for the heavyweight title in Miami Beach on February 25, 1964, Malcolm X, then Ali's friend and Muslim mentor, sitting in Room 15 in the Hampton House, Miami, cautioned this writer:

"Don't pay any attention to all the noise he (Ali) makes. My biggest job is injecting confidence into him."

After Ali "beat" Liston – on the official cards, the fight was all even when Liston failed to come out for the seventh round, claiming an arm was injured – and with succeeding victories, mushrooming world fame, public adulation, mass genuflection, and spiraling income, no one ever again questioned Ali's confidence. But it now may be wise to remember Malcolm X's words.

Also, it may be wise to remember that few, if any, pretty-boy fighters "like" to be slugged in the face and head. The vast majority of them, admit it or not, are vain about their looks. Mess with their faces, babe, and they cut out. Of the handsome fighters, only Sugar Ray Robinson was an artist.

Yet, the previously-quoted "close friend" swears the broken jaw "hasn't had any big effect on Ali mentally" and Dundee says, "Through my experience with broken jaws, the jaws get better."

Dundee claims that Ali suffered the broken jaw because "he had no teeth in the bottom gum and that weakened the jawbone. He's having a bridge put in and that will strengthen the jawbone."

The dental bridge will strengthen Ali's jawbone, according to Dundee, but can it erase Ali's memory of the injury, the terrible pain of it, the ninety-minute operation to repair it, the weeks of living with a "wired" mouth?

Only time will tell.

And while we're talking about damage, physical and mental, done by cannon shots to the head, still another question begs for an answer:

Has Ali suffered any lasting effects from the barrage of head and body blows he received in his fight with Joe Frazier, that vicious shot, in particular, which sent him to a New York hospital with jaw and cheek ballooned with accumulated blood?

For months after that fight, Ali claimed *he* had done permanent damage to Frazier's exterior and interior head. It was something like saying Frazier had won the battle but lost the war. Now Frazier, turning the tables, says he softened Ali up!

The next question is focused on another facet of the age factor: Is Muhammad Ali too old to beat Ken Norton, who is twenty-eight?

Ali, as said, is thirty-one years old. And, as he declares, he should be in the peaking period of his career.

Joe Louis was thirty-four when he "retired" as the undefeated champion. Thirty-seven when he quit fighting. Jersey Joe Walcott was thirty-seven *when he won the heavyweight title*. Archie Moore was either thirty-six or thirty-nine – depending on whom you accept as the ultimate authority on his birth, Archie or his mother – when he won the light heavyweight title, forty-nine or fifty-two when he quit fighting!

But Eddie Futch, Norton's erudite trainer, makes this point: "Ali has been fighting, amateur and pro, almost twenty years. That grind gets to you."

George Parnassus, who has promoted boxing matches for 50 years and who, by the way, rates Joe Louis as the greatest of all heavyweights, says: "Fighters can't last forever. Motors wear out, human bodies wear out."

Muhammad Ali no longer possesses the halo of invincibility. Joe Frazier has beaten him and Ken Norton has beaten him. The common thread running through those two bouts, and through Ali's narrow, ten-round victory over Doug Jones in New York on March 13, 1963, is . . . *pressure.*

All three opponents pressured Ali constantly. Two of them beat him. The third, Jones, was "sure" he had won!

For some time now, Ali has been able to "stay up on his toes" and flee from danger like a scalded dog only about 25 per cent of the time; that is to say, during three rounds of a twelve-round bout. He can't beat Norton *that* way.

How, then, in summary, does one answer the question: "*Is Muhammad Ali washed up?*"

One says: Probably not. Joe Louis, his poor overall record as a prognosticator notwithstanding, probably has read Muhammad Ali correctly. Will Ali beat Norton on September 10? Possibly, yes. Most probably, no.

Ali says he is a "spiritual fighter" and he is now reconverted to the straight-and-narrow.

That very well may be true. But Ali, like all other pugilists who have claimed or sought ecclesiastical support, must accept this fact. Neither God nor Allah has the time or the inclination to take sides in an event so mundane as a professional fist fight.

PART 7
THE RUMBLE IN THE JUNGLE

Bundini Brown, the Witch Doctor at the Court of King Ali

Neil Allen

The Times, Friday, 25 October 1974

Every king has his court and, depending upon the monarch, the courtiers will sometimes tell much about the character of the ruler they serve. Around Muhammad Ali, as he has run and sparred and sweated for so long for next week's match with George Foreman, are three vital men, plus a dozen or so others who have brief, walk-on parts. They make a tight, usually contented family as they watch old films, laze in the African sun and teach the Zairois boys bad language under the pretence that it is polite English conversation.

Luis Sarria never says anything, so far as I have witnessed. He is the wrinkled, brown masseur whose magic hands have rubbed and kneaded and smoothed a hundred aches and pains from the body of the great gladiator. Sarria, who probably communicates clearly only with himself in some private, sombre world, speaks solely with his fingers and knows Ali's massive body better than any man who ever fought him. It is ironic that this week Sarria, the healer, should be suffering from a serious infection of the feet.

The friend who knows the eratic moods of Ali best is Drew "Bundini" Brown, assistant trainer, court jester, motivator and high priest of the "Ali is the greatest" movement. Bundini – he got the nickname from a Lebanese family and does not know what it means – is a tall, hyper-emotional black man in his forties who can so often be heard in Ali's corner, shouting pleading and praising. Chris Dundee, brother to Angelo, Ali's trainer and virtual manager, once said, long before the camp ever dreamed of coming to Africa, "Put a headdress and beads on Bundini and you'd have a witch-doctor. And I don't mean that in any negative sense. There's good witch-doctors, you know."

If the history of boxing could find no other postscript for Bundini Brown it would still have to record that he thought up the slogan "Float like a butterfly, sting like a bee" which has captured Ali's tormenting style. Bundini wears it on the back of one of the tee-shirts he sells. I bought two from him the day in Las Vagas when, weeping, he was allowed to return to Ali's side after one of several periods of banishment.

"Bo-dini", as Ali calls him, has been out of favour for several different reasons. He declined to join the Black Muslim faith even though their leader, Elijah Muhammad, was quoted as saying he would rather convert Bundini than 12,000 other men. He has a white wife and he has sometimes been an embarrassment to the Ali camp with his historionics in the corner – notably the first, unforgettable match in 1971 with Joe Frazier. When Ali went down in the fifteenth round from a tremendous left hook, Bundini excitedly threw water into the ring and was subsequently suspended by the New York State Athletic Commission.

Bundini is still incredulous about the suspension. "I was trying to revive my soldier. My, you'd think I'd climbed into the ring to get Frazier with a baseball bat." He is a gentle man when the fists are not flying, but it is impossible to forget that while serving in the United States navy he got a dishonourable discharge for attacking an allegedly racist officer with a meat cleaver. For this act of violence he has an explanation.

"He was the ignoratest (sic) man I ever met. I was just a nigger to him. I'm a defender, not a fighter and I waited for him to make a big move. Finally, I went for the cleaver to cut his head off. The officer made it to the deck and jumped overboard. Any man would jump overboard when he is facing death. The worst part about the discharge was they wouldn't let me keep the uniform."

When Ali starts preaching negritude here, Bundini Brown becomes ecstatic. As Ali sits on the ring apron, frustrating his French Interpreter with his speed of speech, Bundini crouches just below, clutching at Ali's leg and moaning "The world will know, the whole world will learn", while his eyes fill with tears of love. Standing only inches away, it is impossible not to be moved a little by the devotion of the disciple, he explains: "I feel sick before he fights, like a pregnant woman. I give the champ all my strength. He get hit, it hurts me." He is an exotic but his involvement is complete.

No one is cooler, more detached, of those closest to Ali, than Angelo Dundee, the dapper, smart-alec trainer from Miami who has happily survived what he has called "Life in a hot corner". Because Dundee is not black he has not received all the credit due to him for the times he has talked Ali into victory, helped him with his "poetry" and diplomatically persuaded him to improve his boxing technique.

Out at the N'sele training camp this week Dundee was amazed when someone quoted Ali's boast that he now weighed only 208 pounds. "Four pounds lighter than when I fought Sonny Liston the first time". Dundee shakes his head sadly. "You don't actually believe what he says, do you? He's about 218 right now. My guy's trained longer and harder than ever before, maybe running nearly nine miles a day. But he's putting you on about the weight."

The weeks of isolation at N'sele bore down hard on Dundee. A fast-talking extrovert who sadly missed the American way of life. "I tell you there were times when I nearly took off for the States with the excuse of doing some publicity crap. But how can you leave the guys on their own?"

The Rumble in the Jungle

George Foreman

When George Foreman flattened Joe Frazier in just two rounds to claim the heavyweight title on 22 January 1973 in Kingston, Jamaica, Smokin' Joe joined the long list of KO victims that had fallen to Foreman's prodigious power. The new champ defended his title twice in emphatic fashion, dismantling Joe Roman in a single round before smashing Ken Norton in two rounds in Caracas. At the time he met Ali, Foreman had only been held to the final bell three times in forty professional fights. Frazier and Norton had both beaten Ali and neither had lasted so much as six minutes with Foreman. For those raised on the modern incarnation of Foreman as the smiling, gentle giant who runs a youth centre, preaches the gospel and sells grills, it is all too easy to forget the terror he once struck in his opponents. In 1974 he was the personification of intimidation, a dour, apparently humourless man whose lack of boxing finesse was more than compensated for by the sheer destructive force transmitted through his hands. He was the meanest heavyweight champ since Sonny Liston. The following comes from Foreman's own autobiography, By George, *which shows him beaming happily on the cover. How times have changed.*

Having demolished Joe Frazier, I didn't expect to hear doubts about my skill. But there they were. "George fought a tomato can," some people said after the Joe Roman fight. "What's he so scared of?"

I realized such comments were motivated by my growing reputation as the champ you loved to hate. But I couldn't ignore them. In too many ways I was still the kid from Fifth Ward, fighting to be king of the jungle. I intended to convince every last doubter. *I'm going to kill one of these fools*, I decided. *Then everyone'll shut up.*

The "fool" I chose was Ken Norton. He'd just lost a close decision to Ali, though as a ringside witness I judged the judges wrong. Earlier that year, in the spring, he'd taken their first fight decisively, breaking Ali's jaw in the process. While Ali's victory in the second fight skipped him to Number 1 contender, he himself was in no hurry to get in the ring with me. That was just as well. In my opinion, Norton at the time was the better fighter: tougher and, certainly, much stronger, and as big as me. He deserved the shot. Besides, killing a man like that would undoubtedly earn me universal respect.

That's what I thought. In reality, I didn't have a clue what I needed. I suffered a terrible emptiness that the next accomplishment – first, becoming champ or, now, killing Norton – was supposed to cure. But in fact, the championship had worsened the emptiness by putting the lie to the belief that winning could make me whole. Meanness flowed into that vacuum; I grew meaner by the day. My sparring partners endured malicious beatings. Being nice to my ex-wife in order to arrange weekends here and there with Michi took all my self-control.

Good news, however, came from my lawyers in San Francisco. They'd gotten my corporate contract invalidated through a legal loophole after discovering that professional fighters must have all such contracts approved by the boxing commission in the state where the boxer resides. And that hadn't been done. With pleasure, I paid back all that the partners had advanced me a year and a half before, and got in return their hefty fifty percent proceeds from both the Frazier and Joe Roman fights. Better than the money was the sense that I was not an indentured servant. Funny, though I still blamed Dick Sadler for steering me wrong, freedom immediately defused much of my fury. Before the Frazier fight I'd relieved Sadler of his status as my manager; with Archie Moore brought in, Sadler was trainer in name only. But now, after the court win, I found myself leaning toward a renewal of our relationship. More and more, I listened to Sadler's advice during training, and less and less to Archie's. That was my usual pattern. Whoever got in my good graces last, got my ear.

The Norton fight was to be held in Venezuela in March 1974. I trained with single-minded devotion, as though he were the champ and I the challenger. That included abstaining from female companionship beginning seventy-five days before the fight, not just fifteen. For a twenty-five-year-old whom beautiful women targeted for their affections, this was immensely difficult. Every time I felt my willpower weakening, I ran to the nearest mirror and checked that little bump on my cheek. By the time we finally got to Caracas for the fight, my meanness was magnified by all that suppression and frustration.

Archie no longer needed to coach me on the art of intimidation. I stared at Norton with the intensity of that laser beam Goldfinger aimed at James Bond. *I'm going to kill you.* Kenny refused to look back at me. If I entered a hotel elevator at the same time, he quietly got out.

Not until I climbed into the ring and gazed across at him did I finally see Kenny's eyes. *My God, they're green.* Realizing that I'd never really noticed them before scared me for a moment. Of course, he'd always refused to exchange stares. But I also noticed, probably for the first time, what a remarkable physical specimen Ken Norton was. With muscles rippling everywhere, he looked more like a weightlifter than a boxer. It was going to be tougher to kill him than I'd planned.

We met with the referee at center ring. Lost in a daydream, I picked out my spots on Kenny's head. I know he knew what I was doing because I saw his fear. The crowd must have sensed it too. Their boos rained down on me.

The bell rang.

Unlike my fight with Joe Frazier, whom I'd gone after immediately, I stalked Kenny Norton – a patient predator, in possession of the ultimate weapon, savoring the anticipation of the conquest.

He saw my head up and threw a hook. Missed. Then another. Missed. I hit him in the side, a shot that felt solid the way a bat feels when you hit a home run. He tried another hook. Missed. I followed with a right to the head. Down he went. As he fell against the ropes I swung and connected again. The referee issued a warning before counting. More boos. Kenny got up in time. Round One ended.

In Round Two, I became a vicious thug, swinging wildly, connecting with almost every punch. The next time he fell, the referee stopped the fight. Nearly unconscious, Kenny was helpless. "Why are you stopping the fight?" I asked, upset because I hadn't finished him.

I looked down at Muhammad Ali, who was at ringside working the fight as color commentator with Howard Cosell. "I'm going to kill you," I said. I hadn't killed Norton, so I figured I might as well kill Ali. All week he'd been taping segments claiming that Norton was a better fighter than I; that Norton had once beaten him and would therefore beat me; that George Foreman hadn't fought any top fighters; and that if by chance I won, he'd whip me to regain the title. Having won a tough twelve-round decision over Frazier just two months before, he was full of typical Ali bluster. I repeated myself louder amid the boos, "I'm going to kill you." This time, I saw fear in him.

The next day I took a limo to the airport with my publicist, Bill Caplan. The rest of my team was still breaking down camp and would follow in a few days. We got to the Pan American counter, where our tickets were being held. For some reason the agents began whispering to each other in Spanish. Then two guys in bad suits showed up. Now everyone was whispering. Of course, they could have spoken aloud in Spanish, since neither Bill nor I understand the language. Finally, one of the agents said, "I'm sorry, I can't give you your tickets."

"Why?" Bill asked.

"Well," she said, tilting her head toward the suited men, "because these two gentlemen are representatives of the Venezuelan government. They say that Mr Foreman cannot leave the country until he pays his Venezuelan income tax."

Bill explained that this violated our written agreement with the government, which had promoted the fight to draw the eyes of the world via satellite as a means of attracting recognition and tourism. In exchange, they'd agreed to waive all income taxes. Which was of course the reason we held the fight there. "That was the deal we made," Bill repeated.

"That deal," one of the men said, "was with the old president. We have a new president now."

I guess the government had changed and we hadn't noticed. Now all bets were off. The Venezuelans demanded $255,000 in taxes before they would let me leave. In today's dollars that would be about a million bucks.

Bill, who's a clever guy with a booming voice, recognized several prominent American sportswriters on their way home from the fight. "What," he yelled, "you mean to tell me that you're holding the heavyweight champion of the world for ransom? This is outrageous!"

Sure enough, all the writers began running for telephones. This caused the Pan Am agents enough embarrassment that they threw up their hands and gave us the tickets.

We hustled upstairs to the boarding lounge. All that separated us from the plane was passport control – and there were the same two guys in bad suits. "I'm sorry," one said, "I can't let you through until Mr Foreman pays his taxes." Now Bill, his eyes bugging out, really started a scene. The suits made no effort to stop him. Nor did I – until a squad of Venezuelan soldiers in battle gear, bearing weapons, marched up the stairs. Bill was still carrying on when I leaned over and said, "You'd better cool it, man. Haven't you noticed these guys've got guns? That's enough."

We walked back out of the airport and into the limousine, which took us to the American Embassy. For five days, the ambassador tried but was unable to work out a settlement. It became clear that for us to leave the country the money would have to be paid. But I wasn't going to pay it. Since an agreement in principle had already been reached for me to fight Muhammad Ali in Kinshasa, Zaire, later that year, I insisted that Don King, who was promoting the fight in Africa, pay the fee. He did. Poor Ken Norton, whose boxing future looked dubious at best, had no such angels. Venezuelan officials forced him to pony up $72,000 before allowing him to leave. Meanwhile, they held ABC's TV truck for fifty grand.

Don King had come to me before the Norton fight. "I can put you together with Muhammad Ali," he said.

"Are you sure?"

He said yes.

I called Ali myself to check. "Do you want to fight me?" I asked.

"Yep."

"You're sure?"

"Yep."

Though he said yes, I thought I perceived some hesitation in his voice.

The next time I talked to Don King he claimed he could get me five million dollars for the fight. That was an extraordinary amount of money, beyond anything I could have imagined. The previous highest purse had been the five million split evenly between Ali and Joe Frazier for their second fight, held in January 1974. "Will you do it?" he asked.

"You sign this piece of paper right here," I said. " 'Five million dollars for George Foreman.' Then you've got me."

He came back in a few days. "Muhammad wants five million also," he said.

"Go ahead, give it to him," I said. "I don't care what he gets, so long as I get my five."

I had a feeling Ali wouldn't have fought for less – not as a matter of honor, but because he was afraid of me. He got more afraid, I'm sure, after the Norton fight. Word later came through Don King that the Muslims, on behalf of Ali, were upset. They requested that I stop saying I would kill him. Everyone could see that I meant what I was saying, and that upset them. They asked me respectfully to cool it, because, "you know, Ali's kind of old for boxing. Please."

"Well," I said, "since it's a religious request, I won't say that I'm going to kill him. I'll just say that I'm going to knock him out – in a hurry."

The next time I saw Ali was at the boxing writers' annual banquet, where I was to receive the "Fighter of the Year" award and my W.B.A. championship belt. They'd invited him to be guest speaker. Before we arrived, I told Mr Moore that I planned to get on Muhammad somehow the same way he always seemed to be pulling stupid practical jokes on others. "I'm gonna tear his coat off."

I'd once run into Ernie Terrell, the boxer who was most famous for refusing to accept Cassius Clay's name as Muhammad Ali. "You can whip that guy, but you've got to watch out for the Muslims," he'd said, claiming that a few days before their fight, he answered his hotel door. A group of men in bow ties ran in, picked up every item that wasn't nailed down, put everything down again, and ran out. "Those are the games they play. They do strange things."

I sat back on the dais, watching Muhammad clowning around

behind the podium, snug and smug in his element. These reporters were his prime audience. They loved and appreciated him. His quickness with words made their jobs easier. Me, I grunted and growled. You could have put all my quotable quotes on the head of a pin and still had room left for my sense of humor.

"And now," Muhammad said, picking up the W.B.A. belt, "I'm going to present this to George." Then he stopped for a moment. "Hmm. On second thought, I'm gonna keep it." They were still laughing as I marched over to pick up the belt. Biding my time, I sat down again. *I'll get him at the next joke.* My chance came a minute later. I sneaked behind him, put one hand on each side of the vent of his expensively elegant jacket, and ripped upward.

Muhammad went berserk. Contorting his face into an angry mask, he grabbed me but didn't swing. I'd grown up with guys who'd knock your head off if you messed with them that way. Of course, that was instinct, this was theater. "You Christian!" he screamed. "You blankety-blank!" *Christian? What does he mean – that I'm an American?*

Trying to get his hands off of me, I was laughing, because evidently no one had seen me rip his coat. "What's wrong here?" everyone kept asking. "What happened?" Finally, three or four guys managed to pull him away. Still enraged, he continued spewing an endless stream of obscenities, then picked up some bottles off the dais and threatened to throw them.

Ali's reaction offered insights. I knew without doubt that he didn't like me, but now I saw through his game. Like Joe Frazier protesting that I shouldn't tell him to shut up, Ali's grabbing me – but not taking a swing – gave me an advantage. Also, I began disbelieving his religious commitment. I figured a man who swore so effortlessly and creatively wasn't exactly God-fearing, at least not in the way I understood or wanted to understand.

Later, still wondering why Ali had spit the word "Christian" at me like a curse, I recalled a meeting I'd had the previous year with representatives of Saudi Arabia about a possible deal to endorse Saudi sports.

"What do you hunt for there?" I'd asked.

The answer came through an interpreter. "Christians," he'd said. "We hunt for Christians." Then laughter.

So maybe that's what Muhammad Ali meant: Christians were animals, and the word "Christian" was a slur.

This was discouraging, because at the time I'd been giving Islam serious thought, sort of trying it on for size. In fact, as far back as 1969, *Muhammad Speaks*, the newspaper published by the Nation of Islam, had influenced me to stop eating pork. If I discovered that someone in my kitchen had cooked bacon or ham or pork ribs, I'd throw out all the pans and utensils and buy new ones.

There was something appealing about what the Nation's polite, clean-cut, self-disciplined young men in suits and bow ties represented. And while I wasn't completely ready to adopt their ways, in this time of great emptiness I'd inched closer toward becoming a Muslim – until Ali's poor manners ended my flirtation. I figured if a religion couldn't make you into a better person, it had no purpose at all, and if his was the true face of Islam, I didn't want to see it in my mirror.

Naturally, this didn't end my search for something, anything, to fill the emptiness. Around the same time I became infatuated with the television show *Kung Fu*, which starred David Carradine as a priest from an ancient order of Buddhist martial artists. Each episode contained nuggets of philosophy, sandwiched between the action sequences, that seemed to stick in my mind. *Now this is something I can relate to.* I wondered whether I might be able to learn that religion and become as wise as David Carradine appeared to be – until I saw him and his wife interviewed by Dick Cavett and she breast-fed their infant on camera. *Never mind.*

Before the Ali fight, scheduled for October 1974, in Kinshasa, Zaire, reporters from every major publication in the country – and outside it – came to interview me at my ranch in Livermore, California. One of them was my old hero Jim Brown, on assignment from ABC, the network that would broadcast the event from Africa. I took him on a complete tour – swimming pools, horses, houses, and guest houses. When the cameras stopped rolling and we were alone he said, "Man, George, you've really got it together. I'm going to get it together like you one day."

Like me? Jim Brown's going to get it together like *me*?

I was awestruck. He didn't know what he was talking about. This was Number 32, who'd starred in the first football game I'd ever watched on television, bulling his way over people and pulling five or six of them into the end zone. I hadn't even known who he was then. But I knew I wanted to walk like him. And I wanted my shoulders to be broad like his. And then when he took off the helmet, I saw the face that I wanted to wear. For me Jim Brown had ranked up there with Roy Rogers and John Wayne and *The Rifleman*, Chuck Connors. As a boy, I would close my eyes and pretend to be them. And now one of them was saying that I had it together and he didn't. The world had turned upside down.

Still looking for answers, I took a Bible to Zaire. It had been given to me some months before, when I'd visited a church that was supposed to have a lot of "nice, pretty girls" in the congregation. Nice was the operative word, since pretty girls were constantly throwing themselves at me; some even offered me money. "Is there anyone new to our church who would like to join?" the preacher had asked. To make the proper impression, I'd raised my hand and mounted the dais. Afterward, the preacher had handed me a new Good Book. "Here, George," he said. "In case you ever run into trouble, this will be your strength." I'd never looked at it, but I took it to Zaire. Embarrassed by it, however – feeling that if I was going to cling on to religion that it ought to be an African religion – I hid my Bible from view. Still, I knew it was there in my room, my good luck charm. I even uttered a prayer now and then: "God, help me to get this knockout." But I guess He had other plans.

I was miserable in Zaire, not least because of the food. Tyree Lyons, my cook who'd worked at the Job Corps site in Pleasanton, scoured Kinshasa for edible chow (he eventually came down with some mysterious ailment that swelled his hands and eyes) and found little. But I hated more than the absence of cheeseburgers. My first quarters were an old army base infested with rats, lizards, and insects. Surrounded by cyclone fencing and barbed wire, it was patrolled and inhabited by rowdy soldiers who drank a lot more beer than I like to see in people toting loaded rifles. Finally I found a suite at the Intercontinental Hotel. Worried about someone coming in and messing with me and my things, I hired guards to keep a twenty-four-hour watch outside the room. This was clearly Muhammad Ali country. Sentiment in his favor colored how everyone looked at me – and they did so incessantly, their eyes following me everywhere. Most people wanted him to win back the title as much as he did. As far as he was concerned, he said, George Foreman held the championship taken from him for refusing to register for the military draft. And who was I? The goof who'd waved the American flag. I realized that no matter what happened in the ring, I couldn't win for losing. If I knocked him out, the most I'd get would be grudging respect for vanquishing a legend. And if I lost, there'd be a big crowd at the station, jeering me back to Palookaville.

Two weeks after my arrival in Zaire, and five days before the fight, I was cut over the eye during a sparring session; I had walked into an elbow my partner raised to protect himself from my savagery. Blood spurted. "Hey, I'm cut," I yelled.

"No, you're not," Sadler said. "You're all right."

"Stop everything," I insisted. "I'm cut."

That raised a flag in me. The trainer's job is to protect his fighter. Many's the time less serious finger cuts have caused lengthy postponements, for the simple reason that a championship contest is intended to be a match between both men at their best. Distrusting local doctors, I had Sadler place a butterfly adhesive over the cut in anticipation of flying to Belgium or France for proper medical treatment and regrouping. But, fearing that I wouldn't return, Zaire president Mobutu Sese Seko, who had cut the deal with Don King to sponsor the fight, refused to let me leave until after the bout, which he intended to be a showcase for his country. The month's postponement we did get wasn't nearly long enough for me to heal properly and begin the training cycle again, since the doctors forbade me from sweating for a minimum of ten days. No sweating, obviously, means no sparring or road work.

Like the lazy fox who couldn't reach the grapes, I convinced myself that I didn't need sparring and road work anyway; knocking out Muhammad Ali was a mere formality. Despite his crowing, I still believed he was afraid. I remembered the fear in his eye when I beat Ken Norton. He'd tried to cover with bravado, but having grown up with that stuff, I could spot it across the street. His not swinging at me when I tore his coat meant there was no reason to psych him out further. Yeah, he was scared. I saw it again when I ran into him and his friends at a Kinshasa night-spot.

I thought we were covered. Dick Sadler came to me for $25,000 to slip the referee under the table. I asked why. "Because," he said, "you've got a habit of hitting people when they're down, man. I want to make sure he doesn't disqualify you." I gave him the money, because that's how the game was played. Whether Zack Clayton ever received it, I don't know.

As usual before fighting, I was thirsty. Years before, Sadler had insisted that I dry out before the weigh-in and fight. Hungry to learn and determined to do what's right, I didn't question the wisdom, even though heavyweights aren't disallowed for tipping the scales. One time after a weigh-in I ate the usual poached eggs and toast breakfast with Charley Shipes, who was also on that evening's card. *Man, he must not want to win*, I thought when he drank glass after glass of water. I figured drying out was some secret Sadler weapon to build strength, the way marathon runners would later load up on carbohydrates before a race. Since Sadler had trained or worked with other heavyweight champs, I also figured he must know something.

"Ready for your glass of water?" he'd always ask in the dressing room just before the fight.

"Yeah, give it to me."

"Okay, take a nice drink."

I'd swallow the contents in two big, refreshing gulps.

"How was that?"

"Great."

"Okay, good. Now here's a couple pieces of ice."

A treat.

The feeling of near dehydration, relieved only partially by the short drink and ice chips, contributed to an overall mood Sadler created. I was thirsty, in more ways than one. He'd wind me up with curse after vicious curse, describing the destruction of that evil blankety-blank waiting in the ring. By the time he turned me loose, I'd become an exploding monster. The result: forty fights and forty victories, thirty-seven of them by knockout, most in the early rounds. Why question success?

At four o'clock in the morning, on October 30, 1974, I awaited my fate in the locker room. Later I would read that Muhammad Ali's arrival in the ring was greeted by tribal drumbeats and a crowd roaring "Al-ee, Al-ee." But I was aware of none of that. My thoughts were elsewhere. I wanted to end the fight, collect my money, and get home. Who'd ever fought at four a.m.? But it wasn't four in the morning where it counted: back home. There it was prime time. And we were live via satellite, the focus of the world's attention.

"Are you ready for your water now?" Sadler asked. We'd kept Muhammad waiting in the ring long enough.

"Yep," I said. Just like always.

I took a big swallow and almost spit it back into the cup. "Man," I said, "this tastes like medicine. This water have medicine in it?"

"SAME WATER AS ALWAYS," he yelled.

"All right," I said. I drank the rest, which tasted just as medicinal.

With the aftertaste on my tongue, I climbed into the ring accompanied by tepid cheers and scattered boos. I looked over at Muhammad in his corner, clowning around. When he wouldn't return my stare, I knew for sure that he was afraid of me.

Muhammad's introduction by the ring announcer brought an ecstatic ovation. He was incredibly popular, maybe even more popular than their president, Mobutu. Muhammad Ali was their man. In fact, Muhammad Ali was everyone's man. Everywhere he fought, his opponents faced the same disadvantage I did, receiving polite applause that seemed even more sparse in contrast.

While referee Zack Clayton gave us the instructions, Muhammad finally looked me in the eye. We glared at each other. My only thought was to knock him out early.

At the opening bell, Muhammad became a rabbit. He'd flick a jab at me and run. Me, I rushed him like a tiger, throwing hard shot after hard shot, going for that early shower. But he was one tough rabbit to catch, even for a tiger. Somehow, we always ended up on the ropes or in the corner, with me whaling away and him covering up. I'd jab, jab, jab, then throw several knockout punches that couldn't find their mark. He'd hold on to me, and the ref would break us apart. Still, though, he'd hold on, pressing his elbows against my back as I bent over.

His only offense was that famous flicking jab. It came so fast, you could barely see it, let alone counter it. Each time he threw one, I'd think, *Man, that's a quick jab.* I soon figured out that he was trying to open the cut over my eye. But I wasn't worried. Any minute, I knew, he was going down, just as every other opponent of mine had.

For the first two rounds I unleashed a torrent of punches, none of which really found its mark. Muhammad was a master at covering up. Not until the third round did I land a solid blow. It was a wicked right hand that struck home just under his heart. Blows like that can drive the wind – and the will – out of a man. Muhammad looked at me as if to say, "Hey, I'm not going to take that off you." That made me happy, because I thought then that he'd finally stand toe to toe with me, his pride getting the better of his intelligence. No way could he win a slugging match with me; we both knew that. But when I charged after him, his intelligence prevailed. He backed into the ropes and began covering up to avoid another barrage of heavy shots. I beat on him mercilessly, trying to connect with one of those home-run punches.

At the sound of the bell ending the round, Muhammad's face looked like he'd just seen a miracle. He had: his own survival – he was still on his feet.

Back in my corner, Sadler and Archie Moore insisted that I keep up the pounding. But I was already nearly exhausted. I couldn't understand why. I'd fought only three rounds, yet felt that I'd gone fifteen.

In the next round, we continued playing predator and prey. He'd hit me with one shot – usually the jab, but sometimes a right – then run. He had to, because when he faced me I placed my left foot between both of his feet. That means his alternatives were to either stand in front of me and fight or move backward. So of course he moved backward and covered up. He was helped by an apparently loose top rope, which allowed him to lean way out of the ring, his head beyond my reach. No one in my camp had checked the ropes before the fight. Why bother? For years now, my fight plan had been to take off my robe, get a quick knockout, put the robe back on, and return to the dressing room. Who worried about the tautness or slackness of the ropes? Now Muhammad was the beneficiary of that lack of attention to detail.

In that fourth round I was able finally to land a thundering right on the back of his neck. It weakened him, and I knew that if I could land another one like that, he'd go down and out. But when I loaded up the weapon and cocked it, I saw something that made me pull back instead. That sight is, in fact, the image I recall most vividly from the fight. It was the face of a "friend," sitting at ringside, who happened to be directly in my line of vision. (What he did bothered me so much that I've put him out of my mind forever; I can't even remember his name.) Between when I threw the first shot and prepared to throw the second, he began waving his arms wildly and screaming, "Bull! He hit him behind the neck. He's cheating." A man I'd considered family was rooting against me. In a state of shock, I couldn't deliver the punch that probably would have ended the fight right there. For the rest of the night I wondered whether he'd do the same thing every time I threw one.

My hurt and disappointment, and that thinking, lessened whatever power I had left. And there wasn't much of it. I wondered what had happened to my stamina, let alone my strength. No matter what the sportswriters said, stamina was never one of my problems; I'd had plenty of it. But because they'd not seen it – with my fights usually ending in the early rounds – they'd assumed I lacked it. I guess they hadn't noticed that I'd gone the distance three times before, and had even once scored a tenth-round knockout (of Gregorio Peralta).

It seemed that this was turning into a déjà vu nightmare of my amateur fights against Clay Hodges. Man, was I tired. I could barely get off the stool between rounds. Even so, Sadler was instructing me to continue my fearsome attack. This contradicted his usual advice, which was to slowly and carefully build to the knockout. "Get him," he said. "He can't last another round."

Archie Moore wasn't as insistent as Sadler; at least, he didn't say as much. This man of great pride had been disturbed and hurt, I think, by my pushing him to the side in favor of Sadler

again. If either guy had told me to change tactics, I would have.
They could have said to back off a round or two, catch my breath,
and let him come to me; he'd have to, if he wanted to win,
because by then he was far behind on points. But because these
guys counseled me to attack, attack, attack, I did. Their job was
to give advice. Mine was to take it.

Every time I went to hit Muhammad, he'd cover up, strike me
with that one quick jab or right, then run. The sad part was that
my blows, which numbered at least five to one over his, were met
by the crowd with either silence or, worse, the reaction of my
"friend." Meanwhile, each one of Muhammad's little jabs
brought tumultuous cries. I was winning these rounds, but
Muhammad Ali owned their hearts and minds more completely
with every punch he absorbed. For them, this had become a
morality play: Muhammad was good and I was evil. And yet, it
was because of me, as champion, that this fight had been staged
in Zaire. George Foreman, not Muhammad Ali, had tried to do
something grand for Africa, had brought the television cameras
to show off Africa to the world, had made the Africans proud of
themselves. I'd wanted them to love me, too – and for some
reason they didn't. I vowed never to go back.

In the seventh round, Muhammad noticed that I was getting
tired, that my shots weren't hurting as much. He said, "Come
on, George, show me something. Is that all you got?"

Knowing that he was whistling in the graveyard, I figured,
*Okay. I'm just going to play around now, catch him talking, and let
him try to hit me. When he tries, I'll knock him out.* As tired and
weak as I felt, I always believed that I still had enough for that
one shot to end it all. All I needed was the chance, the opening.
If Muhammad made the mistake of coming to me, it would be
his last mistake that night.

Angelo Dundee, Muhammad's trainer, must have divined my
plan. He yelled out, "Don't play with the sucker, don't play." A
few years before, he'd been present at a fight of mine in Lake
Geneva, Wisconsin, and had seen the ferocious beating I'd given
a tough Jamaican boxer. So he understood the damage I could
do.

Angelo's warning seemed to sober Muhammad a little. He
stopped playing around and talking.

In the eighth, I tried to entice Muhammad to come to me. Dropping my hands, I followed him around the ring, as if daring him to step into my web; there was no way he could hurt me. When we neared the ropes, I began pummeling him again. He was knocked backward near the corner, then bounced to the side. Off balance, I turned to follow him and was leaning his way when he threw a left-right combination whose power was multiplied by both my leaning toward him as I tried to re-balance myself, and his momentum off the corner.

As the combination struck ground zero on my chin, I remember thinking, *Boy, I'm going down.* Muhammad, I'm sure, was as surprised as I was.

My fall to the mat felt that much harder because my legs had been twisted while I was off balance. On my back, I lifted my head and not only was I alert and uninjured, I was actually excited and hopeful: *This guy hasn't mixed it up with me all night. Now, when he thinks he can come in and finish the job, I'll be able to get him. It doesn't matter how tired I am – I've still got enough to put him down when I get the chance. And now I will.*

Though I could have, I didn't get up immediately. Because in the days when there were no standing eight-counts that would allow a boxer to clear his senses before reentering the fray, the custom developed to stay down until eight. Instead of watching the referee's count, you were supposed to look for your cornermen's signal. Even as I did, I could hear Zack Clayton's count. He said "eight" and Sadler motioned me up. I stood at once, but Clayton waved me off with a quick count – nine and ten became one word to me.

It was over.

Clayton guided me to my corner as Ali and the crowd began celebrating. My God, it was over. It was really over. I felt disappointed, less for losing than for not getting a chance to mix it up. Then the magnitude of the loss began to hit me. I would be sorting it out for a long time.

"All right?" Sadler asked.

"Yeah."

Back in the dressing room, the mood was funereal. While dejection had set in, I was still more tired than anything else. Lying there on the training table, letting the thoughts just come and go, I heard questions – impertinent questions – from sportswriters they wouldn't have dared to ask even twenty-four hours before. Now these guys believed they could get away with anything. *So that's how it is? You're either on top, or you're nowhere.*

In short order, I would become depressed beyond recognition, and this fight would go down in boxing history; no less than Norman Mailer wrote an entire book about it.

Muhammad began bragging about his great strategy – letting me punch myself out before delivering the crowning blows. But I know, and he knows, he had no such strategy before the fight. To say he did is to shoot an arrow into a barn and then paint a bull's-eye around it. Muhammad's only strategy had been survival. When I cut off the ring from him, he had nowhere to go but the ropes, and nothing to do but cover up. What's more true than his concoction of some brilliant strategy is that I fought a foolish fight by not letting him come to me more, especially when I was tired and far ahead on points. I hadn't done that because I couldn't let anyone think that George Foreman was afraid of Muhammad Ali, and because my trainers told me to give it my all.

"Rope-a-dope" the fight got nicknamed when I mentioned to a writer that I believed my water may have been mickeyed. What else, I asked, could account for that medicinal taste and my terrible tiredness? What else could account for how sick and sore I felt for a month afterward?

So was there "medicine" in my drink? I can't say for certain. Later, I heard that Sugar Ray Robinson, watching the fight at home in the States, had commented to a friend that I seemed drugged. Maybe sportswriter Jim Murray, aiming for a laugh, was closer to the mark than he realized when he wrote that I looked like "a drunk trying to find a keyhole."

If I had been slipped a mickey, why? I can't answer with certainty there, either. Only afterward, when I thought about Sadler and my relationship with him, did it seem somewhat plausible. I remembered some stories he used to tell about boxers who belonged to gangsters – how the fix would be in for this guy or that to lose in order to set up a bigger payday or better betting odds down the line.

Such stories poured out of him when we were on the road and bored. We laughed about them. I was young and considered

Sadler a father figure. Was he joking? I don't know. But surely his message between the lines was that he'd protect me from such nastiness.

There was the tale Sadler told of an aging heavyweight who threw a fight to an up-and-coming champ. After the third round, the trainer put the stool out for his aging heavyweight, who angrily kicked it over backward. That told the trainer that his fighter was going down. A man who's soon to hit the canvas doesn't need the rest.

"I felt so bad," the trainer said. I thought he felt bad because he believed his man had thrown the fight. Then he clarified: "He could've at least given *me* a chance to make some money on it too."

The years since the fight have not answered the question for me of whether I was indeed doped. One verifiable fact is that Muhammad had been the heavy underdog until a late flurry brought down the odds. Was that money bet with the heart? I know only that this fight featured more unexplained happenings than any event of my life, and that in the grand scheme of things the loss ultimately helped to make me a man. Back then, however, I believed that the sky had fallen. I wasn't champion anymore. I didn't know what I was.

As for that Bible I'd taken to Zaire, the one given me by the preacher: I put it away where I wouldn't see it anymore. What good was a Bible if it didn't bring you luck?

Walking With Kings

Reg Gutteridge

*"Or walk with Kings – nor lose
the common touch"*
　　　　　　　Rudyard Kipling

You would think that a boxing contest that was covered by some
of America's leading modern literary figures and was the subject
of an award-winning film, first shown nearly twenty-five years
after the event it portrays took place, would deserve the hysterical hype that claims it is – in the words of that most abused of all
sporting epithets – "The Fight Of The Century".

Well, quite frankly, the "Rumble In the Jungle" as it also
became known, did not deserve it. As an exhibition of the "sweet
science" it failed even to rate in this "commoner's" top ten.

"The Greatest" himself, however, would hotly dispute my
verdict. After knocking out George Foreman in the eighth round
in Kinshasa, Zaire, on 30 October 1974, to regain the world
heavyweight championship, he said: "This was a real scientific
fight, a real thinkin' fight. For me it was, anyway. Everythin' I
did had a purpose."

But I think Foreman was nearer the mark when he told me
years later: "Ali didn't beat me, I beat myself. I punched myself
out."

No matter, as an atmospheric event, this epic was out on its
own in the history of the prize-fighting ring. The leading players,
the venue, and the shock climax made it almost as unforgettable
as those Ali-Frazier sagas. The almost superhuman way in which
Ali absorbed Foreman's powerful but ponderous blows convinced
some fans that he could, indeed, walk on water.

Millions of words have already been expended on

describing this unique occasion, so I do not propose to add my two penn'orth. But I would like to mention the disquiet I feel over the way it was depicted in the recent film *When We Were Kings*.

The American brothers who were responsible for this box office hit turned it into a hymn of praise for black America while, in my opinion, somewhat patronising their African cousins and totally disregarding some white "faces" who had something to do with staging the event in the first place.

The most glaring omission in this respect concerned the two men who put up the letters of credit, promoters Hank Schwarz of New York Video Techniques and Londoner John Daly of Hemdale Leisure Corporation. The now departed despot President Mobutu had site rights but did not attend on the night for fear of being bumped off.

Don King, heavily featured in the film, was only the match-maker. Schwarz and Daly were the promoters, a fact which could not have escaped the film makers' attention since both mens' names figured prominently in the posters and programmes in Kinshasa. There was no sight on screen either, of Ali's indispensable white trainer, Angelo Dundee.

The film, which is reported to have taken twenty-three years to edit, had a crew of one hundred who spent fifty-five days in what was once the old Belgian Congo because of a postponement when Foreman suffered a cut eye in training.

They painted a canvas that was as much to do with a musical carnival of brothers as it was a world boxing title fight. The invading American musicians and their motley crew of companions had a very limited understanding of or rapport with either the language or the culture of the French-speaking Zaireois.

I feel some sympathy for one of the musicians I became pals with. I must confess that this guy had me completely fooled. When I saw him accompanying Foreman on the heavy bag with his frenzied bongo drum beating, I thought he was, at the very least, one of those Leopard men who used to cause mayhem in those parts a few years earlier. He was done up in the most elaborate tropical gear you could imagine, complete with gaudy head dress. Thinking that he would make a great subject for an interview, I tentatively approached him and said in stupid, slow, pigeon English: "What is your name and where are you from?"

He looked down at me and drawled: "I'm Black Mack from LA. And I'm working the lounge at The Inter-Continental Hotel."

But it was Foreman's manager, Dick Sadler, who best summed up the whole circus when he looked at a group of these imported crew one day and remarked to me: "I can't wait to get away from my African brothers and home to my American mothers."

My special pal throughout this special trip, however, was an old Cockney sparring partner of mine, a throwback of an old pro who fought for many years out of Blackfriars. He was Tom Daly, father of the young promotional entrepeneur John who is still currently producing big buck award winning films for Hemdale in Los Angeles.

I was so close to Tom that I broke a rule of a lifetime and secured an interview for boxing nut John when he was a teenager with a view to his becoming my tea boy at the *Evening News*. He failed to turn up and I gave his old man a right coating over it. Tom had the last laugh, though, when he sat beside me, as his son's guest of honour, in a ringside seat in deepest Africa all those years later.

John Daly also came to the rescue of many of the British journalists, whose proprietors were reluctant to fund a second trip after the initial postponement, by underwriting their travel costs.

As the then chairman of the British Boxing Writers Association, I was nominated to do this deal with Mobutu's media chieftan, a gentleman by the name of Tshimpumpu, who wore a large fur hat in temperatures that would have done justice to a greenhouse.

When it came to organising things, Tshimpumpu turned out to be one of the world's slowest administrators and I had to doorstep him practically day and night to get the appropriate air tickets to England.

Talking of briefs, this was the performance above all others that paid for Ali's ticket to ride to immortality. Approaching thirty-three years of age and after a prolific number of fights, he was universally tipped to be not just defeated but destroyed by the ferocious Foreman, who had recently smashed Joe Frazier to the canvas six times inside two rounds.

Like many of my Press pals, I had let my head overrule my heart and tipped Foreman to win, too. If there had been the faintest doubt in my mind this was expelled by the pre-fight quote Foreman gave me. Due to TV programming demands in America the bout was due to start in the wee small hours. When I asked Foreman whether this bothered him, he simply gave an evil grin and said: "When I was a kid in Houston, Texas, I won all my fights in the early hours of the morning." Then, as if I needed any more convincing he added that Houston had the highest crime rate in the USA. How strange then that this mean, impolite sinisterly handsome man of very few words has metamorphosed into the fat jolly grandfather who was still boxing, commentating and, miraculously, bible punching when this book went to press.

I became convinced, way back then, that a miracle of a different kind was about to happen when, just before the first bell, I was on the receiving end of an extraordinary verbal reprimand from Ali himself. He leaned over the top rope, wagged his finger at me and said: "I hear you been telling the people in England that I'm gonna lose – shame on you. This nigger can't whip my arse!" I knew then that I had tipped a loser, but I felt like shouting for joy because, just like the entire population of Zaire, I loved "The Greatest" too.

As for big George, he presented me with the silver microphone, which the American Boxing Writers Association awarded me for "Excellence in Broadcasting Journalism" twenty years after Zaire. He told me then that his one big regret about those early years was that "I wish I had been nicer to people".

He also surprisingly revealed to me on another occasion that he sometimes felt genuine physical fear before a fight. Straightfaced, he swore: "I was so afraid when Joe Frazier and I were psyching each other out eyeball to eyeball in the ring before our fight, that I was hoping he would not drop his eyes in case he saw my knees knocking." Good on you, George.

Floyd Patterson, too, who happened to have the fastest hands of any heavyweight champ including Ali, told me when we were commentating together in South Africa that he had felt fear in his first disastrous fight with the Swede Ingemar Johannson back in the 1960s. "I had overtrained," he said: "And suddenly knew I couldn't do justice to myself and froze."

Nice guy Floyd was so sincerely patriotic that, for weeks afterwards, he donned a beard and false moustache whenever he went out to "disguise my shame for letting down my country".

PART 8
THE LONG FALL
FROM GRACE

The Thrilla in Manila

Ferdie Pacheco

FIGHT OF THE CENTURY
MUHAMMAD ALI   VS.   JOE FRAZIER
champion   challenger
HEAVYWEIGHT CHAMPIONSHIP
MANILA, PHILIPPINES
OCTOBER 1, 1975
ROUND 14

In the mid-1970s the United States was recovering slowly from the social upheavals of the sixties. Political protests shook the public into an awareness that the nation's involvement in Vietnam had been badly misguided. The war finally ended with the withdrawal of US embassy personnel in 1975. Assassination attempts on prominent figures continued to be an unsettling fact of American life, as President Ford survived two failed attempts on his life. The public's spirit was leavened in 1975, however, by baseball's World Series, as the Cincinnati Reds edged the Boston Red Sox four games to three in one of history's most exciting Fall Classics.

Meanwhile, the world's population passed four billion. In a historic first, the Soviets' Soyuz craft linked in space with the Americans' Apollo 18, inaugurating an era of cooperation in space by the two superpowers.

In boxing, Muhammad Ali continued to take his Ali Circus to various foreign countries. In 1975 the traveling spectacle set sail for the Philippines and what was expected to be an easy fight with an old adversary, Joe Frazier.

It would turn out to be anything but that.

The Background

The greatest fight of the century was not considered much of a fight when it was made. It seemed like an "oh, by the way" kind of promotion by Don King; an afterthought.

King had found yet another country badly in need of a divertissement. He would provide it, in the form of a sporting event that would capture the world's interest while distracting the Filipino people's attention from the rebels in the country's mountains, the nation's sagging economy, and the humid heat of October. President Ferdinand Marcos would be grateful for the opportunity to host a happening featuring the charismatic world heavyweight champion, Muhammad Ali. For his part Ali was eager to get out of his own country. He sought escape for the oldest of reasons: love. Ali needed to escape the bonds of his marriage.

In Africa the previous year Ali had met a gorgeous girl, Veronica Porche, and had fallen head over heels in love. The relationship grew increasingly serious in the ensuing months. Belinda, Ali's long-suffering wife and the mother of his children, seemed powerless to stop the affair. Ali was a man in lust.

A fight in the Philippines would allow Ali to be alone with Veronica for at least six weeks. Belinda would be left behind to tend to the children. This was too good to pass up. Ali enthusiastically signed the contract.

Joe Frazier's stock had fallen to a low point since beating Ali in their first fight, in 1971. In 1973 Frazier had entered the ring with George Foreman, who treated Smokin' Joe as his personal yo-yo, bouncing him off the canvas until he knocked him out in the second round. In a return match with Ali in Madison Square Garden in 1974, Joe had been beaten handily in losing a twelve-round decision. Joe Frazier was on the skids.

Muhammad Ali is a loving man. He cannot hold a grudge. He always treats former opponents with great warmth and affection, and he had an especially soft spot in his heart for Joe Frazier. His first encounter with Frazier had been one of the greatest fights in his career, even though he had lost the fifteen-round decision in a superb contest of wills. Now Ali, the victor in the '74 rematch, felt sorry for Frazier. He wanted to give him a going-away present. Frazier would come to the Philippines, take his beating, and go home with a truck load of retirement money. Ali and his people agreed it would be a decent thing to do for the man who had provided Ali such invaluable, high-profile exposure. In his singular way, Ali loved Frazier. Frazier forced him to fight at the top of his form.

Says Angelo Dundee, "Joe Frazier wasn't a safe opponent for anybody. Frazier on any given night could lick any given fighter because he was – he was for real. The only problem he had was that Muhammad Ali was around, and Muhammad Ali could always beat Joe Frazier."

In Frazier's corner there was no love lost for the opponent who proclaimed himself the Greatest. Joe Frazier truly despised Ali. Joe was a tough man from the mean streets of Philadelphia. His road to the top had been hard; his fights typically were brutal slugging matches. However tough, Frazier was an honorable man, a noble warrior who loved his family. Physically, he was the antithesis of Ali: short (a shade under six feet), heavily muscled, and frequently scowling. As such, he was the perfect foil for Ali, who loved to tease his opponents, often focusing his barbs on an aspect of their appearance. Frazier had a deep, glowing pride in who he was and what he had become. He saw nothing funny about his looks, but Ali did. Ali called him "the Gorilla."

For Joe, this fight wasn't about money. He took what was offered; there wasn't even a meaningful negotiation. Ali was guaranteed $4 million against 43 percent of all fight-generated income. Frazier would end up with half of Ali's eventual take of $6 million.

Frazier requested accommodations for seventeen people in Manila. Ali said he needed plane tickets and lodging for fifty, and by the time his full entourage had arrived in the Philippines, it numbered considerably more than fifty. You see, Joe Frazier was in Manila on business. Muhammad Ali was there on holiday.

The Ali Circus, which had seriously begun to gather steam in Zaire, reached its zenith – or nadir, depending on your perspective – in Manila. The increasingly bloated size of the Circus was not the result of Ali's generosity, although that was legendary. What made these sideshows possible was the governments of the countries hosting the fights, which provided airline tickets and hotel accommodations at no cost. At that price Ali invited the world, and his world came to consist of an eclectic group of ex-fighters, boxing managers, agents, pimps and their whores, movie stars between pictures, beauty queens, rock stars, writers, painters, facilitators, tourist guides, politicians, gangsters, procurers, drug dealers, and garden-variety con men.

All we lacked was a priest, but we had an entire college of cardinals in the form of the Muslim hierarchy led by Herbert Muhammad, who was Ali's manager and the son of the Right Honorable Elijah Muhammad. We didn't lack for spiritual help.

The presence of such a glut of parasites might be expected to have an adverse effect on a boxing champion who is preparing to defend his crown. In this case there were other deleterious distractions for the fighter: he was on a secret honeymoon, he seriously underestimated his challenger, and he viewed his visit to Manila as an all-expenses-paid, six-week vacation. Put these together and you have a formula for disaster.

As soon as Don King announced the fight, he labeled it the "Thrilla in Manila," which Ali impishly amended to the "Thrilla in Manila with the Gorilla." He even brought a toy gorilla doll to the press conference and gleefully punched it as cameras clicked.

Whenever Joe Frazier made the mistake of letting himself get caught seated beside Ali in a television studio or at a press conference, the results were painful to behold.

"I'm gon a . . ." Frazier started to say in one interview.

"I'm going to . . ." Ali enunciated clearly, correcting Joe as if he were a dumb ghetto kid. "Not 'I'm gonna.' Talk intelligent," Ali said, smiling patronizingly at Joe, who reacted badly; you could almost see smoke issuing from his ears. Doggedly, determined not to let Ali deflect his train of thought, Joe plowed on.

"I'm gonna go inta training . . ."

"Not *inta*," Ali interrupted. "*Into*. Say, how far did you go in school?"

"As far as you went," Frazier snarled.

"You don't look that way. Why do you say *dat-uh*?" As the crowd of photographers and writers began to laugh openly, Ali gathered momentum. "*Dat-uh* – what is that, Joe? What's *dat-uh*? The word is *that*, not *dat-uh*. Say *that*."

At this point it looked like Joe would explode and cold-cock Ali right there, but he was restrained before he could attack.

Knowing that he was well under Joe's skin, Ali pulled out the little black-rubber gorilla doll and began to recite his doggerel to a delighted audience:

> "It will be a Killer
> And a Chiller
> And a Thriller
> When I Get the Gorilla
> In Manila."

Then he began to punch the gorilla doll – bip, bip, bip, bip; five, six, seven times.

"All night long," Ali sang out, and from behind him Bundini Brown echoed his sing-song refrain, "All night long!" Ali punched the doll again for good measure, then added, "Come on, Gorilla, this is a thrilla; come on, we in Manila."

Joe Frazier was hurt, bewildered, and angry. At the door of his limousine, he faced the reporters' microphones. "He's talking now," said Joe, "but the time comin' when he gonna hear the knock on the door, when it's time to come in the ring, and then he's gonna remember what it's like to be in with me, how hard and long that night's gonna be!"

Frazier had accepted this fight in a state of cold fury. He had beaten Ali in the first fight, yet never got the glory he believed that he deserved. Sure, some people complimented his victory as workmanlike, but somehow the glory had accrued to Ali, who had only recently returned to action following his exile. People made excuses for him: he had come back too soon, he wasn't ready yet for a championship bout. Moreover, some boxing scribes and other observers thought that Ali had won that '71 encounter in New York, despite having been knocked down by Frazier. Joe went into the hospital for six weeks after the fight, they pointed out. As for the second fight, Joe blocked it out of his mind as a bad night, an aberration.

Ali, meanwhile, was basking in the sunshine of overwhelming public adoration and enjoying the forbidden fruits of his Asian tryst with Veronica. He escorted her openly around Manila, enjoying the envious looks cast by other men. He made his big mistake, however, when he took her to the Presidential Palace to meet Marcos and his comely wife, Imelda.

Ali introduced the radiant Veronica as his wife.

"Your wife is quite beautiful," said Marcos, himself a connoisseur of fine ladies.

"Your wife ain't so bad herself," shot back Ali, his handsome face leering at Imelda, who smiled back.

A *Newsweek* article soon described the meeting to the world. Belinda exploded in all directions when she saw it. Her first act of vengeance was to board a plane to Manila. By the time she landed there, she knew that her marriage to Ali was over.

For Ali, training seemed to run a distant third among his priorities, behind public appearances throughout the Philippines and his torrid affair with Veronica. All eyes were on the champion and his extravagant activities. Even the rebels stopped fighting and filtered into Manila to watch the Ali Circus in action.

The stage was set. Ali, laughing and taunting "the Gorilla," anticipated an easy fight. Joe Frazier, dressed in workingman's denim and snorting fire, couldn't wait for the first round to arrive, freeing him to attack and destroy his nemesis, the only man on this planet to make fun of his looks and even demean his blackness. Frazier didn't just want to win and wrest Ali's title from him. He wanted to kill Ali.

The fight would be held at 10:30 a.m. at the Philippine Coliseum, in downtown Manila. It seemed pointless to announce an attendance figure, since by the time the fight started, Filipinos had oozed into every nook and cranny of the steaming arena. There were no longer aisles, just a wall-to-wall carpet of sweating people. The more athletic and daring spectators had even crawled out onto the rafters. The line of windows at the top of the arena was blocked by the uppermost edge of the throng.

There was no air conditioning. The high humidity in surrounding Manila and the temperature in the arena made breathing nearly impossible. Under the ring lights it was even hotter. Never before in my forty years of boxing involvement had I experienced heat like this. I survived the corner work by wearing a towel that was soaked in cold water and filled with ice cubes on top of my head. Even this didn't help much.

The fighters were called to the middle of the ring by Carlos Padilla, a diminutive Filipino referee. My first thought was, "Oh God, how is that midget going to control these two giants?" It wasn't an idle thought.

Frazier stared hard at Ali. Smoke seemed to emanate from Smokin' Joe's nostrils, and he pawed the canvas with his foot. He looked like he wanted to hit Ali during the introductions. He was ready to go.

Ali looked serene, as if he were expecting a game of tennis. His mouth was still running, still joking at the expense of the Gorilla. His eyes twinkled. This, he thought, was going to be fun.

But it wouldn't be fun. It would be a battle nearly to the death, an epic struggle in three stages: stage one, which might be called Ali's Easy Time; stage two, Frazier's Turn; and stage three, The Shootout.

The Three-stage Struggle

Ali came out on fresh legs at the opening bell, easily dodging Frazier's bull-like rushes. He blocked Joe's punches on his shoulders and gloves or slipped out of range, causing Frazier to swing wildly in the air. Ali was beautiful, and Joe . . . well, Joe was the Gorilla. Enough said. This was going to be easy.

In the second round Ali suddenly decided to fight flat-footed and go for the knockout – to shock and amaze the world. He rained blows on Joe, whose ability to take a punch had been questioned since Foreman had bounced him around like a basketball a year ago in Jamaica. Now Frazier kept coming, cannonball shots caroming off his iron jaw, and then he suddenly was staggered. Frazier was in trouble! Ali saw this and pursued him relentlessly. After Frazier had made it safely to the bell, Ali began to view him in a different light. This wasn't going to be easy after all. Joe banged his gloves together in his corner as he waited for Round Three to begin.

The third round was more of the same. Ali would flick a powerful jab at Frazier, who seemed mesmerized by the punch. Then Ali would connect with a pile-driving right. Frazier's head would snap back, sweat flying, as his knees buckled. Twice more he seemed ready to fall, but he did not. Ali returned to the attack, confident that no man could take this punishment for long.

By the fourth round Ali's punches had lost their zing. He was tiring. The heat; the bright lights; the muggy, oxygen-deprived atmosphere; and the toughness of his opponent were wearing him down. It showed in small ways. Ali's customary composure lapsed at the end of the round when, with Frazier still on his feet, glowering like a wolf through his bloody mouthpiece, Ali snapped, "You dumb chump, you!"

"Around the fourth round, when Joe started cooking. I knew we were in for a long night," says Angelo Dundee.

Questions hung in the air. How much more could Frazier take? How much more did Ali have to give? His long days and nights of partying and lovemaking had suddenly become a factor. Frazier had trained to go fifteen hard rounds if necessary. Ali hoped to be back at his hotel suite with Veronica by the end of Round Five. But here was Round Five, and Joe Frazier was still there in front of him and, worse, now advancing on him, wind-milling damaging body punches.

While Ali continued to win the rounds on points, the momentum was slowly shifting. Now Ali backed into a corner and stayed there, permitting Frazier to pound his arms and body. It was the African rope-a-dope again, only this time his opponent, unlike the quickly exhausted Foreman, was ready to go the distance. Our corner yelled, "Quit playing!" Angelo, up on the top step, hoarsely yelling to be heard above the din, exhorted Ali, "Get out of the goddamn corner." But Ali stayed in a corner, on the ropes. Perhaps he couldn't get himself out of there.

Stage one ended around the close of Round Five, whereupon stage two, Frazier's Turn, began. Joe Frazier's fights had their own rhythm and style. Frazier often took a beating in the early rounds, but then his hard heart took over. Discouraged opponents caved in as Joe turned on his afterburners and launched his relentless, all-out attack.

Frazier's heart, his determination to win, surfaced during Round Five. His trademark evil left hook began beating a tattoo on Ali's ribs and kidneys. Frazier put his head on Ali's chest, pushed Ali back using his powerful thick legs, and let fly punches to Muhammad's body. Ali winced and tried to dance away from the mayhem, but Frazier's head seemed sewn to Ali's sternum. They embraced each other in a grotesque tango, Ali receiving steady punishment as the two fighters lurched across the ring. Suddenly, at the end of the fifth, Ali's legs were visibly turning to rubber. He knew he was getting into trouble, entering a zone he called "the dark room where you are searching for the light switch."

"Lord, that man can punch," gasped Ali as he joined us in the corner. We all looked at one another. He'd never said anything like that to us – not while fighting Sonny Liston, not while battling George Foreman, and not while tussling with Frazier in their two previous bouts. Our spirits sagged upon hearing this confession.

But no one ever doubted Ali's courage. His heart was big and his balls were even bigger. He went out for more in the sixth. Frazier, sensing the change in the tide, stepped up his attack. Joe was brutally effective. Ali sucked it up and took the punishment.

Near the end of the seventh round, Ali, with his back to the ropes, grabbed Joe by the back of the head and pulled him into a clinch. He yelled in Frazier's ear, "They told me you was washed up, champ."

Joe gritted his teeth, hammered his hardest punch to Ali's kidney, and growled, "They lied to you, champ. They lied!"

Stage two – Frazier's Turn – lasted until the end of the tenth round. By consensus, the fight was even to that point. Ali had taken the first five rounds, Frazier the second five. Ali had Frazier in trouble early but couldn't knock him down; then Frazier had knocked Ali from one side of the ring to the other, but, he, too, had been unable to score a knockdown.

Now came the most brutal test of two equally matched human beings I have ever seen. We held on to a bit of hope in our corner. Ali is at his best when he is out on the end of a limb, we reminded ourselves. Somehow, by some unusual means, he always finds a way to win. That is why he is the definitive champion.

Frazier and his cornermen held out a similar hope. He'd beaten Ali once, so he could do it again. There were only five rounds to go. The "Championship Causeway, Route 10 to Route 15," as a fight's final rounds were sometimes called, belongs to the man who wants it the most. It is the ultimate test of wills. Ali had a strong will, but so did Joe Frazier. Who would win out in the end?

Stage three, The Shootout, began with tough trench fighting at the start of the tenth round. In the corner, before the bell, Ali had looked like a beaten man. His chin drooped on his chest. His eyes rolled back in his head when we gave him water. Bundini, his witch-doctor-amateur-psychologist-cheerleader, was in hysterical tears, imploring Ali, "Force yourself, champ!" Angelo calmly issued simple commands. These directives made all the boxing sense in the world to someone who wasn't fighting Joe Frazier right now and whose tank wasn't running perilously low on gas. Ali rose wearily to answer the bell for the tenth, the needle of his gas gauge hovering near *E*.

By Round Eleven, Frazier seemed at the height of his power. He fought like a devastating force of nature. He pinned Ali in a corner, where Ali stood helpless as he absorbed shot after shot.

"Lawd, have mercy!" cried Bundini on my shoulder. I could only respond, "Oh, God." Angelo continued to scream, "Get outta there. Ali, move, move." Angelo screamed again and again, but Ali stayed on the ropes, pinned there by Frazier's incessant pummeling. Joe sensed the kill.

"When Ali came to the corner, his arms went down at his sides instead of being on his lap like always," Angelo Dundee recalls. "Then I knew I had to get the ice bucket, put his head in it, and squeeze the ice on him. I knew I had to work because it was such a grueling fight. We were tired in the corner just going up and down the steps; that's how hot it was in that primitive arena with its tin roof, and the heat was multiplied with the lights. I don't know how Joe Frazier and Muhammad were able to fight that day."

In the corner Ali seemed to experience a rebirth. In sports it's called finding your second wind. In Ali's ring career it denoted the moment when the genial man-child turned into a killer. It's a frightening thing to see. When the bell rang for Round Twelve, the killer had emerged. He started popping his hard jab, Frazier's head bobbing back like a cork in a pool of turbulent water. Now, with Frazier bobbing and weaving and trying to deflect that jab with his gloves, Ali knew the time had come to drop his lethal right hand. Suddenly, long rights began to hammer the oncoming Frazier. Spittle and blood flew from Frazier's slack jaw. He was like a stunned, blinded bull at the end of a corrida.

As Frazier reeled to his corner, his trainer, Eddie Futch, gasped at the damage done to his man. Frazier's face had become disfigured, a mass of bumps, bruises, cuts, hickeys, and swellings. His eyes were closing.

"Can't take much more of this," said the kindly Eddie Futch to Joe.

Angelo greeted Ali with a shower of ice-cold water. Angelo was all smiles, excited by the evidence before him.

"You got him, champ. He ain't got no more power," said Dundee. Ali gave him a withering look that seemed to say, "Oh yeah? Then you go out and finish him."

Round Thirteen saw Ali throw every bit of his remaining strength at the sagging Frazier. Joe staggered but kept coming, barely able to see his tormentor through the slits that were his eyes. Yet still he attacked, still driving forward, throwing punches. It was an awesome display of one man's indomitable spirit. Joe Frazier would not be beaten. Ali would have to win this fight outright.

Ali continued his battering of Frazier through Round Fourteen. There was a palpable sense that life and death were hanging in the air in that arena. There is a limit to the amount of trauma a man's brain and body can absorb and still function. Boxers occasionally exceed this limit and, tragically, leave their lives in the ring. Tonight, amid suffocating heat and humidity, Joe Frazier had sustained a terrible beating. While his warrior heart, his implacable will, told him to go on, it remained for a saner voice to tell him that he must not.

That voice belonged to Eddie Futch, who said, "Joe, I'm going to stop it."

"No, Eddie, no. Don't do this to me," Frazier mumbled, his words barely comprehensible, uttered as they were through split lips and with a thick tongue and a clouded brain. Joe kept pleading to continue, but on this night and as always, Eddie knew best. In his quiet, authoritative voice, Futch finally said, "Sit down, son." His hand rested lightly on Joe's shoulder, preventing him from leaving the stool. "It's all over," said Eddie. "The world will never forget what you did here today."

Says Angelo Dundee, "When Eddie got Joe back in the corner, he knew the guy had nothing left. He was empty. If he'd got up, he'd have got knocked out for sure. Frazier could have been hurt very easily, because in that condition, that's when a fighter gets hurt. He had nothing to go with, no resiliency."

The Thrilla in Manila was over. For two reasons it was a good thing that Eddie Futch kept Joe Frazier from coming out for another round. First, Smokin' Joe might have died in the ring. Second, Ali would have had to go out there again, too, and he might not have lasted long himself. He was near the end of his rope.

Afterward, back at the hotel when we had all recovered, Futch said, "Joe puffs up; he don't cut, but he blows up. By the thirteenth he could barely see. His whole face was puffed up, nicked, cut, and bruised. His face was a mess, and I wanted to stop it then, but he wanted one more round. I let him; it was his fight, he had to finish it. Also, to tell the truth, Ali hit him so much and so hard, I thought maybe he had punched himself out, so what the hell, maybe Joe had a chance. But when I seen the whipping he took and how he barely got back to the corner, I said no, it ain't worth getting his brain scrambled. He's got a fine family and a great future, and I stopped it. I ain't sorry. Joe just couldn't take one more round of that hell."

As usual, Ali summed it up best. Reclining, exhausted, on his training table in the steaming dressing room, he said, "I always bring out the best in the men I fight, but Joe Frazier, I'll tell the world right now, brings out the best in me. That's one helluva man, and God bless him."

Aftermath

What we saw in Manila – a fight to the finish between two great heavyweights, with intense emotion flowing; a grim battle of character and the will to win – was the fight of the century, in my book. I simply cannot think of a more entertaining fight, given all of the surrounding circumstances and the meaning of the fight to both contestants, and given its historical significance.

"What that fight goes to show you is two things," says Angelo Dundee. "Number one is that Ali was never physically the same fighter after he lost those three and a half years of his career, quite honestly. But he won two more titles because of his character, and it his character that allowed him to go on in that fight. The other thing it shows you is how bad Ali felt. He later told *Sports Illustrated* that it was the closest he ever felt to dying, and after the tenth round, when Frazier made that great comeback, he thought about quitting. So it tells you that even the great ones, they might think about quitting, but what counts is what they do."

Ali went on to be designated the athlete of the century. No one achieved his magnitude of worldwide fame. His long championship run, during which he won a heavyweight crown three times, included extraordinary fights with the toughest of opponents: Sonny Liston, George Foreman, and Joe Frazier, among others.

Ali also was a symbol in the days of social upheaval in the sixties and seventies. He became a global hero, worshipped on every continent. He was a deeply religious man too, a man who truly loved his fellow human beings.

Ali fought on for too long. When should he have quit? Personally, I would have been ecstatic had he retired after defeating Joe Frazier in Manila. Frazier effectively retired at that point – he fought just twice more – and he is in reasonably good shape today. Frazier has continued his involvement in boxing in Philadelphia, developing young fighters including members of his family. He is revered in the sport's circles, where his stature is assured by his epic fights with Ali.

Ali suffers from mid-brain damage in the form of advanced Parkinson's disease. He handles it like he handled a tough opponent; he will not submit easily to it and in his resistance he sets a worthy example for his fellow sufferers. He travels far and wide and still captivates his audiences with his charismatic personality. He never questions God's will, and he lives enveloped by a serenity of spirit and a peace of mind that many seek but few attain.

Don King went on to become the premier promoter in boxing history. Chronically beset by legal problems and attacked by the press, he hires the best attorneys, smiles his dazzling smile, and holds his arms aloft as he cries out in his deep, sonorous voice, "Only in America!"

As for the rest of the cast from that unforgettable morning in Manila, Eddie Futch remained at the top of his profession until his death in 1999; Ali's cornermen Bundini Brown and Luis Sarria have also passed away; and Angelo Dundee remains active in boxing.

With that final fight against Frazier, Ali achieved a little-noted distinction. Through one climactic fight with each of them, Ali effectively terminated the careers of three seemingly invincible champions: Sonny Liston, George Foreman in his first incarnation, and Joe Frazier. Each fought again, more or less briefly, before calling it quits for good, but none was ever again a contender, except Foreman in his long-delayed comeback. Ali, the apparent winner of this four-way round-robin, was, ironically, the loser. He continued to fight, ultimately at the cost of his health.

For those of us who played a role in the historic sporting event that transpired in Manila on October 1, 1975, and for many of the millions who watched it on television, the fight remains unforgettable. It was the Fight of the Century.

Postscript: Ali's Injury

The question that hung in the air after Manila was how much more of this type of punishment could Ali take? He had absorbed some monstrous beatings. While his opponents retired, one by one, he kept fighting. But why? Didn't we see the damage being done to him?

Did Angelo Dundee encourage him to call it quits?

"No, at no time," says Angelo, "because if I brought up the subject, he'd just say, 'I know what I'm doing.' That's Muhammad Ali. He did what he wanted to do with his life."

As his physician, I told Ali and the people around him that he should retire. I pointed out the slowing and slurring of his speech, his diminished reflexes, the beginning of a shuffling gait, and a barely perceptible thickening of his voice. These are all signs of mid-brain damage, which, when it reaches maturity, becomes the "punch-drunk syndrome." In time this syndrome usually progresses to Parkinson's disease. I voiced my concerns, but none of the members of the Ali Circus would heed my warnings, least of all Ali.

The matter of money loomed large in the background. The cost of maintaining his entourage and his growing roster of ex-wives was astronomical. Ali simply had to fight to pay off all his debts. The members of the Ali Circus were in the same straits. Not one of them had an alternative source of income commensurate with what they received when Ali fought three times a year. No one wanted to kill the Golden Goose.

It's easy to have principles and morals when you have a positive bank balance and independent wealth. It's often different when you are broke and dependent on someone else's ability to generate income.

In the mid-1970s I was a very successful doctor in Miami, with two clinics. I had made good investments and was financially secure. I would like to think that if this had not been the case and I needed Ali to keep fighting in order to support me, I would have had the moral courage to maintain my position, which was that Ali should retire.

Ignoring the subject of brain damage, the Ali Circus trundled on, with no fewer than five fights in 1976. He had fought once in 1977—winning a fifteen-round decision in May over the unheralded Alfredo Evangelista—when my conscience could take no more. Ali's health was deteriorating. Even the press, which is often blind to such things, noticed the worsening of his symptoms. Ali blissfully overlooked his declining boxing skills and his obvious physical impairment. But Herbert Muhammad and the rest of the boys wanted one more fight for him that year; an easy one, they emphasized.

They matched Ali up with Earnie Shavers in Madison Square Garden on September 29, 1977. Earnie Shavers! Mother of God! An easy fight? No, this fight was an act of criminal negligence. In Shavers they had picked the heaviest hitter in boxing. The man could knock down a building with one punch. Oh, he was fierce.

So much for the notion of an easy fight! The hell with it, I said to myself. This is Ali's last fight or I leave. My conscience was throbbing. They were killing this kid.

Ali waged a wonderfully courageous fight that night in the Garden. In Round Four Shavers caught Ali with his best shot. Ali was momentarily out on his feet. He fell back against the ropes into his rope-a-dope stance. Shavers eyed him warily. Then Earnie backed off, not believing what he saw. Was Ali faking? No, he was out on his feet, in serious trouble, but once again, his habitual good luck rescued him.

The bout came down to the final round, which in those days was the fifteenth. This fight was being televised by NBC, which had decided to report the judges' scoring while the fight was in progress.

Ali was ahead by three points. All he needed to do in Round Fifteen was box, run, and clinch, and he would win the fight. But Angelo was unaware that we were ahead by three points. He believed that the fight was very close, so he dispatched an exhausted Ali to duke it out in the last round with the heavy-fisted Shavers.

Round Fifteen was a battle of epic proportions, every bit as violent as Round Fourteen of Ali-Frazier in Manila. Both men took turns landing haymakers. The bell rang and Ali collapsed in exhaustion in the corner.

"Did I win the round?" he asked.

"Yes," someone told him.

"Did I win the fight?"

Yes, he did, by four points—much more than enough. That fifteenth-round war of attrition had been needless. For me this was the last straw. Slow murder, pure and simple, was being committed.

The next morning I was summoned to the New York State Athletic Commission offices, where I met a grim-faced Dr Edwin Campbell. He held the results of lab tests in his hand.

"Ferdie, based on these results and what I saw last night, I'm recommending that we never license Ali to fight again in New York."

I smiled in relief. We both knew he was right. He showed me the lab results.

"After a tough fight like that one, you expect a little blood in the urine, but look at these tests," said Campbell. I took a look and winced.

"These results show not only whole blood cells, but entire columns of cells that line the renal tubules," he continued. "The filtration cells that strain the blood in order to produce urine are completely gone, destroyed. There is no filtration system. Ali's kidneys have been injured, and kidney damage will lead to major incapacitation and, eventually, kidney failure and death."

I made five copies of the lab report. I then sat down and wrote a formal letter. I sent copies of my letter along with the lab report to Ali; his wife, Veronica; his manager, Herbert Muhammad; his spiritual adviser and "master," the Honorable Elijah Muhammad; and, of course, Angelo Dundee.

I mailed each package separately, in a return-requested envelope, so as to be sure each person had received the message.

Everything that I experienced in boxing had occurred through the generosity and help of Angelo Dundee and, to a large extent, Chris Dundee. For years I found it hard to place any of the blame for the damage to Ali's health on Angelo. Yes, he was there. Yes, he let it happen, but in all fairness I understood why and how such a kind and loving man could not bring himself to stop Ali from committing self-destruction.

Remember, I left Ali's camp after the Shavers fight in September 1977. In December he fought an exhibition with Scott LeDoux. On February 15, 1978, Ali lost his title to a virtual amateur, Leon Spinks, in a fifteen-round decision in Vegas. On September 15, 1978, he won the title back from Spinks in New Orleans, by way of a fifteen-round decision. Both Spinks bouts were hard-fought affairs. Ali's kidneys took a beating and his brain damage progressed, yet still no one around him uttered the word *retirement*.

Ali himself, finally aware of the extent of his decline, retired in 1979. The boxing world heaved a sigh of relief. I was happy, but I knew Ali and his love of the spotlight, and I knew the parasites of the Ali Circus. In 1980, a big-money opportunity presented itself in the form of a bout in Las Vegas against one of Ali's former sparring partners, Larry Holmes, the current heavyweight champion. This fight had Major Disaster written all over it.

The over-the-hill Circus gang convened in Vegas. In my place they brought Herbert's doctor, who loaded Ali with amphetamines to lose weight; a diuretic to get the water out of his system; and, to top it all off, thyroid medication, for no discernible or justifiable reason. What little chance Ali had to win this fight evaporated amid that cocktail of pharmaceuticals, which would inexorably sap his muscular strength.

The beating inflicted by Holmes lasted into the eleventh round. Ringsiders felt the fiasco should have been stopped by Round Three. I didn't think Ali should have answered the opening bell.

Let's pause for a moment to examine Angelo Dundee's reasons for sticking with Ali.

Says Angelo, "I was the manager from the get-go, and I was his trainer at the end. I'm his trainer and friend today. So I feel good about it. Our relationship was 100 percent, and it's 100 percent today. I wanted to stay there in the corner to protect him. I wasn't gonna let him get hurt. If I was there, I could stop it."

Angelo's reasoning is sound, but it doesn't jibe with the reality of what happened. If his purpose was to protect Ali, why let him fight Holmes in his drug-weakened condition? Why not stop the fight by the third round, when it was evident that Ali had nothing to offer that night? The answer to these questions is that Angelo didn't have the power to stop the fight. That responsibility had always belonged to Herbert Muhammad and the Muslims.

They always had a lot more to lose than a fight. Ali's career was irretrievably enmeshed in his blackness and in Muslim politics. Herbert didn't have the balls to stop the Holmes fight early. Don't kid yourself: Angelo had nothing to do with it!

And if, after such a disgraceful performance, Angelo saw the light, he hid it well, for he allowed Ali to suffer further humiliation, at the hands of a vastly inferior opponent, Trevor Berbick, who handed Ali yet another defeat, on December 11, 1981, in Nassau, the Bahamas.

And people still wonder whether Ali's brain damage is due to boxing?

Before I leave my role in the tragedy, let me try to clarify a point. Angelo Dundee is not only a close friend of mine, but the godfather of my prized daughter, Tina. We remained close after I left Ali's camp. I understood that Angelo's character is such that he could not stand up to the Muslims and leave Ali.

"If I left, Ali would have just gotten someone else and continued to fight," Angelo says, and that rationale works for him.

I say in reply, "Yes, but it's your conscience that I'm speaking of. How can you look at yourself in the mirror and say, 'I'm letting Ali go on and continue to be damaged. It's on my head. I have to live with it.'"

Such thoughts may never have passed through Angelo's head. Angelo is the baby of his family. He was programmed to obey, not to think. Older brother Chris was the boss. A tough survivor of the Depression, Chris had little sympathy for the idea of boxers quitting. They fought till they couldn't fight anymore. When Angelo picked a beautiful Georgia-born peach, Helen, a model, to be his wife, he had two bosses he did not contradict. He also fell in love with a beautiful legend, Muhammad Ali, and he acquired another boss along the way, Herbert Muhammad and the Nation of Islam. Angelo found himself surrounded by bosses, all of them wanting or needing the Ali Circus to cruise along indefinitely.

Is there any wonder that Angelo's conscience was overwhelmed? Angelo did as he always had done: he took the path of least resistance. His rationale is weakly persuasive, but for all the wrong reasons. If Angelo was there to protect Ali from serious harm, then why was he there in Vegas for the Holmes fight, or in the Bahamas for the Berbick travesty?

Poor Angelo; he took as big a beating as Ali did, for if ever one man loved another, Angelo truly loved Ali. And no matter what kind of face he puts on it, Angelo bitterly hates what boxing did to Ali.

Thomas Hauser observes, "Ali wanted to fight. It was what he defined himself by. The three greatest fighters of all time were Muhammad Ali, Sugar Ray Robinson, and Joe Louis. All fought longer than they should have. They wound up in their later years in less than ideal condition. There's a message in that for anybody.

"But what Ali showed in Manila, more than in any other fight, was that he was a warrior. He was a gladiator. Underneath that sweet exterior was a mean, tough son of a gun at work. In that fight he said to all those people who called him a pretty boy who would fold when the going got tough, 'Here I am. This is my courage.' Ali and Joe Frazier weren't just fighting for the heavyweight championship of the world that night. They were fighting for something much more important. They were fighting for the championship of each other. They both knew that this would be the last time they would face each other, and that whoever won that night would be recognized by history as the greatest fighter."

My final observation on Ali's life is that his luck still holds for him.

He is hurting badly. His Parkinson's syndrome or disease is advancing steadily, even accelerating. Yet Ali sails blithely on, boarding one airplane after another, making appearances throughout the world, spreading hope and joy and his message that love conquers all.

How else to explain the attention and the emotions that focused on his lighting the torch at the opening ceremonies of the 1996 Olympic Games in Atlanta. This was vintage Ali. What a chance he took! What a gamble! Once more, he shocked and amazed the whole wide world. Through his electric, riveting presence, he delivered his message, "Never give up! Never! Never!"

Can "Old Man" Ali Accomplish the Impossible?

Gregg Simms

Ebony Magazine, September 1978

After the torture of the contest in Manila, Ali's next opponents would have put Joe Louis's Bum Of The Month Club to shame. In February 1976, the hopelessly overmatched Jean-Pierre Coopman of Belgium fell in five rounds. Jimmy Young proved more durable, going the distance in April. The following month the lightly regarded Richard Dunn was dispatched in five rounds before Ali travelled to Tokyo in June for the nadir of his career – a bizarre match against professional wrestler Antonio Inoki. The Japanese grappler spent most of the match lying on his back kicking Ali in the leg. Over fifteen rounds Ali threw six punches. The fight was declared a draw, but all agreed it was a disgrace. In Sports Illustrated, *Mark Kram called it a farce.*

In September Ali returned to boxing to win a highly suspect decision over Ken Norton in New York, but the decision in his favour was a gift. It couldn't last. Ali went fifteen rounds against Alfredo Evangelista in May 1977 and was lucky not to get knocked out by the heavy-handed Earnie Shavers in September, with the champion taking another decision that was too close for comfort. Looking for softer opposition, Ali signed to defend his title against the unheralded Leon Spinks on 15 February, 1978 in Las Vegas. With just seven pro fights to his credit, Spinks had no business fighting for the crown, but he seized his chance with both hands and outworked an out-of-shape and ageing Ali to win by split decision. The deposed champ vowed to regain both his belt and his pride and the rematch was booked for 15 September 1978.

An Aging Gladiator Seeks to Win Title
for the Third Time

On the Fourth of July, Muhammad Ali got up at 4:30 a.m. just as he had for the preceding seven days. It was a holiday but the world's greatest fighter and former heavyweight champion of the world could not afford any holidays. He showered and dressed and by five o'clock was in the small cabin converted into a Muslim mosque near the entrance to his training camp in Deer Lake, PA. After a quiet thirty minutes reading the Koran, Ali varied his usual routine slightly. The rain was too heavy for his usual hour of running, so he settled for a massage and some exercises before his 9:45 breakfast. After breakfast, he walked to the camp entrance to "walk down my food" and, an hour later started chopping down the first of four trees that were to fall that day. After that came a nap and by early noon he was hard at work in the gymnasium – skipping rope, punching the bag, shadow boxing, sparring with his partners. After the workout, he talked to the literally hundreds of fans who had braved the weather to visit his camp. At six, he had dinner, then took a short walk. From seven to ten he talked with his friends and family and at ten p.m. he went to bed in his own cabin some 75 yards away from the one occupied by his wife, Veronica, and their children.

If this sounds as if Muhammad Ali was really serious about his training for his September 15 championship bout against newly-crowned heavyweight champion Leon Spinks, then it sounds right. Ali is attempting the impossible. An aging fighter who has already lost to a strong young fighter almost never wins the rematch—and, at thirty-six, Ali is by every count an aging fighter. He was only twenty-two when, as Cassius Clay, he lifted the crown from Sonny Liston's head in February, 1964. Now, fourteen years and thirty-eight fights later, he is forced to prepare himself for another battle, this one probably the most important of his entire career. Not only is he trying to defeat a brash, young champion in his physical prime, he is trying to make boxing history by becoming the first man ever to win the heavyweight crown three separate times.

But age is not Ali's only drawback. It is true that the years have slowed his hands a bit and that he is not quite as fleet of foot as he was in his younger years. His punches seem to have lost a bit of their steam and he finds himself missing a few openings each fight because his reflexes are not razor sharp and his eye is perhaps not quite as keen. His desire, perhaps, is also not quite so keen. He has been everywhere, done almost everything he ever wanted to and he has enough money and note to last him the rest of his life.

There's a world of difference between Muhammad Ali and Leon Spinks. The young champion is hungry. Neither his fame nor his fortune approaches Ali's instant worldwide recognition or the more than $50 million Ali has grossed with his fists.

At twenty-five, Spinks has tasted success and he enjoys its sweetness. He enjoys his six-door, white-on-white Lincoln Continental limousine, his steel-gray Cadillac Seville, and he enjoys dancing the "Freaky-Deaky" in the country's top discos. And he wants more.

Ali, on the other hand, wants for nothing. His charisma is unmatched in sports and in most other fields. He can use the $3 million he will get for his rematch with Spinks, but he is already a multi-millionaire without it.

While Spinks hasn't yet psychologically emerged from the bowels of the inner city, Ali has made the world his toy. "I know sixty-two presidents of nations," he brags.

This is not the first time that Ali has been faced with the "impossible." When Ali was indicted by a Federal Grand Jury for refusing to accept induction into the Army on May 9, 1967, he was immediately stripped of his heavyweight title by both the World Boxing Association and the New York Boxing Commission. It looked like the end of his career but he came back despite a 1971 loss to champion Joe Frazier to become the second heavyweight champion ever (Floyd Patterson was the first) to regain a heavyweight world title. He did it the hard way in Zaire against a young and powerful newly-crowned heavyweight champion by the name of George Foreman in Oct. 1974. Despite his 32 years at that time, Ali honed himself into such a fine condition that he was able to outlast and eventually to out-punch the younger, stronger Foreman despite the terrific heat and humidity of tropical Zaire.

Before the Foreman fight, a number of Ali's aides feared that their champion was going to lose. And they would not let him get too complacent during his training for Spinks. Ali and his manager, trainer and handlers know well that Spinks took an over-confident Ali and they would not let him forget it. They often talked about Spinks and sometimes they would tell Ali quite frankly, "Leon kicked your butt good."

Their needling seemed to work as Ali trained harder than ever before.

"You almost get in shape yourself, just following him," says C. B. Atkins, an Ali aide. "I know he will be ready if he keeps going at this rate."

Aides such as Atkins are very important to Ali, not only because of the work they do but because of the atmosphere they create. Atkins, Drew (Bundini) Brown, Wali Youngblood Muhammad, Lloyd Wells, former heavyweight champion Jimmy Ellis, Gene Kilroy and others provide a relaxed feeling of urgency.

The messiah of Deer Lake faces his toughest ordeal on the training table in a tiny room with the quiet Cuban known only as Sarria. Between massages, the ex-champ does exeruciating exercises to toughen his stomach muscles.

On July 4th, he went through his grueling table workout as Lloyd Wells, formerly a scout for the National Football League's Kansas City Chiefs, looked on.

"That table is the toughest thing in sports," Wells expounded. "That table is what made (wide receiver) Otis Taylor quit football. He said he couldn't take it anymore."

Each day, it was on that table where Ali himself dealt with the coming confrontation with Spinks.

While Sarria massaged, Ali slipped into a semi-trance and recited his visions of what was to come.

"I will be 220 pounds, by August first," he said. "When I go to New Orleans I will be 215. The night of the fight, after I eat dinner I will go in the ring at about 217 pounds."

He slipped deeper into the trance. The bronze hulk's eyes were half closed, his naked body gleamed with abolene cream, and the lights were out.

His vision was inside the 85,000-seat Superdome in New Orleans. He saw himself and Spinks in the ring.

"'In this corner, weighing 215 pounds, Muhammad AALEEEE.' The Superdome is full. I come out jabbing, dancing." Lying on his back, Ali shot out two left jabs, a right, two more left jabs, and all the time Sarria kept rubbing like it all wasn't happening.

Two more lefts, another right and more words. "People see me dancing. People see that it's gonna be different this time.

"Right now I am in better shape than I was when I fought Spinks the first time. On July the 4th I weigh 233."

From his trance, he acknowledged that he must keep his mind right to beat the charging bull. "I won't go near a hotel in New Orleans. I'd be crazy to do that. All the pimps and the girls and people asking me for tickets. I will stay in a little house somewhere or a trailer. I have to walk and think."

Later, at dinner, Ali talked about the first match. "I gave him the first six rounds, thinking he would get tired, but he didn't. But even so, it was still a close fight.

"This time it will be different. I will stop him. It will not go the distance. This time I'm hungrier. I only really fight when I'm an underdog or when somebody's good. Sonny Liston, the first two times. I got up for them. George Foreman the impossible. (Joe) Frazier, the first fight, I was favored. The second two I got ready.

"The first (Ken) Norton fight; who's Norton. I lost it. The second two Norton fights, I came back. Think about that. Against Rudy Lubbers in Indonesia and Al Blue Lewis in Ireland, I looked bad. Jurgin Blin in Germany, I looked bad. Jean Pierre Coopman in Puerto Rico, I looked bad. I've got to have the pressure.

"Now here's a good one. Three-time champion."

Still, with all the training and all the psyching, the fact remains that time won't wait for a heavyweight championship fight. That means physically Ali is slipping downhill while Leon Spinks is maturing and getting better.

Forget all the talk about Leon not training properly. When he was "out of shape," he weighed 198 pounds. When he beat Ali, he was 197 pounds. He plans to fight at 193 or 194 the second time. And his discoing, if nothing else, kept him very active.

His tactics will be the same simply because they worked before. He will work on Ali's shoulder to slow the jab and lead his attack with one of the most versatile right hands of any heavyweight.

Ali's task will be to keep Leon off with his left jab. Ali will have to punch constantly whether he dances or not because Leon will come in and just keep coming.

As he himself says over and over, Ali's most serious mistake was not fighting in the early rounds. That meant Spinks took no punishment until the fight was half over.

The importance of that mistake is graphically apparent in films of Spinks's ten-round fight with Scott LeDoux who launched a pitched battle with Spinks from the first round. After six rounds Spinks began to tire and LeDoux fought him to a draw.

If Ali does the same, launches an offense early, his chances of winning the heavyweight title for the third time will be very real. Spinks walks into punches, and he can take them well. But he is no Joe Frazier. Whether Ali has the stamina to fight another intense fifteen-rounder is a question that worries boxing promoter Don King, who badly wants Ali to win. He made a short visit to Deer Lake to tell Ali that he would bring in WBC heavyweight champion Larry Holmes to work with him. "I don't want anyone telling you you are in shape and training well if you are not," King told Ali. "We will be honest with you."

Ali appreciated the concern but he did not seem worried enough to think the offer was important. He was quite pleased with his training pace and with his ability to rise to the challenge. He just smiled a smile starting from wherever his magic lives and said, "For mortal men, I'm about as bad as they're gonna get."

McIlvanney on Boxing

Hugh McIlvanney

Leon Spinks v. Muhammad Ali, New Orleans, 15 September 1978 Dreaming of Another World

Nowhere, not in Kuala Lumpur or Manila, beside the log-cabin mosque at his camp on a Pennsylvania mountain or by the turgid sweep of the Zaire River, has Muhammad Ali ever contrived a less likely or forgettable setting for the utterance of his dreams. He was lying naked under the stars, stretched on a quilt that was laid out behind the low hedge that screens the brick-floored patio from a patch of neat lawn at No. 463 on a street called Topaz in a middle-class suburb of New Orleans. It was shortly after five o'clock on Thursday morning and he had just run for thirty minutes through the heavy Louisiana night, pounding out three or four miles along the shores of a nearby lake as part of the unwontedly rigorous training schedule he has imposed on himself in preparation for what the T-shirts of the faithful are hailing as the Third Coming: his attempt next Friday night to win his return match with Leon Spinks and so become the first man ever to reign three times as heavyweight champion of the world.

Now, as the insects whirred in the trees along Topaz, anticipating the muted sound of the water sprinklers that would go to work when the hot dawn came up, he was a sprawling shadow outside the front door of the house he had rented to take him away from his besieged suite and the thronged lobbies of the Hilton Hotel downtown. As always, he had remained modest enough to leave a small towel draped across his thighs, although he had no company here other than a couple of bodyguards from the New Orleans police department (who seemed about as sensitive as the guardians of the law usually are in the Deep South), his Cuban masseur, Luis Sarria, two of the bucket-carriers from his entourage who had come hustling out from the Hilton after being left sleeping when the boss started his run even earlier than usual, and two reporters from London who had ridden the helpers' coat-tails in the knowledge that Ali is at his least strident and most captivating if caught in those still and private hours when most of the world is abed.

Sarria rubbed the soles of Ali's feet and, as he relaxed, that compartment of his head that is constantly engaged in the production of his own Superman cartoons began to work overtime. His voice was a soft, confidential drone as the images of dramatic happenings, past and to come, crowded his imagination. He started quietly by insisting that he really meant it this time when he said that the defeat of Spinks would be his last fight. It was true that several earlier threats of retirement had rapidly dissolved but now, with his thirty-seventh birthday only four months away, the cruelty of training was becoming unbearable and the need to translate himself into a new and wider context was too urgent to be denied, he told us. To achieve that translation ideally, however, it was necessary to assert yet again his uniqueness as a boxer, necessary to put the twenty-five-year-old upstart Spinks in his place, reduce him to the role of a bit-player in the cosmic events enacted around The Greatest.

Ali's voice became animated, vivid with prediction. "So I'm out there with him in the Superdome, and the world is amazed. This ain't the fat man that took him casual in Las Vegas last February, that didn't train or eat good, that listened to all the talk about how easy he would be, saw him as just a kid out of the amateurs with seven nothin' pro fights to his name, a novice who didn't belong in the ring with the best heavyweight of all times. No, this is the real Ali, lookin' beautiful and movin' fast, goin' for him from the first bell, attackin', attackin', no rest, crowdin', hurtin', pop, pop, with the jab, then the right hand, the hooks, the combinations, pressure he can't take. It's a mismatch, by seven or eight it can't go on, the referee is jumpin' in to stop it. It's all over. Muhammad ALLEE is champion of the world for the third time. This is a miracle . . . and then I go and pick up my briefcase, get in my Lear jet and fly off to see some President of a country somewhere."

"Can I go?" asked Lloyd Wells, who is one of the twenty-two

people here on Ali's payroll for this fight and was getting ready at that moment to list in a notebook the sequence and number of punishing abdominal exercises his employer would soon perform on the rubbing-table.

"Yeah," said Muhammad absently, while Sarria's hands fluttered, black as crows, over the oil he had spread in a glistening film on a body already looking harder and more athletic than it has done in three years. At one point Sarria hovered like a diviner above the stomach, then tapped gently to elicit a hollow sound.

"Water," he said, using one of his few words of English.

"I know," said Ali, "from now till the fight we'll cut it right down, dry out and lose five or six pounds more and go in there about 218. No more of Dick Gregory's juice and vitamin mixtures. They're keepin' weight on me."

"I could kiss you for that," said Lloyd Wells, leaving the outsider to wonder if the reaction was unconnected with resentment of Gregory, the comedian turned humanitarian activist and nutritional expert who has been advising Ali on diet and advocating in particular the virtues of lemon and lime juice and of kelp. Jealousies are intense and bitter among the motley group that draw sustenance from the great fighter's generosity and, although Gregory can be financially independent of the intrigues and hypocrisy, he cannot escape being a target for the backbiting.

Stretched on the table, placed like an incongruous fugitive from a gymnasium in the middle of the well-furnished suburban living-room, Ali was letting his thoughts drift up and away from such squalid trivia as pay cheques. "Think of what it will mean to be the first man ever to win the heavyweight title three times. That's somethin' worth taking a lot of hurt for. It's somethin' I'll have for the rest of my days. Each morning when I wake up, whether the sun is shining or there's rain or snow, that will be there. You can lose an arm or your health, your wife or your life, but they can't take that away from you. Nobody could deny I was the greatest, greater than Marciano or Louis, greater than Jack Johnson. Wherever I went, people would say, 'There he goes, there ain't never been nobody like him.' Think of how it would help me in my work with my new project, my real life's work, the WORLD organisation."

WORLD (the initials stand for World Organisation for Rights,

Liberty and Dignity) is a little something he dreamed up while hob-nobbing with Brezhnev on his recent visit to Russia. The concept envisages persuading tens of millions of his admirers around the globe to pay a membership fee of $25 a head to provide the basic financing for a headlong assault on every major problem on earth, from famine to leprosy to racism. Earlier, on the patio, soliloquising about a scheme he claims is so far advanced that the US Government should be approving tax exemption "in about a week's time", he indicated that, naturally, he would be putting all his accumulated resources at WORLD's disposal and that he had been promised specific assistance by friends as diverse as folk-singer Johnny Cash and President Muammar Gaddafi of Libya. "Most of the hatred on the earth is because people don't understand each other. Americans hate Russians but maybe they wouldn't if they'd been there like I was. Ain't it somethin' that Brezhnev knew about me, that the hell I'd raised had reached him and he wanted to meet me? He made me a kind of ambassador to let folks in America know more about his country. I found there was a lot of peacefulness over there. I never saw so much peace in my life. In a grocery store you can put your money down on the counter and nobody will grab it. You can walk in a park at night and nobody will bother you. I'm not sayin' I'd like to live there. There's a lot that's dull about it. The clothes is dingy but it's for sure that everythin' ain't bad."

The wonderful naïveté of his interpretation of life in the Soviet Union, like the simplistic optimism that sees WORLD as something between his own United Nations and the Red Cross ("It would take a thing as big as that to give me fulfilment after what I've already done"), seems at first to make stark contrast with the intensity of his professional effectiveness as a boxer. But both are fed by the deep reservoir of dreams in his nature. The difference is that as a boxer he has the will and the equipment to transmute fantasy into fact. Whether the alchemy will work once more at the age of thirty-six, when he is faced with an opponent who is the living embodiment of fierce and hungry youth, is a question only the foolish answer glibly. Ali's respect for the question is declared in the extreme dedication he has brought to his training over the past two months. His attitude was exemplified at the house on Topaz on Thursday morning when the presence of myself and a colleague encouraged him to shatter his record for the total of abdominal exercises completed in a session, driving himself through more than five hundred without a hint of cheating.

From the early summer days of running and chopping trees in Pennsylvania to roadwork, callisthenics and serious sparring here in New Orleans, he has sweated in a way that has been alien to him since his third meeting with Joe Frazier in Manila in October 1975. When he disrobes at the Superdome next Friday the world will see his body just about as fit as he can make it at his age. But it is the erosion that remains invisible that will threaten him. Can all the systematic honing of his physique restore the swiftness of reflex, the judgement of distance and sharpness of timing that once made other heavyweights look as if they had sludge in their veins?

It is unlikely. For a long time now he has been reachable even with crude and ponderous punches and there has been no notable reversing of the trend in the latest sparring with a series of moderate partners. "Guys who could only have waved to him in the old days row land solid," says Harold Conrad, a New York aficionado who has been watching him throughout his professional career. "Spinks is a natural fighting animal who just keeps coming with punches. Some are good and some are nothing, but there are so many of them that as long as he is in there he will lay plenty of hurt on Muhammad. He could even do the damage we have all been dreading if he stays there long enough. People say Muhammad threw away the first fight in Vegas with bad tactics, by playing about in the early rounds. But I'm not so sure it was a matter of tactics. With the doubtful condition Ali had then, if he had warred with Spinks early on he would have been knocked on his ass in the later rounds. As it was, he was able to hang on through fifteen but Spinks kicked the shit out of him and won from here to Calcutta.

"This time Ali is in shape. He's worked like a sonofabitch. But that old bum with the white beard will be on the stool along with him and he could take the scythe to Ali's legs long before the fifteenth. So I think it would be crazy for Ali to go for a points win. I think he's got to street-fight this kid. He's gonna be at least 20 lb heavier, he's learned a lot of meanness in fifty-eight pro matches and nobody has more fighting heart than he has. He should go out blasting at the first bell and try to ruin Spinks by halfway. It will be hard, for Leon don't discourage easily. But I believe Ali has one big night left in him and I'd bet on him to do the job."

The diagnosis, the prescription and the prognosis are echoes of my own thinking about a conflict that could be one of the most melodramatic even Muhammad has provided. Leon Spinks, offering a gap-toothed stare of preoccupation under the flaring Afro as he moves through his training to the constant, amplified din of funky disco music (it tows him from the open doors of a van when he runs, shudders in waves about him in his gym at the Municipal Auditorium), is not seeking to con anybody when he presents a different script. His programme has been haphazard and not without its enervating diversions but he is likely to be much the same unremittingly aggressive force as he was last February. At twenty-five, he has not learned the habit of apprehensiveness and perhaps he never will. Ali has had fifty professional fights more than he has but the eleven-year discrepancy in age may be equally important.

"I am a natural fighter and a natural winner," says Leon Spinks. Those are excellent credentials but next Friday night they may be invalidated by a man with more than a trace of the supernatural.

No Nemesis, Just a Novice

There was just too much history bearing down on Leon Spinks in the New Orleans Superdome on Friday night, and he was left feeling as mesmerised and helpless as a boy trying to shovel against an avalanche. Muhammad Ali's Third Coming to the heavyweight championship of the world was an exercise not so much in brilliance as in contrived inevitability. He and half the people on the planet wanted this victory so badly that Ali, having tortured his thirty-six-year-old body in training to the point where it was once again an outrageous instrument of his ambitions, was able to spit on the calendar and turn the fierce youthfulness of Spinks into something humiliatingly self-destructive. Seven months ago, the twenty-five-year-old from the St Louis ghetto looked like an inescapable Nemesis, a force strong and irreverent enough to close an era as he swarmed through the disintegrating remnants of his boyhood hero's resistance to take the title in Las Vegas. On Friday night he looked what his record said he should be: a brave and powerful novice, burdened with inexperience and the extreme limitations of a recently converted amateur.

These fifteen rounds were less of a championship match than a procession, a New Orleans parade without a jazz band. There was scarcely a hint of serious discomfort as Ali established himself as the first heavyweight to take the title three times, and did so, unbelievably, more than fourteen years after he first made monkeys of the forecasters by draining the ogre out of Sonny Liston. Here, after a first round in which his punches were extravagantly mistimed, he swiftly found distance and rhythm and set a pattern that frustrated and all but demoralised his opponent. Even when the three Louisiana officials had taken the fifth round away from Ali because they felt his holding during those three minutes amounted to fouling, none of them could leave him with a total of fewer than ten rounds. The referee, Lucien Joubert, gave ten to Ali, and four to Spinks, with one even, and so did one of the judges, Ernest Cojoe, while the second judge, Herman Duitreix, had it 11–4 with no even rounds. Few of the unofficial cards at ringside could credit the loser with any more, and many gave him less. It was a tribute to the persistence of his spirit that he took the fourteenth, and perhaps the fifteenth, too, as Ali's legs and arms began to tire after forty minutes of astonishing fluency. But, leaving out the question of rule violations in the fifth, it was hard to accept that the defending champion had done more than share any of the other rounds.

Spinks had come to the ring with more handicaps than any young boxer could be expected to carry in only the ninth fight of his professional career. There were about 70,000 people in the soaring vastness of the Superdome (easily the largest indoor crowd boxing has known), and most of them – from the celebrities like Jackie Onassis and President Carter's mother, John Travolta and Kris Kristofferson, to beer-slugging red-necks on upper tiers so remote that they might have been in the next county – were vociferously prejudiced. Spinks was booed as he ducked through the ropes as champion, and, as if Ali's friends weren't enough of a problem, his own corner was such an over-crowded Babel of confusing advice that the one man most likely

to provide a constructive theme between rounds walked away
from the chaos after the sixth. George Benton, an outstanding
middleweight when he fought out of Philadelphia, and now a
skilled tutor who did much to channel Spinks's natural violence
into profitable aggression in Las Vegas, had said during the
champion's haphazard training that he was being prevented from
offering maximum assistance. "They're cutting my throat, stopping me from helping the kid," he had said then. Now, as he
moved disconsolately through the hysteria of the ringside audience, he muttered: "What can I do? There are ten people up
there in that corner. What can I do? There are too many amateurs
up there."

That was true, and the sad fact was that the boy wearing the
gloves looked like one of them. Spinks had affected an unworried
grin, showing the gumshield like a surrogate denture, as Ali
danced away from his charges or repelled him with flicking jabs
and single and double hooks in the early rounds. But his depression became blatant as Ali's strength refused to wane, as the
older man blended glimpses of his former foot-and hand-speed
with punishing improvisations learned over eighteen hard years
against the toughest men in the world, tricks that enabled him to
war as well as box with such as Liston, Frazier and Foreman.
Spinks felt the heel of the glove and the bare hardness of the
forearms more than once. Above all, he found his most hopeful
rushes smothered at birth by the holding that Ali has developed
to a level where it has less in common with a boxer's survival
technique than a wrestler's belligerence. Lucien Joubert, perhaps
responding to the collective desire that came down in waves
from the rim of the arena and with silent force from the countless
committed millions beyond, permitted far more of that clutching, hauling and spinning than had been seen last February, and
the challenger benefited from the referee's leniency.

But such questionable passages would have been rendered
insignificant if Ali had not linked them with surges of selective,
effective attacking, circling fleetly and watchfully, jabbing with
increasing confidence and accuracy, sometimes hooking off the
jab, releasing the occasional brisk combination of hooks and
uppercuts, looking to land overhand rights, always adding to his
overall control, causing his victim's eyes to cloud with the

realisation that the discrepancy in class was irreversible. "Get him, Lee," a female member of the Spinks party at the ringside shouted repeatedly in a voice that grew more shrill as her man slid hopelessly behind. "Beat him on his head. Give him what he give you." "I think he'll need something from that black bottle Ali reckons he used last time," a sarcastic reporter suggested. By that stage, Leon looked in need of a soda siphon, and a chance to break it over Ali's skull.

Spinks had indicated during the preliminaries a heavy awareness of what an ordeal the evening would be. Ali was solemnly, almost morosely, undemonstrative, and any Muslim praying he did was unaccompanied by conspicuous gesture (he may, of course, have been relying on the celestial canvassing of his manager, Herbert Muhammad, son of the founder of the Black Muslims, who spent the entire contest with his eyes cast down and his lips moving silently while Angelo Dundee gave brisk advice and Bundini Brown and the others in the corner jabbered and whooped). After dropping on to his knees and closing his eyes for a long Catholic prayer, Spinks spent nearly a full minute before the bell embracing his brother, Michael, a fellow Olympic champion in Montreal. He appeared uncharacteristically conscious of the weight of the occasion, and that impression was reinforced later when he admitted to interviewing journalists that he had been unable to concentrate with the intensity that a title defence demands. "My body was ready, but my mind wasn't on the fight," he said, and quickly became bellicose when pressed on the strangeness of that omission. "Maybe it was because I had a lot of other things on my mind, a lot of problems that come with the heavyweight championship," he offered, eventually. "Who knows? I don't. That just wasn't me in there, period. But I won't cry because I have lost once, it won't keep me from sleeping or from going back to the gym."

Nor did it keep him from congratulating Ali or declaring that the master is still his idol. Ali in turn described Spinks as a gentleman and made the familiar prediction that the man he had just outclassed would end up as champion after he had gone. He made it clear, however, that he was in no hurry to step aside. "The title is too hard to get," he said. "I'm not goin' to give it up without thinking. I'm going to sit down for six or eight months and think about it. Then I'll decide whether to fight again. I would never want to go out a loser. I've always wanted to be the first black man to retire undefeated, and to do it now after being champion three times would be somethin' no one could ever equal. I have made suckers out of all of you. I was training three months before you knew it.

"That couldn't have been Ali in that ring tonight. It couldn't have been the old man, the washed-up thirty-six-year-old fighter dancin' through fifteen rounds against a twenty-five-year-old boy. M-a-a-a-a-n, that was a miracle, and can you imagine what it means? I was great in defeat, what will I be to the peoples of the world after this? I'm going to get on with settin' up my WORLD organisation to help the poor folks of the world, to help the hungry and those with diseases and famines and all kinds of problems.

"If you think I have done something now, wait till you see what I do as president of WORLD. We now have tax exemption, we now have a charter. We're going to have offices all round the world, an office in the Kremlin, an office in Bangladesh. I'm going to Moscow in about another month to see President Brezhnev. I told him I'd go back to see him after I regained my title. About sixteen presidents have now given their approval to WORLD. It's going to be helping people all over the globe."

When he listed the sources from which he had drawn help in beating Spinks, he began with Allah and moved by way of Dick Gregory and his vitamin-charged juices to the doctor who had prescribed "half a pint of ice-cream and a big hunk of honey, thirty minutes before the fight". There were plenty of smiles around the room, but few sneers. If he put on wellingtons to cross the Okinawa Deep we'd have to rate his chances at only slightly odds against.

Larry Holmes v. Muhammad Ali, Las Vegas, 2 October 1980

Shooting for Immortality

For nearly twenty years Muhammad Ali has been imposing an extravagant fantasy upon his life but somewhere, surely, reality is crouching in ambush, waiting to take revenge. It would seem that Larry Holmes is about to give reality some vigorous assistance. Ali has come back, less than four months short of his thirty-ninth birthday and after two years of debilitating retirement, insisting that next Thursday the most remarkable fist-fight ever to break out in a car park will make him the heavyweight champion of the world for the fourth time.

When he beat Leon Spinks in September of 1978 to become champion for the third time, the feat was unprecedented. But that match was for the World Boxing Association version of the title and Spinks was a raw upstart, lately out of the amateurs. This week it is the World Boxing Council championship that is at stake and Holmes, at the age of thirty, is a mature and brilliantly equipped heavyweight who his won all thirty-five of his professional fights and stopped twenty-six opponents, including the seven who have challenged him since he took over his title slightly more than two years ago. If Ali can give eight years and a beating to such a man, we shall have to stop insulting him with words like miraculous.

He is, of course, joyously aware of the dramatic outrageousness of what he is attempting. As he leaves his training sessions at Caesars Palace Hotel in Las Vegas he is apt to part his white robe theatrically and declare: "This is the first miracle." The condition of his body is indeed astonishing. He has shed 30 lb, ridding his torso of the fat that enveloped it like a greasy, shapeless quilt a few months back. The pendant breasts have gone and as the skin has tautened across his chest and midriff the planes of his face have regained their previous handsome definition. To complete the impression of rejuvenation, he has used a black-blue dye on his hair and the overall effect is enough to make an ordinary thirty-eight-year-old man hide in a geriatric ward. Angelo Dundee, who has worked with Ali since the teenage days in Louisville, Kentucky, is not exaggerating when he says that the most vital appurtenance of his preparation for this challenge has been the mirror. Simple narcissim has always been a major tributary to the deep mainstream of his pride and there is no doubt that through the bleak slog of running and bench callisthenics and punishment in the gym he was sustained by the mirror's daily testimony that he was beginning to look pretty once again.

But the event scheduled for Thursday evening in a temporary outdoor arena specially constructed in the parking area of Caesars Palace (at a cost of $800,000 and with an attendance of

24,000 and gate receipts of $6 million in mind) is not a beauty
contest. The question that only violence can answer is whether
Ali's physique, which looks just about as trim and imposing as it
did when he stunned the boxing world by making a physical and
psychological wreck of the awe-inspiring George Foreman six
years ago, still possesses the power, flexibility and capacity to
endure that it did in Zaire and again in 1975 against Joe Frazier
in Manila. That fierce collision in the Philippines with the noblest
of all his rivals offered the most recent convincing glimpse of the
greatness of Ali. He fought eight more times between that night
and his retirement as a reigning champion in 1978 but none of
the performances, not even the reversing of a humiliating defeat
by Spinks, represented him at anything like his best. When he
bowed out of the game it was with the acknowledgement that
Holmes, already the holder of the WBC title, was the best heavyweight in the world and that fighting him would not be a good
idea. How can anyone logically conclude that the intervening
couple of years have improved Ali's chances? Yet in the betting
shops along The Strip in Las Vegas Holmes can be backed at
odds of 9–5 on, which is not a cripplingly short price for an
ostensible good thing. Anybody who wants to bet on Ali can
have no better than 7–5 against.

Some have sought to explain these odds by reference to the
inevitable rumour that the fight has been made the subject of an
arrangement, carefully choreographed to give Ali victory, set up
a return and so on and on and on. Holmes dismissed these sinister fairy tales with bitter simplicity. When asked his price for
throwing the fight, he said: "My life." It is unthinkable, he adds,
that there should ever be a day when his three daughters would
go to school and have other kids baiting them because their
father couldn't beat Muhammad Ali when he was thirty-eight
years old. "I'll tell you – if there was some dirty business, Don
and I would find the mother that did it and git him." The Don
in question, who flows about as quietly as Niagara, is Don King,
the promoter of Thursday's little *divertissement* and a man who
has steadily been making himself more central to Holmes's career
than the champion's official manager, the far-from-gruntled
Richie Giachetti. King talks of Holmes as "my son" but the hard
facts of drawing power have obliged him to pay Ali $8 million

while asking Larry to be content with $3.5 million plus a percentage of the revenue from the closed-circuit televising of the match across North America and in forty or fifty countries around the world, including Britain.

On the basis of fatherly affection and economic self-interest, King would have no reason to look kindly on an "arrangement" and his determination to be regarded as Mr Clean can only be intensified by the awareness that his name has already been linked with the FBI investigation into alleged wrong-doing in boxing. The promoter, who used a four-year prison sentence to extend his education and change the direction of his life after a manslaughter conviction interrupted his activities in the Cleveland numbers rackets, speaks freely about the investigation, as he does about anything else that is mentioned to him. Apparently believing that oratory begins and ends with vocabulary, he loads his sentences with dubiously pronounced polysyllables and then sprays them over his audience like buckshot. But he can be amusing on the FBI. "I say I'm a bad nigger but I don't think I'm bad enough to take on the FBI. So don't put me in that position, that's a very untenable position for me. I don't want to play J. Edgar Hoover. I don't wanna mess with his spirit. I wanna leave him alone, let him lie quiet."

The tone was less lighthearted when King turned to stories carried in a British Sunday newspaper that quoted a Harley Street neurologist as saying that films of Muhammad over the years betrayed symptoms of brain damage. King argued heatedly that such a long-range diagnosis should be challenged by the medical profession and by Muhammad himself, perhaps through a $2 million court action. Earlier, Dr Donald Romeo, who was appointed by the Nevada State Athletic Commission to examine Ali before this fight, referred scathingly to claims that the great boxer's kidneys and brain had been permanently damaged in the ring. "So he takes some blows to the region of the kidneys and there's blood in his urine – big deal," said the good doctor, who seems to have learned his bedside manner from James Cagney. "It clears up in a day or two, end of story. They talk of brain damage? That's also a bunch of bunk." Anyone who had just come from the Los Angeles hospital where young Johnny Owen lies desperately ill after suffering

severe brain injury in his bantamweight title fight with Lupe
Pintor was bound to wince at such words. Boxing can ill afford
to be smug about this issue.

Somewhat more reassuring is the fact that three days of
comprehensive tests at the famous Mayo Clinic in Rochester,
Minnesota, gave Ali clearance to fight. When he went there on
22 July he weighed 237½ lb. The bound diary that records that
information traces his daily progress in detail, work done and
weight lost since he started serious training at the beginning of
April. He was 251 lb on the fourth of that month (1 lb under 18
stone) and he was down to 221 lb last week. But is the stream-
lining merely cosmetic, or is he genuinely strong and fit? The
best case for an affirmative answer is made by a bare, functional
rubbing-table that is a jarring interloper in the main bedroom
of Suite 301–2 at Caesars Palace, where the orange furnishings
cosset everything but the eyes. It was on that kind of table that
Ali toiled through an endless series of abdominal and back
exercises to build the condition that made him too much for
Spinks in New Orleans. Even more relentless torture has
followed the runs he has been taking before dawn on a Las
Vegas golf course. Two days ago the diary showed that an
aggregate of 13,947 exercises had been completed. The statis-
tic may have limited significance but it is an important symbol
to Muhammad Ali, proof that he has paid his dues yet again
and is ready to rumble. "Look at me," he said, dancing around
the bedroom carpet in slacks and fitting shirt, throwing left jabs
and crossing rights to within an inch or two of a nervous interviewer's face. "Isn't that somethin'? I was a fat man, up to 253
lb. I wanted to get money in the bank. So I tricked Holmes into
fighting me. If I had looked like this, he would never have
agreed to fight me. My mother, my wife, everybody closest to
me, they're all shocked by the change in me. I'm about as thin
as I was when I fought Henry Cooper. No sugar, no soda, no
soft drinks, no milk – just water, that and six months of steady
work, that's what's done it.

"Now they're saying I only look good. Well, we'll see. That's
their latest excuse. First I was too old and too fat. Now they're
saying, 'He's skinny and he looks pretty but he's not strong.'
That's as crazy as saying I've got brain damage. They'll find

out on the night. Holmes is supposed to have a great jab but on a scale of one hundred I'd say mine is ninety and his is seventy-five. His combinations don't mean nothin'. I'll just cover up and wait till he gets tired.

"He runs out of gas by about the eighth or ninth round and I'll pressure him, wear him down. He'll look for me to dance, run, rope-a-dope. But I'll go straight for him from the first bell. If I can get that jab out and keep my distance, it's my fight. Holmes can jab but sometimes it don't come all the way. When that happens, pow! I'll get him with my straight right over the top.

"I'm shooting for immortality and I'm on the doorstep. Holmes can't beat me."

While in Ali's suite, it is hard to remain insulated against his optimism. The place is charged with life, filled with his scurrying, chattering children and his womenfolk and sometimes with the less attractive presence of vying members of a bloated entourage, characters whose only visible quality is adhesion. The man supports enough people to populate a small country and he gives the impression that the well will never run dry.

But Larry Holmes can kill that illusion. All he has to do is fight to the true limit of his ability. He is magnificently fit and he knows that the threat to his mind is the most crucial. The heat exerted by Ali's personality can reduce an opponent's brain to a puddle of confusion. If Muhammad undermines him psychologically, then Holmes's one discernible physical deficiency, that tendency to run out of energy prematurely, may be disastrously exacerbated. The champion's attempts to compete verbally with Ali have been clumsy failures but he insists convincingly that it will be different in the ring. "He was a great fighter but he has stepped out of his time into my time," said Holmes. "I was his sparring partner for four years and I know all there is to know about how he fights. Whatever he tries, I'll do what is needed to beat him, to knock him out. At a distance, I'll be too fast for him. I'll out-jab him. If he covers up, I'll break his ribs or murder his kidneys. If he wants to rassle, I'll show him a few holds. I'm going to stop him, retire him for good."

Picking against Ali, the greatest hero figure modern sport has known, is extremely painful. But here it would be cowardice and hypocrisy to do otherwise. I believe the mirror is telling him lies. He may be the most celebrated victim of a looking-glass since the Lady of Shalott.

A Legend at Hazard

The ring activities of Muhammad Ali now have all the grace and sporting appeal of Russian roulette played with a pump-action shotgun. If he seriously considers inflicting on himself and his admirers across the world another experience like Thursday night's disaster in Las Vegas, there may be a case for taking him into protective custody. To go on trying to sustain the illusion that his middle-aged body can fight as effectively as it did ten years ago is, clearly, to risk grave physical harm, and that is not the only danger. His pride and his legend would also be at hazard, for there can be no doubt that if Ali, the most electrifying athlete of his and perhaps of any generation, ever again earned millions as negatively as he did last week he might begin to be mistaken for a fraud and a bore.

The talk about mounting another ill-advised and unjustifiable challenge for "that other half" of the heavyweight championship currently held by Mike Weaver should be smothered immediately and for ever. Official prohibition of any such mad adventure is not easily achieved in a sport where supervision is ludicrously fragmented and altruism is giving away too much weight to the dollar. However, there should surely be particular efforts made by any who have a claim to leverage – from journalists and broadcasters to members of governing authorities – to preserve Muhammad Ali from the penalties of his own fantasies and the avarice of some who might mislead him. It is impossible to exaggerate the pathetic discrepancy between the bankrupt Ali who succumbed so helplessly to Larry Holmes, failing to last the distance for the first time in his life, and the thrilling master who was too much in his time for such forbidding heavyweights as Sonny Liston, George Foreman and Joe Frazier. The unquestionable lesson is that it is no longer his time.

In the open-air arena at the Caesars Palace Hotel, all the emotional support from a naïvely optimistic majority in the crowd of 25,000 could not lift him out of his chronic torpor. As

Holmes jumped the left jab into his mouth and patiently identified openings for crossing rights to the head and hooking attacks to the body, the man who had three times been champion of the world was reduced to making faces. And even those defiant expressions gave way to a betrayal of pain and confusion as each successive round brought nothing but more systematic punishment. Holmes has learned a great deal on his journey from the role of Ali's sparring partner to that of holder of the World Boxing Council heavyweight championship, with a professional record that showed thirty-five straight victories before this fight, and his cool, sharp, unhurried aggression piled discomfort on a challenger who was soon looking every day of his thirty-eight years. But, before the evening was over, all of us who have a special attachment to Ali had reason to be grateful that the old man was being taken apart unvenomously by a pro (one who feels respect and even love for him) and not by a young slugger out to make a name through dramatic mayhem. "There are a couple of kids around who might have killed Ali if they had been in with him as he was tonight," one of the most knowledgeable American boxing writers said late on Thursday.

Ali's own ability to remain standing when hit by punches that would fell other strong heavyweights only increases the long-term threat to his well-being. "Me being so proud, I wouldn't fall and I probably would have got hurt," he acknowledged in a hoarse, weary voice on Friday morning. "I didn't like the idea of stopping the fight at the moment they did. I didn't know who stopped it. Now I realise what happened and what *would* have happened to me, I'm glad they did stop it. I was gettin' tireder each round, I was gettin' weak. I've never been so drained in my life." The fact that the steady slaughter was ended in the interval between the tenth and eleventh rounds was, in large measure, Ali's reward for retaining the calm expertise and objectivity of Angelo Dundee in his corner throughout his career. There was some controversy and no little distortion afterwards when reporters sought explanations of the blatant rowing that took place at the time of the stoppage between Dundee and Drew "Bundini" Brown, the erratic black man who has been corner-hand and amateur sorcerer to Ali over the years.

Brown's version was that he had wanted to pull Ali out two

rounds before Dundee, as chief second, was ready to do so and that eventually he, Brown, had terminated the fight. But from a position a few yards away and on that side of the ring this observer gained the firm impression that Bundini's interventions had precisely the opposite motive. Dundee endorsed that view convincingly and with good humour. "Did I stop the fight? Is the Pope a Polack? Sure I stopped it. It was my right. I was in charge of the corner. Bundini was grabbing at my sweater, hollering 'One more round, one more round' but the well had run dry, there was nothing there to give. I'd told Ali as early as the fifth that if he didn't start throwing punches I was going to stop the thing. Then, when he took a really bad beating in the ninth, I knew that one more round was the absolute limit he could have, however much he wanted to go on. When the tenth just brought him more hurt, that was it. I didn't care what Bundini or anybody else said. They're saying that Herbert Muhammad as manager stopped the fight from the ringside but I didn't have to wait for word from Herbert. He gives me *carte blanche* when I'm in there."

While the arguments swirled around his head after the relentless suffering of the tenth round, the loser sat silent and apparently remote on his stool, staring blankly ahead of him. He admitted next morning that he had not realised what was going on until he looked across the ring and saw Holmes's seconds lift their man off his seat and hoist his arms in a winner's salute. Ali made a miserable picture as he was assisted away from the ring. The flesh around both eyes was badly bruised and swollen and his face was a confession of exhaustion. Once back in Suite 301–2 of Caesars Palace he was given the drug ananase to help disperse the bruising and went to bed desperately worn out.

But he had enough spirit to joke quietly with Holmes when the champion came in to sit on the edge of his bed for a quarter of an hour. There was an unforced warmth in their banter.

"Man, you're bad," said Ali.

"Look at the teacher I had," Holmes answered. "Hey, you ain't gonna fight again, are you?"

"Oh yeah, I'm comin' back for Holmes . . . Holmes . . . I want Holmes."

"You wanna go a few more rounds now?"

"No, I'm tired."

He was that all right but it did not keep him from being up again and on the apron of the ring at 4.40 a.m. Las Vegas time to perform for breakfasting New Yorkers (at 7.40 a.m. in their city) on the "Good Morning America" show. A few breakfasts may have been spoilt when he borrowed from General Douglas MacArthur and declared: "I shall return." Many of us would be glad of someone to play the part of Harry Truman, who put MacArthur out to grass. Ali's lawyer, Michael Phenner, advised him to cut back on his speculation about meeting Weaver or the South African Gerrie Coetzee, who challenges the WBA champion in Bophuthatswana later this month, in any statements he made to the press on Friday. He agreed. "I know they could chew up my ass," he said. But his overall tone was chirpy enough. "I feel pretty good," he told Phenner, and added archly: "We got the money all right, did we?"

He was still cheerful later in the morning when he came out wearing a black shirt, grey slacks and dark glasses to talk to those of us who had been permitted to pass through his private security force into the suite. "I felt a lot worse after losing to Frazier and Norton and after beating Foreman," he insisted. "Frazier in Manila was terrible. I couldn't get up for the press conference. Psychologically, I am all right. You have to be a champion in losing as well as winning. If your attitude is controlled by your condition then the condition will conquer you. My attitude is in control. I make you think I'll die if I lose, that I'll jump off a building. But it don't bother me."

That claim was as hard to accept as his rationalisations of why he had lost. The weight reduction that he had been hailing as a miracle a couple of days before was condemned as disastrous. "I'd have fought better weighing 250 lb. Going from 260 to 217 was too much. I was slim, looking like I was when I started out, but I was weak. I was dehydrated. In ten rounds in that heat I didn't perspire. There was no sweat in me. I wasn't right at all. If I told you all the problems I had it would sound phoney and I don't like making excuses. One trouble was with my left arm, a pulled muscle. I couldn't throw my jab. In the gym I felt weak and the last two days I couldn't jog a mile. I didn't win a round. His sparring partners could do better than I did. I knew I was in trouble after round one. I sat on the stool and said to myself: 'I'm in big trouble.'" The memory produced the slow, warm smile that was to light up his abused face frequently during the day. "I was dead tired after that one round and there were fourteen more to come."

He refused to commit himself about a comeback. "I'll wait about a month, get my weight back, stay in shape, then go into the gym with Matthew Saad Muhammad, the light-heavyweight champion, and Mustafa Muhammad, the contender who is going to fight him. I'll do about seven fast rounds with each of them and I'll know if I should carry on.

"If I do, I'll train with heavyweights and have wars in the gym. I won't just be playing. This time I didn't throw punches in training, got into the habit and didn't throw them in the fight. In the condition I was in, Holmes was great. He fought a good fight."

There was nothing but mutual generosity at the crowded final press conference attended by the two fighters. Ali had pleasant greetings for Holmes and his wife Diane and kisses for their baby daughter Kandy. When someone shouted that he was "still the champion in my heart", Ali said quietly, "I want to take your heart and turn it over to Larry. He *is* the world champion."

Said Holmes, "Ali does not owe boxing anything. Boxing owes Ali everything it is possible to owe. Without him there would be no million-dollar pay-days and no Larry Holmes as he is today. I love the man and I truly respect him."

"Then why did you whup me back there?" Muhammad called from the other side of the platform. It would have been nice if we could have believed that he was riding out of the hardest game on the swell of laughter.

Muhammad Ali v. Trevor Berbick, Nassau, The Bahamas, 11 December 1981 Falling Idol in Paradise

He continues to recite the commentary for an epic but what we are seeing is not so much a B-movie as a cruel cartoon. Muhammad Ali can still preach and philosophise, boast and charm and predict. What he can't do is fight, at least not within a light-year of how he once did. The genie is gone from the bottle forever and Ali is ready to be dumped along with the rest of boxing's empties.

To do a little dumping at the Queen Elizabeth Sports Centre in Nassau next Friday night, Trevor Berbick won't have to prove himself an exceptional heavyweight. He will just have to show that he is fairly good at being young. When he leaves his stool to begin the sixty-first fight of a professional career that has spanned twenty-one years and made him the only man in history to hold the heavyweight championship of the world three times, Ali will be five weeks and two days short of his fortieth birthday. Much more than half of his life has been punctuated by physical ordeals, and the wearing effects are both blatant and considerable. Berbick, a Jamaican based in Canada, only recently turned twenty-eight and has strength and willingness to compensate for the crudity of his technique. If he does not make easy work of the old champion, any laughing Berbick allows himself on the way to the bank should be done behind a false beard and dark glasses. He says the promoters of Friday's ill-conceived event, a consortium headed by an Atlantan called Jim Cornelius but operating closely if not always effectively with the Bahamian Government, wanted him to act anonymous from the start. "They pushed me over to Freeport on Grand Bahama, 150 miles from Nassau, gave me inferior training facilities and tried to make me feel like I was a second-class citizen," he complains, with as much bitterness as the friendly island voice can manage. "Cornelius is an Ali man. But it didn't work out the way they wanted. I'm living better than Ali is. I got a villa at the Bahama Princess Hotel and the manager lets me train there in comfort. That's why I said it's like a vacation, man."

As Berbick expressed his contentment between prolonged yawns, lying back on his bed in Villa No. 2 at the Princess, he was offering a reminder of the one lifeline that may be available to Ali now that he has been set helplessly adrift by his own fantasies and the greed of others. It is not the least of the ironies associated with what is happening here that the central figure's best hope of avoiding serious harm is his utter loss of credibility. Berbick is 16 st 3 lb – compared with 15 st 5 lb when he laid the basis of a reputation by brawling confidently through fifteen rounds with Larry Holmes, the World Boxing Council heavyweight champion, last April – and he insists that he will be unconcerned if his weight stays as high as it is. His preparation seems to have been as desultory as Ali's own. Both give the impression that they wouldn't run if they had diarrhoea and there is more sparring on the average Saturday night in a Glasgow pub than has been seen around either camp.

Of course, the two men have very different reasons for keeping the traditional masochism out of their schedules. Berbick cannot help feeling that he can afford to be lenient on himself. Ali does so little because that is all he is able to do. The fat rolls and creases around his middle and the muscles whose strength and elasticity and endurance were once the wonders of the sporting world are clogged with a fatigue that will never leave them. He shed most of the fat abruptly and unnaturally before he challenged Larry Holmes in Las Vegas fourteen months ago and found that his appearance of reasonable fitness was a terrible illusion. He was stopped after ten rounds by a champion who took him apart without enthusiasm or a hint of cruelty.

Ali says that he went into the ring with Holmes at around 15 st 2 lb and the effort of making himself as light as he was in his fighting youth and the effect of pills he had been taking for a suspected thyroid condition combined to make him sick on the night, leaving him short of breath and with a racing pulse. Four days after that painful débâcle, he had the first of three intensive examinations by medical specialists at the University of California, Los Angeles. Their declaration that he has suffered no appreciable damage to his body or his brain during two decades of professional boxing – that, in fact, his "current health status is excellent and there is no evidence from a health standpoint that he should be limited whatsoever in his activities" – has been used in a leaflet raid on newspaper editors and television executives by the promoters of the so-called Drama in Bahama. The doctors' testimony is indeed reassuring, and that of the neurosurgeon and the neurologist is especially so to those of us who have been alarmed over recent years by the diminished physical presence of the man and a mumbling diffuseness of speech that seemed to be something quite apart from the whispered monologues that were always an element of his routine in better years. "The patient tended to talk softly and to almost mumble his speech," the doctors reported. "But when questioned about this, he was able to speak appropriately without any evidence of a speech disorder. He was evaluated by both a neurosurgeon and neurologist who felt that his speech pattern was not pathologic."

That is great news but all the report means at the end of the day is that Muhammad Ali is in good shape to mow the lawn or to help his wife carry the groceries. When it comes to judging how well he is equipped as a forty-year-old for fighting ten rounds against somebody a dozen years younger, Angelo Dundee might be a better witness than the lads at UCLA. "He's scared," Ali says quietly of Dundee, whose hustler's coolness and mastery of emergency procedures in the corner have been Ali's perennial safeguards against the destructive hysteria of his parasitic entourage. "Angelo thinks I shouldn't be fightin'. He's coming in to work the corner but he thinks I'm shot, my legs have gone. But Angelo's not me. He don't know what I've got."

At that point what he had most conspicuously was comfort and temporary insulation from the dangers ahead. He was reclining on the blue and white floral cover of his bed in Suite 642 of the Britannia Beach Hotel on Paradise Island, a resort enclave linked by a bridge to the spread of mainly nondescript buildings that sustain Nassau's identity against constant counter-attacks by the sand and greenery that were there before them. The curtains were drawn to close out the morning glare as well as the noise of seaplanes roaring under the supports of the bridge on their way to take-off and the more sociable din made by the clinking of bottles as they were carried to the fancy yachts moored at the marina. It was a difficult place for warlike thoughts to flourish and Ali, wearing only a pair of brown slacks and looking handsomely overfed, did not present the image of a man about to storm another impossible peak of athletic achievement. But that, he told us, was what he was about to do. He was going to clear Berbick out of his path inside the ten rounds allotted for the purpose and then he would take care of Mike Weaver, the World Boxing Association heavyweight champion, and, probably, he'd go on to prove to Larry Holmes and the rest of us that he had been an invalid in Las Vegas last autumn. By taking the world title for a fourth time, he would make us think hard about the saying that records are made to be broken. "They'd have to change that and say, 'Records are made to be broken, all but Muhammad Ali's.'"

He repeated that amended version several times, intoning it with an actor's clarity. No one has been able to explain to him that fooling around with dreams of immortality can shorten your life, and lying back on the bed he was dreaming of nothing less. "When a man does something like I'm doing it's always unpopular until he does it. Then they make statues of him. He's got a name that never dies." When he sought to put next Friday into a manageable perspective, as much for himself as the two or three others in the room, he went to the sources he always calls upon at such times: to his love of attention and his need (an addict's craving) for drama and specifically for the drama of being an aggressively non-conforming black man in a white man's world.

"The hard part was working for the fight before people knew there was a fight, working when the press weren't writing about it. I trained better today knowing you were here, knowing I'm 40, that I'm not supposed to be doing this. Y'see I'm a rebel. Vietnam . . . I didn't go, joined the Black Muslims at a time when negroes were scared to walk to Muslim mosques, on the stands with Elijah Muhammad, preaching the doom of America, standing next to the boldest black man ever to hit America . . . didn't fly the flag in those days, called the white man the blond-haired, blue-eyed devil. Standing right there with BAD Muslims. I'm right there. That's the man. That badder than . . . man, this fight is easy.

"Look at the kind of man you're dealing with. Weigh up my life, you won't be surprised what I do. I'm right there with white people in Georgia and Mississippi, preachin' that America's lynched, slaved, burned, robbed us. Raped our women. White men ain't no good, never be no good. We were preachin' that stuff. That takes more of a man than to fight Berbick. I like controversy, I like drama. I just don't know how to be scared about these things.

"I guess I should be scared, maybe it's gonna hurt me, kill me one day. I've been shot at in Georgia and I've been shot at driving my car down the road in Fayetteville, Arkansas. Bullet went through the windshield, came out the back window. Rentacar."

With that nod to verisimilitude he turned back to the present: "This doesn't look rough to me. Berbick puts his head down and swings like an old woman. I'll eat him up. You must realise I been fighting since I was twelve. This is just another boxing match."

A moment later he yielded to an alternative point of view. "You're right, I'm gamblin'. Yeah, you're right. I'm the world's highest roller. Those guys shootin' for a thousand dollars a roll in Vegas are small-fries. I'm bigger than them. But I don't believe I'm gonna be a shadow of what I was. I believe I'm gonna be right on that night. It's true, I take punches. Look what it's gotten me. I'm rich. I'll probably take some more punches. I have to."

His imperatives and his finances remain equally mysterious to outsiders and what he says about them gives little clarification. He suggests that he will receive $3.8 million for this fight but $1 million is a more convincing figure. (The adversary he has respected most in his fighting life, Joe Frazier, took $85,000 plus expenses to box a draw with Jumbo Cummings in Chicago on Thursday, and left the ring knowing the scorecards had done him a favour.) In any case, according to Ali, the purse is incidental. He has come back to inspire the black peoples of the earth.

He didn't look too inspired himself as he moved at a sauntering pace through the warm, still darkness before Thursday's dawn. His breathing was noticeable on the curves of the Paradise Island bridge and as we took to the cracked streets of Nassau's shopping quarter he slowed enough to give his three Fleet Street escorts delusions of well-being. He had a heavy rubber corset around his middle and he fingered it occasionally for signs of sweat as he talked of the demands made on his time by such as Jimmy Carter and Leonid Brezhnev. Now and then a passer-by was invited to spar but recognition was sluggish and there were no jokers ready to cooperate. It was a strangely melancholy trudge past the shops bravely calling themselves department stores, the cheap restaurants, the dry cleaners, and there was quiet relief when the sun came up. By that time we were passing Peanuts Taylor's Drumbeat Club and heading along a straight road beside the sea. Ali stopped at a T-junction where the side road led to a lumber yard and shadow-boxed perfunctorily. Under his tracksuit parts of his body that used to be taut were bouncing around. Then we piled into the limousine that had been trailing us and rode back to the hotel. A man who has missed the last bus after the bars close takes more out of himself on the walk home than Ali had done with what we were supposed to regard as roadwork.

He had been happier the day before when he ordered a video-machine to be switched on in his room so that he could call some shots against Berbick while the Jamaican rough-housed with Holmes on the screen. "Look at him, he's in hittin' range now and I'm jabbin' – pow, quicker than Holmes, pow, I'm eatin' him up. I can't miss him. He comes at you, puts his head down and swings like an old woman. He's easy."

His standard training session is depressing: some half-hearted slamming of the heavy bag and a couple of rounds of poignantly ordinary shadow-boxing. Easily the best part is his patter to the tourists who turn up to watch. His humour has worn better than his boxing and it is made irresistible by the warmth that comes from his sense of being a continuous presence in millions of lives for nearly twenty years. "Y'know, all people twenty-five years old have been hearin' about me since they were seven," he said to a few of us the other day. "My wife is twenty-five. She heard about me changin' my name when she was eight. The whole generation that's now in power – governors, mayors, policemen, cab drivers, all the people at the prime of life – all of them been following me since they were babies."

It's true and it's enough to make you hope that next Friday Trevor Berbick won't be a competent heavyweight, that he won't even be good at being young.

The King Who Went Out on a Dustcart

Graceful exits are rare in professional boxing but few great champions have gone out more miserably than Muhammad Ali in the Bahamas on Friday night when he lost on points to Trevor Berbick in a thoroughly inept fight that was the melancholy centrepiece of a memorably shabby promotion. The most remarkable career the game has ever known was, we must earnestly hope, brought to its final close by a tinny rattle from the Bahamian cow-bell that was dredged up from somewhere to impersonate the timekeeper's instrument the bungling organisers of the event had neglected to provide. When the incongruous noise signalled the end of the tenth round Ali, who had been forced to acknowledge the full, sad cost of serving more than half of his forty years in the prize-ring as he laboured unsuccessfully to hide the decay of his reflexes, timing and athleticism, was well behind on the scorecards of all three judges.

Berbick is the kind of lumbering, slow-armed swinger he would have first embarrassed and then demolished in his dazzling prime but even the additional sluggishness imposed on the Jamaican's work by conspicuous idleness in training could not save this pathetically diminished Ali. Against an opponent who, as a twenty-eight-year-old, at least had youth to compensate for dubious fitness and extreme crudities of technique, the man who set a record by winning the world heavyweight title three times, scuffled quietly and with decreasing conviction towards a defeat that only the prejudiced in his own camp could seriously question.

To see him lose to such a moderate fighter in such a grubby context was like watching a king ride into permanent exile on the back of a garbage truck. The one blessing was that he was steadily exhausted rather than violently hurt by the experience. But even that consolation was worryingly diluted when most of his inner circle, from his wife Veronica to his manager Herbert Muhammad to his recently acquired friend, John Travolta, thrust distorted and dangerously reassuring interpretations of the fight into his head. "I don't want him to fight but you people are brainwashing him into thinking he did badly tonight," Veronica told reporters in Ali's dressing-room afterwards. "You had made up your mind about the fight you were going to see before you came here." She insisted that her man had done more worthwhile punching than Berbick, who had been barely hitting him. The theme was parroted by a chorus of voices of which Herbert Muhammad's was the most significant. "You done good," said Herbert. "I don't agree with that decision." "Everybody knew you won," said Veronica, talking again into Ali's left ear. For someone who didn't want to invite further exposure to physical hazard, she was making free with the illusions.

Her words had an effect on Ali that some of us found alarming. He was sitting on a wooden bench against a whitewashed

wall and when she sat down beside him he was a slumped, infi-
nitely weary figure, answering questions in a drained whisper as
beads of sweat formed on his chin and dropped on to the folds of
flesh around his middle. Even his wife's arrival did not animate
him noticeably as he admitted that out in the ring he felt old for
the first time in his life (a statement to remind us that he believes
genuine illness contributed substantially to his helpless passivity
when he was stopped after ten rounds by Larry Holmes in Las
Vegas fourteen months ago).

"Father Time caught up with me," he said so faintly that only
the two or three of us at the front of the crowding group of interviewers could make out the words. "I feel tired. Berbick was too
strong, more aggressive. I just had the feeling I could do this
thing. My mind said do it. But I know I didn't have it out there.
I did good for a thirty-nine-year-old, did all right considering I'll
be forty in five weeks.

"I thought Berbick was shorter than he is. I didn't know he
was so strong. He tagged me with a couple of hard ones and they
tired me a bit. There's nothing to worry about, this is not going
to bother me. But I think it's too late to come back. I always say
that after fights these days but who knows how I'll feel next
week."

That last sentence was liable to stir misgivings in many around
him but the resigned, exhausted tone kept our concern in check
until John Travolta, crouching at his feet, and Veronica at his
side fed him their views about how well he had done. Ali quoted
his wife and the actor immediately as if they had touched an
optimistic nerve in himself. "Veronica and John Travolta, they
tell me it was so close, that I won. Was it close?" A smile spread
across his aching face, obscuring for a moment the slight bruising beneath his left eye and the tiny area of discoloration by the
right one. The fatigue seemed to be lifted briefly from his body.
There was in those few seconds the definite threat of another
nightmare up ahead, the bleak possibility that the words he was
hearing would nourish his own capacity to dream away reality.

But yesterday he indicated firmly that he will be steered
towards unambiguous retirement by the memory of how feebly
he coped with the modest problem set by Berbick, the realisation
of how far he has declined from the towering standards of the

past, how totally he has lost the blurring hand-speed, the dancing mobility, the entire thrilling range of virtuosity that made him unique among heavyweights. His brilliance was always idiosyncratic, shot through with outrageous improvisations that blithely violated tenets of the game most fighters regard as sacrosanct. Imagination, balance, elasticity and blinding quickness enabled him to use techniques – such as constantly pulling his head away from punches instead of moving inside them, punching while his feet and body were eccentrically positioned – that would have brought disaster to less inspired performers. But his days of being a magnificent heretic belong to another time.

Once his speed and co-ordination deserted him, he was bound to look worse than ordinary because he did not have the remnants of an orthodox method to hide behind. At the Queen Elizabeth Sports Centre in Nassau he was just an ageing, overweight ex-champion who was no longer troubling to keep the grey out of his hair, no longer able to keep Trevor Berbick's clumsily directed blows out of his face. Much of the action in the early rounds was so riddled with ponderous incompetence that scoring it was largely a negative exercise, but Berbick was marginally less ineffective than Ali and edged ahead. The great man could neither measure nor synchronise his punches convincingly and generally he was reduced to pawing flurries. Just occasionally, as in the fifth, which he won, he managed a fleeting semblance of the old sharpness and caught Berbick with left jabs and passable imitations of right crosses. In between these limited rallies, however, he allowed himself to be bulled to the ropes and when the referee, Zack Clayton, refused to let him hold and wrestle, too many of the younger boxer's haphazard hooks and swings thudded against his head.

Assaults of that kind gave Berbick clear, if unimpressive, superiority in the fourth and seventh and what happened in the eighth was a tribute to the courage Ali will never lose. In that round he went up on his toes and bravely attempted to jab and dance, stick and move. The crowd, swollen to a sizeable, noisy audience in the dusty baseball stadium by the promoters' willingess to sell tickets at a fifth of their face value, chanted his name in their eagerness to be persuaded that they might see a small miracle. It did not come. Ali took the eighth but was soon settling heavily on his heels again and when he was on the wrong end of the undistinguished doings in the ninth and tenth there could be only one result. The two judges who gave the verdict to Berbick 99–94 may have been a touch generous to him but the official who had it 97–94 was scarcely exaggerating.

When Ali mumbled afterwards that Berbick would need to make only reasonable improvement to have a favourite's chance of winning the world championship, he was unlikely to find widespread support for the opinion. The Canadian-based West Indian had looked far more fit and vigorous in his brawling fifteen rounds with Larry Holmes last April but it is hard to imagine that he will ever be more than a strong rough-houser.

On Friday, Berbick was glad enough to get a night's work done and collect his wages for it. He had held out until nearly six o'clock, the hour when the first match was due to start at the stadium, to secure what he considered to be ironclad guarantees that James Cornelius, the tall, belligerent black man from the United States who heads the promotional consortium, would pay the outstanding balance of his purse money. Cornelius – who has been publicly accused by Don King, currently the biggest operator in the fight business, of having led a group of five men who beat him up and threatened his life over a contract wrangle in Freeport last week – is not too brisk at coming up with the ironclads. While reporters from around the world milled about endlessly at the fight press centre on Paradise Island awaiting developments, somebody joked that Cornelius's arrival had been delayed because there was some difficulty over raising the $2 toll needed to get across the bridge on to the island. What was obvious was that the malodorous enterprise billed as the Drama in Bahama had not been quite the source of prestige the Bahamians had anticipated. In the end they must have felt that they needed it the way Bermuda needs the Triangle. Or Muhammad Ali needs another comeback.

Apart from being discouraged by his own decay, Ali may have found the seediness of Mr Cornelius's arrangements inclined to sour him against the sport that has dominated his life. The programme began nearly two and a half hours late with gloves in such short supply that some pairs had to be unlaced rather than cut off the fighter's hands, so that they could be used again.

Down-the-bill boxers had to strip in cramped proximity to one another in ludicrously overcrowded dressing-rooms before going out to answer the cow-bell. It was all a disgraceful mess and the flavour of it was not improved by the violence with which Ali's strong-arm battalion repelled pressmen and broadcasters who tried to follow the loser into his dressing-room.

Inside, there was a contrasting tranquillity, especially when Ali's attractive eleven-year-old daughter from his previous marriage squirmed on to his knee to hug and kiss his battered head. His mother, too, squeezed through the jostling cluster of interrogators to embrace the most famous son in the world. "Good try, honey," she said and then to us: "I didn't cry. I'm glad he didn't get hurt. I'm glad that's it. I'm no worried about his losing. I'm just glad he didn't get hurt." Angelo Dundee, who has run Ali's corner for twenty years, was another who was happy about that but one or two on the fringes of the entourage looked as if they suspected they were about to be hurt – by being deprived of regular swellings around the cash pocket.

Everyone in that room was having thoughts about how it would be when Ali had left this scene behind for ever. A wire-service reporter was being more pragmatic. He was asking the fighter if, when he had quit, he would find time to talk President Gaddafi out of sending Libyan hit-squads after President Reagan. With Muhammad Ali that is supposed to be a practical inquiry. As was said after that Roman heavyweight was done in, when comes such another?

Pal Ali

Reg Gutteridge

"If you can dream – and not make
dreams your master"
Rudyard Kipling

The last time I met Ali, was as his guest in Las Vegas for his fifty-seventh birthday. We hugged, then he grinned and whispered in my ear: "We can't keep doing this in public – they'll all think we're a couple of fairies."

Those words and the irony in them brought tears to my eyes. For if there was one person on God's green earth who could have made me believe in fairies, and leprechauns or Father Christmas even, it was this man among men – this fearless, fragile man child.

Tragically, his body had been vanquished by his own surreal dreams of – if not out-and-out divinity – then indestructibility, but those dreams will never master the free spirit in him.

What compelling dreams they were! The most accurate description of this extraordinary man comes from that doyen of sportswriters, Hugh McIlvanney: "At the heart of the hypnotic appeal which his personality has for so many of us is an irrational suspicion that here is a man capable of willing his own outrageous image of himself into reality" wrote Hugh at the time when "The Greatest" was in his prime.

None of us were to know then, of course, the horrible consequences of his manic invitations to mighty men such as George Foreman and Larry Holmes to punch either his or their own lights out, as George did but Larry didn't. The stark conclusion of these fearless acts of folly inevitably proved that he was not invincible, but they sure as hell earned him immortality.

In 1989 when I was lying critically ill in a Hammersmith hospital with septicaemia and pneumonia, Ali came and sat on my bed, took my hand in his and said a prayer for my recovery. My mind sped through the emotional gearbox from surprise to gratitude, humility and then downright terror. I thought: "Blimey! If he's come all this way to pay his last respects, I must be on my way out any minute."

In truth, my old pal and rival Harry Carpenter had just driven Ali from the BBC TV centre to visit me. He had been there taking part in a show and, as Frank Bruno's sidekick Harry tells it, he kept asking: "Where's Reggie?"

We go back a long way, Pal Ali, and me. And it's been a journey in which he's had me laughing, crying, holding my breath, saying my prayers and cursing the fates for him: but mostly laughing.

As a broadcaster, Ali ruined me for everyone else. He was like a highly trained Alsatian. Providing he took a shine to you, he would do anything for you. Sometimes he did things you did not particularly want him to do, just to feed his insatiable appetite for mischief and, of course, to keep you on your toes.

None of his antics with me were quite as bizarre as the time he got bored in the middle of a fight and requested me to interview him between rounds. Although, as I shall illustrate, there were plenty of other incidents that came close.

He got bored in this particular fight because it took place in Jakarta and Ali did not know many people there on a personal level. "The Greatest" was not the only vain fighter I have met, in fact, they are all vain, to a man.

Just like every other performer, there is a longing to be universally loved deep inside every one of them. Although I must confess that while punching people on the nose is a sure way to get yourself noticed, it is hardly an appropriate way of showing peace and goodwill to all men.

As he matured from an uncertain braggart into a philosophical adult, however, Ali had a need not just for public acclaim, but for one-to-one communion.

The reasons he seemed to take me to his bosom may sound shallow, but for him they were valid. First he liked me because I was British and the British Boxing Board were the last official body to strip him of his title when he refused to fight in Vietnam.

Second, he liked my British manners. Saying "please" and "thank you", unlike so many of his American compatriots, were important gestures of respect as far as he was concerned.

Perhaps more significantly – and I blush to say this – he just found me a nice, cuddly little geezer.

In Jakarta, in 1973, he was fighting a man called Rudi Lubbers and he was toying with him. Now, this happened to be an important occasion for me as a commentator, because it was the first satellite show, sporting or otherwise, to come out of Jakarta to the Western world.

Between rounds, he suddenly leaned over the rope and said: "Get up here, Reggie." Flabbergasted, I told the people back in the *World Of Sport* studio in London about the little bit of history to which Ali was about to treat them. Talking to sportsmen before and after events was by now old hat, admittedly. Chatting them up in the middle of a match, however, was unheard of.

But, wouldn't you know it? The director, David Scott, with a news sense second to none, says in my ear, in the most matter-of-fact tones imaginable: "You'll have to hold on, old boy. We've got an interview with a winning jockey at Catterick after this race. So yours will have to wait."

When I called back to Ali that I'd talk to him later, he was, understandably, not best pleased. Luckily, after the next round he still had not put his man away yet and he shrugged off his sulks long enough to yell into the microphone while he was sitting on his stool. This is what he told millions of viewers in Britain: "I want to apologise to all my friends in Great Britain for not putting this bum away yet. Years ago, I would have finished him off by now. But I'm getting old and tired, so you'll just have to excuse me, please, folks."

Gloriously, and tragically, he was to go on fighting for another eight years.

After this fight, though, my old guv'nor, Head of Sport John Bromley, was so flushed with success at the unexpected coup that he asked me to follow it up with a highly unlikely piece. In the 1970s soccer panels were an all-the-rage novelty on TV here and there was one due on screen immediately after the big fight.

If memory serves, it comprised Malcolm Allison, Paddy Crerand, Derek Dougan and Brian Clough. The star of the show was Cloughie, of course, and "Brommers" asked me whether I could get Ali to gee Cloughie up for the viewers' entertainment.

Now, old Big 'Ead may not be too flattered to hear this right now, but Ali did not know him from Adam. So, in the middle of the usual after-fight *mêlée* in the ring, I said to Ali: "We've got a white guy in football back home who pops off a lot. Just shut him up for me, will you." "Pop off" is an American expression for talking too much. I added that the man's name was Brian Clough, not for a moment expecting that Ali would remember it. Good as gold, he looked straight at our camera and said. "I hear there's a man in England who's worse than me for poppin' off." Then he pauses and puts his gloved hand to his chin, as if he is deep in thought. At this point, I was going to yell "cut" and prompt him.

Suddenly, he resumes speaking: "Brian Clough – I hear you talk a lot. Well, Clough, that's enough. There's only one man in the world who's allowed to pop off and that's me. So, do you hear me, Brian Clough, that is enough."

When the two men eventually met in America, Ali was shocked at how small Brian was. He had expected him to look like one of those American grid iron giants.

For sheer broadcasting excellence, though, Ali surpassed himself during the build-up to that first fight with Joe Frazier. There was so much adulation surrounding him that he could not get out of the hotel during the day. The only privacy he got was on his early morning run. One day I got a message to him that I needed him. Incidentally, with one exception, he never demanded or even requested payment from my TV company. Ali got word back to me that I would have to come round very early in the morning after the road running.

When I got to his room I was confronted with a floor full of snoring sparring partners and Ali was lying prostrate on the bed with a sheet pulled over him, apparently well and truly in the land of Nod.

The interview was to go out live in London and the guys in the studio were biting their nails when I reported that Ali appeared to be fast asleep.

All of a sudden, he pulled the sheet away from his face and sat up in bed. I mouthed the words *World Of Sport* at him, and I knew he was in the starting blocks. That esteemed award-winning journalist, Ian Wooldridge of the *Daily Mail*, did the telephone interview and after Ian had wished him a "good morning" and asked after his well-being, Ali was off and running: "Is this *World of Sport* in Britain?" he asked. When Ian informed him that it was Ali continued: "Well, *World of Sport*" – and with this second piece of free advertising he gave me a knowing wink – then continued: "Yours is the best show in all of Britain, but I'm getting irritated with you, *World of Sport* 'cos you're making me nervous before the big fight." Then he gave them a five-minute monologue and I had to make frantic signals for him to wind up.

He signed off with: "I've got to go now, but I'm goin' to shock and amaze you against Frazier." Then he imitated the hit records of the time, which faded out repetitively and slowly: "The satellite's leavin', the satellite's leavin'," and then, in a whisper, "the satellite's leavin'."

With that, he handed the telephone back to me, pulled the sheet back over his head and I tiptoed my way out through the hulking prostrate bodies.

Ironically, the only time Ali ever asked me for money was when I lost him to the opposition – the BBC. He was in this country and in his prime at a time when TV companies were sometimes spending millions on a single show. He wanted a paltry £1,000 to be interviewed as a personality and not just a sportsman for an hour.

The programme controller at Thames TV at the time was a nice man named Brian Tesler. I suggested that a big name interviewer like David Frost or Eamon Andrews could do the job. Brian said he would very much like to, but that Jeremy Isaacs was doing a series in Bangladesh that was going to take up all his time and manpower.

So Ali went to the BBC instead and gave what Michael Parkinson or "Parky" still says was his most entertaining interview ever.

During a second Parkinson-Ali interview "The Greatest" memorably lost his temper. The main reason for that, I can now reveal, is that that some boxing people over here who should have known better wound Ali up beforehand by telling him that

Michael was anti-boxing, mainly because he frequently ridiculed Joe Bugner.

Whenever I've been on the wrong end of Ali's temper, he has always been playacting, although he can make the act look frighteningly real, as he did once when we were sitting beside a swimming-pool in Las Vegas.

I had a bottle of beer under my deck chair and Ali asked for a swig. Just as he was taking it, he saw his manager, the black Muslim Herbert Muhammad, approaching us. Ali used his famous fast hands to such effect that within seconds he had thrust the bottle into my hand and was screaming at me: "Put that bottle down! I don't like people drinking near me. You should know better!" He was bursting to laugh as he said it; but just like a naughty schoolboy, he was afraid of the headmaster.

Unsurprisingly, Herbert Muhammad and the rest of his Muslim cronies eventually disappeared into the sunset.

Yet, in my opinion, Ali was the most devout one among them. He was the most generous-spirited man I've ever known. He was constantly giving unsolicited and unpublicised financial gifts to poor kids in the street and he had an unerring eye for spotting and helping people who were really in need.

The one thing that Ali would not put up with at any price, though, was anyone who tried to take advantage of his generous nature by attempting to take the mickey out of him.

On another visit to this country, I warned him against appearing on a TV show with Freddie Starr because of that comedian's penchant for taking the mickey. Sure enough, this was confirmed for him soon after when he was taking a bow at a Joe Bugner fight when Freddie Starr, who was in the audience, stood up and began baiting him. When the thunderclouds started appearing in Ali's eyes, Mickey Duff tried to placate him by telling him that this man was the famous comedian. Ali simply fixed Freddie with an imperious stare and shouted back: "They tell me you're famous. Well, I've never seen or heard of you, so sit down. This is my show." Freddie sat down sheepishly, but this little story had a happy ending when the two men became pals later – strictly on Ali's terms, though.

Maybe, he couldn't take to Freddie at first because he fancied himself as a bit of a comedian, too. He wasn't half bad, either.

He once gave me a wrist watch with a picture of himself on it. The next time he saw me, he asked: "Have you still got the watch?"

When I replied that of course I still had it, he cracked: "Well, all those niggers are smarter than you, they sold it."

For me, that was vintage Ali. His sense of humour outside the ring was as impeccable as his sense of timing inside it.

The only way I can even attempt to come to terms with the suffering he has endured since his fabulous career took him a fight or two too far and Parkinson's disease compounded that error, is to find scant consolation in a lyric from a Don Maclean song about Van Gogh, which goes: "This world was never meant for one as beautiful as you . . ."

The Lost Legacy of Muhammad Ali

Thomas Hauser

In 1960, shortly after the Rome Olympics, a Soviet journalist asked Cassius Marcellus Clay, Jr. how it felt to win a gold medal for his country when there were restaurants in the United States that he was forbidden to eat in. Clay's response was short and sweet: "Tell your readers we got qualified people working on that problem. To me, the USA is the best country in the world, including yours."

Seven years later, that same young man was one of the most vilified personages in America.

People today understand that Muhammad Ali defied the United States government and alienated mainstream America because he stood up for his principles. But they don't know what those principles were. Generally, they are aware that, after beating Sonny Liston to capture the heavyweight championship in 1964, Clay announced that he had accepted the teachings of a religion known as the Nation of Islam and changed his name to Muhammad Ali. Thereafter, he refused induction into the United States Army during the height of the war in Vietnam. But to younger generations, Ali today is famous primarily for being famous. There has been a deliberate distortion of what he once believed, said, and stood for. History is being rewritten to serve political, social, and economic ends.

Thus, it's important to revisit the Muhammad Ali who, in the words of author Dave Kindred, was "as near to living flame as a man can get."

In the early 1960s, when Ali first entered the public consciousness, sports was considered one of the few areas where black Americans could compete on equal footing with whites. But in reality, sports reflected the old order. Black athletes could become stars, but only within guidelines dictated by the establishment. And away from the playing fields, as Ali himself once noted, "Many colored people thought it was better to be white." Black Americans were scorned, demeaned, and denied even self-love.

In 1961, while in Florida training for a fight, Cassius Clay met a man named Sam Saxon. Saxon was one of a small group of adherents (known to the media as "Black Muslims") who attended Nation of Islam meetings at a Miami temple and followed the black separatist teachings of a self-proclaimed "messenger" named Elijah Muhammad. Clay accepted Saxon's invitation to attend a Nation of Islam service, and thereafter was indoctrinated with the tenets of the religion.

The Nation of Islam taught that white people were devils who had been genetically created by an evil scientist with a big head named Mr Yacub. It maintained that there was a wheel-shaped Mother of Planes one-half mile wide manned by black men in the sky, and that, on Allah's chosen day of retribution, fifteen hundred planes from the Mother of Planes would drop deadly explosives destroying all but the righteous on earth. Neither of these views are part of traditional Islamic thought or find justification in the Qur'an. Moreover, while the concepts of Heaven and Hell are central to traditional Islamic doctrine, the National of Islam rejected both.

Herbert Muhammad, one of Elijah Muhammad's sons, later explained and sought to defend his father's teachings as follows:

Black people knew their life was bad. They wanted something to make it better. And my father's message was to gain dignity and self-respect and make black people the master of their own needs. As long as other people controlled what we needed, then these people would be able to control us. So my father sought to make black people self-reliant and take them away from gambling, alcohol, prostitution, and drugs. He taught us that the answer to what black people need is in God and in ourselves. And you have to ask what it was that enabled my father to get a man or woman off drugs when right now the whole government can't do it. You have to ask what it was that could bring a man out of prison, and the next month have that man be clean-shaven, wearing clean clothes, completely clean.

You see, my father saw that black people had a deep inferiority complex. He saw that white people had a great superiority complex. And by the whites being in an upper-hand position, blacks would never come up unless someone gave them a philosophy that they were better than whites.

From 1964 through his conversion to orthodox Islam in 1975, Muhammad Ali was the Nation of Islam's most visible and vocal spokesman in America. Nation of Islam teachings were at the core of who he was at that time in his life. Among the positions Ali preached were:

On integration: "We who follow the teachings of Elijah Muhammad don't want to [be] forced [to] integrate. Integration is wrong. We don't want to live with the white man; that's all."

On intermarriage: "No intelligent black man or black woman in his or her right black mind wants white boys and white girls coming to their homes to marry their black sons and daughters."

On the need for a separate black homeland: "Why don't we get out and build our own nation? White people just don't want their slaves to be free. That's the whole thing. Why not let us go and build ourselves a nation? We want a country. We're forty million people, but we'll never be free until we own our own land."

On brotherhood: "We're not all brothers. You can say we're brothers, but we're not."

Ali was black and proud of it at a time when many black Americans were running from their color. "He lived a lot of lives for a lot of people," said social activist Dick Gregory. "And he was able to tell white folks for us to go to hell."

For more than a decade, Ali was the gloved fist of John Carlos and Tommie Smith every day of the year. The establishment media, and sportswriters in particular, came down hard on him.

Jim Murray of the *Los Angeles Times* labeled Ali the "white man's burden." Jimmy Cannon of the *New York Journal American* called his ties to the Nation of Islam "the dirtiest in American sports since the Nazis were shilling for Max Schmeling as representative of their vile theories of blood."

A lot of white liberals and black Americans also took issue with Ali. "I never went along with the pronouncements of Elijah Muhammad that the white man was the devil and that blacks should be striving for separate development; a sort of American apartheid," said Arthur Ashe. "That never made sense to me. It was a racist ideology, and I didn't like it."

Joe Louis added his voice to those opposing Ali and opined, "I'm against Black Muslims. I've always believed that every man is my brother. Clay will earn the public's hatred because of his connections with the Black Muslims. The things they preach are just the opposite of what we believe."

Former heavyweight champion Floyd Patterson concurred with Louis, declaring, "I've been told that Clay has every right to follow any religion he chooses, and I agree. But by the same token, I have every right to call the Black Muslims a menace to the United States and a menace to the Negro race. I do not believe God put us here to hate one another. I believe the preaching of segregation, hatred, rebellion, and violence is wrong. Cassius Clay is disgracing himself and the Negro race."

Still, whether or not one liked what Ali represented, it was clear that his demand for full entitlement for all black people was on the cutting edge of an era. And to many, he was the ultimate symbol of black pride and black resistance to an unjust social order. In that vein, Jeremiah Shabazz, who was one of Ali's first teachers within the Nation of Islam, recalled, "When Elijah Muhammad spoke, his words were confined to whatever city he had spoken in. But Ali was a sports hero and people wanted to hear what he had to say, so his visibility and prominence were of great benefit. His voice carried throughout the world."

Outside the ring, Ali was never violent. His threat to the status quo was one of ideas, which is ironic because he himself was never a "thinker." But beneath it all, there was fear within the establishment that the ideas Ali preached could be converted to rebellion in the streets. Indeed, one can make the case that Ali and the Nation of Islam frightened the powers that be in America into embracing the agenda of moderate civil rights leaders as a way of muting the cries of those who wanted more.

Arthur Ashe later recalled, "I can tell you that Ali was very definitely, sometimes unspokenly, admired by a lot of the leaders of the civil rights movement, who were sometimes even a little bit jealous of the following he had and the efficacy of what he did. There were a lot of people in the movement who wished that they held that sort of sway over African-Americans but did not."

"Muhammad was probably the first black man in America to successfully break with the white establishment and survive," posited civil rights pioneer Andrew Young.

And before Cassius Clay ever changed his name, Malcolm X maintained, "Clay will mean more to his people than Jackie Robinson, because Robinson is the white man's hero but Cassius is the black man's hero."

"It's very difficult to imagine being young and black in the sixties and not gravitating toward Ali," Bryant Gumbel later recalled. "He was a guy who was supremely talented, enormously confident, and seemed to think less of what the establishment thought of him than about the image he saw when he looked in the mirror. And to people who were young and black and interested in tweaking the establishment, and in some cases shoving it up the tail of the establishment, you had to identify with somebody like that. The fact that he won all the time made it even better. You know, for all our passions of those years, we didn't have a lot of victories. More often than not, we were on the losing side, so the fact that Ali won was gravy. He was a heroic figure plain and simple. In every sense of the word, he was heroic."

The civil rights movement and Ali as a fighter both peaked in the mid-1960s. Then the war in Vietnam intervened.

In 1964, Ali had been classified 1-Y (not qualified for military service) as a result of scoring poorly on a Selective Service mental aptitude examination. Then, in early 1966, with the war expanding and manpower needs growing, the test score required for induction into the armed forces was lowered, leaving him eligible for the draft. Ali requested a deferment, but on February 17, 1966, his request was denied and he was reclassified 1-A (available for the draft). Several hours later, a frustrated Ali blurted out to reporters, "I ain't got no quarrel with them Vietcong."

The following day, Ali's outburst was front-page news across the country, and the sporting press raged against him. Red Smith of the *New York Times* harangued, "Squealing over the possibility that the military may call him up, Cassius makes himself as sorry a spectacle as those unwashed punks who picket and demonstrate against the war." Jimmy Cannon continued the assault, proclaiming, "Clay is part of the Beatle movement. He fits in with the famous singers no one can hear and the punks riding motorcycles with iron crosses pinned to their leather jackets and the boys with their long dirty hair and the girls with the unwashed look and the college kids dancing naked at secret proms held in apartments and the revolt of students who get a check from dad every first of the month and the painters who copy the labels off soup cans and the surf bums who refuse to work and the whole pampered style-making cult of the bored young."

Ali wasn't a political thinker. His initial concern over being drafted wasn't religious or political. It was that of a twenty-four-year-old who thought he had put the draft behind him and then learned that he was in danger of having his life turned upside down.

"Muhammad never studied day-to-day current events like the thousands of white kids who opposed the war," Jeremiah Shabazz later acknowledged. "But even though he was unsophisticated in his thinking, he knew it was a senseless unjust war. And of course, in addition to that, Muslims following the Honorable Elijah Muhammad decided long ago that we weren't going to fight the white man's wars. If he starts them, he can fight them."

On April 28, 1967, citing his religious beliefs, Ali refused induction into the United States Army. "Clay seems to have gone past the borders of faith," Milton Gross wrote in the *New York Post*. "He has reached the boundaries of fanaticism."

Less than eight weeks later, on June 20th, Ali was convicted of refusing induction into the armed forces and sentenced to five years in prison. He was stripped of his title and precluded by state athletic commissions throughout the country from fighting. His "exile" from boxing lasted for more than three years.

Ali's refusal to accept induction was part and parcel of a schism within the civil rights movement. "The more conservative black leadership was troubled by his opposition to the war," Julian Bond later recalled. "The civil rights movement at that time was split. There was one group of people who said, 'Let's not have any opinion about the war because this will alienate us from the powers that be, from President Johnson and successor presidents.' And there was another group that said, 'Listen, this war is wrong. It's killing black people disproportionately; it's draining resources that could be applied to the war on poverty; it's wrong in every respect.' So people in the first group were horrified by Ali. They thought he was a dunce manipulated by the Nation of Islam. And those in the second group felt entirely differently about him. Still," Bond continued, "it's hard to imagine that a sports figure could have so much political influence on so many people. When a figure as heroic and beloved as Muhammad Ali stood up and said, 'No, I won't go,' it reverberated through the whole society. People who had never thought about the war before began to think it through because of Ali. The ripples were enormous."

Andrew Young had similar memories in recalling the reaction of his own mentor, Martin Luther King, Jr., to Ali's decision. "Martin made his most publicized speech against the war in Vietnam at Riverside Church [in New York] on April 4, 1967; exactly one year to the day before he was assassinated," Young remembered. "It was soon after that speech that Muhammad refused to take the step forward, and I know Martin was very proud of him."

However, others within the black community took a lesser view of Ali's conduct. "He's hurting the morale of a lot of young Negro soldiers over in Vietnam," said Jackie Robinson. "And the tragedy to me is, Cassius has made millions of dollars off of the American public, and now he's not willing to show his appreciation to a country that's giving him a fantastic opportunity." Joe Louis was in accord with his baseball counterpart, saying, "Anybody in America who don't want to fight for this country; I think it's very bad, especially a guy who has made a lot of money in this country. I was champion at the time World War Two started; and when my time came up, I had to go. I think that he should fight for his country."

More significantly though, Vietnam deflected attention from Ali's racial views and put him in a context where many whites and white opinion-makers could identify with him. There had been an ugly mood around Ali, starting with the assassination of Malcolm X in February 1965. Thereafter, Ali seemed to take on a bit of the persona, not just the ideology, of the Nation of Islam. But when the spotlight turned from Ali's acceptance of an ideology that sanctioned hate to his refusal to accept induction into the United States Army, he began to bond with the white liberal community which at the time was quite strong.

Thus it was that Ali was martyred and lived to talk about it. Ultimately, he returned to boxing. After wins against Jerry Quarry and Oscar Bonavena, he lost a historic fifteen-round decision to Joe Frazier at Madison Square Garden. Then his conviction for refusing induction into the United States Army was reversed by the United States Supreme Court on a procedural technicality. After that, Ali reeled off ten more victories but suffered a broken jaw in a twelve-round loss to Ken Norton. That made him an "underdog" in the eyes of America. People who had once bristled at his words and conduct began to feel sorry for him.

Ali earned a measure of revenge against Frazier and Norton with victories in hard-fought rematches. Then, on October 30, 1974, he dethroned George Foreman to recapture the heavyweight championship of the world. But more importantly, by that time, America had turned against the war in Vietnam. It was clear that Ali had sacrificed enormously for his beliefs. And whether or not people liked the racial component of Ali's views, there was respect for the fact that he had stood by them.

On December 10, 1974, Ali was invited to the White House by President Gerald Ford. It was an occasion that would have been unthinkable several years earlier and marked a turning point in the country's embrace of Ali.

Then, on February 25, 1975, Elijah Muhammad died.

"After Elijah died," Ali said later, "his son Wallace took over as leader. That didn't surprise us, because we'd been told Wallace would come after his father. But what surprised some people was, Wallace changed the direction of the Nation. He'd learned from his studies that his father wasn't teaching true Islam, and Wallace taught us the true meaning of the Qur'an."

Elijah Muhammad's death marked a seismic shift for the Nation of Islam and foreshadowed a significant change in Ali's public pronouncements on race. In the past, the public and private Ali had seemed almost at war with one another over whether white people were truly evil. Now Ali was able to say openly, "I don't hate whites. That was history, but it's coming to an end."

Some of Elijah Muhammad's adherents refused to accept the teachings of his son, Wallace. Ministers like Jeremiah Shabazz and Louis Farrakhan maintained that Elijah had been a prophet and continued to preach what he had taught them. Meanwhile, Ali's religious views were evolving and he later acknowledged, "When I was young, I followed a teaching that disrespected other people and said that white people were devils. I was wrong. Color doesn't make a man a devil. It's the heart and soul and mind that count. What's on the outside is only decoration. Hating someone because of his color is wrong. It's wrong both ways; it don't matter which color does the hating. All people, all colors, got to work to get along."

Ali is now a living embodiment of Martin Luther King, Jr's message that all people are deserving of love. As Jerry Izenberg, one of America's foremost sports journalists, observed, "Ironically, after all he went through, the affection for Ali is largely colorblind. Late in his career, he developed a quality that only a few people have. He reached a point where, when people looked at him, they didn't see black or white. They saw Ali. For a long time, that mystified him. He expected black people to love him and crowd around him, but then he realized white people loved him too; and that made him very happy."

Ali's love affair with America and the world reached its zenith in 1996. Fifteen years earlier, his public profile had dropped after his retirement from boxing. Thereafter, if Ali appeared at an event, those in attendance were excited but he wasn't on the national radar screen.

Then Ali was chosen to light the Olympic flame in Atlanta. It was a glorious moment. Three billion people around the world watched on television and were united by love and caring for one man. But there's a school of thought that the 1996 Olympics carried negatives as well, for it was in Atlanta that corporate America "rediscovered" Ali. And since then, there has been a determined effort to rewrite history. In order to take advantage of Ali's economic potential, it has been deemed desirable to "sanitize" him. And as a result, all of the "rough edges" are being filed away from Ali's life story.

"Commercialization is a natural process in this country," says Jerry Izenberg. "But the Ali I fell in love with wasn't for sale. He fought the good fight in and out of the ring, and that was payment enough for him. He wasn't looking to get paid in dollars, and the true worth of the stands he made wasn't commercial. Then corporate America latched onto Ali at the Olympics," Izenberg continues, "and he became a gravy train for everyone who wants to make a movie or sell something to the public. But the public gains nothing when Ali is commercialized and marketed the way he is today."

No event crystalized the commercialization of Ali more clearly than his appearance at the New York Stock Exchange on December 31, 1999. That was an important day. By most reckonings, it marked the end of a millennium. The Ali who won hearts in the 1960s could have been expected to celebrate the occasion at a soup kitchen or homeless shelter to draw attention to the plight of the disadvantaged. Many hoped to see Ali spend December 31, 1999, in a spiritual setting. Instead, the man who decades earlier was a beacon of hope for oppressed people around the globe and who refused to become a symbol for the United States Army became a symbol for the New York Stock Exchange.

"If it [the stock market] goes up, then you will have been blessed by my presence," Ali told the assembled financial elite. "If it goes down, I had nothing to do with it." As the clock struck midnight, Ali was in Washington, DC, dining on beluga caviar, lobster, and foie gras. That saddened a lot of people. Ali makes his own decisions, but those decisions are made based on how information is presented to him. One can be forgiven for thinking that, had the options been explained differently to him, he would have chosen to serve as a different symbol that day.

The commercialization of Ali is also typified by the 2001 feature film that bore his name. The movie *Ali* represented a unique opportunity to depict its subject for generations, now and in the future, that didn't experience his magic. It cost the staggering sum of $105,000,000 to make and was backed by a multinational promotional campaign that cost tens of millions of dollars. But instead of being faithful to its subject, *Ali* rewrote history.

Ali featured countless factual inaccuracies for "dramatic purposes," as though Ali's life to date hasn't been dramatic enough. The screenplay was disjointed, and the film suffered from the hard reality that no one but Ali can play Ali. But the biggest problem with the movie was that it sanitized Ali and turned him into a virtual Disney character.

"I hated that film," says director Spike Lee. "It wasn't Ali."

"The movie was appalling," adds Robert Lipsyte, who for years covered Ali as a *New York Times* reporter. "They got the plastic covering on Elijah Muhammad's living-room furniture right, but that's about all."

"Will Smith playing Ali was an impersonation," adds Jerry Izenberg; "not a performance."

Also, in an effort to remove all of the warts from Ali's character, *Ali* the movie painted a portrait of its subject – and in the process, of America – that was flat-out wrong. Some of this sanitization, such as reducing Ali's profligate womanizing to a single meaningful relationship, is understandable. Ali's penchant for the opposite sex, while at odds with his public religious pronouncements, was not at the core of his public persona. But other omissions were far more damaging to the historical record and integrity of the film.

For example, Ali's cruelty toward Joe Frazier was completely ignored. In real life, Ali played the race card against Frazier in a particularly mean-spirited way. For the entertainment of white America, he labeled Joe as ugly and dumb. And at the same time, speaking to black America, he branded Frazier an Uncle Tom, turning him into an object of derision and scorn within the black community. The latter insult was particularly galling. Joe Frazier is a lot of things, not all of them good. But he's not an Uncle Tom. Yet to this day, there are people who think of him as a less-than-proud black man because of Ali's diatribes more than three decades ago.

"One of the many paradoxes about Ali," says historian Randy Roberts, "is that he embraced an ideology that disparaged white people; yet he was never cruel to white people, only blacks. Except for occasional humorous barbs, Ali's white opponents were treated with dignity and respect. But things got ugly with Floyd Patterson, Ernie Terrell, and Joe Frazier. And sure; Patterson and Terrell might have asked for it because of things they said. But Joe was innocent. And to deny the cruelty of what Ali did to Joe Frazier is to continue to be cruel to Joe."

In truth, it takes a certain amount of cruelty to be a great fighter. Let's not forget; Ali beat people up and inflicted brain damage on them as his livelihood and way of life for years. And the time when he was at his peak as a fighter coincided with the time when he was most openly angry at the circumstances he found.

Thus, the biggest problem with the film was not its portrayal of Ali's conduct but its misrepresentation of his thoughts. In an effort to create a simple conflict between good and evil (with Ali being good), the movie ignored the true nature of the Nation of Islam. Watching the film, the audience was left with the impression that Nation of Islam doctrine is Islam as practiced by more than one billion people around the world today. *Ali* depicted only that portion of Nation of Islam teachings that highlighted black pride, black self-awareness, and self-love.

Moreover, in promoting the view that America turned against Ali in the 1960s because he was a "Muslim" – as opposed to a member of the Nation of Islam – the makers of *Ali* fed into the dangerous view that America is "anti-Islam." The truth is, there were people who assailed Ali because they thought he was unpatriotic. There were people who assailed Ali because he was spouting a racist ideology or because they thought he was an "uppity" black man who didn't know his place. But Americans did not assail Ali because he was a Muslim. Other public figures such as Lew Alcindor, who converted to orthodox Islam and changed his name to Kareem Abdul-Jabbar, were not vilified for their religious beliefs.

In sum, Ali is now being retroactively turned into a forerunner of Michael Jordan and Tiger Woods. "A bargain has been struck," says Robert Lipsyte. "Ali and the people around him get their money. And I'm glad Ali is making money. He's showing great gallantry in the face of his physical condition, and he never made what he should have made before. But the trade-off is, Ali is no longer threatening. He's safe; he's comfortable. He's another dangerous black man who white America has found a way to emasculate. You know, white America still hasn't figured out how to deal with powerful black male figures who don't play football or basketball other than to find ways to tame them and take away any real power and influence they might have. So the bottom line is, if we can control Muhammad Ali, it makes us more powerful. And at long last, we've brought Muhammad Ali under control."

Mike Marqusee, author of *Redemption Song; Muhammad Ali and the Spirit of the Sixties*, is in accord with Lipsyte and observes, "Ali's power in the third world grew precisely because he was a symbol of defiance against racism and the use of United States military power abroad. And those issues are very much alive today; so it means a lot to the powers that be if Ali can be used to suggest to the rest of the world that they aren't problems anymore. Governments and corporations have this incredible power to incorporate imagery and attach whatever meanings they choose to that imagery in pursuit of their goals. Nothing can take away Ali's past. It happened; it's part of history. But that history is now being plundered and deliberately obscured to sell commercial products and, more significantly, ideas. Ali is being reduced to serving as a mouthpiece for whatever ideas and products those with influence and power want to sell. And the people guiding him are letting it happen for narrow financial reasons."

"Most great athletes can sell Wheaties," notes Ramsey Clark. "But they can't impact upon social and political issues. It's very hard, if not impossible, to do both."

Clark's voice is significant. As Attorney General of the United States, he oversaw as a matter of duty the 1967 criminal prosecution of Ali for refusing induction into the United States Army. However, he has long been aligned with liberal causes and has worked closely with Ali on a number of occasions.

"There's a common tactic among the dominant opinionmakers," says Clark. "They want to influence the population

they're communicating with, so they transmit information
selectively and create an image that's unreal but very powerful.
On the one hand, they'll demonize their subject. Or in the other
direction, they'll overlook the sins of someone they want to
popularize and focus on the aspects of that person's life which
reflect values they want to promote. It's a question of what
those in power want to impose and consider safe. And what we
have now in many of the depictions of Ali is the portrait of a
man who is heroic, well-intentioned, and good – all of which he
was and still is – but who is presented to us in an unreal artificial manner."

Ron Borges of the *Boston Globe* has followed Ali and the
American scene for decades. "It's not uncommon for historical
figures to slip out of focus when removed from their time by
several generations," says Borges. "But this is something more.
There's a deliberate distortion of what Ali's life has been like
and what his impact on America really was. Maybe someone
thinks that this sort of revisionism makes Ali more acceptable.
But acceptable to whom and for what purpose other than selling products and making money? They're cutting out all the
things that made him Ali. Frankly, I wonder sometimes what
Ali is about these days other than making money. I know that,
underneath the facade, Ali is still there. But to a lot of people,
it's like he's a ghost. Twenty-year-olds today have no idea what
Ali was about. As far as they're concerned, he's just another
celebrity. That's what it has come to, and it steals Ali's true
legacy."

Dave Kindred authored a number of ground-breaking stories
about Ali for the *Atlanta Constitution* and *Washington Post*. "In
the past," says Kindred, "there were reasons, a lot of them, for
admiring and respecting Ali. Now you're asked to admire and
respect him because he's a living saint. And I never thought of
Ali as a saint. He was a rogue and a rebel, a guy with good qualities and flaws who stood for something. But now, it seems as
though he stands for everything and nothing. All of the barbed
edges have been filed down. His past is being rewritten. They're
trying to remove any vestige of Ali that might make it harder to
use him to sell automobiles or expensive watches or whatever
other product he's endorsing at the moment. That, to me, is the

heart of it. Ali today seems to be blatantly for sale. He's trotted around to high-profile events and events where he's paid large sums of money for being there, and often I find myself asking, 'What's he doing there?' I assume he enjoys it. I'm sure he likes the attention. His need for the crowd has always been there and he's entitled to the money. But the loss of Ali's voice is very sad. And I'm not talking about his physical voice, because the people around Ali have figured out a way to deal with his infirmities and still keep him center stage. I'm talking about content and hard edge and the challenge that attached to some of the things Ali said in the past. There was a time when Ali forced us to think about race and religion and many of the other fundamental forces that affect our lives. He was right on some things and wrong on others, but the challenge was always there. And that Ali is gone now, with the result that there's a whole new generation – two generations, actually – who know only the sanitized Ali, and that's very sad."

Jeffrey Sammons, a professor of African-American studies at NYU and author of *Beyond The Ring: The Role of Boxing in American Society*, is in accord. "What's happening to Ali now," says Sammons, "is typical of what has happened to so many black figures. It's a commodification and a trivialization. Maybe the idea is that, by embracing Ali as a society, we can feel good about having become more tolerant. We can tell ourselves that we're not like those bad people in the 1960s who took away Ali's title and his right to fight. But by not showing what Ali was, we're also not showing what American society was at that time. And if the rough edges on Ali are filed down, you have the revision of history in a very dangerous way. By distorting America's past, you make it impossible to understand the past. And if you can't understand the past, then you won't be able to understand the present or the future."

None of the above comments is intended to take away from Ali's greatness. Each of the speakers is a longtime admirer of Ali. Each of them would no doubt agree with the assessment of boxing maven Lou DiBella, who says, "In many respects, the way Ali is portrayed today is simply a reflection of how well-loved he is and the fact that he's a great person. All of us are open to adoration and, in Ali's case, he deserves it. He's older, wiser, and mellower now than he was decades ago. He enjoys being who he is. And whatever good things he gets, he deserves them."

Still, Ali's legacy today is in danger of being protected in the same manner as the estate of Elvis Presley is protecting Elvis's image. New generations are born; and to them, Ali is more legend than reality, part of America's distant past.

Meanwhile, 2004 has brought more of the same. The year began with IBM, Gillette, and Adidas featuring Ali in multinational commercial campaigns. Taschen Books published an Ali coffee-table tome bound in silk and Louis Vuitton leather that retails for $3,000 a copy with a "special edition" that sells for $7,500. The book is entitled *GOAT*, which is an acronym for "Greatest of All Time" and also the name of Ali's personal company.

"I think it's significant," says Jerry Izenberg, "that the book is named after Ali's corporation and not Ali." Then Izenberg adds, "For those who didn't live through the 1960s, it takes some work to understand the true importance of Ali. And people are lazy; the media is lazy. No one wants to read and study. So they take the product that's given to them by IMG, Columbia Pictures, and others, and accept it whole cloth. The result is that, the further removed in time we become, the more Ali is distorted. And I get very angry about that, because the distortion of history breeds ignorance. If Ali isn't remembered as the person he truly was, we'll all be poorer. It will wipe out some very important lessons that America learned. Let's face it; most people today don't have at clue about Ali. They have no idea what Ali and the country went through in the 1960s. Ali isn't the same person now that he was then. Like most of us, he changed as he grew older. But I don't worry about the changes in Ali. I worry about the misperception of what Ali stood for. Ali can be all things to all people but, unless there's truth, it's worthless."

Ali in the 1960s stood for the proposition that principles matter; that equality among people is just and proper; that the war in Vietnam was wrong. Every time he looked in the mirror and preened, "I'm so pretty," he was saying "black is beautiful" before it became fashionable to do so. Indeed, as early as March 1963, *Ebony* magazine declared, "Cassius Marcellus Clay – and this fact has evaded the sportswriting fraternity – is a blast furnace of racial pride. His is a pride that would never mask itself with skin lighteners and processed hair, a pride scorched with memories of a million little burns."

And Ali's role in spreading that pride has been testified to by others:

Arthur Ashe: "This man helped give an entire people a belief in themselves and the will to make themselves better."

Reggie Jackson: "Muhammad Ali gave me the gift of self-respect."

Hosea Williams: "Ali made you feel good about yourself. He made you feel so glad you are who you are; that God had made you black."

In sum, the experience of being black changed for millions of men and women because of Ali. But one of the reasons Ali had the impact he did was because there was an ugly edge to what he said. And by focusing on Ali's ring exploits and his refusal to serve in Vietnam, while at the same time covering up the true nature of Nation of Islam doctrine, the current keepers of Ali's legacy are losing sight of why he so enthralled and enraged segments of American society. And equally important, by rewriting history and making Ali out to be in the mainstream of the black civil rights movement, the revisionists demean Ali's personal struggle because they gloss over the extent to which he was cut off from mainstream support.

Thus, Ramsey Clark warns, "Legacies are important but they have to be true. The distortion of a legacy is a distortion of public truth and a disservice to history, as are all distortions of values and character."

Ali himself once recalled, "For three years, up until I fought Sonny Liston, I'd sneak into Nation of Islam meetings through the back door. I didn't want people to know I was there. I was afraid, if they knew, I wouldn't be allowed to fight for the title. Later on, I learned to stand up for my beliefs."

Ali's views have changed since then, but he is unrepentant regarding what he once believed. "Elijah Muhammad was a good man," Ali has said, "even if he wasn't the Messenger of God we thought he was. Not everything he said was right, but everyone in the Nation of Islam loved him because he carried what was best for us in his heart. Elijah taught us to be independent, to clean ourselves up, to be proud and healthy. He stressed the bad things the white man did to us so we could get free and strong. If you look at what our people were like then, a lot of us didn't have self-respect. We didn't have anything after being in America for hundreds of years. Elijah Muhammad was trying to lift us up and get our people out of the gutter. I think he was wrong when he talked about white devils, but part of what he did was make people feel it was good to be black. So I'm not apologizing for what I believed."

It's the ultimate irony then, that so many of the people shaping Ali's legacy today are "spin-doctoring" with regard to his beliefs. Ali stood up for his convictions and sacrificed a great deal for them. Indeed, in a recent commercial for IBM's Linux system, Ali speaks the words, "Speak your mind; don't back down." So why hide the true nature of what Ali's principles were?

Also, it should be said that, in 2004, there's a particularly compelling reason to mourn the lost legacy of Muhammad Ali.

We live in an age marked by horrific divisions amongst the world's cultures and religions. If we are to avoid increasingly violent assaults and possibly a nuclear holocaust, the people of the world must learn to understand others with alien beliefs, find the humanity in their enemies, and embrace that which is good in those they abhor.

Muhammad Ali is the ideal messenger for this cause. He is a man who once preached an ideology that was anathema to most Americans; an ideology that he himself now rejects in significant measure. Yet America has found the humanity in Ali, embraced the good in him, and taken him into its collective heart. And vice versa.

Also, it should be noted that, were he so inclined, Ali is still capable of influencing public debate. All he would need to say is two words regarding the current war in Iraq: "*It's wrong!*" That wouldn't dictate what people think, but it would have a significant impact on what a lot of people thought about. However, instead, Ali has held to the theme advised by those around him and advanced when he was asked about al-Qaeda in June 2002.

"I dodge those questions," Ali told David Frost on *HBO Reel Sports*. "I've opened up businesses across the country, selling products, and I don't want to say nothing and, not knowing what I'm doing, not [being] qualified, say the wrong thing and hurt my businesses and things I'm doing."

It's hard to imagine Muhammad Ali in the 1960s declining to comment on war and racism for fear that it would hurt his business ventures.

Great men are considered great, not only because of what they achieve, but also because of the road they travel to reach their final destination. Sanitizing Muhammad Ali and rounding off the rough edges of his journey is a disservice both to history and to Ali himself. Rather than cultivate historical amnesia, we should cherish the memory of Ali as a warrior and as a gleaming symbol of defiance against an unjust social order when he was young.

Muhammad Ali's Professional Boxing Record

56 Wins, 5 Losses, 37 KOs/TKOs
Born: Jan. 17, 1942 – Louisville, Kentucky, USA

1960

29 Oct – Tunney Hunsaker, Louisville, KY – Win, unanimous decision, 6 rounds

27 Dec – Herb Siler, Miami Beach, FL – TKO Round 4

1961

17 Jan – Tony Esperti, Miami Beach, FL – TKO Round 3

7 Feb – Jim Robinson, Miami Beach, FL – KO Round 1

21 Feb – Donnie Fleeman, Miami Beach, FL – KO Round 7

19 Apr – Lamar Clark, Louisville, KY – KO Round 2

26 Jun – Duke Sabedong, Las Vegas, NV – Win, unanimous decision, 10 rounds

22 Jul – Alonzo Johnson, Louisville, KY – Win, unanimous decision, 10 rounds

7 Oct – Alex Miteff, Louisville, KY – TKO Round 6

29 Nov – Willi Besmanoff, Louisville, KY – TKO Round 7

1962

10 Feb – Sonny Banks, New York, NY – TKO Round 4

28 Feb – Don Warner, Miami Beach, FL – TKO Round 4

23 Apr – George Logan, Los Angeles, CA – TKO Round 4

19 May – Billy Daniels, New York, NY – TKO Round 7

20 Jul – Alejandro Lavorante, Los Angeles, CA – KO Round 5

15 Nov – Archie Moore, Los Angeles, CA – TKO Round 4

1963

24 Jan – Charlie Powell, Pittsburgh, PA – KO Round 3
13 Mar – Doug Jones, New York, NY – Win, unanimous decision, 10 rounds
18 June – Henry Cooper, London, UK – TKO Round 5

1964

25 Feb – Sonny Liston, Miami Beach, FL – TKO Round 7 (won world heavyweight title)

1965

25 May – Sonny Liston, Lewiston, ME – KO Round 1 (retained title)
22 Nov – Floyd Patterson, Las Vegas, NV – TKO Round 12 (retained title)

1966

29 Mar – George Chuvalo, Toronto Canada – Win, unanimous decision, 15 rounds (retained title)
21 May – Henry Cooper, London, UK – TKO Round 6 (retained title)
6 Aug – Brian London, London, UK – KO Round 3 (retained title)
10 Sep – Karl Mildenberger, Frankfurt, Germany – TKO Round 12 (retained title)
14 Nov – Cleveland Williams, Houston, TX – TKO Round 3 (retained title)

1967

6 Feb – Ernie Terrell, Houston, TX – Win, unanimous decision, 15 rounds (retained world heavyweight title)
22 Mar – Zora Folley, New York, NY – KO Round 7 (retained world heavyweight title)

1970

26 Oct – Jerry Quarry, Atlanta, GA – TKO Round 3
7 Dec – Oscar Bonavena, New York, NY – TKO Round 15

1971

8 Mar – Joe Frazier, New York, NY – Lost, unanimous decision,
   15 rounds (for world heavyweight title)
26 July – Jimmy Ellis, Houston, TX – TKO Round 12
17 Nov – Buster Mathis, Houston, TX – Win, unanimous
   decision, 12 rounds
26 Dec – Jurgen Blin, Zurich, Switzerland – KO Round 7

1972

1 Apr – Mac Foster, Tokyo, Japan – Win, unanimous decision,
   15 rounds
1 May – George Chuvalo, Vancouver, Canada – Win, unanimous
   decision, 12 rounds
27 Jun – Jerry Quarry, Las Vegas, NV – TKO Round 7
19 July – Al Lewis, Dublin, Ireland – TKO Round 11
20 Sep – Floyd Patterson, New York, NY – TKO Round 7
21 Nov – Bob Foster, Stateline, NV – KO Round 8

1973

14 Feb – Joe Bugner, Las Vegas, NV – Win, unanimous decision,
   12 rounds
31 Mar – Ken Norton, San Diego, CA – Lost, split decision, 12 rounds
10 Sep – Ken Norton, Los Angeles, CA – Win, split decision, 12
   rounds
20 Oct – Rudi Lubbers, Jakarta, Indonesia – Win, unanimous
   decision, 12 rounds

1974

28 Jan – Joe Frazier, New York, NY – Win, unanimous decision,
   12 rounds

30 Oct – George Foreman, Kinshasa, Zaire* – KO Round 8 (won world heavyweight title)

1975

24 Mar – Chuck Wepner, Cleveland, OH – TKO Round 15 (retained title)

16 May – Ron Lyle, Las Vegas, NV – TKO Round 11 (retained title)

30 June – Joe Bugner, Kuala Lumpur, Malaysia – Win, unanimous decision, 15 rounds (retained title)

1 Oct – Joe Frazier, Manila, Philippines – TKO Round 14 (retained title)

1976

20 Feb – Jean-Pierre Coopman, San Juan, Puerto Rico – KO Round 5 (retained title)

30 Apr – Jimmy Young, Landover, MD – Win, unanimous decision, 15 rounds (retained title)

24 May – Richard Dunn, Munich, Germany – TKO Round 5 (retained title)

28 Sep – Ken Norton, New York, NY – Win, unanimous decision, 15 rounds (retained title)

1977

16 May – Alfredo Evangelista, Landover, MD – Win, unanimous decision, 15 rounds (retained title)

29 Sept – Earnie Shavers, New York, NY – Win, unanimous decision, 15 rounds (retained title)

1978

15 Feb – Leon Spinks, Las Vegas, NV – Lost, split decision, 15 rounds (lost world heavyweight title)

15 Sept – Leon Spinks, New Orleans, LA – Win, unanimous decision, 15 rounds (won world heavyweight title)

* *Now the Democratic Republic of Congo*

1980

2 Oct – Larry Holmes, Las Vegas, NV – Lost, TKO, 11 rounds
(for world heavyweight title)

1981

11 Dec – Trevor Berbick, Nassau – Lost, unanimous decision,
10 rounds

Acknowledgements and Sources

The editor has made every effort to locate all persons having any rights in the selections appearing in this anthology and to secure permission from the holders of such rights. The editor apologizes in advance for any errors or omissions inadvertently made. Queries regarding the use of material should be addressed to the editor c/o the publishers.

"A Look at Cassius Clay: Biggest Mouth in Boxing" by Alex Poinsett, from *Ebony Magazine* March 1963. Courtesy Johnson Publishing Company, Inc. All rights reserved.

"God Save the King, God Save Boxing", "He's Just a Little Boy in the Dark and He's Scared", "What the Hell is This? What Did They Do?" from *Liston and Ali: The Ugly Bear and the Boy Who Would Be King* © 2010 by Bob Mee. Printed by permission of the author.

Chapters 8, 17 and 20 from *Man of Destiny* by John Cottrell, published by Frederick Muller. Reprinted by permission of The Random House Group Ltd.

"Legacies", "Walking With Kings", "Pal Ali" from *King Of Commentary* © 1998 by Reg Gutteridge and Peter Batt. Printed by permission of John Blake Publishing Ltd.

The Devil and Sonny Liston © 2000 by Nick Tosches. Printed by permission of the author.

"Intimate Look At The Champ" by Isaac Sutton, from *Ebony Magazine* November 1966. Courtesy Johnson Publishing Company, Inc. All rights reserved.

"Negroes and the War" from *The Times*, 22 June 1967. Printed by permission of NI Syndication.

"Beyond the Confines of America" from *Redemption Song* © 1999 by Mike Marqusee. Printed by permission of the author.

The Editor wishes to thank the following for their invaluable assistance over the course of this project: Sara Andersdotter, Danny Baror, Bill Campbell, Ashleigh Clarke, Vickie Dillon, Cathy Furlani, Thomas Hauser, Mike Marqusee, Sarah McMahon, Evan Olsen, Su Olsen, Duncan Proudfoot, Caroline Rush, Ben Smith, Craig Tenney, Catherine Trippet, Rosie Virgo, Vickie Wilson.